Property Law FOR DUMMIES®

By Alan Romero

WILEY

John Wiley & Sons, Inc.

Property Law For Dummies®

Published by
John Wiley & Sons, Inc.
111 River St.
Hoboken, NJ 07030-5774
www.wiley.com

For general information on our other products and services, please contact our Customer Care Department within the U.S. at 877-762-2974, outside the U.S. at 317-572-3993, or fax 317-572-4002.

For technical support, please visit www.wiley.com/techsupport.

Wiley publishes in a variety of print and electronic formats and by print-on-demand. Some material included with standard print versions of this book may not be included in e-books or in print-on-demand. If this book refers to media such as a CD or DVD that is not included in the version you purchased, you may download this material at http://booksupport.wiley.com. For more information about Wiley products, visit www.wiley.com.

Library of Congress Control Number: 2012954764

ISBN 978-1-118-37539-6 (pbk); ISBN 978-1-118-50323-2 (ebk); ISBN 978-1-118-50246-4 (ebk); ISBN 978-1-118-50322-5 (ebk)

Manufactured in the United States of America

10 9 8 7 6 5 4 3 2 1

WILEY

About the Author

Alan Romero is a professor of law at the University of Wyoming College of Law. He has been teaching Property Law and related courses at various law schools since 1998. He earned a BA *summa cum laude* in English and Political Science from Brigham Young University. He then graduated with honors from Harvard Law School in 1993, where he was President of the *Harvard Journal on Legislation*. Along the way, he unexpectedly discovered the wonders of property law. He's been thinking, researching, practicing, teaching, and writing about property law ever since.

Dedication

To Amy, for all the reasons that can't be written down in words.

Author's Acknowledgments

Pretty much everything in this book I learned from others. Thanks to all the teachers, scholars, judges, and lawyers from whom I have kept learning about property law. And thanks to the many students who have helped me learn how to learn property law.

Writing this book also required a lot of help. Thanks to the Wiley editorial team who made this book so much better: David Lutton, my acquisitions editor; Jen Tebbe, my project editor; Danielle Voirol, Amanda Langferman, and Jessica Smith, my copy editors; and John Martinez, my technical editor.

Most of all, thanks to Amy and our kids for encouraging me, giving me the time to write this book, listening to me talk about it, and helping me remember what matters.

Publisher's Acknowledgments

We're proud of this book; please send us your comments at http://dummies.custhelp.com. For other comments, please contact our Customer Care Department within the U.S. at 877-762-2974, outside the U.S. at 317-572-3993, or fax 317-572-4002.

Some of the people who helped bring this book to market include the following:

Acquisitions, Editorial, and Vertical Websites

Project Editor: Jennifer Tebbe

Acquisitions Editor: Erin Calligan Mooney

Senior Copy Editor: Danielle Voirol

Assistant Editor: David Lutton

Editorial Program Coordinator: Joe Niesen

Technical Editor: John Martinez

Editorial Manager: Christine Meloy Beck

Editorial Assistant: Rachelle S. Amick, Alexa Koschier

Cover Photo: © iStockphoto.com / DNY59

Cartoons: Rich Tennant (www.the5thwave.com)

Composition Services

Project Coordinator: Patrick Redmond

Layout and Graphics: Melanee Habig

Proofreaders: Lindsay Amones, The Well-Chosen Word

Indexer: Sharon Shock

Special Help

Amanda M. Langferman, Jessica Smith

Publishing and Editorial for Consumer Dummies

    Kathleen Nebenhaus, Vice President and Executive Publisher

    David Palmer, Associate Publisher

    Kristin Ferguson-Wagstaffe, Product Development Director

Publishing for Technology Dummies

    Andy Cummings, Vice President and Publisher

Composition Services

    Debbie Stailey, Director of Composition Services

Contents at a Glance

Table of Contents

Part IV: Acquiring and Transferring Property Rights ... 217

Chapter 13: Acquiring Rights by Finding and Possessing Personal Property...................................219

Chapter 14: Becoming an Owner by Adverse Possession 233

Introduction

*P*roperty is everywhere around you. Wherever you go in the United States, the part of Earth you're on is the property of some person, entity, or government. If you look around you, almost everything you see is property — and it's not just the land. Almost everything visible and tangible is property, except for the people themselves. Even some things you can't see are property. Property law touches all of it.

Property law is about your relationship to all those things around you. It determines what you can do with those things and what you can stop other people from doing with those things. It governs how you acquire a right to possess and use a thing and exclude others from it. It directs how you can give that right to others.

You may be very familiar with property but not so familiar with property law. I wrote this book to help you understand those legal rules that are shaping the world around you in so many ways.

About This Book

Property Law For Dummies gives you the short and simple version of the property rules that are generally the subject of first-year law school courses in property law. I don't cite many cases or include footnotes, so this book doesn't look much like other law books. My goal is to organize, simplify, and clarify the basic rules of property law to make the subject easier to understand.

If you're a law student, you know that your job in law school isn't just to learn legal rules. You're also learning how and why those legal rules are created and changed and how to apply them and make persuasive arguments about them. You're learning how to figure out what the rules are by reading cases, statutes, and regulations. But you may find that in the process of reading cases, making arguments, considering possible rules and approaches, and exploring the reasons for rules, you sometimes have a hard time simply identifying what the rule is. That's where this book can help.

You don't have to read through the whole book in order to understand each part. You can turn to any issue you're studying and find what you need to know. Some issues relate to other issues, of course, so often you find references to other chapters that you can turn to for more detail.

Conventions Used in This Book

I use the following conventions throughout the text to make things consistent and easy to understand:

- ✔ New terms appear in *italic* and are closely followed by an easy-to-understand definition.

- ✔ I use **bold** to highlight keywords in bulleted lists and the action parts of numbered steps.

What You're Not to Read

Most of this book is just the basics. But sometimes I've included additional details, historical background, related rules, and the like. I think all the info is interesting and worth reading, but you can understand the subject without reading the extra stuff. I've set the skippable, nonessential info apart in two ways:

- ✔ **Sidebars:** Sidebars are shaded boxes that give more background or details about the subject.

- ✔ **The Technical Stuff icon:** This icon indicates information that's interesting but that you can live without.

Foolish Assumptions

You may be interested in property law for all sorts of reasons. Even so, I've written this book assuming the following things about you:

- ✔ You're studying property law for the first time. Or you've forgotten it. You may be preparing to answer property law questions on the bar exam. Whether you're learning property law for the first time or reviewing what you've studied before, this book can be a helpful reference and survey of property law issues.

- ✔ You're mostly interested in *real property* — land and buildings and other things attached to the land. Like most property law courses, this book covers some law related to personal property (and many of the rules for personal and real property are the same), but you won't find a lot of info on cars and autographed baseballs or intellectual property like patents and copyrights.

✔ You're familiar with the law generally. You're a law student or at least know the basics about the court system, lawsuits, remedies, the common law system, and so on. If this is a foolish assumption about you, you may benefit from a legal dictionary to help explain unfamiliar terms that I've assumed you know.

✔ You're not looking for cases and other authorities to cite in a brief or some other legal document. You just want to understand the basic rules. If you're looking for supporting authorities to research and cite, you'll need a hornbook or other treatise.

How This Book Is Organized

Each chapter of this book deals with some particular area of property law. I've grouped chapters dealing with the same types of issues into parts. Here's what each part is about.

Part 1: Introducing Property Law

Part I introduces the subjects I cover in Parts II, III, and IV and gives you some foundation to help you understand those later parts of the book. Chapter 1 introduces the subject of property law generally: what property law is, what property is, how you come to own it, and forms of ownership. Chapter 2 talks more about what property is: the types of property and the various rights — and corresponding remedies — that constitute property. Chapter 3 talks more about how title to property originates and is transferred and how ownership of property may be shared simultaneously or divided up over time.

Part II: Understanding Real Property Rights

This part develops the basic ideas from Chapter 2, that property is legal rights in relation to things and that those rights can be adjusted in various ways. In other words, this part is about what a property owner can do with her land and about the sources of such rules.

Chapter 4 describes the basic common law rights that come with ownership of land. The next two chapters then examine two ways in which landowners can adjust those rights by private contracts: covenants and easements.

Finally, Chapters 7 and 8 study how public regulation can change those rights and look at the statutory and constitutional limitations on such regulation.

Part III: Looking at Shared and Divided Property Ownership

Part III considers how two or more people can share the ownership rights that I describe in Part II. People can own property concurrently, as I explain in Chapter 10. Marriage partners share property ownership in unique ways, as you examine in Chapter 11.

Two or more people also may share ownership of the same property successively, over time. For example, Chapter 12 studies the law related to leases of real property, in which both the landlord and the tenant have a legal interest; however, the tenant has the right to possess the property during the lease term, and then the landlord has the right to take possession when the lease ends. Chapter 9 talks about other ways property ownership may be divided up over time.

Part IV: Acquiring and Transferring Property Rights

This part considers how someone comes to have ownership rights in the first place. Sometimes a person may become an owner of moveable things simply by taking possession of them, as Chapter 13 explains. A person also may become an owner of land or other kinds of property by possessing the property as if she owned it for a long period of time; Chapter 14 talks about this rule, called *adverse possession.*

Most of the time, however, people come to own land by acquiring it from others who owned it before. Chapters 15 and 16 talk about contracts to buy and sell land and deeds that actually transfer ownership. Chapter 17 introduces the legal systems for notifying the world of a change in ownership. Often, buyers need to borrow some money to buy land, and they give a mortgage to a lender to ensure repayment of the loan. Chapter 18 talks about the law of mortgages, including how default on a mortgage loan can lead to a foreclosure sale that transfers ownership of the property to someone else.

Part V: The Part of Tens

The last part is a *For Dummies* tradition: The Part of Tens. This part includes three lists of ten that I hope you'll find helpful as you study property law. Specifically, the Part of Tens fills you in on ten important property cases that are worth remembering, ten mistakes that law students often make in applying the property law I cover in this book, and ten property law subjects commonly tested on bar exams.

Icons Used in This Book

To make this book easier to read and simpler to use, I've included some icons that can help you note key ideas and otherwise find what you're looking for.

This icon appears next to information that can help make the law easier to understand or easier to apply.

Any time you see this icon, you know the information that follows is especially important — the stuff you should read if you're skimming and the stuff that's most worth remembering.

This icon flags information that can help you avoid mistakes or misunderstandings.

This icon appears next to information that's interesting but not essential. Feel free to skip these paragraphs.

This icon indicates an example of how a rule or concept works. You can skip examples if you're just skimming for the rules or focus on examples to better understand how the rules work.

Where to Go from Here

If you're a law student studying property law, this book is a supplement to a casebook and maybe other things that you're reading for class. You know what you're studying and what you need help with, so you can just look at the table of contents or the index, find what you're looking for, and start reading.

If you're using this book as your primary source of learning property law, I suggest you start with Chapter 1, which offers a basic foundation for the whole book and can help you get a big picture of the subject before you start studying details. Chapters 2 and 3 likewise introduce some basic perspectives to help you understand the later parts of the book.

Ultimately, where you go from here doesn't really matter — as long as you go somewhere. Each part stands on its own, and the chapters cross-reference each other to help make sure you don't miss anything. So dive in wherever you think is best.

Part I

Introducing Property Law

"Well, all the papers are in order. The only thing left is to have you pee on the side of the house, and it's yours."

In this part . . .

Property law is about the legal rights that come with owning things. In this part, I help you think about what property is and introduce the types of laws that shape property rights. You find out about the basic rights that come with property ownership, how private agreements and public laws can change those rights, and the legal remedies that courts can give you when your rights are invaded. You also get an overview of how property rights are acquired, transferred, shared, and divided over time.

Chapter 1

Getting the Lowdown on Property Law

*P*roperty law is the law about property. Okay, that's probably not helpful, but I have to start the book somehow.

Maybe it's not that helpful, but it's true. Because property law is law about property, understanding what property law is requires understanding what property is. In this chapter, I explain the types of legal rights that constitute property and what the two big categories of property — real and personal — include.

I also describe the ways that ownership may be shared and divided up over time, and I identify ways people may become property owners and transfer their ownership to other people.

Defining Property

Because property law is simply all types of laws about property, describing property law requires defining property. That's the organizing principle, the common denominator, for law school courses about property law and for this book. The following sections explain how property means having certain types of legal rights in relation to a thing and introduce the two main types of property.

Viewing property as legal rights

Property may refer to things that people own, but from a legal perspective, thinking of property as legal rights in relation to things is more accurate. A legal right is essentially a right that a court will recognize and enforce. (Chapter 2 introduces the ways that courts enforce property rights.)

Although you can be much more specific about the legal rights that constitute property, all property rights fit in four basic categories:

- **Rights to possess:** The owner of land has the right to occupy it. The owner of other kinds of property has the right to physically control it.

- **Rights to use:** The owner of property can use it in all sorts of ways. Of course, the right to use can't be absolute because one person's use of her property may interfere with others' use of their property.

- **Rights to exclude others:** An owner can keep others from using or invading her property.

- **Rights to transfer:** An owner can transfer her legal rights in whole or in part to other people.

Describing property law

Unlike other traditional first-year law subjects (namely contract law, tort law, criminal law, constitutional law, and civil procedure), property law is organized by the subject matter of legal rights rather than the type or source of legal rights. Property law includes the study of some contracts, torts, constitutional clauses, procedures, and maybe even some crimes — grouped together because they all concern property. The following list illustrates and explains:

- **Torts:** Interferences with property rights are torts. Torts related to property law include nuisance, trespass, *conversion* (taking or wrongfully keeping someone else's property), and waste.

- **Contracts:** Much of property law is about contracts that transfer and shape property rights. Covenants and easements contractually adjust property rights.

Contracts transferring property rights include leases, purchase agreements, deeds, and mortgages.

- **Statutes:** Property law also includes some statutory law related to property, including oil and gas laws, zoning laws, marital property laws, landlord/tenant laws, finders statutes, recording statutes, and mortgage and foreclosure laws.

- **Constitutional protection:** The U.S. and state constitutions protect private property against governmental intrusions. An owner's property rights therefore include constitutional rights against the government. These rights include the rights to substantive due process, just compensation for taken property, and equal protection. See Chapter 8 for details on these three constitutional property protections.

None of these rights are absolute; they're simply categories and types of legal rights that constitute property ownership. But owning property means having these four rights to some extent.

The extent of these rights for any particular owner depends on the combined effect of all the sources of legal rights and rules. Specific property rights are determined by the following:

- **Common law:** The common law describes traditional property rights that constitute property ownership, created and shaped by judicial decisions over time. Chapter 4 talks about some of the main common-law property rights.

- **Rights created by contract:** Property owners can adjust their rights by private agreement with others. Under the common law, for example, a property owner has the right to exclude others from entering her land, but she can contractually give another person the property right to enter her land. Such rights are called *easements,* which I discuss in Chapter 6. Similarly, the common law may give a property owner the right to run a business on her land, but she can give away that legal right through a contract called a *covenant,* which promises someone else that she will or won't do certain things in connection with her land. Chapter 5 discusses such covenants.

- **Statutory rules:** Legislative bodies may adopt statutes and ordinances to create new property rights or adjust existing property rights. Zoning ordinances, which I cover in Chapter 7, restrict the types of buildings and uses permitted on the land, which limits the rights that property owners would otherwise have to use their property. Chapter 8 talks about constitutional restrictions on the legislative power to adopt new property rules by statute.

Categorizing property as real or personal

Even though having the legal rights to possess, use, exclude, and transfer in relation to any kind of thing that can be owned is property, there are two main categories or types of property:

- **Real:** Real property means property in land and things attached to land, like buildings.

- **Personal:** Personal property means any property that isn't real. More specifically, personal property includes *chattels,* which are tangible things not connected to land, and *intangible property,* which includes things like intellectual property in ideas, patents, copyrights, and trademarks.

Chapter 2 talks more about these types of property and the differences between them.

Applying the same rules to real and personal property

Even though some rules are different for personal property and real property, many of the rules are basically the same. Here are some examples from this book:

✔ Chapter 9 examines estates in real property, but a person may generally create estates in personal property subject to the same rules.

✔ Chapter 10 discusses concurrent estates, in which two or more people own the same property at the same time. That chapter focuses on co-ownership of real property, but people can co-own personal property in the same way.

✔ Chapter 11 talks about marital property rights that may apply to both real and personal property.

✔ Chapter 14 talks about acquiring title to real property by adverse possession, but the same principles apply to personal property.

Law school property law courses (as well as this book) mostly talk about rules concerning real property. Chapter 13 is the only chapter in this book that focuses on rules unique to personal property — rules about the rights and duties of people who find chattels.

Describing the Duration and Sharing of Ownership

An individual can own all the legal ownership rights in an item of real or personal property. But often, more than one person has some ownership rights in a particular property.

Sometimes different people have the legal right to possess and use the same property at different times: One person has the right to use the property for a certain time, and then another person has the right to the property, then another, and so on. Estates and leaseholds are forms of successive ownership rights like this:

✔ **Estates:** An *estate* is ownership of property for some amount of time. A person can own property indefinitely, for a lifetime, for a specified number of years, and for other time periods. For example, one person may own the property for her lifetime, and then another person gets it when she dies. Chapter 9 describes how estates may divide property ownership over time.

✔ **Leaseholds:** A *lease* is a contract between a landlord and a tenant that gives the tenant the present estate (which may be called a *leasehold*). The tenant has the right to possess the property for a time, and the landlord has the right to take possession back when the leasehold ends. Chapter 12 covers landlord-tenant law in detail.

Different people also may share ownership of the same property at the same time rather than successively. Such ownership may be called *concurrent ownership* (Chapter 10 covers the forms of concurrent ownership of property and the rights and duties that co-owners have in relation to each other). Married couples may share ownership of property in unique ways. (Chapter 11 describes how spouses share property.)

Acquiring Original Property Rights

Anything that's owned must have a first owner. Here are some of the ways that a thing first becomes owned as property:

✔ **Sovereign acquisition:** In the U.S. legal system, all land was originally owned by a government. As Chapter 3 explains, federal, state, and foreign governments originated title to lands in the U.S. by asserting sovereign claims based upon discovery and conquest.

✔ **Adverse possession:** If a person possesses property as if she owned it openly and continuously for a long period of time, she acquires title to the property. This is called *adverse possession.* Even though someone else formerly owned the property, the theory of adverse possession is that the adverse possessor acquires a new title instead of getting title from the former owner. Chapter 14 examines the doctrine of adverse possession in detail.

✔ **Creation:** People can create new personal property. Much personal property is originally owned by the person who creates it. Even then, she probably has to acquire raw materials from someone else. But if she gets the raw materials, she can create a new thing, like a hat, and she's its first owner. Similarly, a person can create intangible property like an idea and become its first owner.

✔ **Capture:** Some things exist in nature but aren't privately owned until captured. Chapter 13 talks about acquiring original ownership in this way. For example, wild animals aren't owned until someone captures them. Similarly, underground water, oil, and gas may not be owned until someone lawfully draws them out from underground, as Chapter 4 explains.

✔ **Taking possession:** Even when someone else already owned personal property, a person can acquire original ownership rights by taking possession. If the former owner abandons the property, for example, whoever finds and possesses it first becomes its owner, without acquiring ownership from the former owner. Even if the former owner doesn't abandon the thing, a finder or the owner of the property where the thing was mislaid may acquire ownership rights against the rest of the world — and maybe even against the former owner. See Chapter 13 for details on acquiring ownership by taking possession.

Transferring Property Rights to Another

One of the basic rights of property ownership is the right to transfer your rights to other people. An owner can give away just some of her rights but remain the owner, such as by giving someone an easement to use her property. An owner also can transfer her entire ownership — the basic rights to possess, use, and exclude. Following are some ways she can transfer her ownership rights:

✔ **Deed:** An owner can transfer her ownership by delivering a valid deed to a grantee. Chapter 16 talks about deeds in detail.

✔ **Will:** An owner can transfer her ownership at her death by a will. Chapter 3 covers wills.

✔ **Mortgage:** In some states, a mortgage is treated as a conveyance of title to the mortgagee; in others, it's merely a *lien*, the legal right to sell the property to satisfy an unpaid debt. In either case, if the mortgagor defaults on the debt that the mortgage secures, the mortgagee can foreclose, hold an auction sale, and have the title transferred to the high bidder. Chapter 18 talks about mortgages.

When an owner transfers property to another person, the new owner wants to be sure that the world knows she now owns the property. She does that by recording her interest with the county clerk or other public officer who maintains records related to real property. If she doesn't, as Chapter 17 explains, state recording statutes may allow someone else who buys the property without knowing about her interest to become the owner instead.

Chapter 2

Defining Property in Legal Terms

. . . .

In This Chapter

▶ Classifying types of property

▶ Examining the basic rights that constitute property ownership

▶ Introducing ways in which ownership rights are adjusted

▶ Considering legal remedies for violations of property rights

. . . .

*Y*ou may call the things that you own your "property." The law also sometimes uses the term *property* in this sense, referring to things that are owned. Lawyers love to categorize things, and, of course, they've categorized different types of things that may be owned. The first part of this chapter examines the categories of property.

Of course, the law isn't really about things; it's about legal rights in relation to things. So it's no surprise that lawyers generally think of property as legal rights in relation to things rather than as the things themselves. A thing is property not because of its attributes but because we recognize certain kinds of legal rights concerning it. Although you could make a long list of different legal rights that are property rights, this chapter examines the basic types of rights that constitute property ownership. It also introduces the idea that those rights may be changed by private agreements and governmental regulation.

Distinguishing between Real and Personal Property

Anything that can be legally owned may be called property. All property can be grouped into two main categories: real property and personal property. Personal property can be further classified as chattels and intangibles. One reason to know these categories is simply to understand what other lawyers are talking about. Of course, knowing the categories can also help you decide which rules should apply to a particular item of property and which remedies are available for violations of property rights.

State statutes may define different categories of property for different purposes. So whenever the categorization of property makes a difference in legal rights or remedies, you should first search for relevant statutory definitions.

The following sections describe real property and the two types of personal property.

The real world: Land and buildings

Real property describes land and things that are attached to the land, which is why land is sometimes called *real estate* or *realty.* Even though wood, steel, and other building materials aren't land themselves, when they're built into structures attached to the land, they become real property, too. Trees and other plants naturally growing on the land are also part of the real property. But plants that require regular human cultivation and labor, such as grains and vegetables, sometimes aren't treated as part of the real property.

This book focuses on the law related to real property, but many rules apply to real and personal property alike.

A personal touch: Everything else that can be owned

Personal property is all property that isn't real property. That's a big category. It can be further divided into two subgroups, chattels and intangibles, which I describe next.

Chattels

The term *chattel* sometimes refers to all kinds of personal property, but often it refers only to tangible personal property (such as nose flutes and toenail clippers) as opposed to intangible property.

A chattel, such as a furnace, can be affixed to land and become part of the real property. Such chattels are called *fixtures.* However, fixtures may retain their quality as separate personal property for certain purposes. For example, at the end of a lease term, the tenant generally has the right to remove fixtures she installed even though she doesn't have any more right to the real property when the lease ends.

Intangibles

Intangibles are all kinds of personal property that aren't tangible, that can't be seen or touched. So you can say this kind of property doesn't involve a "thing" at all; it involves only a legal right. The mere existence of such a category of property is a reminder that, in the law, property most accurately refers to legal rights, not to things.

Neither real nor personal: Things that can't be owned

Some things can't be owned at all and therefore can't be private property. Some of these things, such as light, air, and the high seas, can't be owned because they naturally seem communal.

Other things, such as rivers and coastal waters, can't be owned because they belong to the public. And some things can't be owned because they're illegal, like heroin.

A person can own all sorts of intangible "things," including the following:

- ✔ Bank accounts
- ✔ Franchises and licenses
- ✔ Insurance policies
- ✔ Intellectual property such as patents, copyrights, and trademarks
- ✔ Stocks, bonds, promissory notes, and similar documents that aren't themselves valuable but merely represent intangible rights; currency is sometimes treated as an intangible

Describing a Property Owner's Rights

Owning something means you can enforce legal rights concerning it. It doesn't take a lawyer to identify the basic categories of rights that come with property ownership. If you own property, you have the right to do the following with it:

- ✔ Possess it
- ✔ Use it
- ✔ Exclude others from it
- ✔ Transfer it to someone else

The following sections discuss the meaning and significance of these basic rights.

Possessing property

Possessing property basically means intentionally exercising physical control over it. If you own real property, you have the right to occupy the land and structures on it. Similarly, the right to possess personal property is the right to physically control it. In other words, you can handle it and take it places.

Possession is a basic right of ownership, but it's also a condition to having certain rights and duties with respect to property. For example, someone who possesses real property for a long period of time and satisfies other requirements obtains ownership of the property even though it wasn't hers before. This is the doctrine of *adverse possession,* which I tell you about in Chapter 14. Even though possession always means basically the same thing, the required proof of possession varies with different legal rules.

Using property

Property has value because the owner can use it somehow. You can use real property all sorts of ways, such as building things on it, keeping personal property on it, and doing whatever it is you do — eating, sleeping, studying. (Maybe that's all you do lately.) And of course, there are countless types of personal property and countless ways to use it.

Excluding others from your property

You don't need property law to allow you to possess and use property. Even if property laws didn't exist, you could still possess and use land and things. The problem is, so could others — and they might want to possess and use the same things you want to possess and use. As a result, the property would be much less useful to you; it might even be useless.

Excluding others is really what makes property *property.* You generally can keep others off your land. You can keep your things to yourself so they're available for your own use as you choose. If you can't generally exclude others from using a thing, it probably shouldn't be called your property. And if you can exclude people, you can fairly call it property. Even people's ideas and personal attributes, such as voices, have been called property because the law has recognized the right to exclude others from using them.

Transferring property

You can exclude others from your property, but you can also choose not to exclude them. If this book is your property, for example, you could let someone else read part of it or the whole thing. You could let someone else read it for a day, a week, or a year. In fact, you could let her possess and use it from now on. And if you did that, you could also give her the right to exclude others from now on. In short, you could give her your book. This power to give your property rights to others is the right to transfer, which lawyers sometimes call the right to *alienate.*

The right to transfer property is so fundamental that courts invalidate some attempts by private contract to restrict the right to transfer. Not only is this right a basic attribute of private dominion over a thing, it's also important to society because the freedom to transfer is essential to wealth-producing market transactions. (See Chapters 5 and 9 for examples of how courts limit contractual restrictions on transfers.)

Limiting a Property Owner's Rights

The rights to possess, use, exclude, and transfer property sometimes conflict with other people's rights or the public interest. Therefore, these rights aren't absolute. Property law attempts to reconcile competing rights and interests by means of default rules, contractual rules, and public regulations.

Declaring default common law rules

One large part of property law consists of the common law rules that generally describe the extent of property rights. I walk you through some of these rules in Chapter 4.

Suppose one person wants to use her land to raise pigs, but that use may seriously interfere with the adjoining landowner's desire to use his land for his house. Instead of simply declaring that everyone can do whatever they want on their own land, property law sets default rules that limit owners' respective rights. In this example, the law of *nuisance* declares a default rule that a property owner is entitled to be free from unreasonable interference with the use and enjoyment of her land. Likewise, she may not unreasonably interfere with others' use and enjoyment of their land.

Modifying property rights by contract

Even though the law declares default rules that reconcile competing interests, as I explain in the preceding section, people can agree to change those rules. Just as a property owner may transfer her entire property to someone else, she may transfer just some of her rights to someone else.

For example, if the law of nuisance gave a residential property owner the right to prevent a pig farm next door, that owner could enter into a contract with the neighboring property owner to allow a pig farm on that land despite the default nuisance rule.

Covenants and easements are two types of contractual agreements that adjust parties' respective property rights. I tell you more about covenants and easements in Chapters 5 and 6, respectively, but here's a quick breakdown of these contractual agreements:

- ✓ A *covenant* is a contractual agreement that limits a property owner's freedom to use her land in some way or that requires her to do something on her land. For example, one common type of neighborhood covenant is a promise not to use land for nonresidential purposes.

- ✓ An *easement* is typically a contractual agreement allowing someone else to use the owner's land somehow, such as an agreement allowing a neighbor to drive across the owner's land to get to the neighbor's land. A *negative easement,* on the other hand, is a contractual agreement that restricts the property owner's freedom to use her property.

Publicly regulating property

Federal, state, and local governments all have some power to regulate how land is used, and these regulations can further reshape property rights. For example, even though a property owner may have a common law right to use her property as she wishes (as long as she doesn't unreasonably interfere with others' use and enjoyment of their land), local zoning laws may further restrict that freedom by specifying that property in certain areas may be used only for residential purposes. (See Chapter 7 for details about zoning laws.) Similarly, a property owner may have a common law right to transfer her property as she wishes, but federal laws restrict her freedom to transfer it in ways that are racially discriminatory.

Exploring Remedies for Violations of Property Rights

A property right means nothing if you can't enforce it. If you have the right to exclude others from your land but have no power to actually do so, you're practically no better off than if you had no such right.

Enforcing property rights is what really makes them rights. Even if there were no laws at all, people could take possession of things, use them, give them to others, and do their best to exclude others from taking them away. Property law essentially offers the force of the government to help exclude invaders and specifies the conditions on which the government will do so.

Therefore, fully understanding and describing a property owner's rights in relation to a thing requires consideration of both the right and the *remedies,* which are the ways the law enforces that right. Invoking the power of the government to repel an invader is very different from merely obtaining financial compensation from the invader, for example.

The following sections consider the different kinds of remedies available for different kinds of violations of property rights.

Common law forms of action

Long ago, different common law forms of action evolved to address different kinds of injuries to different kinds of property and to provide different remedies. Almost all U.S. jurisdictions have abolished the old common law forms of action and now provide for a single form of civil action.

However, you still need to be familiar with the predominant common law forms of action. Some of the old labels may still be used to identify claims for relief, some differences in claims and remedies persist, and you may read older judicial opinions that use the old labels.

Real property

Real property is called "real" because of the common law actions that protected and preserved the owner's physical possession of land instead of just providing compensation for the land taken by another. Centuries ago in England, the action of ejectment evolved and took the place of various earlier real actions. *Ejectment* entitled the owner to have a wrongful possessor ejected and to regain possession.

If the wrongdoer entered the land but didn't take possession from the owner, the action of *trespass* provided a damages remedy. And if a wrongdoer didn't enter the land but merely interfered with its use and enjoyment, the action of *trespass on the case* (or just *case*) likewise provided a damages remedy.

Personal property

A "personal" action was an action for damages rather than a judgment directly affecting possession of the property itself. Long ago, there were no "real" actions for property other than land, so such property came to be called "personal property." Over time, however, actions developed to recover possession of personal property rather than to just obtain damages. Some of the actions related to personal property were

- ✔ **Trover:** An action for damages from someone who wrongfully took personal property

- ✔ **Replevin:** Originally only an action to recover chattels wrongfully seized by a landlord for breach of a tenant's duties, it evolved to allow recovery of any wrongfully withheld personal property — or damages if the defendant wrongfully disposed of the property

- ✔ **Detinue:** An action for wrongful withholding of possession of chattels, in which the defendant had the choice of returning the chattels or paying money damages

✔ **Trespass:** An action for damages resulting from interference with land or chattels

Legal and equitable remedies

There's another old remedial distinction that you should know: the distinction between legal remedies and equitable remedies. Property remedies developed in two different court systems in England. The common law courts developed the forms of action I talk about in the preceding section. The two basic legal remedies available to a plaintiff were damages and restitution:

✔ **Damages:** An award of money calculated to compensate the plaintiff for injury to or loss of property

✔ **Restitution:** An order requiring the defendant to return property to the rightful owner

The English Court of Chancery, on the other hand, offered some remedies that weren't available in the common law courts. The English Court of Chancery was a court of "equity" rather than "law," so its remedies were known as *equitable remedies*.

Even though modern courts may grant all the legal and equitable remedies recognized by the law, the terms are still used to distinguish types of remedies.

Here are some important equitable remedies to know:

✔ **Injunction:** This is an order by a court preventing someone from interfering with another's property. Such an order may prohibit someone from doing something, require someone to do something, or both. Today an injunction is generally available if the threatened harm by the defendant would be irreparable or if calculating the harm in monetary terms and awarding compensating damages would be difficult.

✔ **Specific performance:** Specific performance is a particular kind of injunction that compels a party to perform a contract. Like injunctions generally, a court orders specific performance only when an award of damages would be inadequate.

✔ **Quieting title:** Quieting title is a judicial declaration about the validity and state of a person's title to land, resolving disputed claims about interests in the land.

✔ **Rescission:** This is a judicial order that cancels a contract and restores the contracting parties to the position they were in before entering into the contract.

✔ **Reformation of written instruments:** This is a judicial order that changes the terms of a written agreement to be consistent with the parties' actual intentions.

Chapter 3

Considering Property Ownership

In This Chapter

▶ Understanding what title is

▶ Considering ways to get title

▶ Introducing how ownership may be divided over time

▶ Looking at how ownership may be shared

A person who has legal ownership rights in a thing has *title* to that thing. This chapter explains what title is and considers the ways to get title.

More than one person can have an ownership interest in the same property at the same time. This can happen two ways: First, two or more people can own interests (called *estates*) that entitle one person to possess the property in the present and for some defined time into the future, then entitle another person to take possession after her, and so on. Second, two or more people can own an estate together (called *concurrent ownership*). That means they both have the right to possess the property in the present. This chapter describes both estates and concurrent ownership.

Defining Title

Title to real property means ownership of the property. You may think of title as a legal document representing ownership, like title to a car. But title to real property isn't represented by a document. Title to real property is a legal status. If you're the legal owner of real property, you own the title.

People rarely own perfect, complete title to real property. As Chapters 15 and 16 discuss, almost all real property titles are subject to various interests belonging to other people. Typically the owner's interest in real property is subject to things like the following:

 ✔ **Covenants:** A restrictive covenant gives up some of the owner's right to use and enjoy property. A *covenant* is a promise that the owner (or the owner's predecessor in title) makes to someone else about how she'll use the real property. The owner still owns the property, but she can't use the property contrary to her promise. For example, a restrictive covenant may promise that the owner won't use the property for purposes other than a single-family residence. See Chapter 5 for information on covenants.

✔ **Mortgages:** A mortgage essentially gives another party some of the owner's right to transfer the property. A *mortgage* is the right to sell the property and apply the sale proceeds to an unpaid debt that the mortgage secures. The owner still owns the property, but she's given away part of her right to transfer the property. Flip to Chapter 18 for further details about mortgages.

✔ **Easements:** An easement gives up some of the owner's right to exclude others from the property. An easement typically is a right to use someone else's land in some way. So the owner still owns the land, but she can't exclude the easement holder from using her land as granted by the easement. For example, the easement holder may have the right to use a road across the owner's land. Chapter 6 explains how easements work and how they're created.

Even if an owner doesn't own perfect and complete title to property, she still owns the title. Some titles are just subject to more rights belonging to other people. Such rights belonging to others may be called *title defects,* because they're flaws or limitations in title.

Acquiring Title

An owner of title generally acquires her title from someone who previously owned the title, although it is possible to acquire title without getting it from a previous owner. The following sections introduce the various ways you can acquire title.

The first owners: Identifying original government title

Every piece of property has to have a first title owner. In the U.S. legal system, the first title owner of all land was a government, whether the federal government, a state government, or a foreign government.

Ownership of nearly all the land in the original 13 states began with the British crown. The British claimed ownership by discovering, possessing, and conquering the land. Even though they acknowledged that the native inhabitants had a right to occupy the land, they asserted the right to grant the land to others even if it was occupied.

Some individuals acquired private ownership of land from the British Crown before the American Revolution. Some such lands were confiscated after the Revolution. The lands still claimed by the British Crown after the Revolution passed to the states by treaty. Ownership of other lands not within the boundaries of those states was disputed but ultimately settled in the federal government.

The federal government subsequently acquired other lands from various countries, including the following:

- **France:** The United States purchased the Louisiana Territory from France in 1803. This territory extended from the Mississippi River on the east to parts of present-day Montana, Wyoming, Colorado, and New Mexico on the west; from Canada on the north to present-day Texas on the south.

- **Spain:** The United States purchased Florida and parts of Georgia, Alabama, and Mississippi from Spain in 1819. Spain also ceded any claims to the Oregon Territory.

- **Great Britain:** The United States acquired the Oregon Territory, including the present-day states of Washington, Oregon, and Idaho, plus parts of Montana and Wyoming, by treaty with Great Britain in 1846.

- **Mexico:** In 1848, Mexico ceded to the United States its territory from the Pacific Ocean to the western limits of the Louisiana Purchase. In 1853, the United States purchased some additional disputed land that's now part of Arizona and New Mexico.

- **Russia:** The United States purchased Alaska from Russia in 1867.

The federal government didn't keep all this land, of course; it gave many lands to the individual states.

Patents: Conveying government land to individuals

The federal government has transferred many lands to private individuals over the years. Here are some of the ways:

- **Public sale:** Early on, the federal government simply offered surveyed lands for sale. Later, people who had improved the land had the first right to purchase the land.

- **Homestead patents:** After public sales ceased, the federal government transferred 160-acre parcels of land to those who occupied and cultivated the land for five years.

> ✔ **Railroad grants:** The federal government gave a lot of land to railroad companies that built railways. The government generally gave the railroads odd-numbered square-mile sections on either side of the new track for a number of miles, creating a checkerboard pattern of private and public ownership.

The document by which the government officially transfers a land title to another is called a *patent*. States have likewise transferred many land titles to private owners by patent.

Acquiring private land for the public

The government often acquires title from individuals. Of course, a private individual may give or sell title to the government, just as she may give or sell title to third parties. But the government acquires title from individuals in other ways too, including dedication, eminent domain, escheat, and forfeiture.

Dedication

A private owner may give land to the government or to the public by dedication. Under the common law, a *dedication* is a private owner's declaration that she intends to dedicate her land for a public use, such as a highway, a park, or a school. She may indicate her intention by a written instrument, or she may instead indicate her intention by words and actions.

Statutes also may specify circumstances in which a private owner dedicates land to the local government. Unlike common law dedications, statutory dedications actually give title to the government. For example, statutes commonly say that publicly recording a subdivision plat map that shows public streets, parks, or other public areas has the effect of dedicating those lands to the government for the purposes indicated on the plat map.

Eminent domain

Federal and state governments have the inherent sovereign power, called *eminent domain,* to take property from private owners for the benefit of the public. States generally grant this power to local governments and some quasi-public entities like utilities as well. The government may take property for actual public use, such as for a park or school, or for a private use that will benefit the public, such as by economically revitalizing a depressed area.

The Fifth Amendment (which applies to state and local governments through the Fourteenth Amendment) requires the government to pay just compensation for land that it takes by eminent domain. So do state constitutional clauses. *Just compensation* generally means the market value of the property taken. Chapter 8 talks more about the Takings Clause of the Fifth Amendment.

Escheat

If a person dies without validly conveying property by will, state statutes specify the person's heirs who are entitled to take the property. But if the person has no heir who can take the property, the state takes title to it by *escheat*.

Forfeiture

Private owners may forfeit land to the government. Some state and federal statutes say that if someone uses property to commit a crime or buys property with money from criminal activity, such as drug trafficking, the property is forfeited to the government. Some state statutes also provide that if a corporation acquires land in violation of law, the land shall be forfeited to the state.

Conveying title to private land during life

A title owner can voluntarily transfer her title to someone else during her lifetime. Such a transfer may be called an *inter vivos transfer,* meaning a transfer during life.

The *statute of frauds* says that a conveyance of title to real property is enforceable only if it's evidenced in writing. Although there are exceptions to the statute of frauds, a title owner generally must sign a written document in order to convey title.

The written document conveying title is called a *deed.* A deed must include the following to be valid and enforceable:

✔ The names of the grantor and the grantee

✔ A valid description of the land to which title is being conveyed

✔ Words indicating an intent to presently convey the title

✔ The grantor's signature

A deed conveys title only when the title owner delivers the deed to the grantee and the grantee accepts it. Chapter 16 talks about conveyancing by deeds in more detail.

Transferring property by will

A title owner can transfer her title to another party upon her death. The document that transfers title at death is a *will,* and the grantor is called the *testator.* Regardless of how the grantor labels the document, the document is a will if the grantor intends the conveyance to be effective only upon her death.

The following generally must be true in order for a will to be valid and effective:

- ✓ **Signature:** The testator must sign the will, or in most states, someone else may sign the will for the testator if the testator so directs and the person signs it in the testator's presence.

- ✓ **Acknowledgment:** The testator must either sign the will in the presence of witnesses or acknowledge to witnesses that she signed the will. Most statutes require two witnesses; some require three. Under the common law, a person who receives property by the will can't be a witness; today most state statutes allow such a person to be a witness if necessary for the will to be valid but void the grant to the witness.

- ✓ **Publication:** Some state statutes say that the testator must somehow indicate to the witnesses that the document is her will. This indication is referred to as *publication* of the will.

- ✓ **Attestation:** The witnesses generally must *attest* the will by signing it in the presence of the testator and sometimes each other as well.

In some states, a will is enforceable without these formalities if the testator wrote the entire will by hand and signed it. Such a will is called a *holographic will.*

Because a will isn't effective until the grantor dies, the grantor can revoke it any time before she dies. She can simply cancel or destroy the will, or she can execute a new will that expressly or implicitly revokes the old will. Some state statutes say that a will is revoked if the testator subsequently marries or has children, unless the will indicates a contrary intention. A divorce also may implicitly revoke a will in whole or in relevant part.

A grant of real property by will is called a *devise,* so those to whom the will gives real property are called *devisees.* Those to whom the will gives personal property are called *legatees.*

To the heirs: Distributing property by intestate succession

If a title owner dies without a valid will, or if her will doesn't dispose of some property that she owned, state law directs who gets the property. Someone who dies without a will is said to die *intestate.* The person herself may be referred to as *the intestate.* So the statutory distribution of such a person's property is called *intestate succession.* People who receive property by intestate succession are referred to as *heirs.*

Even though state intestate statutes vary, they all provide that a surviving spouse has the right to some of the deceased spouse's estate if she died intestate. Some states that don't recognize same-sex marriages do recognize same-sex civil unions or domestic partnerships, and such partners have the same rights of intestate succession as spouses.

The surviving spouse's share generally depends on which other kindred survive, as follows:

- ✔ If the deceased spouse leaves surviving children or descendants of children, the surviving spouse may get one-third or half of the deceased spouse's property.

- ✔ If the deceased spouse leaves no surviving children or descendants of children, the surviving spouse may get half or all of the deceased spouse's property.

- ✔ If the deceased spouse leaves no surviving descendants, parents, or siblings, the surviving spouse generally gets all of the deceased spouse's property.

As Chapter 11 explains, these statutory shares take the place of the husband's common law curtesy interest and the wife's common law dower interest.

The intestate's property that doesn't go to a surviving spouse is distributed in the following order:

- ✔ **Children:** If the intestate had children, the children take the property in equal shares. An adopted child is a child of both the adopting parents and the natural parents. Stepchildren and foster children, however, aren't included among the intestate's heirs. If a child is dead, the living descendants of the child take that child's share *per stirpes,* meaning that those living descendants collectively own that deceased child's share; they don't each share equally with the living children of the intestate.

- ✔ **Immediate family:** If the intestate has no surviving children or descendants of children, then the intestate's mother, father, sisters, and brothers take the intestate property equally. If a sister or brother is dead, that sibling's descendants take the share per stirpes.

- ✔ **Other family:** If the intestate has no surviving spouse, children, descendants of children, parents, siblings, or descendants of siblings, the intestate's property goes to the intestate's grandmother, grandfather, aunts, and uncles, with descendants of deceased aunts and uncles taking the deceased aunt's or uncle's share per stirpes.

- ✔ **Escheat:** If the intestate leaves none of these heirs surviving, the intestate's property escheats to the state.

Acquiring title by taking possession

Adverse possession is the one way a person can acquire a new title to real property without acquiring the title from someone else. Adverse possession gives a person title to land that she didn't own before if she does all the following:

- ✔ Actually, physically possesses the property

- ✔ Exclusively possesses the property

- ✔ Openly and notoriously possesses the property, in a way that's visible and apparent so that the true title owner could and should be aware that she's possessing it

- ✔ Possesses the property adversely to the owner's title; that is, she possesses the property as if she owns the property rather than by permission of the true title owner

- ✔ Continuously possesses the property without interruption

- ✔ Possesses the property in these ways throughout the applicable statute of limitations period, which might be from 5 to 20 years

Chapter 14 covers adverse possession in detail, examining what each element of adverse possession requires. The basic idea is that if these things are true, the possessor has acted as if she's the owner for a long period of time — so long that the true title owner loses the right to deny that the possessor has title and thus regain possession. So the adverse possessor doesn't get the title from the former owner; the former owner simply loses the right to assert her title against the possessor, so the possessor effectively acquires a new title to the property because there's no one with a superior claim of ownership to interfere with her possession.

Selling property by judicial order

A court or public officer may effectively transfer one person's title to another person — without having the former owner sign a deed or take any other action to accomplish the transfer. Here are some of those situations:

- ✔ **Execution sale:** When a person obtains a damages judgment against another, she may have the person's property sold to satisfy the judgment. The person who wins the damages judgment may be called a *judgment creditor,* and the person who owes damages, a *judgment debtor.* By statute, the judgment creditor has the right to a lien against the judgment debtor's real property in the jurisdiction; the *lien* is a legal right to have the property sold and the proceeds of the sale applied to the unpaid judgment.

The judgment creditor can enforce that lien by getting a *writ of execution,* a judicial order to have a sheriff conduct an execution sale by auction and distribute the proceeds. The sheriff has the statutory authority to convey the title to the buyer by giving her a deed.

✔ **Foreclosure sale:** A person who borrows money from a lender may give the lender a *mortgage* to help ensure repayment of the debt. A mortgage gives the lender, called the *mortgagee,* the right to sell real property at an auction sale if the borrower defaults on her obligations. In some states, a lender may conduct the sale itself, without a lawsuit, if the mortgage (or a comparable document called a *deed of trust*) gives the lender the right to do so. Otherwise, the mortgagee must initiate a lawsuit against the defaulting mortgagor and other affected interest-holders; then the court orders the property to be sold. A sheriff or other public officer conducts the sale and gives a deed to the high bidder upon tender of the purchase price. The proceeds of the foreclosure sale are used to pay off the unpaid debt. Chapter 18 talks about mortgages in detail.

✔ **Tax sale:** If a real-property owner doesn't pay the property taxes on the land, the tax officer or other public official can sell the land at auction, give a deed to the high bidder, and apply the proceeds of the sale to the unpaid taxes. In some states, the deed conveys title free from any encumbrances, meaning that anyone else who has an interest in the land, like an easement, a mortgage, or a lien, will lose her interest when the land is sold for nonpayment of taxes. Such interest holders can protect their interests, however, by paying the taxes or redeeming the land from the tax sale.

✔ **Partition sale:** Two or more people may share ownership of property. Except when the co-owners have a particular form of co-ownership called a *tenancy by the entirety,* any co-owner can ask the court to divide up the property in an action called *partition.* If possible, the court will physically divide the property among the co-owners, giving each co-owner sole title to a portion of the property. Otherwise, the court will order the property sold at auction and the proceeds of the sale will be divided proportionally among the co-owners. You can read more about shared ownership in Chapter 10.

✔ **Judicial orders:** A court's judgment concerning ownership of real property may have the effect of transferring title, without the former owner signing a deed or taking any other action.

Sharing and Dividing Property Ownership

Two or more people may share ownership of the same property at the same time. Two or more people also may own the same property at different times, with one person owning the right to possess for a time, then another person having the right to possess, and so on. The following sections talk about both of these ways to share or divide property.

Defining present and future estates

Ownership of property may be divided up over time. The duration of a person's ownership is called an *estate*. In other words, an *estate* is ownership of property for a period of time. A *present estate* is an estate that entitles the owner to possession in the present. A *future estate*, on the other hand, is an estate that entitles the owner to take possession sometime in the future.

Chapter 9 details the types of estates, but here's the short version. First, states today generally recognize three types of present estates:

- ✔ **Fee simple:** The fee simple is the estate that continues indefinitely. Even when the owner of the fee simple dies, the estate doesn't end; it passes to her devisees by will or to her heirs by intestate succession.

- ✔ **Life estate:** The life estate is a present estate that lasts only until the owner of the estate — or someone else specified in the instrument creating the life estate — dies. If the life estate is for the life of the owner of the life estate, then her estate ends at her death, and she obviously has no more estate to give away by will when she dies.

- ✔ **Leasehold:** The leasehold is a present estate that lasts for a definite period of time, for recurring periods, or until either the landlord or the tenant chooses to terminate it. Chapter 12 describes the types of leaseholds and how they're created.

When a life estate or leasehold ends, someone else owns the right to take possession of the property. Because that person owns the right to possess in the future, her right is called a *future estate*. If the grantor of the life estate or leasehold retains for herself the right to take possession when the life estate or leasehold ends, the grantor's future estate is called a *reversion*. If instead the grant gives the future estate to someone else, the future estate that follows the life estate or leasehold is called a *remainder*.

Any of these present estates may be further limited in time by imposing conditions that will terminate the estate. For example, a grant may give property to person A as long as she uses the property for residential purposes. When such conditions limit the duration of an estate, the estate is called *defeasible*. An estate may be defeasible in the following three ways:

- ✔ **Determinable:** If the estate lasts only as long as a certain condition doesn't happen and then automatically goes back to the grantor if it does occur, the estate is *determinable*. The grantor's future estate — that is, the right to possession if and when the condition occurs — is called a *possibility of reverter*.

- ✔ **On condition subsequent:** Similarly, an estate on condition subsequent is an estate that the grantor may terminate if the specified condition occurs. Unlike a determinable estate, the estate doesn't automatically end when the condition occurs. The grantor (or her successors) has a *right of entry* or *power of termination,* which is the right to choose to take the property back.

✔ **Subject to executory limitation:** An estate subject to executory limitation ends automatically when the condition occurs, but instead of reverting to the grantor, the right of possession goes to someone else. The future estate of the third party who has the subsequent right of possession is called an *executory interest.*

Understanding undivided concurrent ownership

Two or more people can share ownership of an estate. When they do, each of them has the right to use and enjoy the whole property that they co-own. Three forms of concurrent ownership exist:

✔ Tenancy in common

✔ Joint tenancy

✔ Tenancy by the entirety

The following sections introduce the characteristics of each of these forms of concurrent ownership. (For more detailed information on each form, turn to Chapter 10.)

Tenancy in common

Unless the instrument creating the concurrent ownership clearly says otherwise, co-owners are tenants in common. When a group of people share ownership by intestate succession, they're tenants in common with each other.

As with all forms of concurrent ownership, each tenant in common has an equal right to use the whole property. However, they may own different fractional shares of the property. That means, for example, that if they sell the property, they'll receive different fractional shares of the proceeds of the sale.

Each tenant in common may transfer her share of ownership during her life or by will at her death. If she doesn't, her share passes to her heirs when she dies.

Furthermore, each tenant in common may end her co-ownership altogether by a judicial action called a *partition.* In a partition action, the court will try to divide the property physically among the co-owners in proportion to their respective fractional shares. If that isn't possible, the court will order the property to be sold, and the proceeds of the sale will be divided among the co-owners proportionally.

Joint tenancy

Two or more people own property as joint tenants if the granting instrument expressly grants the property to them as joint tenants. Joint tenants must own equal shares; they can't own different fractional shares of the property.

The biggest difference from a tenancy in common is that a joint tenant can't transfer her share to heirs or devisees at her death. Instead, the deceased joint tenant simply doesn't share ownership anymore and the surviving joint tenants own the whole property in equal shares. The right of the other joint tenants to own the share of the deceased joint tenant is called the *right of survivorship*.

However, a joint tenant can terminate the right of survivorship during her lifetime by selling her share to someone else, or in some cases by taking similar action with her own share, like leasing it or mortgaging it. Doing so is called *severance*. Severance doesn't end the person's co-ownership with the others, but it does end their right of survivorship with respect to each other. After severance, the severing joint tenant becomes a tenant in common with the other co-owners, although they remain joint tenants among themselves.

A joint tenant also may bring a partition action, just like a tenant in common may.

Tenancy by the entirety

A tenancy by the entirety is a special form of joint tenancy that can be created only between a husband and a wife. As with joint tenancy, the tenants by the entirety always have equal half-shares in the property. Also like a joint tenancy, the tenants by the entirety have a right of survivorship. When one of the spouses dies, the other owns the property by himself or herself.

Unlike with the joint tenancy, however, one tenant by the entirety can't unilaterally sever his or her tenancy by the entirety and become a tenant in common with the other spouse. In fact, in most states, one tenant by the entirety can't unilaterally convey any interest in the property at all; the two tenants by the entirety must join together in order to convey an interest in the property to someone else. Nor can a tenant by the entirety bring a partition action. Of course, one tenant by the entirety can end the co-ownership by giving her interest to the other or by ending the marriage altogether.

Part II

Understanding Real Property Rights

The 5th Wave   By Rich Tennant

In this part . . .

Owning land means having legally protected rights to possess and use the land, to exclude others from the land, and to transfer your rights to others. In this part, you find out more about an owner's rights to possess, use, and exclude.

First, you discover the basic common law property rights that come with property ownership. Then you see how covenants and easements, which are private contracts, can give away some rights to use and to exclude. You also examine how public regulations can change property rights by adding new rights and taking away existing rights, and you explore the statutory and constitutional limitations on such public regulations.

Chapter 4

Identifying Common Law Rights in Real Property

*A*n owner may use her real property in all sorts of ways. She can build various structures: a house, a convenience store, a chocolate factory, a baseball stadium. She also can do things on her real property: butcher, bake, make candlesticks, and so on. However, other property owners may do the same on their property, and their uses of the properties could conflict — like when one owner wants to use her property for sleeping at night and a neighboring owner wants to use his property for nighttime car racing and rock concerts. The law of nuisance resolves such conflicts, determining when someone's activities invade a property owner's right to use his property.

An owner can also use her property as a source of valuable materials. She can cut down its trees for lumber; draw water from streams and from underground; or extract minerals, oil, and gas. When the product of the land is relatively fixed on or under the surface (such as hard minerals and trees), her extractive use of her property doesn't necessarily affect anyone else's property rights. But if the product of the land is moveable (such as water, oil, and gas), extracting those products prevents them from moving onto someone else's land and being used by that owner instead. So the common law also has rules about the extent to which landowners can use such products of the land.

Using land may involve altering the land itself, such as by digging holes for buildings or mines or leveling the earth to make it more useable. As with other uses, this kind of land use may affect other people's land by removing support for their land, causing the land to sink and maybe damaging buildings. Again, common law rules describe the extent to which one can alter the land in this way and the extent to which one is entitled to continuing support from nearby land.

Landowners are also entitled to exclude others from their land. The law of trespass describes one's right to exclude and the remedies when that right is invaded. To be useable, land must have a vertical dimension above the surface of the earth, so sometimes the common law also must consider when invasion of air above the earth is a trespass.

As you can see, numerous common law rules concern the right to use land and exclude others from it. This chapter tells you more about the common law rules you need to know.

Nuisance Law: Enjoying Property without Unreasonable Interference

A *nuisance* (sometimes called a *private nuisance* to distinguish it from a *public nuisance,* which is a completely different subject) is an interference with the right to use and enjoy real property. Physical invasions onto the property are *trespasses,* so a nuisance can be called a nontrespassory interference with the use of real property.

A property owner doesn't have the absolute right to use her land any way she can imagine. Such a right would be impossible because one person's right to do whatever she wanted on her land would sometimes conflict with another person's right to do whatever he wanted on his land. So the law of nuisance in theory gives every property owner the same right: the right to use and enjoy his or her property reasonably, without unreasonable interference by others.

The following sections talk about when an activity is a nuisance and how courts go about remedying a nuisance.

Determining whether an activity is a nuisance

A *nuisance* is an unreasonable interference with a person's use and enjoyment of her property. Many types of activities may be nuisances, especially ones that cause the following:

- ✔ Noise

- ✔ Odors

- ✔ Dust and smoke

- ✔ Pollution of air or water

- ✔ Bugs, rodents, and other pests

- ✔ Explosions and other vibrations

- ✔ Illness

- ✔ Crime

- ✔ Light

Some activities are generally considered nuisances at law or *per se*. Such activities are always nuisances as a matter of law, regardless of the circumstances. An activity is a *nuisance per se* in the following cases:

- ✔ The activity is illegal. When a statute specifically prohibits certain conduct that affects use of land, engaging in such conduct is inherently unreasonable and therefore is a nuisance.

- ✔ The activity is inherently and unavoidably dangerous to life or property.

Other activities may be nuisances if they're unreasonable under the circumstances. Such nuisances may be called nuisances in fact or *per accidens*. Courts consider all the relevant circumstances to decide whether the activity is unreasonable. The relevant circumstances generally include the following:

- ✔ **The location of the properties and the character of the surrounding area:** An activity may be appropriate in some locations and unreasonable in other locations. For example, a gas station may be appropriate in a commercial area but not in the middle of a residential neighborhood.

- ✔ **The extent of the harm to the plaintiff landowner:** To evaluate the extent of the harm, the court considers

  - The character of the defendant's activity and interference with the use of land

  - How much the activity actually interferes with the plaintiff's land use

  - How often it interferes

  - In some cases, the alternatives available to the plaintiff

- ✔ **The benefits of the defendant's activity:** Courts weigh the harm to the plaintiff against the benefits of the defendant's nuisance-causing activity, not just to the defendant but also to the community. Evaluating the benefit includes considering the cost of alternatives that wouldn't interfere with the plaintiff's land use. The more easily the defendant could conduct its activity without interfering with the plaintiff's land use, the more likely the activity is a nuisance.

✔ **Who was there first:** Courts consider which of the conflicting land uses began first. If the defendant's lawful land use was first, it may seem less fair for the plaintiff to come along later and make the earlier use stop or change because it conflicts with how the plaintiff wants to use her land. But this is just one of many considerations, because it may also seem unfair for a nuisance-causing land use to begin operation somewhere and then forever prevent others from using their nearby land productively because of the pre-existing objectionable use of land.

✔ **Zoning:** An activity is more likely to be a nuisance if it violates an applicable zoning ordinance, and it's less likely to be a nuisance if it complies with an applicable zoning ordinance. I cover zoning in Chapter 7.

Substantially harming the landowner

Even if an activity is unreasonable, it must cause substantial harm in order to be a nuisance. As with the determination that an activity is unreasonable, courts consider all the relevant circumstances to decide whether the activity causes substantial harm. These circumstances may include the following:

✔ The activity significantly impairs the market value of the property.

✔ The activity causes physical injury, illness, or mental suffering to the plaintiff.

✔ The more frequent and longer lasting the harm, the more substantial it is.

✔ The activity prevents basic or important uses of the plaintiff's land.

✔ Avoiding the harm of the activity is difficult and expensive.

Causing or maintaining a nuisance is a tort. Liability doesn't depend upon breach of a duty of care, however. Regardless of how careful the defendant or how much she acted in good faith, if she unreasonably interferes with another's use and enjoyment of his land and causes substantial harm, she's liable for a nuisance and the plaintiff is entitled to relief.

Remedying nuisances

The plaintiff who proves a nuisance is entitled to an award of damages for the injuries that the nuisance has caused her. If the nuisance has permanently damaged the land, the plaintiff can recover the lost market value of her property. If the nuisance and its harms stop, the plaintiff can recover the lost rental value of the property during the time the nuisance was in effect. The plaintiff can also recover damages for personal injuries, such as illness, injury, distress, and discomfort. If the nuisance caused the plaintiff to lose profits, she can recover her lost profits, too.

The successful plaintiff may also get an injunction from the court ordering the defendant to stop maintaining the nuisance. If possible, an injunction won't enjoin the defendant's activity altogether; it will enjoin only the specific aspects of the activity that cause the unreasonable interference and substantial harm. For example, the court may order that the defendant can't conduct her activities during certain hours.

A court won't issue an injunction, however, if the resulting hardship to the defendant and the community would greatly outweigh the benefit to the plaintiff. For example, some cases have held industrial activities to be nuisances but refused to enjoin them because of the large economic injuries that the community would suffer compared to the relatively small injuries of discomfort and inconvenience suffered by the plaintiffs. In such cases, the court instead awards damages for the permanently impaired market value of the plaintiffs' property.

Altering How Surface Water Drains

One way that a landowner may interfere with another's use of her land is by altering how surface water drains, such as when it rains or when snow melts. A landowner may build a building, pave her land, or alter the contour of the land in a way that increases the amount of surface water that drains onto neighboring property or changes where it flows, thus damaging nearby property. Or a landowner may try to protect her property against surface water by filling in her land, causing the water to back up onto her neighbor's land.

Different states follow different rules for resolving this type of dispute. The following sections present the rules that courts have applied.

The reasonable use rule: Altering drainage reasonably

Many states, though probably still a minority, apply the *reasonable use* rule. This rule essentially applies the law of nuisance to alterations of drainage: Landowners may alter the drainage of their land as long as they don't unreasonably interfere with others' land.

As in nuisance cases, courts consider all the relevant circumstances to decide whether a particular alteration of drainage is unreasonable:

- ✔ The value and importance of the plaintiff's and defendant's land uses that will be affected by the drainage of surface water

- ✔ The extent to which the plaintiff's and defendant's land uses will be impaired by the drainage of the surface water if the other party prevails

✔ Whether either or both of the parties could avoid the conflict by some other drainage method

✔ Whether the defendant acted maliciously or negligently in altering the drainage

Although a minority of states has expressly adopted this rule for surface water disputes, opinions in other states seem to be moving in this direction, applying reasonableness and balancing ideas.

The common enemy rule: Protecting your own land

Some states apply the common enemy rule to surface water disputes. The simplest version of the *common enemy rule* is that every landowner has the right to protect herself against surface water however she chooses. Therefore, no one has a right against other landowners, and no one is liable to anyone else for causing damage by alterations to the drainage of surface water.

This rule may promote development of land by protecting landowners from liability for altering the land in ways that change surface drainage. But it also may encourage landowners to divert surface water in ways that most benefit themselves without considering how those actions affect other properties.

Courts that apply the common enemy rule therefore have often qualified and modified the absolute version of the rule. Here are some common exceptions to the general rule that someone isn't liable to others for altering surface drainage. A landowner is liable for damage resulting from her alterations if

✔ The alteration is intended to deflect surface water, as with ditches or pipes, and the alteration discharges more water or directs drainage in a way different from the natural drainage.

✔ The alteration of the natural drainage is unnecessary or isn't for a reasonable purpose.

✔ The landowner alters the natural drainage carelessly or negligently.

The civil law rule: Paying for any harm you cause

In its simplest form, the *civil law rule* says that landowners are strictly liable for altering the natural drainage of surface water. The rule thus is the exact opposite of the common enemy rule I describe in the preceding section. Landowners have no right to alter drainage, and they have the right not to be injured by others altering the drainage.

This rule may discourage development because almost any kind of development alters the natural drainage and therefore exposes the owner to liability. Of course, a developer of land can negotiate with the neighbors to buy the right to alter drainage, but that increases the cost of development.

Because the civil law rule sometimes seems undesirable, courts have made exceptions to this rule, too. Here are common exceptions:

- ✔ The rule doesn't apply in urban areas. In those areas, development is more desirable and appropriate, so the common enemy rule or a version of the reasonable use rule applies instead.

- ✔ Agricultural users can alter drainage if it's good agricultural practice and they direct the drainage through natural channels.

- ✔ A landowner isn't liable if she alters the natural drainage but it doesn't do any more harm than before.

Regulating Water Rights

An owner can use her land to capture water to use. If a lake or stream is on her property, she can draw water out of it. She also can drill into the earth and draw water from underground. But doing so can affect the water available to other landowners. If a stream runs through some land and the owner diverts the water to irrigate her land, people who own land downstream may not be able to draw as much or any water from the stream. If a landowner drills a well and draws out lots of water for an industrial operation, neighboring properties may not be able to draw water from their own wells.

Water moves, whether it's on the surface or underground. It may be present on a person's land for a time, but then it may move on to someone else's land. So a landowner doesn't have a right to use all the water that touches her land. Different states have different rules concerning how much water a landowner can take from a water body or from underground, as I explain next.

Claiming water from watercourses

In most states, owners of land that touches a lake or stream have a property right to use that water. Such land is generally called *riparian* land, although land touching a lake may instead be called *littoral*. So the property rights that owners of such land have in the water may be called *riparian rights*.

In Western states, however, ownership of water isn't necessarily connected to ownership of land that the water is drawn from. Instead, ownership of water comes from making beneficial use of the water before others do. These laws about water ownership are referred to as *prior appropriation* laws.

For details about riparian rights and prior appropriation statutes, check out the following sections.

Natural flow and reasonable use: Considering rights of owners of riparian land

The traditional common law rule, originating in England, is called the natural flow rule. The *natural flow rule* says that all owners of riparian land have a property right in the flow of the water. No riparian owner can alter the natural flow of the water, because doing so would interfere with downstream riparian owners' rights in the water.

Of course, any use of the water at all would interfere with the natural flow of the stream. But the natural flow rule allows riparian owners to use water as long as it doesn't substantially or materially diminish the amount of water or impair the quality of the water. A riparian owner can draw water for domestic purposes such as drinking, cooking, and cleaning as well as to water domestic animals. If any other use substantially or materially impairs the quantity or quality of water, however, the landowner is liable to the downstream owners. And the riparian owner can't draw water out to be used on nonriparian land.

This rule severely limits the amount of water that can be used for agricultural or industrial purposes, which is why courts gradually modified this rule to allow more extensive uses of water. Nowadays, most states follow a different rule altogether: the reasonable use rule.

The *reasonable use rule* allows riparian owners to use water for any beneficial purposes on their riparian land as long as they don't unreasonably interfere with other riparian owners' rights. As with other reasonableness rules, courts consider all the relevant circumstances to decide whether a use is reasonable, including the following:

- ✔ **The relative value of the parties' competing water uses:** Courts consider both the importance of the uses to the individual owners as well as their social and economic importance to the community. Domestic uses are generally considered the most important uses, so domestic uses on riparian land don't unreasonably interfere with nondomestic uses. In some states, irrigation is considered the next most important use.

- ✔ **The extent of the injury to the parties' competing water uses if they lose:** This consideration may include how efficiently the parties are using water and the costs of getting needed water from other sources.

- ✔ **Whether the water is being used to benefit riparian land:** Water may be diverted to benefit nonriparian land, but uses to benefit riparian land are generally favored and more likely to be reasonable.

Water permits: Claiming ownership by prior appropriation

The Western states have *prior appropriation* statutes that govern rights to water. Prior appropriation statutes differ, but the basic rule is that anyone, whether a riparian owner or not, can obtain a property right to keep using a certain volume of water by first applying that amount of water to a beneficial use. Essentially, any productive use of water is a beneficial use.

When a person appropriates water in this way, she applies to a state agency that administers the water rights system. The agency gives her a permit that entitles her to keep drawing that volume of water.

If there isn't enough water for all the permit holders, an earlier permit usually prevails over a later permit. However, most statutes identify preferred water uses and allow the holder of a later permit for a preferred use to take her specified volume of water, but she has to compensate the earlier permit holder.

The prior appropriation system entirely takes the place of riparian ownership in the most arid Western states. But in the coastal states and the states from North Dakota to Texas, the system is combined with the reasonable use rule. Some of those states hold that riparian use prevails in a conflict with nonriparian appropriation rights; some hold that appropriation rights prevail over riparian uses; and some hold that the earlier use prevails.

Drawing water from underground

Most underground water forms reservoirs in permeable sand, rock, and such. These underground reservoirs are called *aquifers,* and the permeating water may be called *percolating water.* Landowners may draw this water from underground through artificial wells, or the water may emerge from natural springs.

As with water in streams and lakes, one person's drawing water from underground may diminish the water available to other landowners. Drawing water from underground also may cause the surface of other people's land to subside. So the law has rules about the extent of individual property rights to draw water from underground. Different states apply different rules and may apply different rules in different circumstances. The possible rules include the following:

- ✔ **Riparian rules:** Sometimes underground water flows in a defined stream just like on the surface. Generally, courts apply the same rules that apply to surface streams if a water user proves that a particular source of underground water is a stream.

- ✔ **English or common law rule:** The traditional rule about ownership of underground water is that anyone can drill wells on the surface of her land and take as much water as she wants to use. However, if she takes water maliciously to injure others, she has exceeded her property right and is liable for damages. Likewise, if she uses water wastefully, like simply letting it pour out on the earth for no reason, she has exceeded her property right and is liable for injury to others. Most states used to apply the English rule but have abandoned it in favor of other rules.

✔ **American or reasonable use rule:** Most states follow the American or reasonable use rule. Even though it's called the "reasonable use" rule, it isn't a balancing test like other reasonableness rules. The rule distinguishes between water used on the land from which it's drawn and water transported elsewhere:

- **Onsite use:** If water is used on the land from which it's drawn, the reasonable use rule is essentially the same as the English rule. Any such use is by definition reasonable, regardless of the type of use or the injury to other water users. The only exception, as with the English rule, is that the user is liable for malicious or wasteful uses of water.

- **Offsite use:** If water is drawn out and then transported elsewhere, the rule is different. Such uses are generally held to be unreasonable if they injure other owners of land overlying the aquifer. In other words, using water offsite generally means one is liable to other owners of overlying lands, regardless of the character of the use or the extent of the injury.

✔ **Correlative rights:** The correlative rights rule is more like the reasonable use rule for surface streams and other reasonable use rules. Under this rule, the owner of the surface is liable for harm that results from taking more than her share of the aquifer. Owners thus have an equal right to draw water from underground, and when there isn't enough water to go around, a court may allocate shares of water among the users. As with the reasonable use rule, a surface owner doesn't have the right to take water from underground and transport it elsewhere if doing so injures others.

✔ **Restatement rule:** Some courts follow the rule described by the Restatement (Second) of Torts § 858. The Restatement rule says that a landowner who draws water from under her surface is liable for resulting injury to others only if she unreasonably causes harm or exceeds her reasonable share of the water supply. Reasonableness is determined considering the same factors as in the reasonable use rule for surface streams.

✔ **Prior appropriation:** Most states with prior appropriation systems for streams and lakes apply the same system to underground water. So a person who applies underground water to a beneficial use would generally prevail in a conflict with a later user from the same aquifer.

Extracting Oil and Gas from Underground

Like percolating underground water, oil and gas move around in permeable layers of the earth. If one landowner drills a well on her land and extracts oil and gas, it may drain oil and gas from under her neighbors' land, too. The neighbors therefore may complain that she has taken their property right in the oil and gas.

The traditional rule, however, is that a neighbor has no claim against one who has drilled a well and drained oil and gas from under her land. More recently, courts and state legislatures have modified this traditional rule to protect the interests of landowners in capturing oil and gas from underneath their surface. The following sections talk about the traditional rule and a few of the common modern modifications of the rule.

The rule of capture: "Go and do likewise"

The common law tradition is that the owner of land owns everything under the surface of her land to the center of the Earth. Many states say that includes the oil and gas under her surface. The surface owner can *sever* ownership of the oil and gas from the surface ownership, however, by conveying the rights to oil and gas to someone else or by reserving them for herself when she conveys the surface to another. Either way, someone owns the oil and gas in a defined area underground.

However, the traditional *rule of capture* is that others may lawfully take that oil and gas if they drill a well on their own land and the well draws the oil and gas away. Everyone knows oil and gas can move around underground, and a well nearby can draw it out without physically invading one's land. So the common law recognized that fact by applying the rule of capture to allow every owner of land to freely drill down from the surface of her land and take whatever oil and gas she could get from the well, regardless of whether it came from under her surface or someone else's surface. If a landowner didn't want to lose the oil and gas under her surface, the answer was to "go and do likewise": Drill your own well and capture whatever you can get from it.

Modifying the rule of capture

Even though the rule of capture is easy to apply and in a way treats everyone equally, it isn't a great way to make the best use of oil and gas. The rule of capture encourages landowners to capture oil and gas as fast as they can before others capture it. It also encourages overdrilling, as landowners drill on their own land to offset drainage from wells on neighboring land, and that means people spend more money on drilling than necessary and in the process may deplete the pressure underground and leave more oil and gas uncaptured.

So states have adopted additional rules intended both to give landowners an equal opportunity to capture oil and gas from their surface and also to maximize the recovery of oil and gas. Here are some of those rules:

✔ **Fair share:** The *fair share* rule, or *correlative rights* rule, is that every landowner has an equal, reasonable opportunity to capture the amount of recoverable oil and gas underlying her surface. That doesn't mean she actually has the right to that amount of oil and gas, however. If she doesn't act diligently in drilling wells on her land, others may drain the oil and gas from under her land, as the rule of capture allows. But if all the owners drill with the same diligence, each owner will generally capture the amount of oil and gas under her surface.

✔ **Proration orders:** State law may authorize a state regulatory agency to set limits on the rate of production from wells, called *proration orders.* These limits help protect each owner's fair share by preventing some owners from drawing out oil and gas faster than others. They also protect against overproduction that would impair the total recovery of oil and gas from the reservoir.

✔ **Well spacing rules:** Even with a proration order limiting the rate of production from a well, one owner could capture more than her fair share by drilling more wells than other owners. So state law and regulations may specify the size of the area in which one well may be drilled, called a *drilling unit,* and where a well may be drilled within each drilling unit. That way, multiple wells won't be drilled when one well could drain the same area, and multiple wells won't be used to overproduce and infringe on others' fair shares.

Avoiding Landslides and Subsidence: Supporting Land

One landowner's use of her property may involve excavating and altering the earth on the surface or underground. A landowner may want to level her sloped property to make it more useable for certain purposes. She may dig into the earth to build structures on the land. She may excavate under the surface to extract valuable minerals.

Excavating and altering the land in these ways may affect adjoining and nearby lands. Leveling a slope on one's land may remove lateral support for adjacent land uphill, causing the hill to slide downward and possibly damaging buildings on the adjacent land in the process. Excavating on the surface likewise may cause the adjacent land to subside because of the loss of lateral support. Excavating underground may remove subjacent support, support of the land from underneath, thus causing the surface of the land above to subside and fall down.

Property rules address such conflicts and decide who bears the cost of avoiding such damage and paying for such damage that isn't or can't be avoided. The common law rules differ depending on three variables:

✔ Whether the support is lateral (from the side) or subjacent (from underneath)

✔ Whether the removal of support would damage the land in its natural condition or damages the land only because of the additional weight of buildings on the land

✔ Whether the damaged land is adjacent to the excavated land or just nearby

The following sections talk about the rules in these situations.

Laterally supporting adjacent land in its natural state

A landowner has a property right to the naturally existing and necessary lateral support from adjacent land. That means that each landowner is strictly liable for any damages resulting to adjacent land because of removing lateral support necessary to support the land in its natural condition. It doesn't matter how careful the landowner is or how valuable her use of the land. A landowner also is entitled to an injunction to prevent removal of naturally necessary support by an adjacent landowner.

This rule doesn't mean that landowners can never excavate their land if it would remove naturally necessary support. Not only could they negotiate with the adjacent landowners for the right to excavate, but they also can provide the necessary support by artificial means, such as retaining walls. As long as an owner continues to provide the naturally necessary support in some way, she hasn't interfered with the adjacent landowner's property right to support of the land.

Most authorities agree that a landowner is liable for damage only if she removes earth that is naturally necessary to support the adjacent land. If she excavates on her land and that causes water or oil to flow out from the earth, which causes adjacent land to subside, she generally isn't liable.

Even though a landowner only has the property right to support of her land in its natural state, an adjacent owner who removes that support is generally liable for all damages that result, not just the damage to the land. Most courts agree that if the damaged land has buildings and other improvements on it, the foreseeable damage resulting from interference with the property right of support includes damage to the improvements, so the one who removed support is liable for those damages, too.

Laterally supporting nearby land and improvements to land

Most courts seem to agree that a landowner doesn't have an absolute duty to maintain naturally necessary support for land that is nearby but not adjacent to her own. However, she is liable for damages if she negligently removes support for nearby land.

Likewise, a landowner doesn't have a duty to support the additional weight of buildings and other improvements on adjacent or nearby land. Even so, many courts hold that a landowner is liable for negligently removing support for buildings. Removal of support may be negligent in the following circumstances:

- ✔ The removal of support is unnecessary for the landowner to use her land as she wants.
- ✔ The landowner removes support without giving adjacent and nearby landowners notice so that they have time to protect their properties from possible damage.
- ✔ The landowner removes support without taking reasonable precautions to minimize damage to other properties.
- ✔ The landowner removes support carelessly, not using reasonably careful techniques or not using appropriate equipment to perform the excavation in a way that will minimize the risk of damage to other properties.

Supporting land from beneath

Ordinarily, the owner of the surface owns the earth underneath, too, so her subsurface property supports her surface. But sometimes the ownership of the surface may be severed from subsurface ownership. In that situation, the subsurface owner may remove support necessary to sustain the surface owner's land, such as by excavating to remove minerals.

As with lateral support, the general rule is that a subsurface owner is strictly liable to the surface owner for removing naturally necessary subjacent support. Some courts go further, however, and hold that the subsurface owner also has a duty not to remove support necessary to sustain buildings and other improvements that were on the surface at the time the subsurface estate was severed from the surface.

In either case, the subsurface owner certainly doesn't have to provide support for improvements made after severance. However, as with lateral support, the subsurface owner is generally liable for any damages that result from removing the support that the surface owner is entitled to. So if the subsurface owner removes naturally necessary support or support necessary to sustain improvements preceding severance, she's liable for all resulting damages, including damages to improvements made after severance.

Courts presume that subsurface removal of support would cause the land to subside regardless of the weight of improvements. So to avoid liability the subsurface owner must prove that the land wouldn't have subsided if it weren't for the improvements on the surface, or the improvements added after severance.

No Trespassing! Excluding Others from Land

The preceding sections examine rights to use land. A landowner also has the general right to exclude others from her land. Some say the right to exclude others is what makes something private property. An invasion of the right to exclude is called a *trespass*.

The following sections consider the extent of the right to exclude others and the remedies for trespasses.

Considering what constitutes a trespass

A *trespass* is an intentional, wrongful entry onto another person's land, without the owner's permission and without a legal privilege to do so. The following sections talk about each aspect of this definition.

Entering the land

One enters another's land if she physically crosses a boundary onto that person's land. She may enter on the surface of the land, of course, but she also may enter above or below the surface, because ownership of land extends below the earth and above the earth for some distance that's reasonably useable in connection with the surface. Therefore, if a miner tunnels underneath the surface and crosses the boundary onto another person's land, she has entered the land. Likewise, if a person flies an airplane low across another person's land, she has entered the land even though she never touches the earth.

A person may enter the land by causing things to enter the land, without actually stepping foot on the land, such as by throwing things onto the property or flooding the property.

Intending to enter

A trespass may be intentional or negligent. A person commits an *intentional trespass* as long as she intentionally takes the action that interferes with the plaintiff's right to exclude. An entry resulting from intentional action is a trespass even if the trespasser didn't mean to trespass or didn't realize that her action would be a trespass, unless perhaps a court feels that the trespasser's mistake was excusable. Such an intentional trespass is always a trespass entitling the rightful possessor to a remedy.

On the other hand, a negligent action that unintentionally results in an entry on the land is a trespass only if it causes harm.

Entering without permission

If the landowner consents to an entry, the entry obviously isn't wrongful and isn't a trespass. The owner's permission to enter the land is called a *license*. The landowner can revoke her permission anytime, however. If she does, the licensee becomes a trespasser if he remains on the land.

Even a person who is lawfully on the property can commit a trespass by exceeding the scope of her license or privilege to be on the property. Here are some examples:

- An easement holder uses the property beyond the scope of her easement by overburdening the servient estate, benefitting nondominant land, going outside the boundaries of her easement, and so on (see Chapter 6 for details).

- A licensee exceeds the scope of her license. For example, a real estate agent uses a house listed for sale for a weekend getaway.

- A person enters in a governmental capacity and exceeds the scope of his authority, such as a law enforcement officer who enters a property lawfully but then steals something from the premises.

- A person enters lawfully but leaves something on the property and doesn't remove it within a reasonable time.

Entering without privilege

A person may have a legal privilege to enter property even though she doesn't have the owner's consent. Privileges thus are exceptions to the property owner's right to exclude. Privileges take many forms, but here are some examples:

- Entering the land reasonably to abate a nuisance if the owner hasn't or won't do so herself

- Entering the land to retrieve one's personal property that's on the other person's land (for example, a tenant's lease may terminate or a licensee's license may be revoked while she still has some of her personal property on the land; she has the right to enter the land within a reasonable time to retrieve her personal property)

✔ Entering the land out of necessity, to prevent serious harm to person or property

✔ A law enforcement officer entering the land with authority

✔ Entering the land as reasonably necessary to perform a duty or exercise authority created by law, such as governmental inspectors or firefighters

A person who has a privilege to enter land may still be liable if she causes substantial harm to the property or exceeds the scope of the privilege.

Remedying trespasses

A landowner or other possessor of the land is entitled to recover actual damages to the land resulting from a trespass. If the damage is permanent, the measure of damages would be the lost market value or the cost to fix the damage. The possessor is also entitled to foreseeable consequential damages that result from the trespass such as personal injuries.

Even if there isn't any actual damage, the possessor is entitled to nominal damages compensating her for the wrongful intrusion. She doesn't have to prove any actual damage in order to win a trespass claim, because the entry itself is a violation of her rights, not just damaging her property.

A landowner also is generally entitled to an injunction preventing a trespass from continuing, such as when the trespass is caused by an encroaching structure. However, if the injunction would harm the defendant much more than it would benefit the plaintiff, the court may deny an injunction. A landowner is also entitled to an injunction preventing an owner from committing a threatened trespass if damages would be difficult to determine or the harm would be irreparable.

If the trespasser has actually dispossessed her, the rightful possessor can bring an ejectment action to regain possession.

Using Airspace

Owning land includes owning the earth under the surface and air above the surface. While ownership under the surface theoretically extends to the center of the earth, ownership of the air above the surface doesn't extend endlessly into space. The following sections talk more about ownership of airspace.

Defining boundaries in the air

A landowner owns as much of the air above the surface as she can reasonably use in connection with the surface. That isn't a clear line, obviously. Land wouldn't be useable at all if one didn't own some of the air above the surface; almost any use of the land requires using some airspace above the surface.

Certainly building any kind of structure on the surface occupies airspace. Because you have the right to reasonably use your land as long as you don't unreasonably interfere with others doing the same, you have the right to reasonably use both the surface and the air above it unless you thereby interfere with someone else's use of property. So even though you may occupy only 20 feet of the air for a long time, under the common law principle, you can later decide to build a 200-foot building unless it would be a nuisance.

Although the upper limit of an owner's airspace isn't clearly defined, it certainly doesn't extend into navigable airspace. The upper airspace belongs to the public and is open to air travel.

Using and protecting airspace

Ownership of airspace is just like ownership of land. The owner can use and enjoy it reasonably. Zoning and other statutes often restrict the height of buildings, as I explain in Chapter 7. Such statutes don't actually declare the unused airspace to belong to the public, however; they merely restrain the owner's use of that space. So landowners may own more airspace than the law allows them to use.

Not only can the landowner use and enjoy the airspace, but she can also convey it to others. For example, a condominium may divide up airspace among individual unit owners. An owner can also give another party, such as a utility company, an easement to use some of the airspace.

An entry into another's airspace is a trespass even if the trespasser doesn't touch the surface of the earth. Airplanes may trespass by flying low over a person's property, for example. An airplane trespasses by flying low enough over the surface to interfere with the owner's reasonable use and enjoyment of her surface. Of course, if the airplane doesn't fly over a person's surface, just nearby, the airplane's interference with the surface because of noise and light wouldn't be a trespass — but it could be a nuisance. And if the government's flying the plane, the landowner could only seek just compensation for the government taking an easement through her airspace, as Chapter 8 notes.

Chapter 5

Adjusting Rights by Private Agreement: Covenants

In This Chapter

▶ Understanding what covenants are and how they're created

▶ Examining the requirements for covenants to run with the land at law and in equity

▶ Interpreting and applying covenants

▶ Amending and terminating covenants

*P*roperty owners can customize their rights and reconcile them with other owners by private agreement. One way to do that is by using covenants. In general, a *covenant* is just a contractual promise from one person to another person. If a covenant doesn't relate to land, it's just a contract, which you can read about in *Contract Law For Dummies* by Scott J. Burnham (Wiley). This chapter is about covenants that relate to land.

When a landowner covenants to do or not to do something on land, not only does she have a contractual obligation to the person to whom she made the promise, but she may also have an obligation to people who acquire that person's land in the future. And people who acquire her land in the future may be obligated to keep performing her promise.

This chapter clarifies how parties may expressly or implicitly make covenants that relate to land and when those covenants burden and benefit later owners of land. It also explains how to interpret, amend, and terminate such covenants.

Introducing Land-Related Covenants

A covenant may relate to the land by promising to do something on land or by promising not to do something on land. Covenants thus may be described as follows:

- ✔ **Negative:** A negative covenant, or *restrictive covenant,* is a covenant that the property owner will not do or allow certain things on her land. For example, a covenant not to use a property for commercial purposes is a restrictive covenant. Most covenants are restrictive.

- ✔ **Affirmative:** An affirmative covenant is a promise to do something. It may be a promise to do something on the benefited land, such as providing heat to a building on the covenantee's land. Or it may be a promise to do something on the covenantor's burdened land, such as maintaining certain types of landscaping features on her land. An affirmative covenant may even be a promise to pay money, like a covenant to pay dues to a homeowners' association.

When covenants relate to land, they create a legal interest in land and therefore must comply with the statute of frauds. The statute of frauds, which Chapter 15 talks about in detail, requires written evidence of an interest in real property, signed by the party that's denying the creation of the interest.

Most covenants are created in instruments granting other interests, such as deeds or leases, and so satisfy the statute of frauds. Even if a covenant isn't in writing, estoppel may allow it to be enforced. Chapter 15 talks about estoppel more, but here's the short version: If a party reasonably expends significant value in reliance on a covenant, she may enforce the covenant even if it isn't written. For example, if the benefited party builds a house, relying on a neighbor's covenant not to build a tall building next door, the neighbor may be estopped from denying the existence of the covenant.

If the covenant satisfies the statute of frauds, the original parties to the covenant can enforce the agreement against each other just like they could enforce any other contract. The covenant doesn't have to meet any special property law requirements for the original parties to enforce it.

But the covenant does have to meet special requirements in order to be enforced by and against subsequent owners of the original parties' lands. The following sections talk about those requirements.

Enforcing a Running Covenant at Law

Covenants that are related to the land can *run with the land.* That means the covenant attaches to the land so that subsequent owners of the benefited land can enforce the covenant against subsequent owners of the burdened land. Of course, subsequent owners could voluntarily accept an assignment of contract rights and duties by their predecessors who originally made the contract. But a covenant that runs with the land binds and benefits successors regardless of whether they agree. In effect, the covenant just becomes part of the land.

If a covenant meets the requirements traditionally required by law courts, it's said to run *at law* and may be called a *real covenant.* (See Chapter 2 for info on the difference between law and equity courts and corresponding legal and equitable remedies.) The practical significance of enforcing a covenant at law is that the benefited party enforcing the covenant may recover damages for breach as well as get a judicial order that specifically enforces the covenant. (If she wants the other party to comply with the covenant and doesn't care about damages, she can seek enforcement at law or in equity — see the later section "Enforcing a Covenant in Equity" for details.)

The requirements for a covenant to run with a parcel of land, whether the benefited land or the burdened land, are as follows:

- ✔ **Intent:** The original parties intended the benefit or burden of the covenant to run with the benefited or burdened land. That is, they intended subsequent owners of that parcel of land to be bound by the covenant, benefited by the covenant, or both, as the case may require.

- ✔ **Touching and concerning:** The covenant touches and concerns the relevant land. That is, if the benefit is to run with benefited land, it must be sufficiently related to the benefited land. If the burden is to run with the burdened land, it must be sufficiently related to the burdened land.

- ✔ **Vertical privity:** The subsequent owner of the relevant land, whether benefited or burdened land, has succeeded to the original party's estate in at least some of the relevant land.

- ✔ **Horizontal privity:** The original parties created the covenant in the instrument transferring the benefited or burdened land, or the covenant relates to legal interests the original parties both had in the same land, such as an easement or a leasehold.

Whenever an original party is involved in an action to enforce a covenant, whether she's seeking to enforce the covenant or another is seeking to enforce it against her, she's bound or benefited by virtue of her contract. It doesn't matter whether the covenant runs with her land. Whether a covenant runs with land matters only when a successor to an original party is involved in an action to enforce a covenant. So the requirements for a covenant to run with the land apply separately to the benefited land and to the burdened land:

- ✔ **If the original benefited party seeks to enforce the other party's covenant against someone who bought the other party's land:** The original party only needs to prove that the burden of the covenant runs with the burdened land.

- ✔ **If a successor to the original benefited party seeks to enforce a covenant against the party who originally made the covenant:** The successor doesn't have to prove that the burden of the covenant runs with the burdened land, because the original party is bound by his contract regardless. She only has to prove that the benefit runs with the original party's benefited land so that she has the right to enforce the covenant as the current owner of that land.

- ✔ **If a successor to the original benefited party seeks to enforce the covenant against a successor to the original burdened party:** The successor to the original benefited party must prove that the benefit runs with the benefited land and that the burden runs with the burdened land.

The following sections examine each of the requirements for covenants to run with the land at law.

Determining intent for a covenant to run

A covenant can run with the land only if the original parties who create the covenant intend for it to run with that land. If they don't intend the benefit or the burden to run with the land, then the covenant is just a personal covenant between those parties and it doesn't bind or benefit successive owners, regardless of whether the other requirements are met. If they intend the burden to run with the burdened land but don't intend the benefit to run with the benefited land, then only the burden can run, and vice versa.

A successor may prove the original parties' intent in various ways:

- ✔ **Direct statements:** Sometimes covenants expressly say that the covenant will run with the land to burden successors to the covenantor, benefit successors to the covenantee, or both. That obviously proves the original parties' intent for the covenant to run.

- ✔ **Indirect statements:** Even if the instrument creating the covenant doesn't say it directly, it may still indicate that the parties intend for the covenant to run with the land. For example, a covenant may indicate intent to run by saying that the covenant will bind (or benefit) the party's "successors and assigns." The parties may even indicate their intent for the burden to run by saying that the covenant will "permanently" restrict the land or using other words like that.

- ✔ **Negotiations:** The circumstances of the transaction and the parties' reasons for entering into a covenant can demonstrate intent. For example, if a seller tells a buyer she wants to include a covenant that restricts the subject land to residential purposes for the benefit of future owners who may develop the seller's retained property, that indicates that the parties intended the benefit to run with the land.

- ✔ **The nature of the covenant:** If the benefit of the covenant touches and concerns the land owned by the benefited party, courts generally presume that the parties intended the benefit to run with the benefited land. Likewise, if the burden of the covenant touches and concerns land owned by the burdened party, courts generally presume that the parties intended the burden to run.

No matter how clear and emphatic the original parties' intent to bind or benefit successors, the covenant won't run with the land if it doesn't meet the other requirements for covenants to run. If the covenant isn't in fact connected to the land, the law won't let the parties attach the covenant to the land even if they want to.

Intent for the benefit to run and intent for the burden to run are separate factual questions, and evidence of one doesn't necessarily prove the other. For example, a covenant may say that the covenant will bind the grantee, her successors, and assigns. That's good evidence that the parties intended the burden to run with the grantee's land, but it doesn't say anything about whether the parties intended the benefit to run with the grantor's land.

Deciding whether a covenant touches and concerns the relevant land

A covenant can run with land only if it touches and concerns that land. That's true both for the benefit to run with benefited land and for the burden of the covenant to run with burdened land. The law simply doesn't allow parties to attach covenants to ownership of land unless the covenant is actually related to the land.

A covenant *touches and concerns* land if the performance of the covenant somehow relates to the use and enjoyment of the land. Authorities sometimes say that the covenant touches and concerns burdened land if it lessens the covenantor's legal rights in relation to the land and makes them less valuable, whereas the covenant touches and concerns benefited land if it increases the covenantee's legal rights in relation to her land and makes them more valuable. This standard can be confusing and circular, however. It's probably best to think of "touching and concerning" generally as meaning that actually performing what the covenant requires has some effect, direct or indirect, on what happens on the land.

Some courts continue to follow an older rule that the burden of a covenant won't run with the burdened land unless both the burden and the benefit touch and concern the respective parties' land. The justifications for that old rule have diminished, and many courts today would say that the burden of a covenant can run with burdened land even if the benefit doesn't touch and concern any land. By the way, courts have never required both benefit and burden to touch and concern land in order for the benefit to run — even if the burden is personal and not related to land, the benefit can run if the benefit touches and concerns the benefited party's land.

The following sections talk more about when a covenant touches and concerns land.

Touching and concerning burdened land

A covenant generally touches and concerns the burdened land if it dictates things that must or can't be done on the burdened land. Following are some examples of how the burden of a covenant may relate to the use and enjoyment of the burdened land:

- ✔ A negative covenant typically touches and concerns burdened land by restricting how the land may be used, such as by prohibiting certain activities or buildings on the land.

- ✔ An affirmative covenant may touch and concern the burdened land by requiring the burdened party to do something on her land, such as maintaining underground drain tile that benefits the adjoining land by helping surface water drain away from it. On the other hand, an affirmative covenant that requires the burdened party to do something on the benefited land may not touch and concern the burdened land at all, unless performance of the act somehow must originate from the burdened land.

- ✔ If the burdened party would have to own the burdened land in order to be able to perform the covenant, the covenant touches and concerns the burdened land. For a simple example, if the covenant is that certain kinds of buildings may not be built on a specified parcel of land, the covenantor would have to own the land in order to keep that promise. On the other hand, except for covenants to pay money (which I discuss in the next section), if the person could perform the covenant even if she didn't own the burdened land, then the covenant doesn't touch and concern that land. For example, a covenant to use a certain raw material only from the covenantee's land in the course of the covenantor's business doesn't require the burdened party to conduct the business in any particular location and therefore doesn't touch and concern the burdened party's land.

Covenanting to pay money

Some affirmative covenants, such as covenants to maintain insurance, pay rent, pay real estate taxes, and pay homeowners' association dues, require payment of money or other obligations rather than to do a thing on the land. Although covenants to pay money don't directly relate to the use of the land (after all, a covenantor could pay promised money even if she owned no land at all), such covenants do touch and concern the land if the payments are used in a way that affects the burdened land.

For example, most courts say a covenant to maintain insurance relates to the land if the covenant says insurance proceeds must be used to restore damage to the land. Similarly, a covenant to pay homeowners' association dues touches and concerns the land if the dues are required to maintain areas that the covenantor co-owns or that she has an easement to use in connection with her land, such as recreational facilities.

A tenant's covenant to pay rent to the landlord is also a covenant to pay money. Unlike other types of covenants to pay money, the covenant to pay rent touches and concerns the land even though the landlord doesn't have to use the money to maintain the premises or in any other way that affects the tenant's burdened estate. Courts seem to reason that the payment covenant is the consideration for the estate in the first place, so it affects the burdened estate by being the means of acquiring and keeping the estate.

Touching and concerning benefited land

A covenant may touch and concern burdened land without touching and concerning benefited land. So don't talk about connections to the burdened land when you're explaining why the covenant touches and concerns benefited land. They're separate questions.

Often the benefit of a covenant less obviously touches and concerns benefited land than the burden touches and concerns burdened land. The performance of a real covenant typically touches and concerns the burdened land because it involves activity on the burdened land. On the other hand, the performance of a real covenant typically touches and concerns the benefited land by somehow making it more useful or enjoyable. Restrictive covenants may prevent activities on the burdened land that would conflict with or impair the benefited party's use of land. For example, a covenant not to use the burdened land for purposes other than single-family residential purposes makes the benefited party's nearby land more enjoyable and valuable as a single-family residence by preventing uses that would bring more traffic and people.

Similarly, affirmative covenants may make the benefited party's nearby land more enjoyable or useful by making the burdened land a safer, healthier, more attractive neighboring property. It also may touch and concern the benefited land more directly, as in a covenant to maintain drain tile on the burdened land to improve drainage of surface water off the benefited land.

In contrast, if performance of the covenant benefits a person and not the land, then it doesn't touch and concern the land. For example, a covenant to preserve an old building on the burdened land might be for the personal benefit of the covenantee, who values the building and doesn't want it destroyed. Such a covenant would touch and concern the burdened land but would not touch and concern the benefited land.

Establishing vertical privity

Vertical privity generally refers to the relationship between an original party, whether covenantor or covenantee, and the successor to that party, who wants to enforce the covenant or against whom someone else wants to enforce it. The required relationship between the successor and the original party differs slightly for the benefit and the burden to run, as follows:

✔ **Running burdens:** In order for the burden to run with the burdened land, the successor to the original burdened party must own the same estate that the original burdened party owned, in at least some of the burdened land.

✔ **Running benefits:** For the benefit to run with the benefited land, the successor must own either the same estate as the original benefited party or a lesser estate that was part of the original owner's estate, in at least some of the benefited land.

The reason for this rule is that covenants actually run with estates, not with land, despite the usual expression about covenants running with the land. An *estate* is a period of ownership of land. In the U.S. legal system, people own estates in land, not the land itself (see Chapter 9 for details). That estate may be permanent, called the *fee simple absolute,* or it may be for a time, like a leasehold or a life estate that ends at death. Because real property owners actually own estates in land, it makes sense that covenants would be attached to their estates, not the land.

In fact, the benefit and the burden of a covenant may relate to the same land but to different estates in that land — that's the situation when a tenant makes covenants to the landlord. The burden of the tenant's covenants touches and concerns his leasehold estate in the land, while the benefit of the covenants touches and concerns the landlord's future estate, the reversion. The burden therefore may run with the leasehold if the tenant transfers the leasehold to someone else, and the benefit may run with the reversion if the landlord transfers her estate to someone else.

A successor to the original party's estate has vertical privity regardless of whether the successor acquires that estate in the entire benefited or burdened parcel of land or just some of it. For example, suppose an owner of 5 acres of land sells 1 acre and the buyer covenants that she'll use the purchased land for residential purposes only. Assuming the parties intended the benefit to run, the covenant certainly touches and concerns the seller's land and therefore would run with that land. If the seller then divides up her remaining 4 acres, selling it to four different people, all four of those new owners would have vertical privity with the seller because they succeeded to the original party's estate in some of the benefited land.

The burden runs to a successor only if the successor acquires the same estate as the original party. Using the same example, if the buyer subsequently leases her property to a tenant, her tenant doesn't own the same estate as the original covenantor (the buyer) and therefore doesn't have vertical privity. The tenant therefore wouldn't be bound by the covenant.

But it's different with the benefit. The benefit runs to a successor even if the successor acquires a lesser estate derived from the original benefited party's estate. So, for example, the benefited party's tenant would have the right to enforce the covenants against the burdened party.

Satisfying the horizontal privity requirement

Whereas *vertical privity* refers to the relationship between an original party and a successor, *horizontal privity* refers only to the relationship between the original parties who created the covenant. Horizontal privity today means that the original parties created the covenant in one of two situations:

- ✔ **In the transfer of benefited or burdened land:** If the parties create the covenant in a deed or other instrument that transfers the benefited or burdened land from one party to the other, they have horizontal privity.

- ✔ **Relating to land in which both parties have an interest:** Regardless of when they acquired their interests, the original parties have horizontal privity if they create a covenant that relates to interests that they both have in the same land. Most commonly, that means that the covenant relates to a landlord-tenant relationship or an easement that one of the original parties has on the other original party's land.

Some states no longer require horizontal privity, and that may be a trend. But often the issue doesn't come up because you don't have to prove horizontal privity in order to enforce a covenant in equity, only at law (see the next section for info on enforcing a covenant in equity).

Horizontal privity is the only one of the requirements for running covenants that can't be satisfied separately for the benefit and burden. All the other requirements for running covenants may be met for one side of the relationship but not the other. But with horizontal privity, the original parties either had horizontal privity — and therefore the requirement is satisfied whether you're considering the running of the benefit, the burden, or both — or they didn't, in which case the requirement isn't satisfied for either the benefit or the burden to run.

However, some courts say that horizontal privity is required only for the burden to run — only if someone is seeking to enforce a covenant against a successor to the original burdened party — and isn't required in order for the benefit to run. In that case, if you're considering the running of the benefit, you don't have to consider horizontal privity at all.

A successor must prove horizontal privity in order to enforce a covenant against a successor, but that doesn't mean she has to prove that *she* has horizontal privity with anyone. By definition, a successor never has horizontal privity because horizontal privity is a relationship between the original parties. A successor just has to prove that the original parties had horizontal privity.

Enforcing a Covenant in Equity

A person may enforce a covenant at law or in equity. The only significant difference today is that if someone enforces a covenant in equity, she probably can't get an award of damages for breach of the covenant; she can only get an order of specific performance requiring the burdened party to comply with the covenant. If she satisfies the requirements for enforcing at law, on the other hand, she can get damages, specific performance, or both (see the earlier section "Enforcing a Running Covenant at Law").

The requirements for enforcing in equity differ somewhat from the requirements for enforcing at law. Historically, chancery courts developed their own rules for when they would enforce a covenant, and those rules were different from the rules followed in the law courts. In fact, covenants enforced in equity got their own name, *equitable servitudes,* which is still used today.

Equitable servitudes aren't different interests from real covenants (covenants that run at law). The same covenant may be enforced at law as a real covenant or in equity as an equitable servitude. The benefited party doesn't have to choose to treat the covenant as one or the other; she may plead and try to prove both theories. The only difference is that she can't get damages if she can't prove the requirements for a covenant to run at law.

In order to enforce a covenant in equity, the benefited party must prove the following:

- ✔ The parties intended the benefit to run to successors. As with enforcement at law, the benefited party may prove this by direct statements or by the nature of the covenant and the transaction. Courts don't seem to require that the parties intended the burden to run.

- ✔ The covenant touches and concerns the relevant land. In general, this requirement is the same as for enforcement at law.

- ✔ The burdened party had notice of the covenant when she acquired the burdened property.

The following sections examine the distinctive requirements for enforcing a covenant in equity rather than at law.

Enforcing covenants without privity

The benefited party doesn't have to prove vertical privity or horizontal privity in order to enforce a covenant in equity. That's the biggest difference in the requirements for enforcing covenants in equity and at law (see the earlier section "Enforcing a Running Covenant at Law"). That means that any covenant, however and whenever created, may be enforced in equity by successors against successors, as long as it touches and concerns the land and the parties intended the benefit to run. And it also means that any possessor of land enjoys the benefit — or suffers the burden, as the case may be — regardless of whether she acquired the estate of the original party.

Requiring notice of the covenant

A court won't enforce a covenant in equity against a property owner who didn't have notice of the covenant when she bought her interest in the land. However, some authorities say that the lack of notice doesn't matter if the burdened party didn't pay value for her property interest in the burdened land.

A person who acquires an interest in the burdened land may have such notice by actually learning that the covenant exists. She may discover the covenant from the grantor, from a title search, from neighbors, and so on.

A buyer of burdened land also may have notice constructively. *Constructive notice* means that a person reasonably should've known about the covenant, even if she didn't actually know about it. The most common source of constructive notice is public real property records. If a reasonable title search would discover an instrument identifying the covenant, then the buyer of the property has constructive notice of the covenant. (For information on constructive notice, go to Chapter 17.)

A buyer of burdened land also may have constructive notice of a covenant from the character of the neighborhood. If the neighborhood appears to be subject to a uniform scheme of restrictive covenants, such as a covenant restricting use to single-family residential use, a buyer may be expected to investigate and therefore may have constructive notice of the covenants. I talk more about this kind of notice later in "Inferring covenants from a common development plan."

Remember that a covenant is the right that one person has to restrict or require some activity by another person. So having notice of a covenant means not just knowing that the property is burdened by a covenant but also knowing who has the benefit of that covenant — who has the right to enforce it. In some situations, a buyer may know that the property is burdened by a covenant but not know that a particular property was intended to have the right to enforce the covenant. In that case, the buyer doesn't have notice of the covenant right belonging to that particular owner and isn't subject to equitable enforcement by her.

Enforcement by homeowners' association

Both the law and equity requirements for running covenants allow only an owner of benefited land to enforce a covenant against burdened land. Today, however, in many residential subdivisions, a homeowners' association may seek to enforce covenants against individual owners. Sometimes the homeowners' association does own benefited land. For example, the homeowners' association may own a recreational facility and seek to enforce a covenant requiring lot owners to pay individual assessments contributing to the cost of the facility. The principles for such a covenant to run with the association land are the same as for any other running covenant.

Other times, however, a homeowners' association seeks to enforce covenants that don't benefit any land owned by the association. For example, it may seek to enforce covenants limiting the number or size of outbuildings on a property. Courts today generally allow homeowners' associations to bring such claims even though they don't own any benefited land, on the theory that an association is an agent or trustee for the individual owners of benefited land.

Suppose that the original parties agree that a neighboring owner will also have the right to enforce the covenant against the buyer and her successors. However, the deed creating the covenant doesn't say that; it just says that the property being sold to the burdened party is subject to a covenant. If that original burdened party later sells the burdened land to another person and doesn't tell that person about the oral agreement that the neighbor also benefits, the new owner may have notice that the land is subject to a covenant (because the covenant is recorded) but not notice that the neighbor has the right to enforce it. In that situation, the new owner of the burdened land isn't subject to an enforcement action by the neighbor because she didn't have notice of the neighbor's covenant rights.

Even though notice of the covenant isn't usually listed as a requirement for a covenant to run at law, the recording statutes have much the same effect as the notice requirement. Chapter 17 talks about recording statutes, which generally protect buyers of land from earlier interests that they didn't know about. So if a person buys burdened land without actually or constructively knowing about the covenant, the state recording act will prevent enforcement of the covenant against her — in some states, as long as she records her interest before the covenant is recorded.

Remedying a breach of a covenant in equity

If a covenant is enforceable in equity, the benefited party is entitled to an injunction requiring the burdened party to comply with the covenant. Damages generally are awarded only if the benefited party meets the requirements to enforce the covenant at law. Most of the time, the benefited party doesn't seek damages because she won't suffer any damage as long as the burdened party stops violating the covenant.

Burdens for the Benefit of All: Enforcing Implied Reciprocal Covenants

Covenants generally must satisfy the statute of frauds, meaning there must be signed, written evidence of a covenant in order to enforce it. However, when a developer of land creates a uniform scheme of covenants that restrict and benefit a group of subdivided lots, the circumstances may imply the creation of covenants. Such implied covenants are enforceable even though they're unwritten. The following sections talk about such implied covenants.

Inferring covenants from a common development plan

A covenant is implied when two things are true:

- ✔ A single owner divides her land and sells multiple lots.
- ✔ The owner sells those lots subject to a common plan of development that includes uniform covenants intended to burden and benefit each of the lots.

Of course, if each of those sales is accomplished by a deed that expressly creates the covenants and says they'll burden and benefit all the owners in the subdivision, then there's no need to imply a covenant because all the covenants are express. But if the parties aren't so clear about their intentions, courts will nevertheless infer the creation of such covenants that benefit and burden each subdivided lot.

It's easy to tell when a single owner subdivides her land; the hard part is figuring out when the owner does so with a common plan of development. The following types of evidence may prove the existence of a common plan:

- ✔ **Previous sales subject to covenants:** The primary evidence of a common plan is that the common owner has sold a significant number of lots subject to the uniform covenants. A single sale, or even a few sales, generally won't prove a common plan for all the lots to be subject to the covenants. But if combined with other evidence of a common plan, they may confirm the existence of a common plan. And if later on, other lots are sold subject to the uniform covenants, courts tend to take that as further proof that a common plan existed earlier.

The covenants don't have to be identical in order to establish a common plan, but they must be generally the same. Nor do the covenants have to apply to every lot in order for a common plan to exist. For example, a residential subdivision may have some lots that are planned for other uses, such as parks or schools.

- ✔ **Compliance with the common plan:** The actual development and use of lots in compliance with the common plan is important to establish that such a plan existed. Although there may be some departures or violations, the actual use of the land must generally comply with the common plan in order for such a plan to exist.

- ✔ **Representations:** The developer may tell prospective buyers, whether directly or through sales agents and marketing materials, that all the lots will be subject to a common set of covenants. Such representations support a finding of a common plan.

Implying reciprocal covenants by the common owner

A deed to a lot in a subdivision may expressly say that the purchased lot is subject to covenants but not say that the rest of the lots are subject to the covenants for the benefit of that buyer. But when the common owner subdivides land with a common plan, the common owner implicitly makes a corresponding covenant restricting the rest of the lots in the subdivision for the benefit of that buyer, even if the deed doesn't say so. For this reason, such implied covenants may be called *implied reciprocal servitudes* or *implied reciprocal negative easements* — the common plan implies that the common owner makes a covenant that's reciprocal to the express covenant made by the buyer of a lot.

In this situation, were it not for this rule, each of the lots would be bound by its express covenant for the benefit of any lots that the common owner still owned at the time. When those lots were eventually sold, those owners would have the right to enforce the covenant against earlier buyers. But the earlier buyers wouldn't have the right to enforce the covenant against later buyers. The earlier lots wouldn't be benefited land because the common owner didn't own them anymore and the later deeds didn't say they were benefited. So were it not for the implied covenant theory, the earlier buyers wouldn't have vertical privity with respect to benefited land, nor would the later buyers have notice of a covenant for the benefit of earlier buyers. The earlier buyers therefore couldn't enforce the covenant against later buyers at law or in equity.

The implied covenant theory makes all the lots in the subdivision burdened for the benefit of all the other lots. When each lot is sold, a reciprocal covenant is implied, burdening all the lots yet to be sold for the benefit of that buyer.

Implying both the buyer's covenant and the reciprocal covenant

The implied covenant theory can imply covenants benefiting and burdening a lot even when the original deed to that lot says nothing about a covenant.

Benefitting third parties

The contract doctrine of third-party beneficiaries is an alternative way to give an earlier lot buyer the benefit of covenants burdening later-sold lots in the subdivision. Under this theory, the common owner doesn't implicitly make a reciprocal covenant each time she sells a lot. Instead, the third-party beneficiary theory is that each time a lot is sold, the benefit of the covenant burdening that lot is not just for the benefit of the lots still owned by common owner but also for the benefit of earlier lot buyers. Such people who are not parties to the contract but whom the contracting parties intend to benefit are *third-party beneficiaries*.

The common development plan is relevant to this theory, too. It's proof that the common owner and the buyer intended to benefit the earlier lot buyers, because the common plan was intended to burden all the lots for the benefit of all the lots. However, a third party may be a beneficiary of a covenant even if there isn't a common scheme, as long as there's evidence that the original parties intended the person to be a beneficiary and the buyer had actual or constructive notice of it.

If the common plan was evident at the time a person bought her lot from the common owner, then she implicitly covenants that her land will be subject to the same covenants that the other lots are subject to, even if her deed doesn't say so. Likewise, the common owner implicitly makes the reciprocal covenant to the buyer.

The common plan may not have been evident from the start, however. The more lots that are sold with uniform, express covenants, the more likely that a court will find a common plan sufficiently manifested. Although other kinds of evidence, such as marketing materials and oral representations by the common owner, can manifest a common plan, a court almost certainly won't find an implied covenant unless the common plan has already begun to be implemented in actual sales — unless a significant number of properties have been sold with express covenants.

Even if a common owner represents that there will be a common plan of development, if the first few properties are sold without express covenants, those properties will almost certainly not be burdened by implied covenants, either. But if the next ten lots are sold with express covenants, the following lot that is sold would almost certainly be burdened by an implied covenant, even if the deed didn't express the covenant.

Implying intent to run

For a covenant to run with land, at law or in equity, the original parties must have intended the covenant to run. Not only may a common plan imply the existence of covenants, but it also may imply the intent for covenants, express or implied, to run with land.

An express covenant doesn't always state the parties' intent for the benefit and burden to run with the relevant land. And, of course, an implied covenant doesn't state such intent, because it states nothing. In either case, the existence of a common plan may prove intent for the benefit and the burden to run.

The existence of a common plan indicates that the covenant was intended to restrict the use of the land, regardless of who owns it. The original parties create a common plan with uniform covenants in order to create and preserve a neighborhood of a certain character. If the covenant only bound the original burdened party, the covenants obviously wouldn't accomplish the purpose of the common plan. So the existence of a common plan implies that the original parties intended the burden to run with each lot.

Likewise, the common plan implies that the original parties intended the benefit to run with each lot in the subdivision, even if the parties didn't say so expressly. The idea of a common plan is that every lot will be burdened for the benefit of all the other lots — the benefit and burden are reciprocal. So the existence of a common plan implies that the original parties intended all the lots to be benefited. It also implies that the benefit would run with the lots, rather than being personal to the original buyers, because the purpose of the covenants is to maintain a neighborhood of a certain character.

Giving notice of implied covenant

The common plan can give lot buyers notice that a covenant burdens the lot and that all the other lot owners have the right to enforce the covenant.

When a covenant is implied rather than express, a buyer obviously can't discover the covenant from a title search. If the seller didn't tell the buyer about the covenant, the buyer might claim she didn't have notice, actual or constructive. In that case, the recording acts and the requirements for enforcement in equity would prevent enforcement of the covenant against her.

But the common plan comes to the rescue, making the covenant enforceable after all. If the common plan is sufficiently evident to the buyer, the buyer has constructive notice of whatever she could discover by making a reasonable inquiry. If she asked neighbors, asked the developer, or even searched the title to other properties, she might discover the existence of a common scheme of covenants.

It may be a difficult factual question whether a common plan is sufficiently evident to prompt a reasonable buyer to investigate further. It usually requires that there are a significant number of lots developed and being used in compliance with the covenants, revealing a pattern of use that might suggest the existence of common covenants. That alone probably isn't enough to reveal a common plan but would have to be combined with a substantial number of express covenants recorded on other lots or knowledge of representations by the developer.

The common plan is like the Swiss Army knife of covenant law; it can do almost anything. The existence of a common plan can imply the existence of a covenant in the first place. It also can satisfy most of the requirements for the covenant to run at law or in equity. It can prove intent to run and give notice of the covenant, as I explain in this section and the preceding one. The common plan also can prove that the covenant touches and concerns the burdened and the benefited land. The uniform covenant scheme is intended to create a neighborhood of a certain character, restricting activities on each lot so that all the lots will enjoy the resulting benefits. The covenants aren't to benefit specific people but to make the properties more useable and enjoyable for their planned purposes. Furthermore, even though the common plan itself doesn't prove horizontal privity, a covenant that's part of a common plan would exist only in circumstances where the original parties have horizontal privity: when the common owner sells the burdened land to a lot buyer. So the only thing a common plan can't do is establish vertical privity.

Interpreting Covenants

Even if a covenant applies to a particular property, the burdened party may still argue that the covenant doesn't prohibit the activity of which the benefited party complains. So there may be substantial arguments about what a covenant requires or prohibits.

Traditionally, courts interpret covenants narrowly because they restrict the use and enjoyment of land. So if a covenant is ambiguous, a court will interpret the covenant in the way that will be less restrictive.

One common example of this narrow construction is interpretation of a covenant that says something to the effect that the property will be restricted to a "single-family house." You might think that means that only a single family can live on the property, because how can you tell whether a house is a "single-family" house except by looking inside to see who is actually living there? But many courts reason that such expressions are ambiguous, because they refer to the structures on the property rather than uses. So applying the preference for narrow construction, they conclude that such a covenant only requires any building on the property to look like a single-family house, regardless of how the building is actually used.

But as with other contracts, courts also say that covenants should be construed in a way most consistent with their evident intentions. So a court may consider the purpose of a covenant in deciding what vague or ambiguous terms mean. Courts often consider the meaning of covenants restricting uses of land to "residential uses" or "residential purposes," for example. Some may reason that the purpose of such a covenant is to prohibit nonresidential uses, meaning commercial activities. If so, the covenant would prevent a home business. Others may reason that the purpose is to prevent activities that are incompatible with the residential character of the area by generating extra traffic, noise, smoke, dust, and so on. From that perspective, the covenant may allow some home businesses that are compatible with a residential neighborhood, such as a daycare business for neighborhood children or a professional doing tax work for clients in her home.

Despite the usual preference for construing covenants to minimize the restraint of land, courts broadly construe beneficial covenants, such as reciprocal subdivision covenants. Even though they restrict the use of each lot, they also benefit all the other lots and make them more enjoyable. So courts tend to construe such covenants liberally to accomplish the purposes of producing a desirable community.

Amending Covenants

In the absence of a contrary agreement, all parties to a covenant must agree in order to amend a covenant. Every benefited party has the right to insist upon performance of the covenant; others can't alter one party's rights without that party's agreement. Nor can others impose a greater burden on a burdened lot without the burdened owner's agreement.

But covenants can include provisions allowing amendment without everyone's consent. As long as a buyer has notice of that amendment power, the buyer is subject to it.

For example, a common owner who is subdividing and developing land may reserve the power to amend the covenants applicable to the lots in the subdivision during the course of development. Any lot buyer who has notice of that reserved power is subject to the changes the developer makes.

Uniform covenants for residential subdivisions often allow for amendments without unanimous consent of the owners. The covenants may say that a board of representative homeowners has the power to amend or create certain types of covenants for the subdivision. The covenants may authorize a majority, or a specified percentage of homeowners, to amend the covenants. Such provisions are valid and enforceable.

However, courts generally recognize certain limits on this kind of non-unanimous amendment power, even if the covenants don't expressly limit the power. Here are some of the recognized limitations:

✔ **The covenants may not be amended in a way that destroys the purpose of the original covenants.** The amendments must further the same general plan rather than fundamentally change the plan. For example, the majority of homeowners probably couldn't amend the covenants to allow apartment buildings if the covenants originally created a single-family residential neighborhood. Each buyer reasonably expected that the covenants were for the purpose of preserving that type of neighborhood, so the buyers didn't agree to the power to create covenants serving a different purpose altogether.

✔ **The covenants must be amended uniformly.** The covenants can't be amended as to some specific owners' property but not everyone else's. Here, too, each buyer reasonably expected that the covenants were a uniform scheme applicable to the entire subdivision. However, some authorities say that if the covenants sufficiently gave notice to buyers that the covenants could be amended non-uniformly, then such amendments are permissible.

✔ **The covenants must be reasonable.** Some courts, and even some state statutes, say that unreasonable covenants are unenforceable. Again, this rule may be explained as an unspoken assumption among the original parties that the covenant-making power created by the uniform covenants wouldn't include the power to do unreasonable things; it would include only the power to make reasonable changes intended to better accomplish the goals of the covenants. In deciding whether a change was reasonable, courts may consider both whether the process was reasonable, involving appropriate consideration of evidence, and whether the outcome was reasonable.

Terminating Covenants

Covenants can end in numerous ways, one of which is by private agreement. Some ways that may happen include the following:

✔ The covenant may say that it lasts only for a certain period of time, in which case it expires by its own terms when that time comes.

✔ Uniform covenants may provide for termination at an unspecified time by the vote of a majority or a specified percentage of lot owners.

✔ Even if the covenants don't say that they will expire on a certain date, or upon certain action by property owners, a benefited party can agree at any time to release her covenant. Of course, she can do so only for herself, not for other benefited parties.

✔ If the same party comes to own both the benefited and the burdened land, the covenant ends because one can't have a covenant on her own land.

✔ Some states have statutes that automatically terminate covenants after a specified number of years.

A covenant instead may end without any sort of private agreement. The following sections cover some of the rules that terminate a covenant or make it unenforceable regardless of the parties' intentions or agreement.

Invalidating covenants that restrain alienation

A covenant not to transfer ownership of the burdened land may be unenforceable. The freedom to transfer land is so fundamental to ownership of property, and so important to society generally in order to maximize the value of land, that restrictions on that freedom must be limited and reasonable, or they won't be enforced.

A covenant restraining transfer is reasonable if it serves a sufficiently important purpose and is limited so that it doesn't restrain transfer beyond what's necessary to accomplish that purpose. For example, landlords have a substantial interest in who possesses leased property, so leases may include covenants preventing or limiting transfer of the leasehold. (See Chapter 12 for further information about such covenants.)

Even single-family homeowners have some interest in who their neighbors are. But the relationship between neighbors is much less direct than the relationship between a landlord and a tenant, who have an interest in the very same property. A covenant might say that owners of lots in a subdivision can sell their lots only to other members of a homeowners' association, and the association has the right to decide who can be a member. Such a covenant would probably be unenforceable because the interest in the identity of neighbors is less significant and because the association's power to decide who can be a member is unlimited.

Terminating a covenant because of changed circumstances

A court will terminate a covenant, or at least refuse to enforce it, when the circumstances in the area, the actual uses of land, have changed so much that the covenant can't achieve its purpose anymore.

Consider a covenant restricting use of a lot to residential uses. If the surrounding properties eventually change from residential uses to commercial uses, the benefited land can no longer get any real benefit from restricting the lot to residential use. So the covenant is unenforceable or terminated.

The same thing may happen with uniform neighborhood covenants. Suppose a neighborhood is subject to residential covenants. If a significant number of the lots come to be used for commercial purposes, eventually a court may conclude that restricting the remaining lots to residential uses won't achieve the purpose of preserving a residential neighborhood. Changes within the area subject to uniform covenants are much more likely to result in termination of the covenants than changes in surrounding areas are, because as long as the neighborhood can be preserved as intended, the covenants can probably still achieve their basic purpose.

Some authorities suggest that the changed circumstances doctrine is an equitable defense to an action to enforce the covenant. The equitable theory is that equity won't enforce a right if the harm to the burdened party greatly outweighs the benefit to the benefited party. If a covenant significantly restricts use of the land and does practically no good to the benefited party because of changed circumstances, then a court may refuse to enforce the covenant. Under this theory, the covenant still exists and the benefited party may still be entitled to damages at law.

But other authorities suggest that the changed circumstances doctrine actually terminates a covenant. One explanation is that the parties intend the covenant to last only so long as it achieves some fundamental purpose. So as soon as the covenant no longer serves that purpose, it no longer exists. The benefited party no longer has a covenant and has no right to any remedy for its breach.

Changed circumstances may make some but not all applications of a covenant ineffective. If they do, the covenant may not be terminated but simply unenforceable for certain purposes. For example, consider a covenant restricting the size and number of outbuildings in a residential subdivision. If many of the lot owners have built storage sheds, changed circumstances may prevent a plaintiff from enforcing the covenant to prevent another owner from building a storage shed. But a plaintiff may still be entitled to enforce the covenant to prevent larger outbuildings that could be used for apartments or businesses, because the circumstances haven't changed so much that the purpose of preventing those kinds of uses can't be accomplished anymore.

Waiving a covenant

A benefited party may waive her right to enforce the covenant in the future if she doesn't enforce the covenant in the present. If she accepts or tolerates violations of the covenant, she may indicate that she doesn't intend to enforce the covenant, and others may reasonably rely upon her apparent waiver of the covenant.

However, a benefited party doesn't waive her right to enforce the covenant by tolerating violations that don't affect her property. If the covenant is a uniform covenant applying to a neighborhood, violations farther away from her property may have little or no effect on the use and enjoyment of her property. Her failure to enforce the covenant in that case doesn't indicate that she no longer cares about the covenant but simply that the violation wasn't harmful to her so she didn't have sufficient reason to take action against the violator.

Similarly, a benefited party doesn't waive her right to enforce the covenant against big violations by tolerating small violations. Imagine a residential covenant that prohibited even home-based businesses. If a benefited party tolerated some smaller violations of the covenant, such as a tax preparation service and a daycare business, she wouldn't thereby waive her right to enforce the covenant to prevent a retail store in the future.

In short, a benefited party waives only her right to enforce the covenant against violations that are similar in effect to violations that she hasn't taken action against in the past.

If the benefited party herself has violated the covenant, the burdened party may raise a different equitable defense called *unclean hands*. The principle of this defense is that if a person wants to enforce a covenant, she must abide by it herself. She can't violate it herself and expect others to follow it. But like the waiver principle, her own small violation doesn't prevent her from enforcing the covenant to prevent a big violation.

Abandoning a covenant

An individual may waive her right to enforce a covenant, but of course she can't waive other benefited parties' rights to enforce the covenant. However, collectively, the group of benefited owners may terminate a uniform covenant by abandoning it.

A uniform covenant is *abandoned* when existing violations of the covenant would lead a reasonable person to believe that the covenant has been abandoned and is no longer enforceable. To determine whether a covenant has been abandoned, courts consider the number, nature, and seriousness of existing violations as well as whether owners have tried to enforce the covenant in the past. As with the changed circumstances doctrine, courts also may consider whether it's still possible for the owners to enjoy the benefits of the covenant despite the existing violations.

The same facts may be relevant to the abandonment defense and the changed circumstances defense, and courts sometimes seem to treat them as the same thing. But the two defenses are based on two different principles. The changed circumstances principle is that the covenant can't achieve its purpose anymore. Maybe a court figures that it won't enforce a restraint on the use of property that won't do any good but merely allows one person to harass another person, or maybe the court figures that the original parties must not have intended the covenant to continue when it was no longer beneficial.

The abandonment principle, on the other hand, is that the burdened party reasonably relies on the impression that the covenant is no longer enforceable. Even though the covenant may be recorded, the burdened party actually didn't have notice that the covenant still burdened the property, because circumstances indicated that the owners had stopped enforcing the covenant. So with abandonment, the emphasis is on what the burdened party would reasonably perceive, not the benefit the other owners would receive.

Refusing to enforce unreasonable covenants

By statute or judicial decision, a court may declare an unreasonable covenant to be void and unenforceable. Different courts and statutes have declared covenants void for the following reasons:

- ✔ **The covenant is arbitrary.** In other words, there's no rational reason for the covenant. It may be irrational because it targets particular owners for no good reason or because it serves no apparent purpose.

- ✔ **The covenant does much more harm than good.** If the burden of the covenant is great and far outweighs any small benefit to the benefited parties, the covenant may be unreasonable and unenforceable. When the covenant is a uniform covenant that applies to a group of properties, the court should consider the benefit of the covenant to the group generally, not just the benefit of its application to a particular party in a particular circumstance. This same balance of burden and benefit may explain the changed circumstances doctrine. But the burden may greatly outweigh the benefit even when the imbalance doesn't result from changed circumstances.

- ✔ **The covenant violates an important public policy.** Covenants that restrict ownership or possession on the basis of race would be invalid and unenforceable for this reason. So might other covenants that restrict constitutionally protected activities. For example, a covenant prohibiting political signs might be invalid because it violates an important public policy. Not only might a covenant interfere with important personal rights, it might interfere with important public interests in how land is used. For example, although most courts have held otherwise, some courts have held that covenants prohibiting group homes in residential areas are invalid because they violate an important public policy in favor of such group homes in residential neighborhoods.

- ✔ **The process of adopting or applying the covenant is unreasonable.** Uniform covenants may authorize a homeowners' association or other group to amend covenants, adopt new rules for the subdivision, and make discretionary decisions about the application of covenants to particular properties. For example, a covenant may prohibit certain types of construction or alteration of buildings without prior approval by the homeowners' association board or other group, which is charged with determining whether the planned design is appropriate and harmonious with the neighborhood. Such discretionary decisions may be unreasonable and therefore invalid if the group makes the decision without consideration of appropriate evidence that supports their decision.

Analyzing a Covenant Dispute

You can reduce the chances of mistakes, confusion, or wasted energy by being methodical in how you analyze a covenant dispute. For example, you don't need to waste your energy talking about whether a covenant touches and concerns the burdened land if the original covenantor still owns that land. Here are the steps for analyzing a covenant dispute:

1. **Determine what the conflict is.**

   Make sure you identify and understand who wants whom to do or not do what.

2. **Consider whether there's a covenant that would govern or resolve the conflict.**

   Is there an express covenant that satisfies the statute of frauds, and would that covenant actually prohibit or require the burdened party to do what the benefited party wants? That may require interpreting the covenant. Consider also whether a common scheme of development may imply a relevant covenant.

3. **If there is a covenant that would govern the conflict, determine whether that covenant applies to the parties you've identified.**

   Does the one party have the right to enforce the covenant, and is the other party bound by the covenant? If either is an original party to the covenant, she's bound by her contract and the answer is easy. But if either or both are successors to original parties, then you must consider whether the covenant runs with the relevant parcel of land. The covenant will bind a successor in either law or equity if

   • The covenant touches and concerns the land.

   • The original parties intended to bind successors.

   • Either the original parties had horizontal privity and the successor has vertical privity with the original burdened party (law), or the burdened party had notice of the covenant for the benefit of the party seeking to enforce it (equity). Remember that if the benefited party wants damages, she must prove horizontal and vertical privity.

4. **If the covenant would apply to the parties, evaluate whether it's enforceable.**

   Consider whether the covenant has been terminated by private agreement or is unenforceable for any reason, including changed circumstances, waiver, unclean hands, abandonment, unreasonableness, or restraint on alienation.

Chapter 6

Giving Others the Right to Use Your Land: Easements

. . . .

In This Chapter

▶ Understanding what an easement is

▶ Discovering how to get an easement

▶ Examining the rights and duties of the parties to an easement

▶ Looking at how easements are transferred and ended

. . . .

*O*wning land means you have the right to exclude others. It also means you have the right to transfer your rights to others. Not only can you transfer your entire ownership of the land, but you can also transfer some of your specific rights in the land while keeping other rights. For example, you could agree to give up your right to exclude your neighbor from driving back and forth over a driveway that passes over your land and onto his. The right you would give your neighbor is called an *easement*.

This chapter tells you all about easements, from how they're created, transferred, divided, and terminated to the rules regulating the relationship between the parties involved.

Grasping the Basics of Easements

An *easement* is a right a landowner intentionally or unintentionally gives to another to use or to control the use of her land in some way, without possessing it (which is why it's often described as a nonpossessory interest in land).

Easements, along with covenants (see Chapter 5), are known as servitudes. A *servitude* is a general term for nonpossessory legal rights in another person's land. The land that is subject to an easement is called the *servient tenement* or *servient estate;* the owner may be called the *servient tenant*. The owner of the easement may be called the *dominant tenant*. If the easement serves other land in some way, the benefited land is called the *dominant tenement*.

Easements always burden some land, so there's always a servient tenement. But easements might not benefit any dominant tenement; they may simply benefit a person. Such an easement is called an *easement in gross*.

Check out the next sections, which explore the attributes of easements and reveal how to differentiate easements from licenses and covenants.

Distinguishing affirmative and negative easements

Most easements are *affirmative easements,* meaning they give a nonowner the right to use the owner's land in some way. Here are a few examples of affirmative easements:

- ✔ The right to cross the owner's land to get to and from neighboring property (often called a *right-of-way*)
- ✔ The right to install and maintain power lines, water pipes, and sewage systems on and under the owner's land
- ✔ The right to hunt, fish, or use recreational facilities on the owner's land

Parties may also create *negative easements,* which give the easement holder the right to restrain or control the use of the owner's land in some way. Traditionally, only the following types of negative easements were enforceable:

Preserving land: The conservation easement

A *conservation easement* is a negative easement that limits use and development of the servient land in order to preserve the land's natural character. A conservation easement may protect and preserve wildlife habitats, views and open space, recreational uses, or even agricultural or historical values. A conservation easement specifies the aspects of the property to be preserved and permits the servient owner to use the property consistent with those conservation interests. For example, a farm or ranch may be subject to a conservation easement that allows continued farming and ranching but doesn't allow more intensive uses and development.

Courts began recognizing and enforcing conservation easements during the past century or so. Because of some questions about their enforceability and transferability, many states have adopted statutes that authorize conservation easements. Such statutes generally authorize and apply only to conservation easements held by governments and private conservation organizations. Furthermore, federal law encourages donation of conservation easements to such holders by allowing grantors to claim charitable contribution deductions from federal estate and income taxes.

✔ To restrain development of the owner's property in order to preserve the easement holder's access to light and air on his nearby property

✔ To restrain development of property to preserve the easement holder's view (according to more recent cases)

✔ To restrain development of the owner's property in order to preserve subjacent or lateral support for the easement holder's property so that it doesn't subside

✔ To maintain the flow of artificial streams

Courts today may also recognize and enforce other types of negative easements that they haven't traditionally recognized. For example, by judicial decision and state statutes, states now generally recognize and enforce *conservation easements,* a particular kind of negative easement that limits development to preserve the land. See the nearby sidebar for details.

Describing profits

A *profit,* or more impressively, a *profit à prendre,* is an easement not just to use the land but to remove natural resources that are part of the land. Easements to remove oil, gas, and timber are profits. Because removing such resources requires access to the surface of the land, whenever someone has a profit, he also has an accompanying easement to use the surface of the land as reasonably necessary to remove the natural resources that are the subject of his profit. Because profits are just a type of easement, they're generally subject to the same rules as easements.

Telling easements apart from licenses

By definition, an easement is an interest in land that lasts either indefinitely or for some specified period of time. A license, on the other hand, is permission to use land that can be revoked at any time.

Because both easements and licenses involve the use of another person's land, they can look similar. If the parties' agreement doesn't clearly specify whether the landowner can revoke permission or whether the grant is durable, a court has to figure out whether they intended to create an easement or a license, which determines whether the landowner can revoke permission.

Courts typically consider the following kinds of evidence to decide whether an agreement allowing one party to use another's land is a durable easement or a revocable license:

✔ **Indications that the grant was to last permanently or for a specific time:** If the parties intended the grant to be permanent or for a specific time, the grant is an easement by definition.

✔ **Designations of the area that the grantee can use:** Because a license is revocable at will, the licensor may not be specific about the area subject to the license. In contrast, because an easement is an interest in land, the statute of frauds may require some specification of the land subject to the easement. Even if it doesn't, the grantor of an easement is more likely to be specific about the grantee's rights, because the grantor can't just change her mind if she's unhappy with what the grantee does.

✔ **The right to make improvements:** If the grantee has the right to improve the land somehow, the parties probably intended to create an easement. A license is more temporary and less substantial, so the licensee is unlikely to make investments in the licensor's land, knowing that the licensor can revoke permission to use her land anytime.

✔ **Payment of consideration:** When the grantee pays consideration for the grant, it's more likely an easement. A grantee is less likely to pay for a license that can be revoked at any time than to pay for an easement that's durable and can't be taken away at will.

Knowing what's an easement and what's a covenant

Both easements and covenants can be affirmative or negative. However, easements are typically affirmative, giving the holder the right to use the servient land, whereas covenants are typically negative, limiting what the burdened party can do on her own land. Distinguishing affirmative easements from negative covenants is therefore pretty easy.

The real trick is distinguishing between negative easements and negative covenants. Both restrain the use of the land they burden for the benefit of someone else. In fact, as Chapter 5 mentions, the two can be so alike that courts sometimes call implied covenants "reciprocal negative easements." Sometimes it doesn't matter whether an interest is called a negative easement or a negative covenant. But sometimes it does, such as when deciding whether an oral agreement is enforceable. Consider the following to help decide whether an interest is an easement or covenant:

✔ **The parties' expressed intent:** The instrument creating the interest may expressly say that the interest is a covenant or an easement.

✔ **Breadth of the restraint:** If the restraint prohibits a particular type of use on the entire burdened parcel of land, it's probably a covenant. If the restraint prohibits only a specified use in a specified part of the land, it's likely a negative easement.

✔ **Character of the restraint:** The parties presumably intend the interest to be valid and enforceable. If the restraint wouldn't be a permissible subject for a negative easement, then it should be construed as a covenant if possible.

✔ **Benefit in gross:** An easement or covenant may be called *in gross* when the benefit of the restriction isn't connected to any land but is personal to the benefited party. At least, many courts would say that a real covenant may not be in gross, whereas everyone would agree that easements may be in gross. So presuming that the parties intended a valid and enforceable interest, a restraint in gross should be construed as a negative easement if possible.

✔ **Oral restrictions:** Though nonpossessory, easements are interests in land and are therefore subject to the statute of frauds, which requires written evidence of the interest. But some courts hold that covenants don't have to comply with the statute of frauds, so an enforceable oral restriction would almost certainly have to be a covenant rather than a negative easement.

Creating Easements

An easement exists only if the parties do something to create one. Parties can create an easement in the following ways:

✔ **Expressly agreeing:** The parties can simply agree to create an easement. The statute of frauds generally requires written evidence of the easement; however, an agreement to create an easement may be enforceable under the doctrines of estoppel and part performance despite noncompliance with the statute of frauds.

✔ **Implying an easement by their conduct:** Three situations may imply the creation of an easement: prior use, necessity, and recording a subdivision plat.

✔ **Acquiring by prescription:** A person acquires an easement over another's land by using the land as if he had an easement for a long period of time. This is called an *easement by prescription.*

The following sections talk about all these ways of creating an enforceable easement.

Looking at express easements

Parties can create an easement by express agreement. The grantor, or servient tenant, can simply sign an easement agreement that conveys the easement to the grantee, the dominant tenant.

The parties also may create an easement in a deed that conveys the dominant or servient land. A deed may grant an easement to the grantee along with the land that it benefits, or the deed may reserve to the grantor an easement over the granted land.

Some courts say that a deed can't reserve an easement for someone other than the grantor. So if the grantor wants to do so, he must reserve the easement for himself and then separately convey the reserved easement to the intended beneficiary.

Avoiding the statute of frauds

The statute of frauds applies to easements because they're interests in land. As with other property interests, most state statutes of frauds don't apply to short-term interests that last for less than a year. Otherwise, the statute of frauds requires written evidence of the creation of an easement, signed by the servient tenant — although today a deed signed by the grantor and reserving an easement for himself may satisfy the statute of frauds. The statute of frauds also requires that the writing define the servient estate or the location of the easement.

If there's no such writing, the statute of frauds makes such an agreement unenforceable. However, there are two exceptions to this general rule, when the parties' express agreement creating an easement will be enforced despite the absence of the required written evidence. The following sections take a closer look at those exceptions.

Enforcing an easement due to estoppel

If the servient tenant agrees to give the dominant tenant an easement but their agreement doesn't comply with the statute of frauds, their agreement creates a license. The statute of frauds won't allow the easement to be enforced, but the grantor nevertheless did agree to allow the grantee to use her land somehow. So the grantee has a license, which by definition the licensor can revoke at any time.

However, the licensor may be *estopped* from revoking the license in certain circumstances. If the licensor can't revoke the license, then the license is essentially an easement. Sometimes courts call this an *equitable easement* or, confusingly, an *irrevocable license.*

Estoppel allows the dominant tenant to enforce an express easement agreement, despite noncompliance with the statute of frauds, when the following things are true:

- ✔ **The parties intended to create an easement.** If the parties expressly agreed that the grant was a license, revocable at will, then the estoppel doctrine can't transform the license into an easement.

✔ **The dominant tenant reasonably relied on the grant of an easement to his detriment.** In other words, the dominant tenant somehow changed his position (by investing in the land or otherwise) in a way that he'll suffer loss if the easement agreement isn't enforced. Some courts say that the reliance must be expenditures on the servient land that are required in order to make use of the easement, such as improving a driveway over the servient land. Other courts say that any substantial reliance can support an estoppel claim.

✔ **The servient tenant reasonably should've foreseen that the dominant tenant would rely as he did.** Even if the parties didn't expressly say that the grant was irrevocable, if the servient tenant should've known that the dominant tenant was expecting an irrevocable interest and was going to invest in reliance on it, then once the dominant tenant does invest, the servient tenant is estopped from denying the existence of the easement.

Because the easement becomes enforceable to avoid harm resulting from the dominant tenant's reliance, some authorities say that the easement by estoppel lasts only until the dominant tenant gets enough value out of the easement to justify his expenditures. After he's got as much value from the easement as he put into the property in reliance, he no longer has an enforceable easement.

Enforcing an easement due to part performance

Part performance allows enforcement of an unwritten agreement on the theory that the parties have performed their agreement enough that a court can be confident they really did enter into an easement agreement, despite the absence of a writing.

The requirements of part performance essentially require alternative evidence that the parties did agree to create an easement. Here are the three categories of alternative evidence that may justify enforcement of the easement agreement, despite noncompliance with the statute of frauds:

✔ **Use of the easement:** If the dominant tenant has actually been using the easement pursuant to the alleged easement agreement for some time without objection by the servient tenant, that tends to prove that the parties really did enter into an easement agreement.

✔ **Permanent, substantial improvements:** If the dominant tenant makes improvements to the servient land, that's persuasive evidence that the parties entered into an easement agreement. People don't normally make improvements to other people's land, but easement holders often do so in order to make better use their easements.

✔ **Payment of consideration:** If the dominant tenant paid consideration to the servient tenant, that tends to prove that the parties really did have an easement agreement. However, there may be other explanations for apparent payment of consideration, so some courts have said that payment of consideration alone isn't enough to excuse noncompliance with the statute of frauds; it must be combined with evidence of use or improvements.

The dominant tenant need not prove all three of these things to establish sufficient part performance to excuse noncompliance with the statute of frauds. Some courts have suggested that the payment of consideration alone can't be sufficient part performance to excuse noncompliance with the statute of frauds. In evaluating part performance claims, consider whether the evidence in each of these categories persuasively indicates that the parties must have had an easement agreement or whether the evidence is consistent with an alternative explanation offered by the servient tenant. If the evidence isn't sufficiently convincing, the part performance exception shouldn't apply.

Don't forget that part performance and estoppel are just exceptions to the statute of frauds. They allow enforcement of an easement agreement without the required written evidence of the agreement, but they don't allow enforcement of an easement when the parties never agreed to create one. The easement-holder still must prove that the parties agreed to create an easement, even though the agreement wasn't properly evidenced in writing. Don't make the mistake of arguing that someone has an easement by part performance because he used an easement and made improvements, even though there's no evidence that the servient tenant ever agreed to give him an easement.

Implying easements three ways

The parties' actions may imply the intent to create an easement without any express agreement. There obviously isn't written evidence of such easements that would satisfy the statute of frauds, but they're enforceable anyway. The law recognizes an implied easement in three situations:

- ✔ Prior use
- ✔ Necessity
- ✔ Subdivision plat

Implying an easement by prior use

An easement is implied by prior use when an owner has been using part of her land in an easement-like way to benefit another part of her land and then transfers one of those parts of her land to another person. The party claiming an easement implied by prior use must prove the following:

- ✔ **Severance of unity:** One of the parties has divided her land and transferred part of it to the other party.
- ✔ **Prior use:** Before and up to the time the grantor transferred part of the land to the grantee, the grantor had been using one of the parts to benefit the other part in a way that would be an easement if the parts were separately owned. For example, a water line passes under the land to a house on the land.

Sometimes an easement implied by prior use is called a *quasi-easement* because it arises only when the grantor has already been using part of her land to benefit another part in the way easements do. But before severance, you wouldn't call that use an easement because an owner can't have an easement on her own property.

✔ **Reasonably necessary use:** The prior use was reasonably necessary to the enjoyment of the benefited part of the land. If the grantee claims an easement implied by prior use, the grantee generally only has to prove that the use was beneficial and convenient to his portion of the severed land. For example, if the grantor had been using a driveway across her land for access to the rear of a building that she subsequently sold to the grantee, use of the driveway over the grantor's land is probably "reasonably necessary" for the grantee if it would cost a significant amount of money to build a new access driveway across his own land to a public street.

On the other hand, if the grantor claims to have reserved an easement implied by prior use over the grantee's land, many courts require the easement to be strictly necessary for the use and enjoyment of the grantor's retained land, not just beneficial and convenient. The grantor could've expressly reserved an easement in his deed to the grantee, and often his deed has warranted that he conveys title free from such easements, so courts are more reluctant to find an implied easement retained by the grantor.

✔ **Apparent use:** At the time the grantor severed ownership and transferred part to the grantee, the prior use was apparent to the parties. An easement is implied in these circumstances because we figure that if enjoying one part of the land already depended on using another part of the land in some way, the parties surely meant for that use to continue, even though they didn't think to say so in their deed. But if the parties weren't even aware of the prior use, then they must not have intended to create an easement.

Even though this requirement is usually expressed as "apparent" use, the essential requirement is that the use was known to the parties, or at least reasonably discoverable. For example, underground water and sewer pipes might not seem "apparent" because they aren't visible on the surface, but courts have held them to be easements implied by prior use when the plumbing indicated that there must be pipes passing somewhere underground and the parties could reasonably discover where they were located.

✔ **Continuous use:** The prior use must have been continuous up until the time of severance rather than merely occasional or temporary. Only in these circumstances would we presume that the parties intended for the use to continue as an easement after severance.

Some courts don't list continuous use as a requirement — the requirements that the use be apparent and reasonably necessary are enough to ensure that the parties must have intended for the use to continue.

If prior use does imply an easement, the dominant tenant owns an easement just as if the parties had expressly created the easement in the deed. The easement continues even if circumstances change and the easement is no longer reasonably necessary for use of the dominant tenement.

Implying an easement by necessity

Similar to an easement implied by prior use, an easement implied by necessity, or just *easement by necessity,* is created only when a landowner divides her land among two or more owners. But an easement by necessity arises only when that division of land causes a newly divided parcel of land to no longer have access to a public street, regardless of whether some of the owner's land had previously been used to access that portion before the division of the land.

A person claiming an easement by necessity must prove the following:

- **Severance of unity:** One of the parties has divided her land and transferred part of it to the other party.

- **Loss of access:** The division of the land caused the claimant's land, whether the parcel retained by the grantor or the parcel granted to the grantee, to no longer have a legal right of access to a public street.

- **Necessity:** At the time the property was severed, the claimant's land didn't border a public street or have any other existing easement over private land to get to a public street. This is the only kind of "necessity" for which one may have an easement by necessity. Some courts hold that an easement is necessary even though there may be some other route to a public street, because the other route isn't feasible or effective.

These circumstances imply that the grantor must have intended to grant or reserve an easement to pass across the other part of the subdivided land to get to a public street. But even if these conditions are met, some courts have held that the easement isn't implied if the parties have otherwise indicated their intent not to create an easement — such as the grantee's acknowledging in the purchase agreement that the land he's buying doesn't have access to a public street.

The owner of the servient land can specify the location of the easement by necessity over her land. But if she doesn't do so within a reasonable time after severance, the dominant tenant can choose the access route over the servient land.

Unlike the easement implied by prior use, the easement by necessity lasts only as long as the necessity lasts. If the dominant tenant acquires an easement over some other land to access a public street, or if the government builds a public street over or adjacent to his land, the easement by necessity ends.

The easement by necessity doctrine is not a general rule that a person automatically has an easement over another person's land if needed to get to a public street. The easement by necessity exists only over land that was divided — over either the grantor's or the grantee's land — and only when the division itself cut off access to a public street. One never has an easement by necessity over someone else's land that wasn't part of the subdivided land. If someone buys land that didn't have access to a public street in the first place, he simply must buy easements as needed to get an access route to a public street — or wait for the government to build a public street adjoining his property.

Some states have statutes that authorize private owners to forcibly buy an access easement from an unwilling owner. If a landowner doesn't have access to a public street, he can petition the local government to identify an access route and determine a fair price that he must pay the owner of the servient land.

Implying an easement by subdivision plat

A subdivision plat may imply the grant of easements to buyers of subdivided lots. A *subdivision plat* is a map showing how a subdivision will be laid out, with streets and individual lots. If the subdividing developer gives the streets to the public, which is automatic in some states, the lot owners generally have no need to claim a private easement over the public streets. But if the streets are private, the lot owners may have implied easements to drive over those streets. Likewise, they may have implied easements to use parks and other neighborhood amenities shown on the plat.

States vary in the extent to which lot owners acquire easements over streets in a subdivision plat. There are three approaches:

- ✔ **Broad rule:** Each lot owner has an easement over all the streets in the plat.

- ✔ **Intermediate rule:** Each lot owner has an easement over all the streets in the plat that reasonably benefit the use of his lot.

- ✔ **Narrow rule:** Each lot owner has an easement over the streets that are necessary to get from his lot to a public street.

Over time: Acquiring easements by prescription

A person may acquire an easement by using the servient land a particular way for a long period of time. Such an easement is called a *prescriptive easement.* The user gets an easement by openly, adversely, continuously, and exclusively using the land for a number of years specified by state statute. The following sections explain each of the elements that someone has to prove to get a prescriptive easement.

Acquiring an easement by prescription today is similar to acquiring title to land by adverse possession (a topic I cover in detail in Chapter 14). The difference is simply that if the adverse use doesn't amount to possession but is merely the use of the servient land, the adverse user acquires an easement to continue that use rather than complete ownership of the land.

Open and notorious use of the servient land

The claimant must have used the land as if he had an easement, in a way that was open and apparent to the servient owner. That way, the servient owner should be aware that the claimant is using her land and can bring a claim to eject him if she believes he doesn't own an easement. In fact, if the owner of the servient land actually knows about the use of her land, it shouldn't matter whether the use is visible.

Only physical uses of the servient land can create prescriptive easements. You can't get a negative easement, such as an easement preserving views or light and air, by prescription.

Adverse use of the servient land

The claimant must act as if he has the right to use the servient land — in other words, as if he has an easement. If the claimant uses the land simply because the owner gave him revocable permission, the use is not adverse.

In general, open and continuous use of another's property is presumed to be adverse. However, courts often say that use of unfenced, undeveloped land is presumed to be by permission of the owner. Maybe that's because they assume that if an owner doesn't fence her land, she's telling everyone that she's neighborly and doesn't mind people using her land while she isn't doing much with it. Or maybe courts figure that an owner of such land shouldn't have to be as diligent in watching for adverse uses, because she's leaving it open and not developing it — by presuming others' use to be permissive, others are much less likely to obtain prescriptive easements over her land.

Although adverse use is sometimes described as "hostile" use, the use doesn't have to be hostile in the sense that the owner of the land opposes the use. The use simply needs to reflect a claim to an easement. If the parties intend to create an easement but it's void because of the statute of frauds, for example, the dominant tenant who uses the easement is acting under a claim of right, adversely to the servient tenant's title, even though the servient owner doesn't oppose the use because she, too, intended to grant the dominant tenant an easement. However, you should know that some courts have reasoned that in such cases, the agreement creates a license, and therefore the use is permissive.

If the claimant uses the land adversely, as if he has a claim of right, the owner can't make the use permissive simply by telling the user that she gives him permission. The owner knows about the adverse claim and must take action to resolve the dispute within the statutory limitations period. However, some states say that an owner can declare a use to be permissive, such as by posting signs giving permission, and thereby avoid creation of a prescriptive easement.

Continuous and uninterrupted use

The prescriptive use must be continuous and uninterrupted. That means that the user makes use of the claimed easement in a way that is regular and normal for the type of easement claimed, rather than occasional and sporadic. It also means that neither the servient owner nor anyone else stops the prescriptive use during the required period of time.

Merely objecting to the use doesn't interrupt the use. Nor does unsuccessfully trying to stop the use.

Exclusive use

Sometimes courts say that the use must be exclusive, which is also a requirement for the analogous doctrine of adverse possession (see Chapter 14). But an easement holder doesn't generally have the right to exclude others from the land. The servient owner can continue to use the servient land as long as she doesn't interfere with the use of the easement.

If this is a requirement for a prescriptive easement, it means only something similar to the requirement that the use be uninterrupted. An easement holder has the right to prevent others from interfering with his use of the easement, so if he does prevent others from interfering, then he has used the easement as exclusively as he can. But if he simply uses the land along with the public generally, then he doesn't acquire a prescriptive easement.

Use for the statutory limitations period

All states have statutes specifying a time period within which a person must bring an action to eject a trespasser and regain possession of land; after that time period has passed, she loses her right to bring such a claim (see Chapter 14 for details). The time periods generally range from 5 to 20 years. To obtain a prescriptive easement, the claimant must prove that he satisfied the elements for a prescriptive easement for the specified number of years. He acquires an easement as soon as he has done so, regardless of whether he continues to satisfy the elements thereafter.

The statute of limitations doesn't run against the government, so a person can't get a prescriptive easement over government-owned land.

Public prescriptive easements: Claiming easements for everyone

Sometimes individuals use property not as if they have the individual right to use the property but as if they share the right to use the property along with the general public. For example, people may use a trail over private land as if the public generally has the right to use the trail.

Some courts have held that the public cannot acquire a prescriptive easement in this way. But today courts increasingly accept the possibility. Some state statutes expressly authorize the acquisition of prescriptive easements by the public. In such cases, individual users claiming a public easement need not claim that they acted as if they had an easement; they need only claim that they acted as if they didn't need permission from the servient owner. They also don't need to prove that the use was exclusive, because the claim is that anyone had the right to make use of the easement, and of course so did the servient owner. But they must still prove that the use was also open, notorious, continuous, and uninterrupted for the statutory period.

Interference and Trespasses: Determining the Scope of Easements

The parties to an easement may specify which part of the servient land the dominant tenant may use, how the dominant tenant may use that land, the purposes for which the dominant tenant may use the land, and which land the easement benefits. If the dominant tenant uses the servient land in a way not authorized by the easement agreement, he has trespassed on the servient land.

But often the parties aren't specific about some or all of these aspects of the easement they create. In fact, when the easement is implied or prescriptive, there's no express agreement defining the scope of the easement at all. In such cases, courts must figure out the extent of the rights owned by the easement holder and determine when the easement holder goes too far and trespasses on the servient land.

The following sections point out how to determine the scope of easements and when one of the parties invades the other party's rights.

Prohibiting interference by the servient owner

The dominant tenant has the right to use the servient land in some way. That means he has the right to prevent others from unreasonably interfering with his use of the servient land. For example, the owner of a right-of-way can enjoin the servient owner from installing a locked gate across the way or building improvements that obstruct some of the width of the easement. Similarly, the owner of an easement to install and maintain pipes underground could have a court enjoin the servient owner from building something on top of the easement that would make it impossible or too difficult to access and maintain the pipes.

However, the dominant tenant doesn't own the servient land and doesn't have the right to exclude people generally. That means that the servient owner can use the servient land in any way that doesn't unreasonably interfere with the easement. For example, the owner of land subject to an easement for underground pipes can still plant grass and play badminton on the surface of the easement, even though the dominant tenant would have the right to tear up the ground when needed to access the pipes. Because the servient owner retains all the rights to use the land that she hasn't given away to the dominant owner, she can also transfer those rights to others. In fact, unless the easement says otherwise, she can even give an easement to another company to maintain pipes in the same area, as long as the presence of the other company's pipes doesn't unreasonably interfere with the dominant owner's access to its own pipes. Of course, if the easement agreement says that only the dominant tenant has the right to install pipes in that location, then the servient owner has given up the right to use that land in that particular way.

An easement agreement that states that no one else may have an easement to use the same land in the same way is considered *exclusive.* However, easements are exclusive in this way only if they say so.

Preventing use that benefits nondominant land

An easement that benefits particular land can't be used to benefit any other land. So if someone acquires a right-of-way to pass across the servient land to get to and from a parcel of land, the dominant tenant can't enlarge the parcel of land that he accesses by means of the easement. That may seem strange, because it doesn't seem like it should matter to the servient owner where the dominant owner goes after traveling over the servient land, but that's the rule. In effect, the servient owner gave the right to the dominant owner to do a specific thing on the servient land: pass across it only to get to another particular parcel of land. If the dominant owner does something else, he's acting beyond the scope of his right.

Using the easement to benefit other land is a trespass. Normally, a landowner is entitled to an injunction preventing trespass, regardless of whether the trespass injures her somehow. She has the right to exclude others even if they don't harm the land or interfere with her use in any way. However, if the servient owner doesn't promptly object to an expansion of the dominant land

and the dominant owner invests in the property in reliance on the easement to access his enlarged property, a court may refuse to enjoin use of the easement unless the servient owner can show substantial injury.

Changing the type or purpose of use

An easement agreement may specify that the easement may be used for certain purposes and in certain ways. For example, an easement agreement might grant only the right to ride across the land on a unicycle to go to costume parties. In fact, lawyers who draft easement agreements ought to be as precise as possible to avoid uncertainty and disputes. If the easement agreement does limit the purposes for which the easement may be used, or the ways in which it may be used, then any use beyond those limitations is a trespass.

But when the easement agreement *doesn't* specify permitted purposes or types of use, or when the easement is implied or prescriptive, the court must decide whether new uses of the easement are within the scope of the easement or whether they're trespasses.

A change in the purpose or type of use is generally within the scope of the easement if the new use is a normal and reasonable evolution and it was reasonably foreseeable. For example, over time, the dominant estate may change from agricultural to residential uses, so cars rather than farm vehicles may travel the right-of-way. Most courts would agree that such a change is a normal, foreseeable evolution in the use of the land and that when the parties created a general right-of-way, whether it was express or implied, they would've intended for the dominant tenant to have the right to use the easement in normal ways over time. Therefore, such a change in the use of the easement is not a trespass on the servient land.

If the easement is prescriptive, a court may ask whether the servient owner would've objected to the new use if it had occurred before the prescriptive period had run. If the servient owner would've objected, then the new use is beyond the scope of the prescriptive easement. (See the earlier section "Over time: Acquiring easements by prescription" for details on prescriptive easements.)

Increasing the burden on the servient land

The dominant owner may trespass by using the easement in ways that increase the burden on the servient land. An express easement may specify the extent to which the dominant owner may burden the servient land, such as specifying the size of vehicles or number of trips per day allowed on a right-of-way or noting the number and size of underground pipes allowed in an easement. Any use of the easement beyond such express limits is a trespass.

Of course, if an easement doesn't specify such limits, the court must try to figure out what the parties intended or would've agreed to. Here are some factors the court may consider:

- **The character and severity of the increased burden on the servient land:** The servient tenant expressly or implicitly agreed to allow the dominant tenant to use her land in some way and thereby to burden her own use of the land to some extent. The servient tenant also reasonably could expect that the use would change over time. But the servient owner presumably wouldn't have expected or agreed to a use that would significantly interfere with her own ability to use and enjoy her property.

- **The benefit to the dominant tenant:** Courts may weigh the burden on the servient tenant against the benefit to the dominant tenant to decide whether a particular increase in use is reasonable.

- **The parties' agreement:** Here are some ways the courts try to figure out the parties' intent for express, implied, and prescriptive easements.

  - If the easement is express, a court considers whether the parties' agreement indicates their intention in any relevant way. The court also looks at the consideration paid and the circumstances in which the parties agreed to the easement, which may suggest an intention about the permissible extent of use.

  - If the easement is implied, a court considers the circumstances that imply the easement to help decide whether a more intensive use of the easement is within the scope of what the parties would've intended.

  - If the easement is prescriptive, the court considers whether the servient tenant would've objected to the more intensive use if it had occurred during the prescriptive period.

- **Foreseeability:** If the use is more intensive in ways that were natural and foreseeable, it's more likely to be within the scope of the easement.

- **Past use of the easement:** The parties' past conduct may suggest their original understanding about limits to use of the easement.

Maintaining the easement

An easement agreement may say that the dominant or servient owner has or does not have duties to maintain the easement. The parties may agree to allocate such duties and expenses as they wish.

In the absence of such an agreement, the dominant owner has a duty to maintain the easement so that it doesn't unreasonably interfere with the servient owner's use of her land. Some courts, however, have held that the servient owner must share the expense of maintaining a right-of-way that the servient owner uses along with the dominant owner.

Beyond her basic duty to the servient owner, the dominant owner also has the privilege to maintain, repair, and even improve the land subject to the easement in reasonable ways to make the easement useful. For example, the dominant owner can pave a driveway over the servient land, unless doing so would unreasonably burden the servient land. The servient owner likewise can, if she chooses, maintain, repair, and improve the land subject to the easement as long as doing so does not unreasonably interfere with use of the easement.

Transferring and Dividing Easements

An easement owner can transfer his easement to another person. And as with other property interests, in some ways an easement owner can divide his easement rights and transfer some of them to another person. Similarly, a servient owner can transfer the servient land to another person.

An easement always stays attached to the servient land, so any transfer of the land also transfers the burden of the easement. The deed transferring the servient land doesn't have to mention the easement in order for the easement to transfer with the land. However, if the new owner of the servient land didn't know about the easement and couldn't reasonably have discovered the easement, then a state recording statute may free the new owner from the easement burden. (I examine how recording statutes work in Chapter 17.)

Look at the following sections for info on transferring and sharing easements and the legal limits on doing so.

Sticking to the land: Transferring appurtenant easements

An easement that benefits particular land is *appurtenant* to that land. For example, a right-of-way to drive across servient land to access adjoining dominant land is appurtenant to the dominant land.

A profit also may be appurtenant to specific land. For example, a profit to remove soil for agricultural purposes on the dominant land would be appurtenant to that land.

An appurtenant easement is part of the dominant land and can't be separated from it. So whenever the dominant owner transfers the dominant estate, the easement passes to the new owner, whether the deed mentions the easement or not. However, if a deed conveying the dominant land says that the grantor doesn't transfer the easement, the appurtenant easement will simply end, because the grantor can't keep the easement separate from the dominant land. An attempt to transfer the easement without transferring the dominant estate is void.

Dividing appurtenant easements

Unless an easement agreement says otherwise, an appurtenant easement attaches to the entire dominant parcel that the dominant owner held at the time the easement was created. So if the dominant owner divides the dominant land among several owners, all those new owners have the same right to use the easement, even though they don't own all of the original dominant parcel.

However, division of the dominant land generally results in more intensive use of the easement. If the increase in use is unreasonable and unforeseeable, then the dominant owners may be guilty of trespass (see the earlier section "Increasing the burden on the servient land" for details). However, because subdivision is common, courts typically assume that subdivision for development is reasonable and foreseeable unless an easement agreement says otherwise.

Transferring easements in gross

Profits in gross are freely transferable, but only some easements in gross are transferable. Courts generally agree that commercial easements in gross — those benefiting commercial operations rather than specific land — are transferable. Examples of such easements include utility easements for pipelines, transmission lines, and telephone lines; railroad easements; and recreational easements for businesses (such as boating, fishing, and hunting rights).

On the other hand, personal easements in gross — created for the easement holder's enjoyment rather than for economic benefit — are not transferable. For example, recreational easements to boat, fish, and hunt may be for the personal enjoyment of the easement holder.

The parties to an easement can agree that an easement is transferable, not transferable, or transferable only in specified situations. Even if the parties don't directly say whether an easement in gross is transferable, they may otherwise indicate their intention. You could say that commercial easements, for example, are transferable because the nature of the easement suggests that the parties intended it not just to benefit a particular person or company but to benefit a particular operation that might later change ownership.

The parties may otherwise indicate their intention to allow or restrict transfer of an easement in gross. For example, an easement agreement may grant an easement to the named grantee and his "heirs and assigns." Some courts say those words sufficiently indicate the intention to make even a personal easement transferable. Others suggest that such indications of intent are just one relevant factor to consider, along with other factors such as

- ✔ How much the easement holder paid for the easement
- ✔ How much the transfer of the easement may increase the burden on the servient estate
- ✔ The relationship between the grantor and grantee and the circumstances in which the easement was created

Some states have passed statutes that make easements in gross transferable unless the creating instrument says otherwise.

Dividing easements in gross

The owner of an easement in gross — one that benefits a person or commercial operation rather than land — may divide the benefit of the easement among multiple owners if the easement agreement says so. But often the easement agreement isn't explicit about division of the benefit, so courts have to decide whether the parties intended to allow such division of the easement. If the instrument creating the easement says it's "exclusive," that generally means that the servient owner can't give that right to anyone else. Instead, the dominant owner can transfer that right in whole or in part to others. For example, the owner of an exclusive pipeline easement could share that easement with other pipeline companies. Similarly, if an easement or profit specifies the extent of permitted use by the dominant tenant, the dominant tenant can share the easement with others as long as he doesn't exceed the specified maximum use.

If the easement isn't exclusive, some courts say that it can't be divided. But most courts would probably agree that the easement can be divided if the grantor somehow indicated the intent for the easement to be divisible.

Courts also may allow division of an easement or profit in gross if the division doesn't increase the burden on the servient estate. Some courts still apply the traditional *one stock* rule, which says that when multiple parties use an easement in gross they exceed the scope of the easement unless they use the easement as one enterprise, such as partners and joint venturers. Most courts, however, allow multiple parties to use an easement as long as their uses don't increase the burden on the servient estate, regardless of whether they act as one enterprise. For example, some courts have held that a utility easement holder could sell to a cable television company the right to install cable television lines on existing utility poles, because doing so doesn't increase the burden on the servient land.

Terminating Easements

An easement is permanent unless the parties agree otherwise. But the parties certainly can agree that an easement will terminate at some point, whether at a specific time or when certain conditions occur.

Here are some examples of how easements may expire:

- ✔ An easement agreement may say the easement lasts for a specific time period or for the lifetime of the easement holder.

- ✔ An easement agreement may say the easement lasts only as long as it's used for a specific purpose, such as for a railroad. If the easement agreement specifies a purpose for the easement, the easement ends when that purpose can no longer be served, even if the easement agreement doesn't say so. For example, a grant of an easement for access to a specific public road ends if the public road is closed.

- ✔ An easement in a building or a structure ends when the building or structure is destroyed.

- ✔ An easement that benefits or burdens less than a fee simple estate ends when the relevant estate ends. (See Chapter 9 for details on estates.)

- ✔ A personal easement in gross ends when the dominant owner dies.

Even if an easement is permanent and will never naturally expire, the owner of the easement may terminate the easement in a variety of ways. The following sections detail how that can happen.

Terminating easements by express release or agreement

You can expressly terminate an easement just like you can expressly create one. The dominant owner can release the easement by deed, thereby extinguishing it. Or the dominant owner can transfer the easement by deed to the servient owner. As soon as the same person owns both the easement and the servient land, the two merge because you can't have an easement on your own land.

Ending easements by merging dominant and servient estates

If the same person acquires the dominant and servient estates, the easement merges with the servient estate and ends. That's true even if the parties don't expressly intend for merger to extinguish the easement, because you can't have an easement over your own land.

Courts generally agree that after merger terminates an easement, the easement doesn't revive if the servient and dominant estates are later owned separately again.

Abandoning easements

Even though the owner of title to real property can't simply abandon ownership, the owner of an easement can terminate his easement by abandoning it. Unlike with abandoned chattels (covered in Chapter 13), an abandoned easement doesn't continue to exist, waiting for someone else to find and take possession of it. It simply ends.

Successfully claiming an easement was abandoned requires proving that the easement holder has

- ✔ Stopped using the easement
- ✔ Clearly indicated that he intends to give up ownership of the easement

Like an owner of title to real property, the owner of an easement doesn't have a duty to use his property interest. He can let it sit unused as long as he wants, and whenever he decides to, he can make use of it again. So an easement holder abandons an easement only if he indicates not only that he isn't going to use it now but that he doesn't want to keep it for possible use in the future.

Here are some examples of how an easement holder can clearly indicate his intent to abandon the easement:

- ✔ The easement holder takes actions that prevent use of the easement in the future. If a railroad owns an easement for railway use and removes all the railroad tracks from the easement, the railroad's actions may sufficiently indicate intent to abandon the easement. Or if an easement holder blocks off his access to the easement by building a structure, he indicates that he intends to abandon the easement.

✔ The easement holder doesn't object to obstructions of the easement by the servient owner for a substantial period of time. However, in some cases, even such acquiescence might not clearly indicate intent to abandon an easement. For example, if the easement holder had two access easements to his property, his failure to object to obstruction of one of the easements might not indicate intent to abandon but simply that he didn't need to use that easement during that time.

✔ The easement holder acquires and uses a new easement that serves the same purpose. In some cases, this has supported the court's finding that the easement holder showed that he didn't intend to use the old easement anymore.

✔ The easement becomes unusable because the easement holder has failed to maintain, repair, and keep it clear.

Express statements of intention to abandon are probably not enough to establish abandonment. Such expressions can help to interpret the easement holder's actions, but most courts agree that the easement holder must take some action evidencing abandonment, not merely express the intent to do so.

Terminating easements by estoppel

Estoppel terminates an easement in circumstances similar to abandonment. But instead of terminating the easement because the dominant tenant has given it up (see the preceding section), estoppel terminates the easement because the servient tenant has relied upon the dominant tenant's conduct that indicates his intent to give it up.

The servient owner must prove the following to establish termination by estoppel:

✔ The dominant tenant indicated that he no longer intended to use the easement, whether by doing the same kinds of things that indicate abandonment or by verbally indicating his intention.

✔ The servient tenant reasonably relied on the dominant tenant's indications of intent.

✔ The servient tenant's reliance would cause her to suffer a material detriment if the easement were not terminated.

A typical termination by estoppel occurs when the dominant tenant somehow indicates that he authorizes a substantial improvement by the servient owner that prevents use of the easement. If the dominant owner doesn't directly indicate authorization but merely hasn't been using the easement for a long time and then doesn't object when the servient owner builds the obstructing improvement, the dominant owner may be estopped if the servient owner's reliance was reasonable and she would suffer significant enough harm if the easement were not terminated.

In some cases, estoppel terminates an easement only temporarily or partially. For example, if the dominant owner authorized a temporary obstruction of the easement for construction, the dominant owner is estopped from using the easement during the period of construction. Or if the servient owner partially obstructs the easement in reasonable reliance on the dominant owner's conduct, the dominant owner can continue to use the easement as far as possible but can't have the obstruction removed.

Extinguishing easements by adverse use

The servient owner can extinguish an easement on her land by adversely using it for the same period of time required for adverse possession or a prescriptive easement. The servient owner must satisfy the following basic elements (see the earlier section "Over time: Acquiring easements by prescription" for more discussion of these elements):

- ✔ **Open and notorious use:** The servient owner must use the property subject to the easement in a way that's open and reasonably discoverable by the dominant tenant.

- ✔ **Adverse use:** The servient owner's use must be inconsistent with the rights of the dominant tenant. Because the servient owner has the right to use the servient land in any way that doesn't unreasonably interfere with the use of the easement, even very substantial uses by the servient owner may not be adverse. To be adverse, the servient owner must use the servient land in a way that unreasonably interferes with the dominant owner's use of the easement.

- ✔ **Continuous and uninterrupted use:** If the dominant owner successfully interrupts the servient owner's adverse use, the easement won't be extinguished by adverse use.

- ✔ **Exclusive use:** The servient owner must use the servient land exclusive of the dominant tenant in order to extinguish an easement. That's because an easement holder doesn't have the right to exclude the servient owner, but a title owner does have the right to exclude a trespasser. So in order to extinguish the dominant tenant's rights and make her a trespasser, the servient owner must exclude her from using the easement. Merely sharing use with the dominant tenant isn't enough.

- ✔ **For the limitations period:** The same limitations period that applies to adverse possession and prescriptive easement claims also applies to extinguishing easements by adverse use.

Chapter 7

Zeroing In on Zoning

Governments can adjust property rights by regulation, so understanding the rights of property ownership requires understanding regulatory restrictions on land use. The most common form of public property regulation is zoning, which is why this chapter gives you the nitty-gritty of how zoning codes work and how zoning restrictions can be tailored for specific properties.

Discovering Who Typically Regulates Land Use

The *police power* is the general power of the states to pass laws for the benefit of the public. This power, which is reserved to the states by the Tenth Amendment of the U.S. Constitution, includes the power to regulate land use within their boundaries. Consequently, the federal government doesn't directly regulate land use on private property. But of course, federal laws may certainly affect land uses.

The states may regulate land use in a variety of ways intended to benefit the public. For example, state law may regulate land use in coastal areas to preserve such sensitive areas for the public. However, state legislatures in every state have passed *enabling acts,* statutes that delegate to counties and cities the authority to regulate land use. As a result, most land use regulation comes from counties and cities.

Regulating the Big Three: Use, Height, and Bulk

Zoning ordinances, the most prominent form of local land use regulation, are laws that group compatible land uses together. These ordinances may preserve quiet and safety in residential areas, minimize and manage traffic, reduce fire risks, maintain open space and views . . . you get the idea.

A typical zoning code has two parts: a textual ordinance that specifies the regulations for all the different zoning district designations and a zoning map that shows the zoning district designation for each parcel of land throughout the city or county.

Zoning ordinances traditionally regulate the following:

✔ **Use:** They limit the uses permitted on certain land.

✔ **Height:** They limit the size of buildings on the land.

✔ **Bulk:** They limit the size of lots and the placement of buildings on those lots.

Modern zoning regulations may include other types of restrictions as well, such as architectural design regulations that are intended to ensure new buildings are architecturally compatible with existing buildings in the area.

The terminology may vary, but a typical zoning ordinance designates residential, commercial, industrial, and agricultural zoning districts. Within each of these categories, an ordinance may include a number of different zoning designations with increasingly permissive use restrictions. For example, a simple zoning ordinance may contain the following residential districts:

✔ An R1 zoning district allowing only single-family homes

✔ An R2 district allowing one- or two-family homes

✔ An R3 district allowing multiple-family dwellings

An ordinance may further refine these zoning designations by specifying different height and bulk limitations in different zones. Common bulk limitations include

✔ Floor-area ratio (the ratio of floor space to lot size)

✔ Minimum floor space

✔ Minimum lot size

✔ Requirements that buildings be set back a minimum distance from lot boundaries

An ordinance may specify several zones allowing the same uses but with different combinations of height and bulk restrictions. For instance, it may specify an R1-21 zone that allows single-family homes on lots no smaller than 21,000 square feet.

The traditional zoning ordinance is *cumulative,* meaning that higher uses (those that are less intensive and less likely to be objectionable) are allowed in lower-use zones. For example, a single-family house may be built in a commercial zone, but a commercial building may not be built in a residential zone. However, modern ordinances commonly make uses *noncumulative* or *exclusive,* meaning that higher uses aren't allowed in lower-use zones. For example, even if they want to, landowners can't build single-family houses in a noncumulative or exclusive commercial zone.

Protecting Nonconformities from New Zoning Restrictions

When a zoning ordinance is adopted or amended, it generally allows preexisting structures and uses of property to continue even if they don't comply with the new restrictions. Such preexisting uses that aren't consistent with the otherwise applicable zoning restrictions are called *nonconformities,* or *nonconforming uses.* For example, if an area is rezoned to a single-family residential zoning designation, an existing apartment building in that zone would be a nonconformity.

Zoning ordinances protect nonconformities because lawmakers feel that compelling a property owner to immediately terminate an existing use or destroy an existing structure is unfair to those who have relied on the previous state of the law. Lawmakers also fear that doing so may be considered a *taking* of private property for public use, meaning the ordinance may unfairly deprive an owner of so much of the property's value that it would require just compensation under the Fifth Amendment.

By definition, nonconformities are inconsistent with the zoning around them and therefore interfere with zoning objectives. Zoning ordinances consequently may restrict nonconformities in a number of ways, both to minimize the negative effect on the surrounding area and ultimately to eliminate the nonconformities. Here are some of the most common restrictions:

✔ The nonconforming use of the property may not be changed to a different nonconforming use. Any new use of the property must comply with the requirements of the zoning district.

✔ Nonconforming structures may not be enlarged.

> ✔ The owner may not rebuild the nonconforming structure or resume the nonconforming use if the structure is destroyed.
>
> ✔ The owner may not resume the nonconforming use after a specified period of nonuse, such as one year.
>
> ✔ The owner must discontinue the nonconforming use after a specified period of time. Such provisions are commonly called *amortization periods*. Courts generally allow amortization periods if they're reasonable based on how the property is used and the financial impact on the property owner.

Permitting Conditional Uses

A typical zoning ordinance specifies not only uses that are permitted in each zoning district but also other uses that may be specially permitted only if certain specified conditions are met. Such uses are called *conditional uses* or *special exceptions.*

A property owner who wants to use her property for such a conditional use must first obtain a *conditional use permit.* Today, most zoning ordinances charge an administrative body called a *planning commission* with the authority to grant conditional use permits, but some ordinances give that authority to a board of zoning adjustment or even to the local legislative body.

The commission or other body holds a hearing, at which the property owner may present evidence that her use of the property meets the specified criteria for a conditional use permit. Other people, typically other property owners in the neighborhood, may attend the hearing and argue against granting the permit. The commission considers the information presented at the hearing, along with the review and recommendations of the locality's planning staff, and decides whether to grant or deny the permit. The commission may grant the permit subject to conditions intended to ensure compliance with the criteria for approval of such a permit.

Zoning ordinances typically make a use conditional when it's considered appropriate in a certain zoning district — but only if it complies with certain conditions that reduce negative effects on the area. A group rehabilitation home, for example, may be considered appropriate in a residential zone as long as it doesn't negatively affect traffic and safety. The local zoning ordinance may include relatively specific conditions, such as that another such use may not be within 500 feet of the proposed use. It may also include relatively general conditions, such as that the use must not impair property values in the area.

If a condition to granting a permit is too general and vague, such as one requiring the use of the property to be "consistent with the public interest," it may be unconstitutional. A legislative body can constitutionally delegate its authority to an administrative body only if it provides sufficient guidance directing the administrative body's decisions; the legislative body can't simply surrender its legislative power. A court may hold that merely telling the administrative body to decide whether a use is "consistent with the public interest" isn't enough guidance about when the legislative body has decided the use should be allowed and therefore is an unconstitutional delegation of legislative power.

Avoiding Unnecessary Hardship with Variances

Administrative exceptions to zoning regulations are called *variances*. Whereas conditional use permits are available for uses that the zoning ordinance specifically allows when the listed conditions are met, variances permit uses that the zoning ordinance doesn't allow. Two types of variances exist:

- ✔ **The area variance:** This variance allows a property owner to depart from otherwise applicable restrictions concerning the height or size of buildings or their location on the property. For example, an area variance might allow a house to be built 15 feet from the front of the lot even though the zoning ordinance says houses in that district must be set back at least 20 feet from the front of the lot.

- ✔ **The use variance:** This variance allows the owner to use the property in a way that would otherwise be prohibited in the zone. For example, a use variance might allow a house in a residential district to be used as a professional office.

Some jurisdictions don't allow use variances. Those that do allow them are commonly more liberal in granting area variances than use variances.

Although the requirements for granting variances differ among jurisdictions, one common statutory standard is that a variance may be granted when, "owing to special conditions, a literal enforcement of the ordinance will result in unnecessary hardship." Whether by judicial interpretation of this general statutory phrase or by more specific expression in the ordinance, jurisdictions generally apply the same three basic requirements for granting variances:

- ✔ The owner can't obtain a reasonable return from the property as zoned.

- ✔ The inability to obtain a reasonable return is the result of unique conditions of that particular property.

- ✔ Granting the variance won't alter the essential character of the locality.

The following sections provide guidance on each of these typical criteria for granting variances.

Demonstrating inability to reasonably use the land as zoned

A variance may be granted if enforcement of the ordinance prevents a property owner from obtaining a reasonable return on her investment in the property. The owner must show that none of the uses permitted by the zoning ordinance is economically feasible, not just that the zoning ordinance is preventing the owner from maximizing the property's value. Some authorities suggest that the economic hardship must be so great that the regulation could be challenged as a taking of private property for public use, requiring just compensation under the Fifth Amendment. (Chapter 8 explains when the Fifth Amendment's Takings Clause requires just compensation for land use regulations.)

A variance may be granted only if the enforcement of the ordinance causes the hardship. So if a property owner's own actions cause the hardship, the board may not grant a variance. For example, if a property owner divides a parcel of land so that one of the divided parcels is too small to feasibly develop without a variance, the board isn't authorized to grant a variance to relieve such a hardship.

Explaining why unique conditions require a variance

Although ordinances differ in their expression of the requirement, a board of zoning adjustment may grant a variance only if unique physical conditions of the land, such as its surroundings or its topography, prevent the land from being reasonably used as zoned. If the hardship isn't due to unique conditions and instead would be a problem for many of the properties in the zone, then making exceptions for all similarly situated property would destroy the entire zoning scheme. In that case, the appropriate remedy is generally not to seek a variance but to seek a rezoning of the area.

Imagine a particular parcel of land in a residential zone with an unusually steep, rocky backyard. Because a house couldn't feasibly be built on the steep, rocky portion of the lot, complying with the zoning ordinance's height limitations and minimum setback requirements from the side and front lines of the parcel would make the house so small that it wouldn't be marketable. In general, the other properties in the zone don't have this problem with steep, rocky backyards. In such a case, the board could grant a variance allowing the house to be taller or nearer to the side and front lot lines.

Avoiding alteration of the essential character of the locality

A board of zoning adjustment may grant a variance only if the variance won't alter the essential character of the area. For example, even if an owner of property in a residential zone shows that her property can't feasibly be used for residential purposes, a board may not grant a variance allowing her to use the property for a retail store if a retail store in that location would harm the essential residential qualities of the neighborhood, such as by increasing traffic too much.

Many statutes expressly require the hardship to be "unnecessary" in order to grant a variance. If the hardship can be relieved without altering the essential character of the area, the hardship is unnecessary because the ordinance can accomplish its purpose without causing such hardship. But if a variance would alter the essential character of the area, the individual hardship is a necessary cost of accomplishing the primary purpose of the zoning ordinance, which is to preserve that essential character. In these cases, the variance must be denied.

 Often boards of adjustment grant variances even though the property owner hasn't met the statutory criteria, maybe because they don't know or understand the law, because they don't care about the law, or because they have personal or political reasons. Although a board of adjustment doesn't legally have authority to grant a variance when the statutory criteria aren't met, no court will review the decision unless some aggrieved neighbor initiates a lawsuit.

Amending Zoning

State law grants city and county legislative bodies (typically called county commissions or city councils) the authority to adopt zoning ordinances. That authority, of course, includes the power to amend the ordinances after they're initially adopted.

The legislative body can initiate consideration of zoning amendments, but often individual landowners petition the legislative body to amend the zoning ordinance to allow some desired use. A landowner may request two types of amendments:

✔ **Map amendment:** A *map amendment* changes the zoning map so that the landowner's property is included in a new zoning district that allows the desired use. For example, a landowner who wants to build an apartment building on property that's included in an R1 single-family residential zone might ask the legislative body to rezone the property to an R3 zoning designation that allows multiple-family residential uses.

✔ **Text amendment:** A *text amendment* changes the restrictions that apply to the property's zoning district to allow the landowner's desired use. For example, an R1 single-family residential zone might require all buildings to be located at least 5 feet from the side boundaries of the lot. A landowner who wants to build an extra detached garage on her R1 lot might ask the legislative body to amend the R1 zoning restrictions to allow such a garage to be built only 3 feet from the side boundaries. Because text amendments change the restrictions for all properties in that zoning district, such amendments are relatively rare.

Many zoning ordinances say that if 20 percent (or another specified percentage) of nearby property owners object to a rezoning, the rezoning will take effect only if three-quarters of the local legislative body votes in favor.

Some courts have held that when an individual landowner seeks a zoning amendment, the legislative body's decision whether to grant the amendment isn't really a legislative decision. Instead, they consider it to be an *administrative* or *quasi-judicial* decision, meaning that even though the legislative body is obviously not a court, it's acting judicially by applying existing rules and policies to a specific landowner's property. Courts that consider rezonings to be quasi-judicial will review a challenged rezoning decision more carefully than they review legislative actions. For example, these courts may require evidence to support the government's claim that the rezoning decision is in the public interest.

In the following sections, you find out about the relationship between zoning amendments and the comprehensive plan for an area as well as what constitutes illegal spot zoning.

Requiring consistency with a comprehensive plan

Zoning enabling acts all contain some version of a requirement that the zoning ordinance be "in accordance with a comprehensive plan." This means that not only must the originally adopted ordinance be in accordance with a comprehensive plan, but so must amendments to the ordinance. This statutory requirement limits local legislative freedom to adopt amendments requested by landowners.

State approaches to interpreting and applying requirements of consistency with a comprehensive plan include the following:

✔ **The zoning ordinance must be rational.** In most states, the requirement of consistency with a comprehensive plan isn't very restrictive. Most courts have interpreted the requirement to mean simply that the zoning ordinance itself must reveal a rational plan of zoning, not that the zoning ordinance must comply with a separate document called a *comprehensive plan.* Therefore, most courts hold that as long as a zoning amendment could rationally be thought to be consistent with the public interest, it's in accordance with a comprehensive plan.

✔ **The zoning ordinance must comply with a written plan.** Some states require that the zoning ordinance be consistent with an actual written plan for the community. Such a requirement is more of a limit on legislative freedom to zone and amend. In some of these states, an amendment to a zoning ordinance simply can't allow something that the comprehensive plan doesn't allow. Therefore, the landowner may need to first seek amendment of the plan before seeking amendment of the zoning ordinance — and some states limit the circumstances in which the plan may be amended or how often it may be amended.

✔ **The zoning ordinance must be in basic harmony with a written plan.** In some states, the zoning ordinance only needs to be generally consistent with a written plan, so the legislative body may amend the zoning ordinance to allow something not allowed in the comprehensive plan — or to forbid something allowed by the comprehensive plan — as long as the amendment is in basic harmony with the purposes of the plan.

✔ **The court reviews a zoning ordinance differently if it's inconsistent with a written plan.** When a zoning amendment is inconsistent with the plan in some respects, some courts have shifted the burden to the government to demonstrate how the amendment advances the purposes of the plan. They may also review the amendment decision to determine whether the evidence before the legislative body could have supported a conclusion that the amendment was consistent with the plan.

Invalidating spot zoning

When the local legislative body rezones a single lot or a small group of lots, a court may find that the rezoning is illegal spot zoning. *Spot zoning* is the rezoning of a small area in circumstances that violate one or more of the following limitations on the zoning power:

✔ **The statutory requirement that zoning be in accordance with a comprehensive plan:** Rezoning a small area may allow uses in that area that are incompatible with the surrounding area and therefore not in accordance with a comprehensive plan for the area. (See the preceding section for details on the comprehensive plan requirement.)

✔ **The constitutional doctrine of substantive due process:** Rezoning a small area inconsistently with the surrounding area (whether more or less restrictively) may be unconstitutionally arbitrary or irrational. (See Chapter 8 for more on the substantive due process doctrine.)

✔ **The constitutional requirement that guarantees equal protection of the laws:** Rezoning a small area may discriminate in favor of the landowner by allowing her to do things on her land that others aren't allowed to do. As a result, the rezoning benefits her rather than the community as a whole. On the other hand, an unwanted rezoning of a small area may discriminate against the landowner by irrationally denying her the right to use her property in the same way nearby properties can be used. (You can read about the Equal Protection Clause in Chapter 8.)

In deciding whether a rezoning is illegal spot zoning, courts generally consider the following:

✔ **The size and ownership of the rezoned area:** The smaller the rezoned area and the fewer the number of owners, the more likely a court will find the rezoning to be illegal spot zoning.

✔ **The extent of compatibility with the surrounding area:** The court examines the uses allowed by the rezoning to ensure they're compatible with the uses permitted in the surrounding area and in harmony with the comprehensive plan for the area. The less compatible the permitted uses are, the more likely the rezoning is illegal spot zoning.

✔ **Who is really benefiting from the rezoning:** The court determines whether the local legislative body genuinely intended to benefit the public or whether the public benefits were merely incidental to the private benefits for the owners of the rezoned land. The more the rezoning was for the private benefit of the landowner, the more likely the rezoning is illegal spot zoning.

A few state courts have held that a local legislative body can rezone a small area only if it can show that the original zoning of the area was a mistake or that conditions in the area have substantially changed in a way that justifies the rezoning.

Chapter 8

Recognizing the Limits of Public Regulation

*E*ven though governments can adjust private property rights to serve public purposes, the power to regulate land use isn't unlimited. In other words, the government can't just do whatever it wants. Both statutes and constitutions limit the government's power to regulate land use. So if you want to know what a property owner can do with her property, it isn't enough to know what the local zoning ordinance allows and prohibits. You also have to consider whether that local ordinance is valid and enforceable. That's what this chapter is about. It fills you in on the most important statutory and constitutional limitations on zoning regulations.

Looking for the Local Power Source: State Enabling Statutes

States generally delegate the authority to regulate land use to cities and counties through state statutes called *enabling acts.* Because the state enabling act is the source of local power to zone or otherwise regulate land use, a local government can exercise that power only as authorized by the state enabling act. If some part of the local zoning ordinance conflicts with the state enabling act in some way, that part of the local ordinance is invalid. In this way, the state enabling act limits local zoning authority.

Most state constitutions give cities, and maybe counties, too, the power to exercise *home rule*. That generally means that a city can adopt a charter specifying local authority it can exercise without specific state authorization. If a city exercises home rule power to zone, it may not have to comply with the state enabling act. But even then, some states with home rule provisions say that because land-use regulation is a matter of state as well as local concern, the local zoning still must comply with requirements of the state enabling act.

All 50 states have zoning enabling acts that authorize local governments to zone. These state enabling acts can differ, of course. But almost all these acts are based on the Standard State Zoning Enabling Act, published by the U.S. Department of Commerce in the 1920s, and therefore share some basic elements:

- **Types of restrictions:** In the words of the Standard State Zoning Enabling Act, a zoning ordinance may "regulate and restrict the height, number of stories, and size of buildings and other structures, the percentage of lot that may be occupied, the size of yards, courts and other open spaces, the density of population, and the location and use of buildings, structures and land for trade, industry, residences or other purposes."

- **Uniformity within districts:** The standard act says that zoning regulations "shall be uniform for each class or kind of buildings throughout each district, but the regulations in one district may differ from those in other districts."

- **Purposes:** Section 3 of the Standard State Zoning Enabling Act lists the permissible purposes of zoning ordinances, which include specific purposes such as lessening street congestion and avoiding overcrowding as well as the broad purpose of promoting "health and general welfare."

- **Power to grant variances:** If the locality chooses, the local ordinance may provide for a board of adjustment. If so, the enabling act specifies the board of adjustment's powers, including the criteria for granting a variance from requirements of the zoning ordinance.

- **Consistency with a comprehensive plan:** The Standard State Zoning Enabling Act says the local ordinance must be "made in accordance with a comprehensive plan." In most states, this doesn't mean the locality must actually adopt a document called a "comprehensive plan"; it just means that the regulation must be a rational and comprehensive way to regulate land use for the benefit of the public. But in some states, the local government does have to adopt a comprehensive plan for the community before it can zone. And in some states, the zoning ordinance must comply with the comprehensive plan or at least be in basic harmony with it. Chapter 7 talks more about zoning in accordance with a comprehensive plan.

A landowner may argue that a zoning ordinance or its application to her property is invalid because it doesn't comply with requirements in the state enabling act. For example, if the state statute authorizes a board of adjustment to grant variances only for the physical characteristics of buildings (like height and location on the lot), a local zoning ordinance that allows variances to permit an otherwise prohibited use (like allowing a commercial use in a residential zone) would be invalid. Therefore, a landowner who's unhappy with a particular zoning restriction should always examine the state enabling act to see whether the local zoning restriction is valid under that act.

Explaining Property Deprivations: Substantive Due Process

The Due Process Clause of the Fourteenth Amendment says, "Nor shall any State deprive any person of life, liberty, or property, without due process of law." State constitutions contain similar clauses. This may sound like only a requirement about the processes or procedures by which the government deprives people of life, liberty, or property. But it's more than that. The doctrine of substantive due process prohibits the government from depriving a person of life, liberty, or property without a good reason. The deprivation must not be arbitrary; rather, it must somehow rationally further some legitimate public purpose.

The following sections help you understand

- ✔ Whether the government has deprived a person of property
- ✔ Whether the government's purpose is permissible
- ✔ Whether the regulation is a rational way to accomplish that purpose

Identifying a deprivation of property

A land use regulation can violate the substantive due process doctrine only if it deprives the owner of property. The first step in making a substantive due process argument, therefore, is to identify what property the owner has been deprived of.

Land use regulations don't deprive owners of their land altogether. They just deprive owners of the right to do particular things on their land. But that's what property is — a bunch of rights in relation to the land. Although taking away ownership of land is obviously a bigger deprivation than taking away the right to build a moat, they're both deprivations of "property" in this sense.

Most courts follow this reasoning and apply substantive due process to any regulation that takes away a property right the owner would otherwise have. So pretty much any land use regulation must be a rational way to further some legitimate public purpose, unless the regulation prohibits something that the property owner never had the right to do in the first place, like maintain a nuisance on her property.

Some courts, however, reason that if a regulation requires someone to get government permission to do something on the land, the owner has a property right to do that thing only if permission ordinarily would've been granted. Only then do these courts apply the substantive due process doctrine and consider whether denying permission is a rational way to further some legitimate public purpose.

Deciding whether a regulation is rational

Courts express the requirements of substantive due process in different ways. In a landmark 1926 Supreme Court case considering a due process challenge to a zoning ordinance, *Village of Euclid v. Ambler Realty Co.,* the Supreme Court used several expressions to describe when a regulation violates the substantive due process doctrine:

- ✔ If it "passes the bounds of reason and assumes the character of a merely arbitrary fiat"

- ✔ If it doesn't have "a rational relation to the health and safety of the community"

- ✔ If it's "clearly arbitrary and unreasonable, having no substantial relation to the public health, safety, morals, or general welfare"

The following sections look at how courts decide whether a regulation — or its application — is arbitrary or irrational.

Considering whether the law is a rational way to accomplish the purpose

Courts presume that regulations are rational and valid, so the challenging property owner bears a heavy burden of proving otherwise. Most courts agree that a regulation is valid as long as the government could've rationally thought that it would advance the public interest somehow. As some courts say, a regulation is valid as long as the perceived public benefit is "fairly debatable." A regulation isn't unconstitutional just because it turns out the regulation doesn't accomplish its purpose. Nor is it unconstitutional just because other means might appear to accomplish the purpose better.

But some courts, especially state courts, are less deferential. These courts consider not just whether a regulation could be expected to advance the public interest but also whether the regulation actually does so. Some cases also consider whether other regulatory choices would make more sense. And some cases find that a regulation is unconstitutionally irrational or arbitrary if the harm to the property owner greatly outweighs the benefit to the public.

Challenging the law or its application

A property owner may argue that the mere passage and existence of a land use regulation violates her substantive due process rights. This argument is commonly referred to as a *facial challenge* because the property owner claims that the regulation on its face is unconstitutional.

In *Village of Euclid,* for example, Ambler Realty Company argued that the passage of the Euclid zoning ordinance significantly impaired the value of its property in violation of the Due Process Clause. The Supreme Court held that the zoning ordinance was a rational way to further legitimate public purposes such as managing traffic and preserving residential values.

However, the Court also noted that even though the zoning ordinance in general was a rational way to serve legitimate public interests, particular applications of the ordinance may not be. Property owners may thus argue that a generally valid zoning ordinance is nevertheless irrational *as applied* to their specific properties in specific ways. As the Court put it, "It is true that when, if ever, the provisions set forth in the ordinance in tedious and minute detail, come to be concretely applied to particular premises, including those of the appellee, or to particular conditions, or to be considered in connection with specific complaints, some of them, or even many of them, may be found to be clearly arbitrary and unreasonable."

So even though facial challenges to the rationality of zoning ordinances are relatively rare, property owners raise a wide variety of as-applied challenges to specific zoning provisions and decisions. For example, a zoning ordinance on its face may rationally separate residential and commercial uses, but the decision not to rezone a specific lot from residential to commercial may nevertheless be held irrational.

Considering whether a regulation advances a public purpose

Substantive due process requires that a regulation be a rational way to serve some legitimate public purpose. Courts generally sustain a regulation that rationally serves such a purpose even if the evidence suggests that it wasn't the government's actual purpose. In fact, even if the evidence suggests the government had an illegitimate purpose, courts generally sustain the regulation against a substantive due process challenge as long as the regulation also serves legitimate purposes.

The next sections give you a breakdown of widely accepted legitimate purposes and some purposes that have been considered illegitimate.

Laying out the typical legitimate purposes

Legitimate public purposes include any benefits to the public health, safety, morals, or general welfare. Cases have identified a long list of public purposes that zoning ordinances may serve, such as the following:

- Public health, such as by avoiding overcrowding or preserving access to light and air
- Public safety, such as reducing fire risks, preventing development in unsafe areas, and facilitating access by emergency personnel
- Preserving the character of existing neighborhoods, especially residential neighborhoods
- Protecting and maximizing property values
- Reducing public costs for street maintenance and other public services
- Preventing *nuisances,* which are unreasonable interferences with another's use of her property (see Chapter 4)
- Generating economic activity, jobs, and taxes
- Protecting the environment
- Maintaining an aesthetically pleasing community

Aesthetic purposes used to be on the illegitimate-purposes list but aren't anymore. Earlier cases sometimes invalidated land use regulations when a regulation's only purpose seemed to be to make the community look nicer. Some courts invalidated restrictions on signs for this reason. But over time, courts came to agree that creating and maintaining a beautiful, aesthetically pleasing community is a legitimate public purpose.

Looking at illegitimate purposes

Because zoning ordinances or other land use regulations can benefit the public in so many ways, listing purposes that courts have said are *not* legitimate public purposes is probably easier. It's a pretty short list:

- **Private purposes:** A private purpose obviously isn't a public purpose. Consequently, a rezoning violates substantive due process if it only benefits a particular private property owner but not the public. However, private benefits often result in public benefits, too. If a private owner can make more money, that may result in more jobs, taxes, and economic activity for the community generally. But sometimes courts find that a particular zoning decision actually harms the public in order to provide a private benefit, and in such a case, the zoning decision violates substantive due process because it doesn't rationally advance any public purpose.

✔ **Preventing competition:** One particular private purpose that some cases have considered is protection from competition. For example, a zoning board of adjustment might deny a conditional use permit for a motel on the grounds that too many motels are in the area already. Most courts have indicated that protecting existing properties from competition is an illegitimate private purpose and not for the benefit of the public. Of course, zoning always restricts competition by limiting the areas of town where certain kinds of uses are permitted. As long as some legitimate public purpose supports the regulation, it's valid even if it also serves anticompetitive purposes.

✔ **Avoiding or reducing just compensation:** Sometimes the government makes a certain regulatory decision as a way to get something else it wants from the property owner. Normally a court wouldn't second-guess the real reasons for a government's regulatory decisions — as long as the court can see legitimate reasons for a decision, what really motivated the government doesn't matter. But sometimes the government's own actions reveal the reasons for its decision.

Consider the case of *Nollan v. California Coastal Commission*. In that case, the government approved a development request on the condition that the owner give the government some unrelated property interest. The Court reasoned that the attachment of the unrelated condition revealed that the purpose of conditionally denying approval was to extort that unrelated property interest from the owner without having to pay for it. The Court concluded that however broad the concept of a legitimate public purpose might be, this isn't a legitimate public purpose.

Similarly, the government might anticipate buying land in the future and try to reduce the cost of that land by zoning it more restrictively in the meantime. Some cases have reasoned that such a purpose isn't a legitimate public purpose.

Compensating for Property Taken for Public Use

Governments may intentionally and formally exercise *eminent domain,* the power to forcibly take title to property or lesser interests in property (like easements) for public use. An exercise of eminent domain may be called a *condemnation.* The Just Compensation Clause (also known as the Takings Clause) found in the Fifth Amendment of the U.S. Constitution requires that the government pay fair market value for the property it takes.

Governments also may indirectly take property through regulations that have a similar effect. Such takings are naturally called *regulatory takings.* In an *inverse condemnation* action, which is a lawsuit alleging a regulatory taking, the court must determine whether the government's regulation amounted to an act of eminent domain and therefore requires compensation. So although the Takings Clause doesn't prohibit any regulatory action, it does require compensation for some regulations and thereby further restrains government land use regulation.

The following sections examine when a regulation is a taking and how a court will remedy such a taking.

Compensating for condemnations

The Just Compensation Clause requires the government to pay compensation whenever it exercises the power of eminent domain, whether it takes a lot of property or just a little bit of property. Obviously, the government must pay more compensation if it takes title to a 10-acre parcel of land than if it merely takes the front 20 feet of that parcel or takes an easement across part of the land. (I cover easements in Chapter 6.) But in either case, the government has clearly "taken" property for public use and must pay compensation for it.

The third part of the Takings Clause: Public use

The Takings Clause says that private property shall not "be taken for public use, without just compensation." Many cases have considered when property is "taken" and what "just compensation" is. Fewer cases have considered what "public use" is. But the Supreme Court has held that the phrase limits the government's power to take property: The government may take property only for "public use."

In the 2005 case of *Kelo v. City of New London,* the Supreme Court considered when takings are "for public use." You may think that means taking the property for the public to use, but not so. The Court held that the public use clause requires only that a taking serve a public purpose — any permissible public purpose. In *Kelo,* the Court specifically considered whether condemning property and then transferring it to private owners for private development is a taking for public use. The Court held that promoting economic development is a legitimate public purpose, and therefore a condemnation for transfer to a private party is "for public use" if it could rationally be expected to promote economic development.

However, the Court said that if the government's "actual purpose was to bestow a private benefit" under "mere pretext of a public purpose," that would violate the public use clause and be invalid. So the public use clause invalidates a taking if the evidence shows that the real purpose of a condemnation for economic development was to benefit the private developer and not the public.

The Court also noted that although this is the extent of the federal constitutional limitation on eminent domain, state constitutions and state statutes may further limit the exercise of eminent domain. Almost all states have done so since the *Kelo* opinion, restraining in various ways the exercise of eminent domain for private development.

Similarly, the government must pay compensation even if it takes property only temporarily and then gives it back to the owner. For example, if the government takes a private laundry facility during wartime, it must pay just compensation for the time it possessed the laundry, even though it returns the laundry to the owner when the war is over.

Figuring out when a regulation is a taking

Although any governmental seizure of land requires just compensation, whether big or small, regulatory takings are different. The government simply couldn't afford to pay compensation every time a regulation takes away some property right from an owner. Besides, people own property subject to the government's reserved power to reasonably regulate.

On the other hand, if the government never had to pay compensation for regulations taking away property rights, the government could practically eliminate private property. So at some point, regulation may interfere with private property so much that the government must pay for it, just like when it physically seizes property.

The hard part of regulatory takings law is figuring out when a regulation is severe enough to require the payment of just compensation. Most of the time, making that call requires a pretty complex consideration of various factors. But in two situations, a regulation is so much like a physical seizure that it's always a taking:

- **The regulation deprives the property owner of all economically beneficial use of the land.** In this case, at least from the owner's perspective, the regulation has the same effect as if the government took the property away altogether.

- **The regulation forces the property owner to submit to physical invasion of the land by other people.** Even though the owner retains other property rights, the right to exclude others is so fundamental to private property ownership that such a regulation is treated as a taking regardless of the magnitude of the invasion.

If a regulation doesn't deprive a property owner of all economically beneficial use of the land or force the property owner to allow invasion of her property, the decision about whether the regulation is a compensable taking is an ad hoc, case-by-case determination. The Supreme Court's opinion in *Penn Central Transportation Co. v. City of New York* described the factors of "particular significance" in this determination:

✔ The "economic impact of the regulation on the claimant," especially "the extent to which the regulation has interfered with distinct investment-backed expectations"

✔ The "character of the governmental action"

Evaluating the magnitude of the regulatory burden

If a regulation prohibits all economically beneficial uses that the owner would otherwise have the right to engage in, it's always a taking. If not, no definite line tells you when a regulation becomes a taking. But the greater the negative economic impact of a regulation on the value of property, the more likely the regulation will be a taking requiring payment of just compensation.

Here are some things to consider in judging the economic impact of a regulation:

✔ **Background principles of state law:** A regulation takes nothing from an owner if it merely prohibits things that the property owner had no right to do anyway under background principles of state property law. So you first have to determine the extent and value of the owner's property rights under background principles of state law. Then you have to compare that to the value of the property as regulated. If long-established state nuisance law never would've allowed a property owner to develop certain sensitive coastal lands, for example, then a regulation forbidding such development didn't really take anything away from the owner.

✔ **Investment-backed expectations:** A particularly important factor in judging the economic impact of a regulation is *investment-backed expectations* — expenditures acquiring and developing property in reliance on the present state of the law. If the law is subsequently changed contrary to those expectations, the property owner suffers not only disappointed hopes for future uses and profits but also an out-of-pocket loss of her past investments. Such an economic impact seems especially unfair and harmful and therefore is particularly significant in judging the economic impact of a regulation. The owner doesn't have to prove interference with investment-backed expectations in order to prove a taking, however.

✔ **Proportion of the total property value:** The economic impact of a regulation can be measured only in relation to the value of the property. If a regulation causes a property owner a $100,000 loss, that loss may be small or large, depending on how much the property is worth. If the property is worth only $100,000, then such a regulatory impact would certainly result in a taking. But if the property is worth $10,000,000, then such an impact is minor.

The Supreme Court has emphasized that property owners can't prove takings by identifying discrete rights that are a subset of the whole property and then showing that a regulation takes all those discrete rights. Rather, you have to compare the economic impact to the value of the property as a whole. For example, in *Penn Central Transportation Co. v. City of New York,* the property owner claimed that a regulation deprived it entirely of the right to build in the airspace above an existing terminal. The Court disagreed, reasoning that the airspace above the terminal is only part of the value of the property as a whole and must be considered along with the value of the existing terminal and the land.

✔ **Duration:** A property's market value reflects not just its present value but also its value over time. If a regulation limits use of property for only a few years, the regulation's economic impact is much less than if the regulation lasts indefinitely. So at least when a regulation is intended to be temporary, like a moratorium on development while the government decides on appropriate regulations, the duration of a regulation must also be considered in measuring its economic impact.

✔ **Benefits to the property owner:** The economic impact of the regulation may be mitigated by values the property owner receives in return. For example, an ordinance may restrict the property owner's freedom to do something and thereby reduce her property value, but it may also enhance her property's value by restricting neighboring owners' freedom as well. In *Penn Central,* the Court considered the value of transferable development rights that the property owner received in evaluating the magnitude of the economic impact on the owner, because those rights allowed additional development elsewhere and that additional development would add value to its property.

Considering the character of the governmental action

The Supreme Court in *Penn Central* said that "the character of the governmental action" is also a relevant consideration in deciding whether a regulation amounts to a taking. The Court suggested a couple of characteristics that would be relevant: if a regulation can be characterized as a physical invasion, it's more likely to be a taking, whereas if the regulation is simply the result of a "public program adjusting the benefits and burdens of economic life to promote the common good," it's less likely to be a taking.

The fundamental principle of the Takings Clause is to avoid unfairly making some individuals bear the expense of accomplishing public purposes. The distribution of the regulatory burden therefore is an important consideration:

✔ If a regulation burdens a relatively small group, it's more likely to be a taking than if the regulation applies widely across the community.

✔ If a regulation targets certain owners simply to facilitate public functions and not because the use of their land is related to the public purpose, such a regulation is more likely to be a taking. For example, a regulation that restricts development of wetlands doesn't unfairly or randomly target certain owners to bear a public burden — it just targets those whose land has the unique characteristics the public wants to protect.

> ✔ If a regulation burdens some for the benefit of others, such a regulation is more likely to be a taking than if the burdened parties enjoy some reciprocal benefit from others being burdened.

Some cases have also suggested that the purpose of the regulation is a relevant characteristic in determining whether the regulation is a taking. Some even weigh the harm to the property owner against the benefit to the public.

Exactions: When the government can demand property in exchange for regulatory approval

One unique circumstance related to takings law is the *exaction*, in which the government gives permission to develop land only if the owner surrenders some property interest to the government. The Supreme Court first held in *Nollan v. California Coastal Commission* that an exaction is unconstitutional if the condition doesn't somehow mitigate the public harms that would justify outright denial of permission. In such a case, the unrelated condition "alters the purpose" of the development restraint to an "out-and-out plan of extortion" to obtain property the government desires without having to pay just compensation for it. That sounds like a substantive due process objection, that the regulation is for an illegitimate purpose; however, when the case was decided, there was a comparable takings law rule, since rejected by the Court, that a regulation is a taking if it doesn't substantially advance a legitimate public purpose.

The Court subsequently considered another exactions case, *Dolan v. City of Tigard.* In *Dolan,* the Court instead explained the requirement of *Nollan* as an application of the unconstitutional conditions doctrine. This doctrine declares unconstitutional a governmental condition that requires the surrender of a constitutional right (such as the right to just compensation for taken property) in exchange for a discretionary public benefit (which is how the Court apparently viewed development permission).

Dolan also added the further requirement that not only must the condition mitigate the harms of the proposed development (often referred to as the *nexus* requirement), but the condition must also be roughly proportional to the public harms threatened by the proposed development. The Court therefore held invalid an exaction that required the property owner to dedicate land to the public for a bike and pedestrian path in order to obtain permission to expand her store. Even though the path could rationally be thought to mitigate the increased traffic that would result from a bigger store, the city had made no individualized determination indicating that the path would at least roughly offset the traffic increase caused by the bigger store.

Remedying regulatory takings: Paying up

In the past, many courts would simply invalidate regulations that they found to be takings without payment of compensation. In 1987, however, the U.S. Supreme Court in *First English Evangelical Lutheran Church v. County of Los Angeles* held that the federal Just Compensation Clause requires courts to award compensation rather than invalidate regulatory takings. The Constitution doesn't forbid the government from taking property, after all; it just requires that the government pay compensation when it does so. So the courts' job is to make sure that the government pays compensation whenever it takes property.

Just compensation is the fair market value of the property on the date the property is taken. Because a regulatory taking typically doesn't take the entire value of the property, the court must determine how much fair market value the owner has lost because of the regulation.

A court order requiring payment of just compensation is of course an order to pay cash to the property owner. But the Constitution doesn't always require payment of just compensation in cash. In deciding the amount of compensation due, courts may consider compensating benefits provided to the owner, such as transferable development rights, as complete or partial compensation for a regulatory taking.

If a court declares a regulation to be a taking and therefore orders payment of just compensation, the government may respond by amending or repealing the regulation. The government certainly can do that. But the Court in *First English* said that repealing a regulatory taking can't excuse the government from the obligation to pay just compensation for the time the regulation was in effect.

Treating Similarly Situated Owners the Same: Equal Protection

The Fourteenth Amendment's Equal Protection Clause requires that property regulations, like other laws, treat similarly situated owners the same. However, zoning ordinances always treat different properties differently: Some properties are zoned residential, some commercial, some industrial. Further differences in treatment result from individualized decisions on whether to grant variances, conditional use permits, and rezonings. So there are many opportunities for property owners to complain that the government has unjustifiably treated their property differently from other properties.

The Equal Protection Clause doesn't prohibit regulating different properties differently. Obviously, all sorts of laws apply to some people differently from other people. But the Equal Protection Clause does require that the government not treat people differently when it doesn't have a good reason to do so. In ordinary land use regulation cases, that means that the government needs a rational reason for treating different properties differently.

The next sections take a look at permissible reasons for differences in treatment and how courts remedy violations of the Equal Protection Clause.

Looking for rational differences in treatment

A land use regulation may treat properties differently as long as a rational person could think that the differential treatment would further or relate to some legitimate public purpose, regardless of the government's actual purpose.

Because the Equal Protection Clause was adopted after the Civil War to remedy racial discrimination, courts require more of a justification for differential treatment on the basis of race or national origin (and in some other circumstances, too). In such cases, the law is invalid unless the law is necessary and narrowly tailored to accomplish a compelling public purpose — which is very unlikely.

The difference in treatment may relate to the primary purpose of the regulation, or it may relate to other legitimate public purposes. But if there is no reason, or if the reason is illegitimate — such as government animosity toward the property holder — the difference in treatment violates the Equal Protection Clause. The following sections explore various rational reasons for differential treatment.

Advancing the regulatory purpose

A difference in regulatory treatment may be thought to directly advance the primary purpose of the regulation. For example, consider a zoning regulation that zones an area for agricultural uses. A primary purpose of such agricultural use restrictions is to avoid conflicts between agricultural activities and other types of land uses, such as residential uses that may be impaired by noise, smells, and dust. The agricultural zone therefore may allow a house only on a lot at least 5 acres in size, whereas in residential zones, a house may be built on a much smaller lot. That difference in required minimum lot size directly advances the regulatory purpose of minimizing conflicts between agricultural activities and residential uses. The regulation would therefore clearly not violate the Equal Protection Clause.

Limiting pursuit of the regulatory purpose

Equal protection challenges are much more likely when a regulation treats properties differently and that difference in treatment doesn't directly advance the regulatory purpose. But differential treatment may rationally relate to legitimate public purposes in other ways. For example, the difference in treatment may result from reasonable judgments about how far to pursue a particular regulatory purpose. Even though a zoning ordinance could completely prohibit a particular type of activity in a zone, the government may reasonably decide to tolerate some less incompatible versions but prohibit more incompatible versions.

For example, a residential zoning district might generally prohibit commercial uses, including motels and boarding houses, but allow rooming houses in which meals aren't served. A property owner could complain that there's no rational reason for allowing rooming houses but not boarding houses. Allowing rooming houses may not advance the purpose of creating a quiet, safe, and attractive residential area and perhaps even interferes with that purpose. But the difference in treatment of rooming and boarding houses may nevertheless be rational if the government could rationally have concluded that boarding houses, at which meals are served, would therefore be more commercial because they're more like restaurants and their residents are more transient, and therefore boarding houses would be more incompatible with a residential area than would rooming houses.

Advancing competing public purposes

A zoning ordinance may rationally treat properties differently because the difference in treatment furthers some different but still legitimate purpose.

Protecting nonconforming uses is a simple example of such a reason for differential treatment. Consider the agricultural zoning district that allows houses only on lots of 5 acres or larger. If someone had built a house on a smaller parcel of land before that zoning restriction was adopted, the zoning ordinance would allow the use to continue as a nonconforming use. A property owner who wants to build a house on a parcel smaller than 5 acres is treated differently from a property owner who already had a house on a smaller parcel. The existing house on a smaller parcel might interfere with the zoning objectives just as much as a new house on a smaller parcel would. But the difference in treatment is still rational because it serves a different public interest: the interest in protecting people from changes in the law that disappoint their reasonable expectations and impair the value of investments they've already made in reliance on a previous state of the law.

Drawing lines that serve a purpose wherever they're drawn

Zoning ordinances by their nature draw lines between different areas and impose different regulatory restrictions on either side of those lines. Sometimes the location of a line is inevitably arbitrary because there's no reason to draw it here or there. When a city zones an undeveloped area, for example, it may have no particular reason to draw the line between residential and commercial uses down one street instead of the next street. The line just has to be drawn somewhere.

Such line-drawing doesn't violate the Equal Protection Clause. Even though the city may not be able to demonstrate a reason for drawing the line down Street A instead of Street B, that's simply because the mere drawing of the line advances the public purpose of separating residential and commercial uses, wherever that line might be. That's why equal protection challenges to the location of zoning map lines, as opposed to the restrictions within zones, are unlikely to succeed.

Remedying equal protection violations

A governmental action violating the Equal Protection Clause is void. If a particular difference in treatment denies equal protection, a court will invalidate that aspect of the regulation. However, in some cases, that remedy isn't very helpful to the property owner, who really wants to be allowed to do something on her land, not just to be treated like other similarly situated owners. That's because the government can simply avoid the equal protection violation by prohibiting other similarly situated owners from doing the thing the successful claimant wants to do.

For example, imagine that a light agricultural zone doesn't allow keeping pigs but does allow keeping other types of animals. A property owner might claim that the government has violated her equal protection rights because it doesn't have a rational reason for allowing some animals but not pigs. If the property owner persuades a court that pigs are no more objectionable than horses and therefore that there's no rational reason for treating the two uses differently, that doesn't necessarily mean the property owner can thereafter keep pigs on her property. Instead, the city may choose to prohibit horses and other animals as well as pigs, thus avoiding the irrational difference in treatment but not accomplishing the property owner's real objective.

Respecting Free Speech Rights

The First Amendment to the U.S. Constitution says, "Congress shall make no law . . . abridging the freedom of speech." Although most land use regulations don't limit speech at all, some do. Some land uses, such as signs and adult businesses, involve protected speech and therefore invoke the protections of the First Amendment. The First Amendment doesn't prohibit land use regulations that restrain speech, but it does limit the government's freedom to adopt such regulations. Check out the following sections to find out how the government can (and can't) regulate freedom of speech through zoning ordinances.

Regulating the land use effects of speech

Land use regulations that infringe on speech often target not the speech itself but the secondary effects of that speech. Local ordinances often regulate billboards and other signs, for example, not to regulate the content of such signs but to minimize distractions to motorists, to avoid visual clutter, and so on. Such regulations are said to be *content-neutral* because they don't regulate the content of the speech, only the location and manner of speech. Sometimes it's hard to tell whether a regulation is content-neutral, but courts will treat it that way as long as the predominant concerns were the secondary, non-speech effects of the regulated use.

A content-neutral regulation is permissible under the Free Speech Clause if it

- ✔ **Serves a substantial governmental interest:** A city's interest in preserving the quality of life and avoiding adverse effects from land-related speech is generally a substantial governmental interest. Although people may debate whether a particular regulation will serve such governmental interests, it's enough that the city has some evidence that leads the city to reasonably believe the regulation will produce the desired public benefits.

- ✔ **Doesn't unreasonably limit alternative avenues of speech:** If a land use regulation limits where or how certain speech may be conducted, the regulation must not unreasonably limit alternative avenues of engaging in such speech. As long as alternatives are available, a regulation isn't invalid simply because it makes locations for that speech more scarce and expensive. But if the alternatives are too expensive for the type of speech and speaker and if the location itself is an important part of the speech, then alternatives may be inadequate and the regulation, invalid.

Regulating the content of speech

Land use regulations may actually regulate the content of speech rather than just the land use effects of speech. The constitutionality of such regulations depends on whether the regulated speech is commercial.

The First Amendment protects commercial speech, meaning speech that proposes commercial transactions, less than other kinds of speech. But it does protect commercial speech, as long as it's truthful, nonmisleading speech about lawful commercial activities. A law that regulates the content of such speech is permissible if it meets three criteria:

- ✔ It serves a substantial governmental interest.

- ✔ It directly advances that governmental interest.

- ✔ It doesn't reach further than necessary to accomplish the purpose.

So, for example, a land use regulation may allow some types of commercial signs but not others if the regulation satisfies this test. In *Metromedia, Inc. v. City of San Diego,* the Supreme Court said that a billboard regulation constitutionally could allow onsite commercial advertising but not offsite commercial advertising. The regulation directly advanced the city's substantial interests in traffic safety and aesthetics and didn't reach further than necessary. It simply prohibited billboards that would cause the identified public harms except when the competing interest in the commercial speech — identifying the goods and services available onsite — outweighed the interest in traffic safety and aesthetics.

If an ordinance regulates the content of noncommercial speech, on the other hand, it almost certainly violates the First Amendment. The government would have to show that there's a compelling public interest in regulating the content of the speech and that the regulation does so in the narrowest way possible.

In *Metromedia,* the Supreme Court held that the sign regulation unconstitutionally allowed only some kinds of noncommercial messages. It also held that regulations can't treat commercial speech more favorably than noncommercial speech. The Court therefore held invalid a regulation that allowed onsite commercial billboards but not onsite noncommercial billboards.

Part III
Looking at Shared and Divided Property Ownership

The 5th Wave   By Rich Tennant

"I just think we need to make provisions in our Will for disposition of our property. Who'll get Park Place? Who'll get Boardwalk? Who'll get the thimble and all the tiny green houses?"

In this part . . .

Here you discover the details of how people can share ownership of property over time and how two or more people can own the same property at the same time. You also see how property law regulates the relationship among people who have legal interests in the same property. In addition, you consider two situations in which people have legal interests in the same property — marriage and landlord-tenant relationships — and the unique law related to those relationships.

Chapter 9

Dividing Ownership over Time: Estates

. . . .

In This Chapter

▶ Identifying the different present and future estates

▶ Understanding limitations on future estates

▶ Considering the transfer of estates

▶ Examining the relationship between present and future estates

. . . .

*O*wning property means having legal rights in relation to it, one of which is the right to transfer rights to others. A property owner can transfer her rights in whole or in part. She can divide them up in all sorts of ways, such as transferring just the mineral rights, transferring 2 of her 20 acres, or transferring an easement.

A property owner also can divide up her property rights over time. She can give a person ownership of her land for ten years but keep the rest of the ownership rights — so she'll get the land back after ten years pass. Or she can give another ownership of the land for that person's lifetime but keep the rest of the ownership rights or give them to someone else. She can even give ownership to another person as long as he uses it for certain purposes. These temporal measurements of ownership are called *estates*.

Even though a property owner will die someday and no longer possess or own the property, while she's alive she can own the property forever. While she's alive — or by will at her death — she can transfer ownership in the future, not just during her lifetime. But because people living in the future will have a greater interest in that land than will the former owner after she's dead, the law limits an owner's power to specify who has the right to possess the land after her death.

This chapter covers the ways property can be divided up over time as well as the limits on creating future interests. It also clarifies how such interests, whether present or future, can be transferred. Finally, this chapter walks you through the rules that govern the relationship between the present possessor and those who have the right to possess in the future.

Introducing the Concept of Present and Future Estates in Land

An *estate* is ownership of the right to possess land for a particular time. Nonpossessory interests, such as easements or mortgages, aren't estates. The idea of estates is pretty simple; the harder part is getting used to the legal labels for different estates, different ways of dividing the land up over time. Fortunately, even though you can imagine an endless variety of ways to divide ownership of property over time, the law of estates groups them into just a few categories with common characteristics.

 The first variable that distinguishes different estates is whether the estate is ownership of the right to possess now or in the future. A person who has the right to possess now has a *present estate*. A person who has the right to possess in the future has a *future estate* or a *future interest*.

If a present estate is unlimited in time, then obviously no one has a future estate in that land. But whenever a present estate is limited in time, a corresponding future estate has the right to take possession when the present estate ends.

Creating and Distinguishing the Present Estates

Four types of present estates exist:

- ✔ Fee simple estates
- ✔ Fee tail estates
- ✔ Life estates
- ✔ Leaseholds

The first three used to be called *freehold estates,* because they came with certain obligations in the feudal system. The leasehold, of which there are several different types, wasn't a freehold estate. Those days are long gone, however, so the distinction between freehold and nonfreehold estates doesn't really matter anymore. But since leaseholds today are governed by so many rules unique to that estate, Chapter 12 talks about leaseholds separately.

The following sections detail the creation and characteristics of the first three kinds of present estates.

Creating a fee simple: No expiration

The *fee simple* is the estate that never expires. If no one ever divides up a property over time, the owner has fee simple. The estate never ends but is passed from person to person over time, whether by conveyance during life or by will or intestate succession at death.

A fee simple exists whenever the instrument creating the estate doesn't otherwise limit the duration of the estate. If a deed or will simply says it conveys property "to A," then A has a fee simple, even if the instrument doesn't say it conveys a fee simple. A deed or will also may grant a fee simple by saying "to A and her heirs." The expression "and her heirs" doesn't give her heirs a separate future estate; it merely indicates that the estate is inheritable. Such expressions that describe the character of the estate may be called *words of limitation*.

Dealing with the fee tail: Direct descendants

The fee tail isn't simple. Like the fee simple, the *fee tail* is inheritable at death; however, only the direct descendants of the owner can inherit it. So if the owner of the fee tail dies without having had children, the fee tail estate expires and the ownership passes back to the grantor and his heirs or to someone else if the deed or will named a third party who would take the property in that event.

A deed or will creates a fee tail by saying words such as "to A and the heirs of her body" or "to A and her heirs, but if A dies without issue, then to B." The distinctive expressions creating the fee tail are "issue" or "heirs of her body."

Only a few states still recognize the traditional fee tail. In the rest of the United States, statutes declare that fee-tail-granting language has some other effect. Here's a breakdown of what these alternate effects may be:

- ✔ The fee tail language is basically ignored, so the grantee has a fee simple.

- ✔ The fee tail language creates a fee simple in the grantee, but if the grant says a third person will get the property if the fee tail owner dies without issue, that third person has a future estate to take possession if the grantee dies without issue.

- ✔ The fee tail language gives the grantee a life estate, and then upon her death, the property goes to her children in fee simple.

- ✔ The fee tail language gives the grantee a fee tail, and thereafter her lineal descendants have a fee simple.

The most important thing to remember about the fee tail is that fee tail language has different effects in different states, so you need to look at the state statute to determine the consequence of such language.

Limiting a present estate to life

A *life estate* is an easy label to understand — it means an estate that expires when a person expires. Usually a life estate ends at the death of the person who owns the life estate, but a life estate can be created to end at the death of any person or persons. When a person owns a life estate that ends at the death of someone else, it's called a life estate *pur autre vie,* meaning for the life of another.

A deed or will may create a life estate by any words indicating that the estate automatically ends at the death of a person or persons. Usually an instrument simply says "to A for life." It could also say something like "to A until her death," or "to A, then at her death to B."

Making Present Estates Defeasible: Conditional Endings

Each type of present estate may be made *defeasible,* meaning it ends if a specified condition occurs. An estate subject to such conditions may be called a *defeasible estate,* whereas an estate that isn't defeasible may be called *absolute.* So a *fee simple absolute* is a fee simple that has no conditions of defeasibility.

Commonly if an estate is absolute, people just refer to it as a life estate or a fee simple.

There are three different kinds of defeasibility:

- ✔ Determinable
- ✔ On condition subsequent
- ✔ Subject to executory limitation

Each type of present estate — fee simple, fee tail, life, and leasehold — may be defeasible in each of these ways. For example, one may create a fee simple determinable, a fee simple on condition subsequent, and a fee simple subject to executory limitation. For the basics on each type of defeasibility, read on.

Determinable estates

A *determinable* estate lasts until a specified circumstance happens or ceases, and then the estate automatically ends and possession of the property goes back to the grantor or to whomever the grantor has given the right in the meantime.

A condition of defeasibility therefore is created by language indicating duration, such as "until" or "as long as." For example, "to A as long as the property is used for residential purposes" would create a *fee simple determinable*. The grant may also say that the property reverts to the grantor after the condition occurs, but the property will revert to the grantor even if the grant doesn't say so, because if the grantor didn't give that future estate to someone else, she still owned it.

Estates on condition subsequent

An estate *on condition subsequent* is subject to a condition that gives the grantor (and her successors) the right to terminate the estate and take possession back.

Unlike a determinable estate, an estate on condition subsequent doesn't automatically expire when the condition occurs. The grantor must exercise the right to re-enter the property and terminate the prior estate by giving notice to the owner of the estate, by beginning a legal action to regain possession, or even by physically re-entering the land. An estate on condition subsequent therefore is created by conditional words, such as "but if" or "on condition that," accompanied by a description of the grantor's right to take possession back. For example, "to A, but if the property is used for nonresidential purposes, the grantor may re-enter and take possession."

In the past, words of condition alone were enough to create an estate on condition subsequent. But today, most courts say that the instrument must expressly create a right to terminate or re-enter, or else the words of condition won't create a defeasible estate; instead they'll create a covenant or some other nonpossessory interest or nothing at all.

Estates subject to an executory limitation

An estate *subject to an executory limitation* lasts until some specified circumstance happens or ceases, but then possession goes to someone other than the grantor.

The difference between an estate subject to an executory limitation and the other two types of defeasible estates (a determinable estate and an estate on condition subsequent) is that an estate is subject to an executory limitation when the instrument creating the defeasible estate gives the future estate — the right to possess after the estate is defeased — to someone other than the grantor. It doesn't matter whether words of condition or duration express the circumstances resulting in the third party taking possession.

For example, a fee simple would be subject to an executory limitation if the grant said "to A as long as used for residential purposes, then to B." Likewise, a grant that said "to A, but if used for nonresidential purposes, then to B" would also create a fee simple subject to executory limitation. In either case, the estate automatically ends when the condition of defeasance occurs; the third party doesn't have to exercise a right of entry like the grantor must with a condition subsequent.

Identifying Future Estates

A *future estate* is an estate that takes possession in the future. But that doesn't mean the owner of a future estate doesn't own anything until she has the right to take possession; a future estate is an interest in real property in the present even though it isn't possessory.

By definition, a future estate follows a present estate. All the labels for future estates correspond to the present estates that they follow. The fee tail, life estate, and leasehold don't last forever, so they have future interests that follow them. And if any type of estate is defeasible, a future interest follows the defeasance of the estate. Table 9-1 lists the present estates, the types of defeasibility, and the future estates that follow each.

The following sections give you the basics on how to identify and describe future estates.

Table 9-1	Present and Future Estates	
Present Estate	*Defeasibility*	*Future Estate*
Fee simple		No future estate follows
Fee tail, life estate, or leasehold		Reversion or remainder
	Determinable	Possibility of reverter
	On condition subsequent	Right of entry
	Subject to executory limitation	Executory interest

Reversionary interests

A *reversionary interest* gets its name because it's an interest that reverts, or goes back, to the grantor. Three of the future estates are reversionary interests:

- ✔ **Reversion:** A *reversion* is the future estate originally retained by the grantor that follows a life estate, fee tail, or leasehold. In other words, it's the grantor's future estate that follows the natural expiration of estates less than a fee simple. A grant may expressly reserve a reversion in the grantor, but even if it doesn't, the grantor retains a reversion whenever a grant creates a life estate, fee tail, or leasehold without giving the future estate to someone else.

- ✔ **Possibility of reverter:** A *possibility of reverter* is the future estate originally retained by the grantor that follows a determinable estate. A determinable estate ends automatically when a condition occurs, so the possibility of reverter automatically becomes possessory when the determinable estate ends. The grant may expressly reserve a possibility of reverter. But even if it doesn't, the grantor retains a possibility of reverter whenever the grant limits the present estate in a way that automatically ends but doesn't specify who gets the property after it ends.

- ✔ **Right of entry:** Sometimes called a *power of termination,* a *right of entry* is the future estate originally retained by the grantor that follows an estate on condition subsequent. The right of entry doesn't automatically become possessory when the condition of defeasibility occurs; the owner of the right of entry must take action to exercise the right, such as giving notice or filing a lawsuit to regain possession. Some courts say that the grantor has a right of entry only if the instrument creating an estate on condition subsequent expressly refers to the grantor's right of entry or power of termination.

Distinguishing a reversion from other future estates is easy because a future estate is a reversion only if it was originally retained by the grantor and it immediately follows the end of a life estate, fee tail, or leasehold.

Distinguishing the possibility of reverter from the right of entry, on the other hand, is harder. If the prior defeasible estate ends automatically, expressed by words of duration, that indicates a possibility of reverter. If the prior defeasible estate doesn't end automatically but says something to the effect that the grantor may terminate the estate and re-enter, then it's a right of entry.

Sometimes the grant isn't that clear. It may use some words of condition that sound like the estate is on condition subsequent but also use some words suggesting that the estate automatically ends upon occurrence of the condition. If the grant is unclear, courts generally will construe the defeasible estate to be on condition subsequent, so the grantor has a right of entry.

Often it doesn't matter whether the grantor retained a possibility of reverter or a right of entry. In either case, when the condition of defeasibility occurs, the grantor has the right to take possession of the property, and if the owner of the former estate retains possession, the grantor (or her successors) must bring a lawsuit to regain possession. But the distinction may matter in some cases, such as the following:

✔ **Statute of limitations:** The possibility of reverter automatically becomes a present estate with the right of possession the moment the condition of defeasibility occurs. So the statute of limitations period — which is also the adverse possession period — begins to run as soon as the condition occurs. But if the grantor instead retained a right of entry, some courts have held that the limitations period doesn't begin to run until the grantor exercises the right of entry, because the possession by the former owner isn't wrongful until the grantor does so.

✔ **Rental value:** The owner of the possibility of reverter has the right to immediate possession when defeasance occurs, so some would say that she has the right to recover the reasonable rental value of the property from the former owner from that time on. But if the future estate was a right of entry, the grantor wouldn't have the right to rental value until exercising the right of entry.

✔ **Waiver:** The owner of the right of entry must exercise her right within a reasonable time after the occurrence of the condition. If she doesn't, some courts say that she waives the right to terminate the defeasible estate. The owner of a possibility of reverter, on the other hand, doesn't have to do anything to assert the right to possession, so she can't waive her right in this way.

All three types of reversionary interests are interests originally created in the grantor. The grantor may even retain such an interest in a devise by will, even though she's dead at the moment the conveyance is effective, so she never actually owns the future estate. After such an interest is created, the grantor may convey it to others by a conveyance during her life, by will, or by intestate succession. Such transfers don't change the label or character of the reversionary interest.

Nonreversionary interests: Creating future estates in others

Only two future estates can originally be created in someone other than the grantor:

✔ **Remainder:** A *remainder* is the future estate created in a third party that immediately follows a life estate, fee tail, or leasehold. That simple definition expresses four requirements, which are sometimes stated as rules for an interest to be a remainder:

- The future estate must follow a life estate, fee tail, or leasehold.

- The future estate must be created at the same time and by the same instrument as the estate that precedes it (the life estate, fee tail, or leasehold). Otherwise, the instrument that creates the present estate, such as a life estate, actually creates a reversion in the grantor, which the grantor may subsequently transfer to another but which will still be a reversion rather than a remainder.

- The future estate must not cut short the prior estate; instead, it must take possession only when the prior estate expires — with a life estate, for example, when the life estate ends.

- The future estate must take possession immediately when the prior estate expires, without a gap of time between the prior estate's expiration and the future estate holder's right to take possession.

✔ **Executory interest:** Any future estate created in someone other than the grantor, and that isn't a remainder, is an *executory interest*. It's the future estate created in a third party that follows a defeasible estate. For example, a grant that says "to A as long as used for a school, then to B," creates an executory interest in B.

Executory interests may be described as *shifting* or *springing* (though the distinction makes no difference in the relevant law; it's just a common way of describing one of the characteristics of the executory interest). A *shifting executory interest* is one that shifts possession from one grantee to another, like in the school example, which shifts possession from A to B. A *springing executory interest,* on the other hand, changes possession from the grantor to the executory interest holder when the condition of defeasibility occurs. For example, the grant may say "to A when she graduates from law school."

Describing the present estate the future estate holder will own

A future estate is the right to take possession at some time in the future, when a prior estate expires or is terminated by a condition of defeasance. When the future estate takes possession, the future estate holder's interest won't be future anymore — at that point she has a present estate, because she's in possession.

The present estate that she takes at that time may be a fee simple absolute. For example, if a grant says "to A for life, then to B," then after A dies, B will own the property without any further limitation in time. In other words, B will own a fee simple absolute at that point. So when this grant was originally made, you could fully describe B's interest by saying that B has a remainder in a fee simple absolute.

But the future estate can be in a lesser estate than a fee simple absolute. The grantor can give a future estate holder a future interest in any present estate she chooses. For example, the grantor could give property "to A for life, then to B for life, then to C." In that grant, B has a remainder that follows A's life estate, but when it becomes possessory, B won't own a fee simple absolute. B will own only a life estate. When B dies, then C will have a fee simple absolute, because the grant doesn't limit the duration of C's ownership. So B has a remainder in a life estate, and C has a remainder in a fee simple absolute.

A full description of a future estate therefore includes two things:

- ✔ The label for the future estate
- ✔ The present estate that owner will have if and when the future estate becomes possessory

If someone has a future estate in less than a fee simple absolute, there must still be someone else who has a future estate to follow that person's estate.

You haven't described all the estates in a property until you identify someone who has a future interest in a fee simple absolute. But there may be several people with future interests in lesser estates whose interests precede that last person in line.

Here's an example of a full future estate description: "to A for life, then to B as long as used for residential purposes, and then to C, but if the property is thereafter used for commercial purposes, the grantor retains the right to re-enter." This grant creates the following interests:

- ✔ **A has a life estate.** Someone always has a present estate, and there can only be one present estate at any time.

- ✔ **B has a remainder in a fee simple subject to executory limitation.** B's future estate is a remainder because it immediately follows A's life estate. When B takes possession, her present estate is subject to a condition of defeasibility that, if it occurs, will transfer possession to a third party, C. So when B takes possession she'll have a fee simple subject to executory limitation.

- ✔ **C has an executory interest in a fee simple on condition subsequent.** C's future estate is an executory interest because it's a future estate in a person other than the grantor that doesn't follow a life estate. When C takes possession, her present estate is subject to a condition of defeasibility, with a right of entry in the grantor. So C's present estate will be a fee simple on condition subsequent.

- ✔ **The grantor has a right of entry in fee simple absolute.** If and when the grantor takes possession pursuant to her right of entry, she'll have a fee simple absolute because the grant doesn't specify any further temporal limits. After you've identified a future estate in a fee simple absolute, you've reached the finish line.

Distinguishing contingent and vested remainders

A remainder may be either contingent or vested, depending on whether conditions have been fulfilled and whether you can identify all the people who have a right to take possession.

Contingencies: Unfulfilled conditions, unidentified people

A remainder is *contingent* if either or both of the following are true:

- ✔ **The remainder is subject to an unfulfilled condition precedent.** A *condition precedent* is a condition that the owner of the remainder, often called the *remainderman,* must fulfill in order to have the right to take possession when the remainder becomes possessory. For example, consider a grant "to A for life, then to her oldest child if he graduates from law school." By the terms of the grant, the oldest child of A will have the right to take possession after A's death only if and when he has graduated from law school. That's a condition precedent that makes the remainder contingent.

- ✔ **The person or people who will have the right to take possession under the remainder can't yet be identified.** For example, consider a grant "to A for life, then to the surviving children of A." Until A dies, you can't tell who the surviving children of A will be. You could also describe that as an unfulfilled condition precedent, that in order to qualify to take possession, a person must outlive A.

A contingent remainder may ultimately fail, meaning no one satisfies the conditions to take possession under the remainder. In this case, the property reverts to the grantor unless the grantor has otherwise specified that someone will take possession in that event. The grantor's interest following a life estate, fee tail, or leasehold is called a reversion. So as long as a remainder is contingent, the grantor also has a reversion, to take possession if the contingent remainder fails.

Vested remainders

If a remainder isn't contingent, it's vested. In other words, a remainder *vests* when any conditions precedent are fulfilled and all the people who will have the right to take possession under the remainder can be named. However, even a vested remainder may be subject to partial or complete *divestment,* or defeasance. Here are the three possible situations in which a remainder is fully or partially vested:

- ✔ **Indefeasibly vested:** An indefeasibly vested remainder isn't subject to any conditions precedent or conditions subsequent. You can figure out who all the takers are, and no one else can qualify to share possession under the remainder. For example, this remainder is indefeasibly vested after A has a child born: "to A for life, then to her oldest child." As soon as A has a child, the remainderman is identifiable and has no further conditions to satisfy in order to take possession at the end of A's life. Of course, A's oldest child may die before A, but that doesn't mean that the remainder is contingent. The remainder belonging to A's oldest child will simply pass to his heirs or devisees when he dies, so if A's oldest child dies first, his heirs or devisees will own the vested remainder and will take possession when A dies.

✔ **Vested subject to partial defeasance:** When a remainder is to a group of people, one or more of them may be identifiable and have fulfilled all conditions precedent, whereas other possible members of the group aren't identifiable and haven't fulfilled the conditions precedent. In that situation, the remainder is vested as to some and contingent as to others. Such a remainder may be called vested subject to partial defeasance, or *partial divestment.*

✔ **Vested subject to complete defeasance:** A remainder that's subject to a condition subsequent is *vested subject to complete defeasance.* A condition precedent must be fulfilled in order for the person to be qualified to take possession, whereas a condition subsequent terminates or defeats the remainder. For example, this grant creates a remainder vested subject to complete defeasance: "to A for life, then to B, but if he graduates from law school, then to C."

Sometimes there isn't any apparent functional difference between a condition precedent and a condition subsequent, but there's still a grammatical difference. If the remainder is stated and then qualified, typically with a clause starting "but if," then it's a condition subsequent, making the remainder vested subject to complete defeasance.

Interpreting grants to heirs

A grant to a person "and her heirs" generally doesn't give the heirs a share in the estate or a separate estate. "And her heirs" are words of limitation indicating that the estate granted is inheritable.

But if she wants, a grantor can actually grant an interest to a person's heirs. For example, a grantor can convey property "to A for life, then to the heirs of B." Until B dies, the remainder is contingent, because you can't know who B's heirs are until she dies. But there's no legal problem with that. As soon as B dies, her heirs will have the right to take possession. If B is still living when A dies, the property would revert to the grantor subject to an executory interest in B's heirs; as soon as B dies, the heirs would be identifiable and take possession.

If a grantor gives a remainder to her own heirs or to the heirs of a person to whom she gives a life estate, however, two traditional rules may dictate how the grant is interpreted. The *Rule in Shelley's Case* relates to grants to a life tenant's heirs, and the _doctrine of worthier title_ relates to grants to the grantor's heirs. The following sections talk about these rules in detail.

The Rule in Shelley's Case

The _Rule in Shelley's Case_ applies when a deed or will conveys a life estate (or a fee tail) to a person and the remainder to that person's heirs. The rule says that the remainder in the person's heirs merges with the life estate, so she actually has a fee simple absolute and the heirs own no interest at all. Only a few states still recognize the Rule in Shelley's Case, although in other states it still applies to older instruments.

The grantor may want the heirs to have a separate interest, however, so that their ancestor can't sell the property during her life and prevent her heirs from getting the property altogether. The grantor can still accomplish this purpose by avoiding the circumstances that invoke the rule. Here are some ways she can do that:

- ✔ Grant the remainder to the children of the life tenant rather than to the "heirs." The Rule in Shelley's Case applies only when the grant is to "heirs."

- ✔ Instead of granting the remainder to the heirs in the same instrument, retain a reversion. Then separately convey the reversion to the heirs of the life tenant.

- ✔ Grant the remainder to someone else in trust for the benefit of the heirs of A. The rule applies only when the life estate and the remainder are both legal or are both equitable, so granting the life estate to A and the remainder in trust for the benefit of the heirs of A avoids the rule.

Doctrine of worthier title

The _doctrine of worthier title_ is similar to the Rule in Shelley's Case but applies when the grantor conveys a remainder to her own heirs. In that situation, the doctrine says that the grant of the remainder is void. Instead, the grantor retains the reversion, and her heirs receive the property by inheritance rather than by virtue of the grant.

Some states have rejected the doctrine altogether, but most states still apply the doctrine as a rule of construction, meaning that unless the grant explicitly indicates otherwise, courts will construe such a grant to retain a reversion rather than grant a remainder to heirs. If the grant is by will, today it makes no difference whether the remainder to the grantor's heirs passes to them by the devise or by inheritance of the reversion. In fact, as a result, most recent authorities say that the doctrine doesn't even apply to devises by will; it only applies to conveyances during lifetime.

A grantor may want to give a remainder to her heirs instead of retaining a reversion for them to inherit at her death, perhaps so her interest isn't available to creditors. She can easily do so by explicitly saying in the grant that she doesn't retain a reversion but intends to give her heirs the remainder. She can also avoid the doctrine by conveying the remainder in trust for her heirs or by conveying the remainder to her children, because the doctrine applies only when the remainder is to "heirs."

Restricting Certain Future Estates via Common Law Rules

Even though future estates aren't possessory in the present, they may significantly affect the value and use of land today. A person obviously won't pay as much for a life estate as for a fee simple absolute. In fact, a person probably won't significantly develop and invest in land that's owned in a life estate, because she'll lose her investment after the life estate ends, which could happen at any time. Instead, she'll first seek to buy the life estate from the life tenant and the remainder from the remaindermen so that she'll have fee simple ownership. But if she can't figure out who those remaindermen are, then she can't buy the remainder and she won't develop the property.

That's just one way uncertainty of ownership can impair the use and value of property in the present. The law favors the productive use of land. On the other hand, the law also respects the right of an owner to transfer property as she wishes, including the right to transfer property to others after her death. The old common law balanced these concerns by destroying contingent remainders if they didn't vest at the expiration of the preceding estate.

Future estates may more directly inhibit the transfer of property to those who will productively use it. A grantor may create a future estate to take possession if the present estate holder tries to transfer ownership. The grantor may want to ensure that her grantees keep the property in the family instead of selling it to someone else. But this obviously conflicts with the law's desire to facilitate the free transfer of land. So in some cases, courts hold that such conditions of defeasibility are void and unenforceable.

The following sections talk further about these two common law rules that restrict the grantor's freedom to convey property as she wishes in favor of the public interest in making good use of the land: the destruction of contingent remainders and invalidation of restraints on alienation.

Destroying contingent remainders

The old common law rule was that a remainder had to vest by the time the preceding estate ended, or else it was simply destroyed. The remainderman couldn't later satisfy the conditions precedent and take possession. Imagine a grant "to A for life, then to B if he marries." Until B marries, the remainder is contingent because it's subject to the condition precedent that he marry. If A dies before B is married, B's remainder is simply destroyed. Even if B gets married later, he won't have the right to take possession. Instead, the property reverts to the grantor and her heirs.

The life estate may even end before the death of the life tenant, and if the remainder hasn't vested yet, it'll be destroyed. The life estate may end earlier by a now-obsolete doctrine called *forfeiture* or by merger. In this context, *merger* refers to the transfer of the life estate and the grantor's reversion to the same person. In that situation, the reversion and the life estate are said to merge and destroy the contingent remainder.

Nearly all jurisdictions have rejected the old common law rule of destruction of contingent remainders. The few states that have applied the rule haven't had occasion to talk about the rule for many years, so they may abandon the rule when they get the chance. But for now, the rule may be relevant to some practicing lawyers and is worth being familiar with at least to understand what cases and authorities are talking about when they refer to the rule about destructibility of contingent remainders.

Invalidating restraints on alienation

A grantor may try to restrain the grantee's power to transfer, or *alienate,* the property in three ways:

- ✔ **Disabling restraint:** A *disabling restraint* is a declaration in the deed or will that the grantee can't transfer the estate. For example, "to A and her heirs. The property may not be conveyed and any attempt to do so shall be void." Disabling restraints are always invalid. The power to transfer an estate is so fundamental to ownership that the grantor simply can't declare that a person doesn't have the power to transfer.

- ✔ **Promissory restraint:** A *promissory restraint* is a covenant not to transfer the property. For example, "to A and her heirs, who covenant not to convey the property to anyone else." Promissory restraints may be valid if they serve a legitimate purpose and are appropriate in scope. (For more on promissory restraints, which are simply one form of covenant, see Chapter 5.)

- ✔ **Forfeiture restraint:** A *forfeiture restraint* is a condition of defeasibility; it says that if the grantee conveys the estate, it will automatically terminate, or the grantor may terminate it pursuant to a right of entry. For example, "to A and her heirs, as long as they never attempt to convey the property to anyone else." A forfeiture restraint may make an estate determinable, on condition subsequent, or subject to executory limitation. It may be valid and enforceable if it's reasonable in light of the following considerations:

- **The type of estate made defeasible:** A court is much more likely to declare a forfeiture restraint invalid if it makes a fee simple rather than a lesser estate defeasible. Forfeiture restraints making leaseholds defeasible are very common — the leasehold says that the landlord may terminate the lease if the tenant transfers the leasehold without the landlord's prior consent.

- **The purpose of the restraint:** The restraint must serve a significant purpose in order to be valid. For example, a restraint restricting transfer of a family farm to people outside the family may serve a significant, legitimate purpose.

- **The scope of the restraint:** The more extensive the restraint, the less likely a court will enforce it. For example, a restraint that terminates the estate if the grantee transfers any interest at all is less likely to be valid than a restraint that terminates the estate if the grantee mortgages the property. The scope must be appropriate for the purpose to be served.

- **The duration of the restraint:** A restraint is more likely to be valid if it's limited in time in a way consistent with the purpose of the restraint. For instance, a restraint for the lifetime of the grantor is more likely to be valid than a restraint with no limitation in time.

- **The harm from the restraint:** The court considers the harm to the grantee and to the public as well as the benefit to the grantor.

- **Consideration:** If the consideration paid by the grantee reflects the restraint on alienation, the restraint is more likely to be valid than if it doesn't.

Limiting Nonreversionary Interests: The Rule against Perpetuities

The rule against perpetuities limits the uncertainty of future ownership, like the old rule of destructibility of remainders. But it's much more complex than the destructibility rule. That's why I'm devoting this section to examining each aspect of the rule against perpetuities in detail. But first, here's the rule:

> No interest is good unless it must vest, if at all, not later than 21 years after some life in being at the creation of the interest.

I recommend just memorizing this common expression of the rule against perpetuities rather than trying to restate it more simply — any version that seems simpler is probably wrong.

Understanding the interests subject to the rule

The first step in applying the rule against perpetuities is to consider whether the rule applies to the interest in question. The statement of the rule says "no interest" is good unless it must vest within the confusingly worded time period. Even though that may sound as if it applies to many types of interests, any interest that's always vested would never violate the rule. It operates only on interests that are *not* vested.

Only two types of estates may be created but not vested:

- ✓ **Contingent remainders:** This includes group remainders that are contingent as to some but vested as to others, which this chapter refers to earlier as *remainders vested subject to partial defeasance*.

- ✓ **Executory interests:** By definition, executory interests aren't vested until the condition of defeasibility occurs and the executory interest becomes possessory.

Some options to purchase are also subject to the rule, but of course those interests aren't estates.

All other estates are always vested. If there were any point to talking about the vesting of present estates, one would have to say they're vested the moment they're created. The person or people must be identifiable to actually take possession. If they don't have the right to take possession already, they don't have a present estate. The reversionary future estates are all considered vested at creation, because they're all retained by the grantor, who is identifiable and doesn't have to fulfill any conditions precedent in order to have the right to take possession if and when those future estates become possessory. And, of course, vested remainders are vested.

So if it makes more sense to you, you can safely say that "no contingent remainder (including a remainder vested subject to partial defeasance) or executory interest is good unless it must vest, if ever, not later than 21 years after some life in being at the creation of the interest."

Determining the moment of vesting

The rule against perpetuities says no interest is good "unless it must vest, if at all," within the specified time period. So after you identify an interest that's subject to the rule, the next step is to figure out when it will vest. You can't figure out a specific date, of course, but you can figure out the event that will cause the interest to vest.

Executory interests are easy to figure out. They vest when they become possessory. In other words, the moment an executory interest vests is when the condition of defeasance occurs and the prior defeasible estate ends. Contingent remainders are a bit harder. They vest when all conditions precedent are fulfilled and when all the remaindermen who will take possession are identifiable. The rule against perpetuities is why the distinction between vested and contingent remainders matters (see the earlier section "Distinguishing vested and contingent remainders").

Of course, an executory interest or contingent remainder may never vest. But that's okay. The rule doesn't invalidate a contingent interest simply because it's uncertain to vest. An interest is good as long as it must vest, *if it ever vests,* within the specified time period. So an interest is good if at the creation of the interest you know that within the time period the condition will either occur or become impossible to occur, in which case the remainder is said to *fail.*

Consider a grant "to A for life, then to the children of A who reach age 21." If A has no children who are at least 21 years old at the time of the conveyance, the remainder is contingent. It may turn out that A never has children or that she has children but all of them die before turning 21. So of course the remainder isn't certain to vest ever. But if it ever does vest, it's certain to vest within 21 years after A's lifetime, because any of her children who reach age 21 will do so within 21 years of her death.

An interest is either valid or invalid at the moment it's created. When the interest actually vests doesn't matter. All that matters is whether, at the moment the interest is created, you can say for certain that if the vesting event is ever going to happen, it will happen within 21 years of the lifetime of someone who's living when the interest is created.

Considering lives in being

The following clause is the hardest part of the rule against perpetuities: no interest is good unless it must vest, if at all, "not later than 21 years after some life in being at the creation of the interest."

The rule says "some" life in being at the creation of the interest because it doesn't matter who. If there's anyone alive at the time of the conveyance during whose lifetime, or within 21 years thereafter, the interest is certain to vest if it ever does, then the interest is good. If you can't identify anyone alive at the time of the conveyance during whose lifetime plus 21 years the interest is certain to vest, if it ever does, then the interest is void.

But even though the rule is satisfied as long as the interest is certain to vest or fail within 21 years of the life of anyone who was alive at the time of the conveyance, practically, the person must somehow be connected to the vesting of the interest. Anyone who isn't connected to the vesting of the interest could die at any time, even the day after the creation of the interest, and not affect when the interest vests. So as you search for a life in being at the creation of the interest within whose lifetime plus 21 years the interest is certain to vest or fail, you only need to consider people who will affect the occurrence of the condition that will vest the interest. Such people may include the following:

- ✔ People who are somehow named or identified in the instrument creating the interest or whose lives are connected to the occurrence of the vesting event

- ✔ Children of a person named in the creating instrument who is dead at the creation of the interest, because by definition, if the person is dead, then all her children are born. As a group, the children of a person who is still alive are not "lives in being at the time of the conveyance," because, as far as the law is concerned, a living person can always have more children until she is dead. (By the way, the rule against perpetuities disregards gestational periods, so even though a man's child may actually be born after his death, the rule in effect considers that all a person's children are born by the moment of his or her death.)

- ✔ The grantor, who of course must be alive at the time of the conveyance or right up until the moment of the conveyance if by will

- ✔ The children of the testator in a will

The interest must be certain to vest, if ever, within 21 years of the life of someone who was alive "at the creation of the interest." The interest is created when it's conveyed. If the interest is created by an inter vivos conveyance (a conveyance during the grantor's lifetime), the interest is created when the deed is delivered and accepted, as I explain in Chapter 16. If the interest is created by will, it's created at the moment the testator dies, not when the testator prepared her will.

The rule against perpetuities requires you to identify at least one person who is alive at the time of the conveyance within whose lifetime plus 21 years thereafter the interest is certain to vest, if ever. That means that, if an interest is valid, you must identify such a person and explain why the interest is certain to vest or fail during that person's lifetime plus 21 years. Your explanation should be essentially in this form: "The interest is valid under the rule against perpetuities because if it ever vests, it will do so within 21 years of the lifetime of X, who was alive at the time the interest was created." Then you explain why that's true. If you can't identify such a person, then the interest is void.

So to explain why an interest is void under the rule against perpetuities, you should say something like this: "The interest is void under the rule against perpetuities because it may vest more than 21 years after everyone alive at the time of the conveyance is dead." It isn't enough to say that the interest may vest more than 21 years after a particular person is dead; the interest is void only if there is nobody alive at the time of the conveyance within whose lifetime plus 21 years the interest is certain to vest, if it ever does. To explain why that's true, you generally should explain why the interest isn't certain to vest within 21 years of the lifetime of the people who might appear to be connected to the vesting of the interest. Then you can note that anyone else who was alive at the time of the conveyance could die at any time and the interest could vest more than 21 years afterward.

Here are examples of how to apply the rule against perpetuities to a valid and an invalid interest:

- ✔ **Valid interest:** Someone's will gives property "to A for life, then to my grandchildren who reach age 21." Unless all the testator's children are dead at the time the testator dies, the remainder to the grandchildren who reach age 21 is contingent or vested subject to open. More grandchildren could still be born. But the interest is valid under the rule against perpetuities because it's certain to vest, if ever, within 21 years of the lifetimes of the testator's children, who are alive at the time of the conveyance. Because the interest is created at the death of the testator, by definition all the testator's children are alive at the time of the conveyance. All their children — the testator's grandchildren — will be born during those children's lifetimes. And therefore all of those grandchildren of the testator will reach age 21 within 21 years of the lifetime of their respective parent, who is alive at the time of the conveyance.

- ✔ **Invalid interest:** Someone's will gives property "to A for life, then to A's grandchildren who reach age 21." The interest is invalid because the interest isn't certain to vest or fail during the lifetime of someone alive at the time of the conveyance. In other words, it could vest more than 21 years after everyone alive at the time of the conveyance is dead. A's grandchildren, of course, could reach age 21 more than 21 years after A dies. They couldn't reach age 21 more than 21 years after their respective parents' lifetimes, because by definition they would be born during their parents' lifetimes. But their parents — the children of A — as a group aren't necessarily alive at the time of the conveyance. Because A is alive at the time of the conveyance, she can still have more children, and those later-born children wouldn't have been alive at the time of the conveyance. A's grandchildren will of course reach age 21 during their own lifetimes, but they, too, as a group aren't necessarily alive at the time of the conveyance: more grandkids could still be born later.

Any other person alive at the time of the conveyance could die the very next day and not affect the vesting of the interest. So there's no one alive at the time of the conveyance within whose lifetime plus 21 years the interest is certain to vest, if ever. If A were to have a child after the conveyance and all A's other children died shortly after the conveyance, then that surviving child of A could have a child 30 years later, and her child — a grandchild of A — would reach age 21 more than 21 years after everyone alive at the time of the conveyance was dead. So even though that may be very unlikely, the interest is not *certain* to vest or fail within the lifetime plus 21 years of someone alive at the time of the conveyance.

Modifying the rule by statute

A substantial number of states have statutes that significantly modify the rule against perpetuities. Those modifications include the following:

- ✔ **Wait and see:** The traditional rule against perpetuities invalidates an interest at the time of the conveyance if it isn't certain to vest or fail within 21 years of some living person's lifetime. But some state statutes instead say that an interest is valid as long as it actually does vest within 21 years of the lifetime of someone alive at the time of the conveyance (or a longer period of years specified by the statute, as long as 1,000 years), even if the interest could have vested later in time. That requires waiting to see when the interest actually vests.

- ✔ **Cy pres:** Some state statutes authorize courts to apply an equitable doctrine called *cy pres* to modify invalid interests so that they comply with the rule against perpetuities.

- ✔ **Uniform Statutory Rule Against Perpetuities:** Many states have adopted this uniform statute, which says that an interest is valid if it's valid under the traditional rule against perpetuities or if it actually vests within 90 years of the conveyance. So even if an interest would be invalid under the traditional rule, you have to wait to see if it actually vests within 90 years before the interest is invalid.

Transferring Present and Future Estates

The owner of a present estate can transfer her interest to another during her life or at her death by will or intestate succession. But she can't transfer ownership of something she doesn't own in the first place. So if the present estate is determinable, for example, the estate remains determinable when she transfers it to another. If she owns an estate for her life and transfers it, the estate will still end when she dies, so the grantee acquires a life estate pur autre vie (for the life of another). And of course, she can't transfer an estate for her life by will or intestate succession, because once she dies, she has no more estate to give.

Today the owner of a future estate also can generally transfer her interest to another during her life or at her death by will or intestate succession. Again, the owner can only transfer what she owns. So, for example, if she owns a remainder contingent upon her graduating from law school, if she dies without having done so, she has no remainder left to give.

However, some states still apply an old common law rule that contingent remainders and executory interests cannot be transferred inter vivos. Even then, exceptions to the doctrine make an inter vivos conveyance effective if it's made by warranty deed for adequate consideration or if it's made to the owner of the present estate. The same is true in some states for possibilities of reverter. Finally, some states have statutes saying that a right of entry can be transferred inter vivos, but most states say that it can't be transferred inter vivos except to the owner of the present estate or in connection with a transfer of the reversion.

If the owner of an estate purports to convey more than she owns, the conveyance isn't void; instead, it will convey whatever estate she actually has the power to convey. For example, if the owner of a life estate purports to convey the fee simple absolute to a grantee by deed, the deed will transfer the life estate that the grantor does own. Furthermore, if the grantor conveyed the estate by warranty deed and she later acquires the estate she purported to convey, the doctrine of estoppel by deed will automatically transfer the newly acquired estate to her grantee.

Governing the Relationship between Owners of Present and Future Estates

Just as property law includes rules regulating the relationship between owners of different land, it also includes rules regulating the relationship between owners of different estates in the same land. You could think of the owner of a present estate and a future estate as neighbors in time. The actions of the present estate owner can affect the future estate owner's future use and enjoyment of the property just as a landowner's actions can affect a neighbor's use and enjoyment of neighboring land. The law of *waste* is the common law doctrine that restricts the present estate owner's use of the property to preserve the value of the future estate; it's kind of like a nuisance rule for temporal neighbors.

Another problem for owners of different estates in the same land arises when one of them wants to sell her interest but her estate isn't marketable or as valuable if sold separately rather than as part of the fee simple absolute estate. If all the estate owners agree to sell, they obviously can do so. But in some circumstances, courts will order that property be sold in fee simple even though one or more estate owners don't want to sell, in order to enable the others to transfer their interest.

The following sections talk about these two rules governing the relationship between owners of present and future estates.

Taking a closer look at waste

The essential principle of waste is that the owner of a present estate must not impair the value of the future interest by impairing the property somehow. The following sections fill you in on how the present estate owner can commit waste and how waste can be remedied.

Committing voluntary or permissive waste

If the owner of the present estate does something to the property that reduces its value, such waste is called *voluntary* or *active waste.* Voluntary waste may include things like the following:

- ✔ Cutting mature and valuable trees, unless needed for fuel or repairs or to cultivate the land
- ✔ Changing the use of agricultural land
- ✔ Extracting minerals from new mines (mining from already existing mines is not waste, however)
- ✔ Destroying or damaging buildings, unless the present estate holder built the building in the first place

Of course, the present estate holder can use the property in any way that's expressly authorized by the instrument creating her estate. The owner of a leasehold often has the express right under the lease to use the property in certain ways, regardless of whether they might constitute common law waste.

The owner of the present estate may also be liable for *permissive* or *passive waste.* Such waste is passive because the present estate owner doesn't actually cause it herself, but she commits waste by allowing the impairment of the property to occur. This primarily means that the present estate owner must repair and maintain the property as needed to prevent deterioration, such as keeping roofs in repair to prevent water damage. The present estate owner doesn't have to repair ordinary wear and tear, however, nor does she have to repair a building to a better condition than when she received her present estate. She also doesn't have to rebuild a building damaged by fire or other casualties for which she wasn't responsible.

The present estate holder doesn't have to invest her own money and resources to prevent deterioration. Her obligation to preserve the property is limited to using the rental income received, or the rental value if she occupies it herself, to maintain and repair the property as needed to prevent waste.

Failing to pay property taxes, insurance premiums, or mortgage interest may also be treated as permissive waste.

Remedying waste

The future estate holder can recover damages from the present estate holder who commits waste. If the future estate holder sues for damages before she has the right to take possession, the damages are the loss of market value due to the waste. But if she sues for damages when the future interest becomes possessory, her damages are the cost of fixing the damage. Some states have statutes allowing the future interest holder to recover a multiple of the actual damages suffered.

A future estate holder who may not ever have the right to take possession, however, may not have the right to damages. So the owner of a contingent remainder, a remainder vested subject to complete defeasance, an executory interest, a possibility of reverter, or a right of entry generally can't sue for damages.

A future estate holder also can obtain equitable relief to enjoin waste. An injunction may compel the present estate holder to make repairs or prohibit her from destroying buildings. A court may also appoint a receiver to prevent waste. Even owners of contingent interests may get equitable relief from the court, unless their interests are very unlikely to ever become possessory.

Forcing the judicial sale of real property in fee simple absolute

If the owner of an estate wants to sell her property, it may not be as valuable or marketable if the others with estates in the property won't join in the sale. By statute or judicial decision, most courts agree that they have the authority to order the property sold in fee simple absolute if necessary to preserve the value of the interests in the land.

If the property is losing value because old buildings are deteriorating and the rental value isn't sufficient to maintain them and pay property taxes, the life tenant could get a court order to sell the property in fee simple even if the remaindermen objected.

The proceeds of the sale may be kept in trust, with the income paid to the present estate holder for the duration of her estate, such as the lifetime of the life tenant, then the principal given to the future estate holder at the end of the present estate.

Chapter 10

Sharing Property: Concurrent Ownership

*M*ultiple people can own an estate concurrently. Three forms of concurrent ownership exist. They all share the same basic characteristics, but two of them come with the right to own the other's shares in the property when they die.

Whatever the form of concurrent ownership, the co-owners have the same right to use and enjoy the property and the same duty to take care of it. One's use of the property can significantly affect the other's use, so various rules govern the rights and duties of the co-owners in relation to each other.

If one or more of the co-owners don't want to continue that relationship, they can change or terminate their co-ownership.

This chapter fills you in as to how more than one person can own the same estate in the same property. It examines how each type of concurrent ownership is created and how they vary from one another. It also looks at the rules governing the relationship among co-owners and how concurrent ownership ends. The last section introduces you to condominium ownership, which combines concurrent ownership of some things and separate ownership of other things.

Concurrent Ownership: Owning the Same Property at the Same Time

Concurrent ownership means that two or more people have the same rights to use and enjoy the same property at the same time. Concurrent ownership has three forms, which may be called *concurrent estates:*

- ✔ Tenancy in common
- ✔ Joint tenancy
- ✔ Tenancy by the entirety

A fundamental characteristic of any type of concurrent ownership is the *unity of possession*, meaning that each co-owner has an equal right to use and enjoy the entire property that's co-owned; there are no physical boundaries among cotenants. Each co-owner has an undivided interest in the whole property. Both real and personal property may be co-owned in these ways, but I focus on real property in this chapter.

Even though the forms of concurrent ownership are sometimes called *concurrent estates,* the concurrent estates are different relationships among co-owners of an estate, not different time periods of ownership. Any of the present estates I cover in Chapter 9 may be co-owned in one of the three forms of concurrent estates. For example, a group of people may own a fee simple determinable in tenancy in common or in a joint tenancy. A group of people also may co-own a future interest, although of course they don't have the right of possession until their future interest becomes a present estate. To help you avoid confusing the present and future estates with concurrent ownership, I generally refer to forms of concurrent ownership rather than concurrent estates.

Concurrent owners may be called *cotenants,* and any of the three kinds of concurrent ownership may be referred to as a *cotenancy*. Sometimes, however, the term "cotenant" is used to refer specifically to tenants in common. In this chapter, I use the term *cotenant* to refer to concurrent owners in any of the three types of concurrent estates.

Getting Familiar with Tenancy in Common

The tenancy in common is the most common form of concurrent ownership. As with all three forms of concurrent ownership, each tenant in common has a right to use the whole co-owned property. However, even though their right to use the property is undivided, tenants in common may own different fractional shares in the property, meaning that they'll receive different shares of profits from the property and different shares of the land or its selling price when the tenancy in common ends. Tenants in common may transfer their shares during their lifetimes and at death by will or intestate succession.

The following sections take a closer look at the creation and characteristics of the tenancy in common.

Creating a tenancy in common

One reason why the tenancy in common is the most common form of concurrent ownership is that conveyances to multiple people create tenancies in common by default. Every state has some version of a statute that says a conveyance to two or more people creates a tenancy in common unless the conveying instrument clearly says otherwise. And when a person dies without distributing property by will, intestacy statutes give property to various relatives as tenants in common. So many tenancies in common may be created by default, without the grantor really choosing that form of concurrent ownership.

Because of the presumption that any co-ownership is a tenancy in common, creating a tenancy in common is simple. Any conveyance of an estate "to A and B" will create a tenancy in common — although in some states, if A and B are married, it may instead create a tenancy by the entirety (see the later section "Examining Tenancy by the Entirety" for more about this type of concurrent ownership). Of course, the grantor may avoid any uncertainty by explicitly conveying an estate "to A and B as tenants in common."

Understanding fractional shares

Unlike with the other forms of concurrent ownership, tenants in common may own different fractional shares in the concurrently owned property — meaning the shares don't have to be equal. For example, an intestate succession statute may distribute a one-third share to the surviving spouse and a two-thirds share to the deceased's children. If there are three children, each of the children would have a two-ninths share.

A conveyance to two or more people is presumed to be in equal shares unless the conveyance says otherwise. Even if the conveying instrument doesn't say otherwise, a cotenant may rebut the presumption and prove she has a larger share by proving all three of the following:

 ✔ She contributed a larger share of the purchase price.

 ✔ She didn't intend to give a gift to the other cotenants.

✔ She didn't have a family relationship with them. If she did have a family relationship, courts presume that her larger share of the purchase price was intended to be a gift.

As long as the unequal contributions were not a gift or the result of a family relationship, the cotenants will own fractional shares equal to the proportion of the purchase price that they contributed. So a person who contributed two-thirds of the purchase price would have a two-thirds interest, and so on. Of course, the parties may agree to make nonmonetary contributions as well as cash contributions, such as investing their labor to fix up the property. Such contributions may be considered in deciding the parties' fractional shares.

Even though tenants in common may own different fractional shares, that doesn't mean a tenant in common is limited to using just her fractional share of the property. As long as the tenancy in common exists, even the owner of a one-hundredth share has the equal right to use and enjoy the whole property. But it does mean that she gets a smaller share of profits from the property and contributes a smaller share of expenses. And if and when the tenancy in common ends, she'll get only her fractional share of the property or the proceeds from selling it. I talk more about those issues later in "Governing the Relationship among Cotenants."

Transferring one's interest

A tenant in common may transfer her co-ownership interest during her life or by will at her death. If she doesn't do so, her share will pass by intestate succession to her heirs.

Absent an agreement otherwise, the other tenants in common don't have any claim to her share of ownership just because they're co-owners. And a tenant in common can transfer her share without the consent of the other tenants in common, because she's transferring only her interest and not changing their interests. She may transfer her property entirely, or she may transfer a lesser interest, such as a lease or a mortgage.

Taking a Closer Look at Joint Tenancy

The joint tenancy is essentially a tenancy in common with equal shares of ownership and accompanied by a *right of survivorship,* which is the right of the surviving joint tenants to take over ownership of a deceased joint tenant's ownership share. However, joint tenants can end the right of survivorship by transferring their shares during their lifetimes or by taking similar actions; ending the right of survivorship in this way is called *severance.*

The following sections examine how to create a joint tenancy and how the right of survivorship works.

Overcoming the presumption of tenancy in common: Creating a joint tenancy

Statutes in all 50 states presume that a conveyance to two or more people is a tenancy in common. In fact, some states have abolished joint tenancies altogether. In the rest of the states, one can still create a joint tenancy but must clearly indicate the intention to create a joint tenancy in order to overcome the statutory presumption of a tenancy in common.

To create a joint tenancy, it's usually enough for the instrument to say "to A, B, and C as joint tenants." But in some states, usually influenced by statutory language, courts have indicated that the grant must rebut the presumption more expressly, such as by saying "to A, B, and C as joint tenants and not as tenants in common." Even that may not be enough, because some courts reason that "joint tenants" is too ambiguous to indicate the intent to create concurrent ownership with a right of survivorship. Instead, the grant must expressly create a right of survivorship, as in "to A, B, and C as joint tenants with right of survivorship." The clearest version, sure to suffice in all states, is "to A, B, and C as joint tenants with right of survivorship and not as tenants in common."

Satisfying the four unities: Time, title, interest, and possession

Most courts still apply the traditional rule that a joint tenancy can exist only when the following four *unities* are present:

- ✔ **Time:** The joint tenants must acquire their interests at the same time by the same instrument. If separate deeds are given to two co-owners, they don't have unity of time and can't be joint tenants.

- ✔ **Title:** The joint tenants must acquire their interests from the same grantor. Two or more grantors can't convey fractional shares to different grantees and create a joint tenancy relationship among them.

- ✔ **Interest:** The joint tenants must have identical interests, which means the following:

  - The joint tenants must have the same fractional shares. For example, if there are three joint tenants, they each must have a one-third share.

- They must have identical estates. One joint tenant can't have a life estate in her share while another owns her share in fee simple. (I walk you through the types of estates in Chapter 9.)

- Their interests must all be legal or all equitable. One joint tenant's share can't be held in trust while another's isn't.

✔ **Possession:** The joint tenants must have an equal right to possess the whole property. This undivided ownership of the whole is the essential characteristic of all concurrent ownership. If the instrument gives parties rights to different physical parts of the land or rights to the land at different times, it doesn't create concurrent ownership of any type.

Traditionally, if an instrument purports to create a joint tenancy but the four unities aren't present, the co-owners will be tenants in common rather than joint tenants, no matter how clear the grantor's intention to create a joint tenancy. Today, however, some courts consider the grantor's intention and interpret the grant in the way most consistent with that intention.

Consider a grant of a two-thirds interest to A and a one-third interest to B "as joint tenants with right of survivorship and not as tenants in common." Traditionally, this can't create a joint tenancy because A and B don't have unity of interest. However, a court might hold that even though the instrument can't have created a joint tenancy, the parties have a tenancy in common for their lives, with a contingent remainder to the survivor of the two. Or a court might even allow the parties to have a joint tenancy with unequal shares, despite the traditional unities requirement.

The four unities themselves don't create a joint tenancy. Even if a deed creates concurrent ownership with unity of time, title, interest, and possession, the concurrent ownership is a joint tenancy only if the deed rebuts the statutory presumption of a tenancy in common and expressly says that the parties own the property as joint tenants. Tenants in common certainly can have unity of time, title, interest, and possession, too; the unities of time, title, and interest just aren't required in order to create a tenancy in common.

Because of the four-unities requirement, an owner of property traditionally couldn't convey property to herself and another person as joint tenants. They wouldn't have unity of time or title. One could avoid this problem by conveying the property to a straw man who would then convey the property back to the owner and her new joint tenant, thus satisfying the four unities. Today, however, some states don't require use of a straw man but allow an owner to convey to herself and others as joint tenants.

Understanding the right of survivorship

The right of survivorship is what makes the joint tenancy different from the tenancy in common. The right of survivorship means that when a joint tenant dies, she simply doesn't share ownership anymore, and the surviving joint tenants share the whole in equal shares. The last surviving joint tenant owns the whole estate by herself.

So if four people have a joint tenancy, they each begin with equal quarter shares. When one dies, her share ends and the other three now have equal one-third shares. When the next dies, the surviving two joint tenants have equal half shares. And when the next dies, the last survivor owns the whole estate.

The right of survivorship isn't a type of inheritance. The surviving joint tenants don't acquire the deceased joint tenant's interest when she dies. Rather, all the joint tenants own the entire property all along, so as some joint tenants die, the survivors don't really own anything that they didn't own before. They just share what they own with fewer people.

That means that a joint tenant can't transfer her fractional share in the property by will, nor will it pass to her heirs by intestate succession. A joint tenant has no further interest in the property when she dies. The last surviving joint tenant, of course, is no longer a joint tenant when all the other joint tenants have died. So when she dies, she can convey the property by will, and it will pass to her heirs by intestate succession.

Severing the joint tenancy

Despite the name, the "right" of survivorship isn't really a right. During her lifetime, any joint tenant can destroy the others' right of survivorship with respect to her fractional share — and in the process also give up her own right of survivorship with respect to the others' fractional shares. She doesn't need the other joint tenants' consent to do so. Therefore, joint tenants don't really own a right of survivorship; they just have an expectation of surviving, as long as other joint tenants don't end the relationship earlier.

Terminating the right of survivorship is called *severance,* because it severs the joint tenancy relationship between the severing party and the rest of the joint tenants. Severance doesn't end the parties' co-ownership; it merely destroys the right of survivorship that comes with joint tenancy. In other words, when a joint tenant severs her joint tenancy with the others, she changes her relationship with them from a joint tenancy to a tenancy in common.

Transferring a share to someone else

In general, a joint tenant severs her joint tenancy by transferring her fractional share of the property, in whole or in part, to someone else. Doing so destroys the four unities required for a joint tenancy (as described in the earlier section "Satisfying the four unities: Time, title, interest, and possession") and thus ends her joint tenancy relationship. She can't change the relationship among the other joint tenants, however. So if there are three or more joint tenants, the remaining joint tenants still have a right of survivorship with each other, but the severing joint tenant becomes a tenant in common with the rest of them.

For example, if there are four joint tenants, one joint tenant may sever her joint tenancy by selling her one-fourth share to someone else. Her buyer will then be a tenant in common owning a one-fourth share; the other three as a group will own a three-fourths share as tenants in common with the buyer, but among those three, they will continue to be joint tenants with each other and have a right of survivorship in their three-fourths share.

Severing a joint tenancy through other transfers

When a joint tenant transfers her entire interest to a third party, there's no question that she has severed her joint tenancy and her grantee is now a tenant in common with the other co-owners. But other types of transfers, such as the following, may also sever a joint tenancy:

- ✔ **Executory contract to sell a fractional share:** If one joint tenant signs a purchase agreement to sell her fractional share of the property and the agreement is specifically enforceable, her interest is severed. That means if she dies before the sale is completed, the other joint tenants won't get the proceeds of the sale by right of survivorship. Instead, the proceeds will pass by her will or intestate succession.

- ✔ **Executory contract to sell all the shares:** Some courts hold that if all the joint tenants sign a purchase agreement to sell the co-owned property, they sever their joint tenancy. Others say that the joint tenancy isn't severed until the parties complete the sale, unless the purchase agreement or other circumstances indicate that the parties intended to sever the joint tenancy earlier.

- ✔ **Lease:** Some courts hold one joint tenant's lease of her interest severs her joint tenancy.

- ✔ **Divorce decree:** A final divorce decree giving one possession ends the joint tenancy relationship. A divorce decree ordering the parties to sell the property also may sever the joint tenancy.

- ✔ **Mortgage:** In some states, called *title theory states,* a mortgage conveys title to the mortgagee. In those states, a mortgage of her interest by one joint tenant severs her joint tenancy with the others. In other states, called *lien theory states,* one joint tenant's mortgage doesn't sever her joint tenancy. However, some courts in lien theory states hold that a mortgage will sever a joint tenancy when the mortgagor dies, to the extent necessary for the mortgagee to foreclose its mortgage against the deceased joint tenant's fractional share and recover the unpaid debt. (Chapter 18 talks about the title theory and lien theory of mortgages.)

✔ **Foreclosure or other involuntary sale:** If a joint tenant mortgages her fractional share and defaults, then as soon as the mortgagee forecloses and sells the mortgaged share, the joint tenancy is severed. Similarly, although the existence of a judgment lien against one joint tenant's share doesn't sever her joint tenancy, the joint tenancy is severed when the judgment creditor executes the judgment lien and sells the property to satisfy the judgment.

✔ **Agreement:** The joint tenants simply may agree to terminate their joint tenancy and become tenants in common.

Examining Tenancy by the Entirety

A *tenancy by the entirety* is essentially a joint tenancy between spouses. The practical difference between the two is that the individual spouses can't sever the tenancy by the entirety and defeat the other's right of survivorship by unilaterally conveying or encumbering their fractional shares.

Most states don't recognize the tenancy by the entirety anymore, but a substantial number still do. The following sections explore the creation, characteristics, and termination of tenancies by the entirety in those states that still recognize them.

Creating a tenancy by the entirety

The states that recognize tenancy by the entirety differ in what the conveying instrument must say in order to create a tenancy by the entirety. Different courts have taken the following positions:

✔ Any conveyance to a husband and wife creates a tenancy by the entirety unless the instrument rebuts that presumption and says they are tenants in common or joint tenants.

✔ An instrument that says it conveys the property to A and B, "husband and wife," creates a presumption that they are tenants by the entirety.

✔ The statutory presumption in favor of a tenancy in common applies to a conveyance to a husband and wife just like any other conveyance. Therefore, the instrument must expressly say that it creates a tenancy by the entirety in order to overcome the presumption.

Traditionally, a tenancy by the entirety can be created only if the four unities — time, title, interest, and possession — are present, just as with a joint tenancy (see the earlier section "Satisfying the four unities"). The co-owners also must have a fifth unity: The parties must be legally married.

Therefore, as with joint tenancies, if a husband or wife owns property and wants to create a tenancy by the entirety with his or her spouse, he or she can convey the property to a straw man, who in turn conveys it to the husband and wife as tenants by the entirety. In some states, however, judicial decisions or statutes allow a spouse to create a tenancy by the entirety by a direct conveyance to the other spouse, or to both of them, despite the traditional unities requirements.

Restricting transfers by tenants by the entirety

Of course, tenants by the entirety together can sell, mortgage, or convey any other interest in their property. But unlike with tenancies in common and joint tenancies, one of the tenants by the entirety doesn't have the same freedom to transfer interests in her fractional share of the property.

The states that recognize tenancy by the entirety have different rules about what a tenant by the entirety can and can't do with her fractional share without the other party's consent:

- ✔ Most states simply prohibit either spouse from unilaterally conveying any interest in the property, voluntarily or involuntarily. Any attempt to do so is simply void. Creditors of only one spouse can't levy against property held by the entirety.

- ✔ Some states allow either spouse to sell or encumber his or her half interest in the property during their joint lifetimes. A spouse can also sell or encumber his or her right of survivorship if he or she outlives the other. Creditors of one spouse can levy against his or her fractional share to satisfy the debt. Of course, if the other spouse is the survivor, then the survivor will own the property entirely and the interest of the deceased spouse's grantee or creditor ends.

- ✔ Some states prohibit any conveyance or levy against the property during the joint lifetimes of the spouses. But either spouse may convey his or her right of survivorship, and creditors may levy against it.

- ✔ Some states allow the tenants by the entirety to unilaterally convey their fractional interests during their lifetime or in their rights of survivorship, but the states prohibit creditors of one spouse from levying against individual fractional shares generally or when the property is the person's principal residence.

Although states vary in the extent to which a tenant by the entirety can transfer interests in her fractional share without the other's consent, none of them allow a tenant by the entirety to impair the other's rights. With a joint tenancy, a joint tenant can sever the relationship and end the right of survivorship. But with a tenancy by the entirety, one spouse's transfer or encumbrance won't defeat the other spouse's right of survivorship.

Till death do us part? Terminating a tenancy by the entirety

A tenancy by the entirety ends when one of the spouses dies. As with a joint tenancy, the other spouse simply owns the entire property at that point; she doesn't inherit the share from the deceased spouse. Of course, in those states that allow tenants by the entirety to sell or encumber the right of survivorship, the surviving spouse may have previously lost or given away her right to possess the property upon the death of her spouse.

Even though a tenancy by the entirety can't be severed in the same way a joint tenancy can be, it can be terminated before the death of a spouse. The following events also terminate a tenancy by the entirety:

- ✔ **Divorce:** Unless the court or an enforceable premarital agreement says otherwise, a final divorce decree generally ends the tenancy by the entirety and changes it to a tenancy in common. If the parties aren't spouses anymore, they can't be tenants by the entirety. But the court or an agreement may preserve the right of survivorship.

- ✔ **Release:** One of the spouses can terminate the tenancy by the entirety by releasing his or her interest to the other.

- ✔ **Agreement:** Although one spouse can't sever the tenancy by the entirety, the spouses together can agree to do so.

- ✔ **Conveyance:** Of course, if the spouses jointly convey the property to someone else, the tenancy by the entirety ends.

Governing the Relationship among Cotenants

Cotenants are the closest of neighbors. They have the right to possess and use the very same property at the very same time. Obviously, conflicts may arise regarding how they use the property, expenses in maintaining the property, and so on. The following sections highlight the rules governing the relationship among cotenants.

Using the concurrently owned property

Each cotenant has undivided ownership of the whole property. She can use and enjoy the property just as any other property owner can. Undivided ownership of the whole may seem confusing, even impossible. If one cotenant wants to use the land to grow peanuts and another cotenant wants to use the land to raise elephants, it may be impossible for both to use and enjoy the property as they wish. If it is, they have to either reach an agreement or end the cotenancy by partition, as I explain later in "Breaking Up: Terminating Concurrent Ownership by Partition."

As long as the cotenancy lasts, each cotenant can use the whole property. That means no cotenant can exclude another cotenant from doing the same. Such exclusion is commonly referred to as an *ouster*. An ouster occurs in the following situations:

- ✔ A cotenant demands to share possession and the cotenant in possession refuses or physically excludes her.

- ✔ A cotenant makes permanent additions that prevent the other cotenants from using the land. However, some authorities say that making improvements generally doesn't oust other cotenants.

- ✔ A cotenant purports to sell the entire ownership of the property to someone else, and that buyer takes sole possession.

- ✔ A cotenant is the only one in possession and she somehow gives notice to the other cotenants that she asserts the right to sole possession.

- ✔ A cotenant receives all the income and profits from the land and denies the other cotenants' right to share in the profits.

- ✔ A cotenant asserts exclusive title and denies the other cotenants' title in court pleadings.

An ousted cotenant has the right to a judicial order that enjoins the ouster and awards money damages. Damages are the value of the cotenant's share of possession, generally the cotenant's fractional share of the profits from the land or the reasonable value of the ousting cotenant's use of the land.

Ordinarily, possession by one cotenant isn't inconsistent with the rights of other cotenants. But if a possessing cotenant ousts the others, denying the others' rights to possess, then her possession is hostile and adverse to the rights of the ousted cotenants. In that case, the cotenant in possession may acquire exclusive title to the property if her possession continues openly and without interruption for the adverse possession period. The ousted cotenants therefore must take some action to regain possession within that time or lose the right to do so. (See Chapter 14 for more on adverse possession.)

Paying expenses

Cotenants share the costs of ownership as well as the burdens of ownership. However, one cotenant doesn't have to share expenses that she doesn't choose to make or agree to share. The following sections talk about cotenants' responsibilities regarding expenses.

Payments to preserve title

Paying a mortgage loan and property taxes may be necessary to preserve title to the property. If the cotenants' collective title is mortgaged, default on the mortgage loan may result in the property being sold in foreclosure. Likewise, if the owners don't pay property taxes, the property may be sold in a tax sale to satisfy the unpaid tax debt.

Sometimes owners are personally liable for payment of a mortgage loan and property taxes. That is, even if the property is sold to satisfy the unpaid debt, they remain personally liable to pay any remaining debt. In that case, any cotenant who pays more than her fractional share of the mortgage or property taxes may recover the other cotenants' shares in a judicial action for contribution.

If the owners aren't personally liable for such payments, a cotenant can't sue the others for contribution of their fractional shares. However, in an action for accounting among the cotenants or in a partition action, a cotenant who pays more than her fractional share is entitled to a credit for the other cotenants' fractional shares that she paid. (See the later section "Fair shares: Accounting among cotenants" for details.)

The rule is different, however, if the cotenant has sole possession of the property. If she ousted the other cotenants, she's entitled to a credit for her excess mortgage and tax payments only if the other cotenants sue to recover the property and damages for her exclusive use of the property. Even if she didn't oust the other cotenants, she's entitled to recover only the amount by which her mortgage and tax payments exceed the reasonable rental value of her exclusive use of the property.

An individual cotenant may mortgage her undivided fractional share, and of course other cotenants wouldn't have any obligation to contribute to those payments. If the mortgagee forecloses on such a mortgage, it would have the right to sell only the cotenant's undivided fractional share, and the buyer at the foreclosure sale would simply take the defaulting cotenant's place as a tenant in common with the other cotenants.

Necessary repairs

A cotenant who pays more than her fractional share of necessary repairs to the property is entitled to a credit for her excess payments in an action for accounting among the cotenants or in a partition action. She also may recover the other cotenants' shares of such expenses in an independent action for contribution if the cotenants have agreed to share such expenses or, most courts say, if she gives notice to the other cotenants before making the necessary repairs.

Improvements

A cotenant can't make other cotenants contribute to improvements of the property. Of course, cotenants may agree to share the cost of an improvement, and a cotenant can enforce that agreement against the others. But in the absence of such an agreement, the other cotenants don't have to share the cost of improvements.

However, if a cotenant pays for such improvements, the improvements may increase the amount of rent or profit received from the property. And if the property is sold, it may be sold for a higher price because of the improvements. In that case, the cotenant who paid for the improvements is entitled in an accounting or partition action to the extra rents or sale proceeds resulting from the improvements.

Renting the property

Each cotenant has the right to use and enjoy the entire property, so in almost all states, a cotenant doesn't have to pay rent to the other cotenants even if she's the only one of the cotenants who uses it. However, a cotenant may be liable for the rental value of her use in the following situations:

- ✔ The parties agree that one cotenant will exclusively possess and pay rent to the other cotenants.

- ✔ The cotenant exclusively possesses the property because she's ousted the others. In that case, she's liable for the rental value of her own possession.

- ✔ A cotenant seeks contribution to expenses from nonpossessing cotenants, in which case they may offset their fractional share of the possessing cotenant's rental value against their share of the expenses.

A cotenant also may lease the property to someone else. Each cotenant has the right to use the property, so each has the right to lease that right to others without the other cotenants joining in the lease. Of course, she can lease only what she owns, so her tenant still has only an undivided interest in the whole and can't exclude the other cotenants from the property.

When a cotenant leases the property to a third party, she must share the rents she receives with the other cotenants according to their fractional shares, even though they aren't parties to the lease. This rule is often referred to as the *Statute of Anne,* an 18th-century English statute that originated this rule. Some states apply this principle more broadly to any income that a cotenant gets from the property, such as income from extracting minerals from the property.

Acquiring interests in the property

Even though a cotenant has no duty to do so, a cotenant may acquire an adverse title or interest in the property from a third party. For example, she may buy a mortgage or buy the property at a tax sale or even buy a disputed claim of superior title. In general, if she acquires such an adverse interest, she can't do so for just herself; she must acquire the interest on behalf of all the cotenants. The other cotenants must contribute their fractional share of the purchase price within a reasonable time after receiving notice of the purchase. If they don't, they lose their right to share ownership of the acquired interest.

This rule regarding acquiring interests in the property doesn't apply in the following situations:

- **Lack of a fiduciary relationship:** This rule is based on a fiduciary relationship between cotenants who acquire their interests at the same time. So if the parties didn't acquire their interests at the same time, or if they don't have a valid cotenancy for any reason, they don't have such a fiduciary relationship and any of them can purchase the title individually.

- **Interests acquired when the cotenancy didn't exist:** Any title or interest one acquires before or after the existence of a tenancy in common belongs to her individually.

- **Interests purchased from another cotenant:** The rule doesn't apply to purchases of interests from one of the cotenants rather than a third party, because such a purchase obviously wouldn't be for the benefit of all the cotenants.

- **Interests that aren't adverse to the cotenants' title:** A cotenant can acquire for herself any interest in the property that isn't adverse to the cotenants' title. For example, if the cotenants own a life estate in common, one of the cotenants can buy the remainder or reversion for herself individually. That future interest isn't part of the estate that the cotenants share.

Avoiding waste

A cotenant has a duty to her cotenants not to commit waste. *Waste* essentially means impairing the value of the property in which others have an interest. Following are some examples of waste by a cotenant:

- Damaging the property beyond ordinary wear and tear is waste.

- A tenant in possession commits waste if she doesn't make repairs necessary to prevent further deterioration, although she doesn't have to restore the property to its original condition or better.

- Some cases hold that new mineral extractions are waste.

- Some cases hold that removing timber is waste or that removing timber for profit or beyond one's proportional share is waste.

A cotenant who commits waste is liable for damages to the other cotenants. If the waste impairs the market value, the cotenants can recover their fractional share of the lost value. If the waste is extracting profit by mining or removing timber, damages may be only the other cotenants' fractional share of the net profits.

Breaking Up: Terminating Concurrent Ownership by Partition

Cotenants can end their concurrent ownership by dividing the property into individually owned parcels or by selling the property and dividing the proceeds according to their fractional shares. Dividing up the property or its value in this way is called *partition*.

The parties may voluntarily agree to partition, either by physically dividing the property or by selling the property and dividing the proceeds. But even if the parties don't agree, any cotenant can get an order from a court ordering partition of her interest. Such a partition by lawsuit is often called an *involuntary partition,* although of course at least one cotenant wants to partition and therefore starts the process; if no cotenant wants to partition, the court never has occasion to order partition.

The following sections offer insight into both voluntary and involuntary partition. They also cover ways partition may be restrained and the final accounting that accompanies partition.

Partitioning voluntarily: Deciding to split property or proceeds

The cotenants may voluntarily partition the property by agreement. They can divide the property into individually owned parcels by giving each other deeds conveying their interests in the parcels that they won't have an interest in anymore.

In fact, even if they don't give each other written deeds, the cotenants' oral agreement to divide up the land will likely be enforceable if they take possession and make improvements on their individual parcels or otherwise detrimentally rely on the oral agreement. Chapter 15 talks about such exceptions to the statute of frauds.

Often the cotenants can't divide the property into individually owned parcels that are equal in value or that correspond to their respective fractional cotenancy shares. But cotenants receiving more valuable parcels can pay money to those receiving less valuable parcels to make the values correspond to their fractional shares. Such payments may be called *owelty,* at least by those who like to make lawyer sounds.

Cotenants also can voluntarily partition the property by sale, of course. They can simply join together in selling the property and then divide the proceeds as they agree.

Compelling partition

If the parties don't agree to partition, or if they don't agree on how to partition, any tenant in common or joint tenant is entitled to a judicial order compelling partition, unless the cotenancy is subject to a valid restraint on partition. A tenant by the entirety can't partition, but she can divorce. That's the only way a tenant by the entirety can compel "partition" if the spouses don't agree.

A *partition action* is a lawsuit by a cotenant against the rest of the cotenants. The lawsuit must name not just the other cotenants but also any other parties whose interests will be affected by the partition. Such parties may include the following:

- ✔ **A person who has an executory contract to purchase the interest of a cotenant:** Even though such a purchaser doesn't own the cotenant's interest yet, the purchaser owns equitable title to that interest. (See Chapter 15 for details.)

- ✔ **A mortgagee of a cotenant's interest:** However, a mortgagee of the entire property, not just one of the cotenants' fractional shares, doesn't have to be included because the partition won't affect the mortgagee's interest.

- ✔ **A lessee of one cotenant:** After partition, the lessee will only have the right to possess the property individually owned by her lessor. The rest of the cotenants aren't bound by the lease.

Court orders: Dividing the property physically or by sale

The court in a partition action may either order the property to be divided physically among the cotenants or sold and the proceeds divided among the cotenants. In either case, the court must determine each cotenant's fractional share in the process of partitioning the property.

Physical division

State statutes governing the partition remedy vary, but all of them favor physical division rather than sale. That's because courts don't want to take away anyone's property if they can avoid it, regardless of whether the person receives its value in money. State statutes may require a court to partition by physical division unless some or all of the following are true:

- ✔ Physically dividing the property is impracticable or inconvenient or would significantly impair its value.
- ✔ A partition by sale would better promote the parties' interests.
- ✔ A partition by sale wouldn't prejudice or harm any of the opposing cotenants' interests.

In general, some courts order a physical division as long as it's feasible, whereas others consider the balance of benefits and harms to the cotenants. The harm of taking away someone's property may be a greater concern than economic loss, however. So even if physical division would make the property worth less than if the entire property were kept intact, some courts may order the property physically divided if one cotenant really wants to keep her property, even for sentimental and emotional reasons, and couldn't afford to buy the entire property if it were partitioned by sale.

Physical division may be impossible or inconvenient for various reasons, such as the following:

- ✔ The property has a house or other building on it, and the land isn't big enough to divide into parcels of equal value. The smaller parcel with the building will still be more valuable than the other parcels.
- ✔ The resulting parcels would be too small to be useable and marketable.
- ✔ Physical division would substantially impair the value of the property.

Even if the court can't physically divide the property into individually owned parcels that exactly correspond to the parties' fractional shares, the court can adjust the values received by requiring some cotenants to pay owelty to other cotenants. But if the values are too far away from being equal, the court will simply order the property to be sold.

If one cotenant has improved the property in some way, a court in a physical partition action will award the improved portion to that cotenant if possible. Because the resulting difference in market value resulted from the cotenant's own investment, the court doesn't have to consider that difference in value in equitably dividing up the property among the cotenants.

The court typically appoints commissioners to inspect the property and determine how the property can be physically divided. The commissioners also may determine the value of the property as a whole and as divided to help determine whether physical division will impair the parties' interests.

Partitioning future interests

Cotenants who share the present right to possess have the right to bring a partition action. Co-owners of leased property also may partition the reversion. Co-owners of other future interests can seek judicial partition only if a state statute authorizes it. Some states have statutes that allow co-owners of indefeasibly vested remainders to partition. (Remainders are the future interests that follow life estates; see Chapter 9 for details.)

The partition of a future interest can't change the rights of the owner of the present possessory estate. So the partition action only partitions the property prospectively for the owners of the future interest. Of course, the owner or owners of the present estate could agree to participate in the partition.

Division by sale

If the court decides that physical division is impossible or inequitable, the court may order that the cotenant wanting to keep the property may purchase the interests of the other cotenants. Some statutes direct that if property is to be partitioned by sale, any cotenant may choose to purchase the property at a value determined by an appraisal process described in the statute. If there are multiple cotenants who want to buy the property, a court may even order a private auction sale among the cotenants.

Otherwise, the court will order a public sale. The statute may specify the sale procedure or the court may have discretion. But either way the usual process, and in some states the only permitted process, is to sell the property at public auction to the high bidder. In some states commissioners will first appraise the property to determine a minimum price. The cotenants may bid at the auction along with anyone else who wants to bid. The proceeds then will be divided among the cotenants according to their fractional shares.

Fair shares: Accounting among cotenants

The partition action includes a final accounting among the cotenants to determine who owes how much money to whom. The accounting may include charges and credits for the following:

- Charges for rents and profits received that were not previously distributed according to the cotenants' fractional shares

- Charges for the rental value of a cotenant's exclusive possession if she has ousted the others

- Credits for payments for necessary repairs beyond one's fractional share

    ✔ Credits for mortgage and tax payments beyond one's fractional share

    ✔ Credits for insurance payments beyond one's fractional share

    ✔ Credits for the increased value of the property resulting from improvements made by a cotenant

If the property is divided physically, a cotenant who has a net credit has a lien against the other partitioned parcels for the money the other former cotenants owe her as determined by the final accounting. If the property is partitioned by sale, the distribution of sale proceeds will simply be adjusted to include the charges and credits from the final accounting.

Restraining partition

The creator of a cotenancy may restrict the cotenants' right to judicial partition for a reasonable time. So may the cotenants themselves.

For example, the owner of property may validly devise it to her children as tenants in common and include a disabling restraint that prohibits any of them from partitioning the property during their lifetimes. Similarly, state condominium statutes restrain partition by condominium owners, prohibiting individual owners from seeking judicial partition of the common areas, which condominium owners hold as tenants in common.

A restraint on the right to partition is a restraint on alienation, so it may be void and unenforceable unless for a reasonable purpose and appropriately limited in time and scope (see Chapter 9 for details). Courts have sustained restraints on the right to partition for a limited time. Presumably the rule against perpetuities period — 21 years beyond the lives of those alive at the time of the conveyance — would be as long a time as a court would find reasonable.

Creating and Owning Condominiums

A *condominium* is a form of ownership in which people individually own some parts and collectively own other parts of the property. All states have statutes enabling the creation of condominiums. The following sections describe the basic features of condominium ownership.

Creating a condominium

State statutes specify the process for creating a condominium. The process generally requires a condominium developer to publicly record the following:

✔ **Declaration of condominium:** This document, which must comply with the state statute's requirements, creates the condominium, defining the units and common areas and specifying the rights and duties of the developer, the unit owners, and a *condominium association,* an entity run by a board of elected unit owners.

✔ **A map of the project:** This map identifies the units and common areas.

✔ **Articles of incorporation, master deed, and/or bylaws:** Among other things, these documents create the condominium association, describe its powers, and specify rules regulating the use and ownership of condominium units and common areas, consistent with the state statute.

✔ **A declaration of covenants that run with the land:** See Chapter 5 for details on covenants.

All the unit owners are members of the condominium association. A board of elected unit owners runs the association and has the authority to take some actions by their own vote. Other decisions require a majority or larger vote of all unit owners.

Owning individual units

A condominium owner individually owns a *unit.* A unit may include the interior space and walls of an individual apartment or even just the space inside the walls. Condominium statutes enable the ownership of such space — even though it may be 20 floors off the ground and not touch the surface of the Earth at all — just as a person can own a plot of land.

The condominium owner thus has the exclusive right to possess and use her individual unit, like any other property owner. However, the unit owner's right to use is limited in various ways for the benefit of other unit owners, and she has duties to the other owners. Condominium bylaws specify rules that bind all condominium owners. Here are some common restrictions on condominium owners:

✔ The unit owner must keep her unit in good repair.

✔ Only a certain number of people may reside in the unit.

✔ Only people of a certain age may reside in the unit. Such restrictions can be a reasonable way to provide a certain type of residential setting for certain groups of people.

✔ Unit owners can't make changes to their units without approval by the condominium association.

✔ Unit owners can't lease their units without prior approval by the condominium association.

✔ Owners can't do certain things in their units, such as operate a day care center, keep pets, or make loud noises at night.

Condominium bylaws also may restrict the freedom to transfer units in various ways to ensure that new owners are good and responsible neighbors. Existing owners may have a *right of first refusal,* the first right to choose to purchase a unit from a selling owner before she can sell to someone else.

Owning common areas

Condominium owners also share undivided ownership of *common areas* as tenants in common. Common areas include everything on the condominium property that isn't individually owned, such as the following:

✔ Exterior walls and roofs

✔ Hallways, lobbies, stairways, and elevators

✔ Common amenities for condominium owners, such as clubhouses, tennis courts, and pools

✔ Plumbing, heating, and cooling systems

✔ Parking areas and garages

Ownership of each condominium unit comes with ownership of an undivided interest in the common areas. The two can't be separated.

Managing common areas

The condominium association generally has the power to manage the common areas on behalf of the unit owners. The association may maintain, repair, and improve the common areas. Within the scope of the authority granted to the association, it can adopt reasonable rules governing the use of the common areas as well as governing the use of individual units.

The association may require individual unit owners to pay *assessments,* their proportional share of common expenses, such as maintenance of the common areas and security services. Even though unit owners have an undivided interest in the common areas, the association may even impose fees for using particular common areas, such as recreational facilities, as a way to pay expenses related to the common area. Unit owners may be personally liable to pay assessments. If they don't pay the assessments, the association may have a lien against their individual units, allowing it to sell the property to satisfy the unpaid assessments.

Chapter 11

Owning Property in Marriage

Spouses have a special and unique interest in shaping their mutual rights in property. They can co-own property in any of the concurrent estates I describe in Chapter 10. Specifically, they can choose to own as *tenants in common* if they want to control property jointly during their lives but want their respective shares to be separately transferable and inheritable. They can elect to own a property as *joint tenants* if they want the surviving spouse to solely own the property. Or they can choose to own as *tenants by the entirety* if they want a right of survivorship that can't be taken away by each other or by creditors.

Spouses also can and do use the estates I describe in Chapter 9 to plan their rights in property in the future. For example, a wife's will may give her husband a life estate in her property and then give the remainder to her kids. And maybe if she doesn't want him to remarry, she'll give him the property subject to a condition of defeasibility that he not remarry. Or she may be unhappy with her spouse and not give him anything at all.

The traditional common law recognized that sometimes people didn't provide for their spouses at death. So over time, the law has taken different approaches to ensuring that spouses are treated fairly. This chapter talks about such rules that are relevant in the states today.

Of course, a marriage may end before the spouses' lives end. The parties can agree in advance about how they'll own property during their marriage and how it will be distributed upon divorce. But the law also regulates the distribution of property when parties divorce. This chapter examines these legal issues as well.

Protecting the Surviving Spouse

Many people's wills provide generously for their surviving spouses, but others don't. The law has traditionally protected the interests of surviving spouses to make sure they get some share of their deceased partners' property even if the deceased didn't provide for them.

In the past, the common law protected the interest of surviving spouses by means of two basic rules:

- ✔ **Curtesy:** A husband who had children with his wife immediately obtained a life estate in all the real property in which his wife held a freehold estate and which was inheritable by their children.

- ✔ **Dower:** A wife who survived a husband wasn't an heir, but she was entitled to a life estate in one-third of any real property in which her husband owned a freehold estate during their marriage, even if he sold it during his lifetime or excluded her from his will. She could agree on the one-third division with the heir or get a court order specifying the third in which she received her dower interest.

Sometimes these rules are referred to as *legal life estates* because they're life estates that the law, rather than the owner, creates. Modern state statutes have changed or abolished these rules, so you don't need to know the details of how curtesy and dower used to work. However, a few states still recognize a limited right of either spouse to dower in the property the deceased spouse owned at death, often as an alternative to the statutory options that are generally more favorable.

Nowadays, most state statutes accomplish a similar purpose by giving surviving spouses the right to take a share of the deceased spouse's estate, as follows:

- ✔ In all states, if a spouse dies without a will, the surviving spouse is now an heir and is typically entitled to half of the estate if the couple didn't have kids or one-third if they did.

- ✔ If a spouse dies with a will, the surviving spouse can take whatever the will gave her, or she can disregard the will and choose to take a *statutory* or *forced share* of the estate, which is usually the same share as if there were no will.

Yours, Mine, and Ours: Community Property Systems

Some states have a statutory system of marital property called community property. In community property systems, spouses own equal shares in all the property they acquire during their marriage; they can also own property separately. The following sections reveal how property is classified as community or separate and describe the parties' rights with respect to community property.

Distinguishing separate property from community property

Any property that's acquired by either spouse during the marriage and that's not shown to be separate is *community property.* If property is separate, spouses generally own it individually as if they weren't even married — they can use it and transfer it as they wish. Separate property includes the following:

- Property that either spouse owned before the marriage

- Property that either spouse receives individually during the marriage by gift, inheritance, or will; such property, which may be called *lucrative property,* is considered separate because it isn't acquired by the efforts of the married partners

- Property that is exchanged for or somehow takes the place of separately owned property

- Ownership shares in property that the spouses own as tenants in common or joint tenants with each other

- Property that either of the spouses earns if they're living separate and apart

- Income from separately owned property, such as rents and profits, except to the extent that those profits result from the parties' labors. (In a few states, however, all income from separate property or community property is community property unless otherwise agreed.) If separate property has increased in value due to the marriage partners' labors, the increase in value is community property

✓ In most community property states, personal injury damages for individual injuries, such as pain and loss of body parts; however, personal injury awards for loss of earnings and expenses are community property

Spouses may convert or *transmute* property from separate into community or community into separate. They may do so by a written document that complies with the requirements for conveying property.

Transferring and dividing property

Each spouse can transfer his or her separate property freely. Each spouse also has an equal and full right to manage and transfer community property. However, community property statutes generally require that both spouses join in certain kinds of transactions, such as real estate transfers and transfers of household necessities.

The spouses may have separate liabilities as well as community liabilities. Creditors who hold community debts may obtain legal satisfaction from both community property and the separate property of the spouse who incurred the debt. However, the creditor may be required to use up all the community property before going after separate property. Creditors who hold separate debts may obtain satisfaction from the debtor spouse's separate property, but in some cases, they also may reach community property.

Unlike property held in tenancy in common or in joint tenancy (which I cover in Chapter 10), community property can't be partitioned during marriage. But, of course, the spouses' property must be divided when the marriage ends, whether by divorce or death. The following sections explain how it's divided up.

Transferring marital property when one spouse dies

The death of a spouse dissolves the marriage. The distribution of the deceased spouse's property differs for separate and community property, as follows:

✓ **Separate property:** The deceased spouse can dispose of her separate property by will however she chooses. Any separate property that she doesn't dispose of by will generally passes by intestate succession just like any other property.

✓ **Community property:** Each spouse can give half of the community property by will to whomever he or she chooses. But if a spouse dies *intestate* (without a will), the statutes vary in how much of the community property the surviving spouse gets. In some states, the surviving spouse gets the deceased spouse's entire half-share of the community property.

Dividing marital property when the spouses divorce

When spouses divorce, the distribution of their property differs for separate and community property, as follows:

- ✔ **Separate property:** In some of the states, separate property must be distributed to its owner. But in others, the court can award alimony or support out of separate property, and it can distribute separate property between the spouses equitably and not necessarily just to the owner.

- ✔ **Community property:** Some states require community property to be distributed equally between the divorcing spouses. Others don't require equality but instead allow the court to distribute the community property as the court decides is fair under all the circumstances.

Protecting Homesteads

All but a few states, by statute or constitution, protect homesteads from creditors to some extent. In this context, a *homestead* is a family residence. You don't have to be married to have homestead protection, so this isn't just a marital property issue. But homestead protections are related to marital property because states adopted homestead laws to protect families by preserving a place for the family to live even if the head of the family gets in financial trouble, and thereby to reduce the chances that the state will bear the burden of caring for the family. In some states, one can claim homestead protection only if she is the head of a family and a married couple shares homestead protection rather than having separate homestead protection.

Homestead statutes protect homesteads by protecting a certain value or size of homestead from forced sales by creditors. When a person owes money to others, creditors normally can recover the debts by obtaining a judgment, which gives them a judgment lien against the debtor's real property in the jurisdiction. The creditor can then *execute* the lien with a lawsuit that forcibly sells the property of the debtor at auction to the highest bidder. The creditor can then apply the proceeds of the sale to the debt owed.

In most states, homestead laws exempt a certain amount of value of the homestead from creditor actions. But some states instead protect a certain maximum size of homestead, regardless of value. Still others include both a value limitation and a size limitation. In any case, the homestead laws don't prevent execution sales of homesteads; any excess value or area may still be sold to satisfy debts.

For example, the homestead law may specify a $10,000 homestead exemption, but a judgment creditor could still execute a judgment lien against the homestead despite the homestead statute. The debtor would get to keep the first $10,000 from the sale of the property, but the rest would be available to satisfy her debts.

Similarly, the homestead law may specify a 1/2 acre maximum size of homestead but not specify a value. Under such a statute, a judgment creditor may execute a judgment lien against any land beyond half an acre if it's severable from the residence.

Nowadays, the statutes that specify a value of the exemption typically don't protect nearly enough value to prevent a homestead from forced sale to satisfy unpaid debts. The homestead exemption amounts range from a few thousand dollars up to $200,000. So today's homestead laws often just protect a certain amount of value for the homeowner.

A family can have only one homestead, and it must be an actual residence. Some states even require the owner to record a written declaration identifying a homestead.

The homestead exemption doesn't protect the owner from creditors who have mortgages securing loans used to purchase or improve the homestead. So a homeowner who defaults on a mortgage loan used to purchase the home won't have any homestead protection against the mortgagee. But generally, if a homeowner is married, both spouses must sign the document creating the mortgage or else the homestead protection still applies.

Homestead protection extends to a surviving spouse. In some states, even if the deceased spouse separately owned the homestead, and even if the deceased spouse gave the homestead to someone else by will, the surviving spouse has the right to continue living in the homestead if she wants to.

Dividing Property upon Divorce

When married partners divorce, they must somehow divide their property between them. They may do so by agreement with each other, of course. But if the divorcing spouses can't agree, a court must decide how to distribute the property. Community property states have their own way of distributing property upon a divorce. (See the earlier section "Yours, Mine, and Ours: Community Property Systems" for details.) This section talks about how the rest of the states divide property upon divorce.

The court's job is to divide the property fairly between the parties. A marriage is similar to a partnership. Each of the spouses contributes to the partnership in different ways: managing the household, earning money, caring for kids, and so on. The general principle that guides property distribution is that the court should divide up the property in a way that reflects the parties' relative contributions to the marriage and the parties' property.

Courts generally try to divide ownership of property so that the divorcing spouses don't have continuing property relationships and the parties have a final resolution of their legal relationship.

Property division isn't directly for the purpose of providing support for a divorced spouse or for the parties' children. A court may award alimony, requiring a divorcing spouse to provide financial support to the other while living separately. A court also may award child support, requiring the noncustodial parent to pay money for the living expenses of the children. Alimony and child support are different from property division. In some states, property must be distributed without consideration of a spouse's need for support. In other states, alimony and property distribution may be considered together, and an award of alimony may influence the distribution of property.

State statutes dictate the process of distributing property upon divorce, which generally includes three steps:

1. **Classify which property is subject to distribution among the parties.**

2. **Value the marital property and then do the math.**

3. **Distribute the property fairly between the divorcing parties.**

I describe each of these steps in the following sections.

Classifying property to be distributed

Different states take different approaches to which property the court must divide between divorcing spouses. Those approaches include the following:

- ✔ In some states, all property of either spouse, whether obtained before or during marriage, is subject to equitable distribution by the court.

- ✔ Some state statutes say that all property is subject to equitable division upon divorce, save for specific exceptions, such as gifts and property received by will or inheritance.

✔ Other statutes require the court to determine whether property is
marital or nonmarital. In these states, only marital property is subject
to equitable division. In general, property acquired by the parties' joint
efforts is marital property, but the courts have broad discretion in
classifying property as marital or nonmarital. Some courts have held
that the court may distribute nonmarital property in certain situations,
such as when the parties both used it during their marriage and when
the non-owning spouse helped care for and improve the property during
the marriage.

The parties may agree by contract before or during marriage that certain
property is separate property not subject to distribution by the court.

Courts construe "property" broadly to include contract rights, intangible
interests, and other things that can be valued and divided. Some property may
even be partially separate and partially subject to distribution, such as when
separate property has become more valuable because of the joint efforts of
the married partners.

Valuing property to be distributed

After classifying property, the court generally must determine the value of
the property before deciding how to distribute it (unless, of course, the court
simply gives each of the parties a percentage interest in particular property).
To help the court determine the value of the property, the parties involved
must present evidence about the property's value. At that point, it's up to the
court to decide the best method for valuing the property and to calculate its
value.

Distributing property

When the court has identified all the property subject to distribution and
has valued it as necessary, the court must equitably distribute the property
as a whole. The court doesn't have to divide up every asset; instead, it may
award some things entirely to one party and other things to the other. The
court may award the present value of property that involves future benefits,
such as retirement payments. But if the value is too uncertain or the couple
doesn't have enough marital assets to pay the present value, the court may
just award a percentage of future payments.

Some statutes require the distribution between the spouses to be equal. Others require the distribution to be equal unless the court finds substantial reasons for distributing property unequally. Most statutes simply require an equitable distribution; however, even then some courts hold that the distribution should be equal unless the court uncovers reasons indicating that an unequal distribution is fair.

Some states have statutes that specify which factors the court may consider in deciding what distribution is fair. In other states, the courts themselves determine which factors to consider. Either way, the factors generally include the following:

- How long the marriage lasted

- Who did what to cause the divorce (although some states say this isn't ordinarily relevant to distribution of property)

- How each of the spouses contributed, both financially and nonfinancially, to the marriage and to the value of the marital property; for example, the court should consider not only the amount each person earned but also the value of managing the household and caring for children

- Actions of a spouse during the marriage that wasted or diminished the value of the marital property

- How the property was acquired and whether it was separately owned

- The relative age and health of the parties; for example, a court may award a larger share of the property to a disabled spouse

- The financial circumstances of the parties, including both their present assets and income and their ability to earn money in the future

- Tax consequences of the distribution of property, such as the tax consequences resulting from sale of marital property

- In some states, the needs of the parties and their children; in other states, such considerations are relevant only to support decisions

- Some courts take alimony and child support obligations into account, whereas others say such obligations shouldn't influence property distribution

Chapter 12

Leasing Property: Landlord-Tenant Law

In This Chapter

▶ Identifying how leases are different from licenses and easements

▶ Getting to know the types of tenancies

▶ Understanding landlords' duties to deliver and maintain the premises

▶ Examining the transfer and termination of leaseholds

*T*he leasehold may be the most common way that property ownership is divided up over time. In estates terminology, which I cover in Chapter 9, the landlord conveys a present estate, known as the *leasehold* or *term of years,* to the tenant and retains a future interest, known as a *reversion.* When the leasehold ends, the landlord has the right to take possession of the premises again.

If that's all there was to it, landlord-tenant law wouldn't need its own chapter. It would just be part of estates. But there's a lot more to it. The landlord-tenant relationship has many distinctive rules — some common law rules that developed over time to govern this unique relationship, some statutory rules that respond to various perceived deficiencies in the law, and some rules that are commonly created by contracts between landlords and tenants.

This chapter examines the types of leaseholds that you can create, the rights and duties of landlords and tenants, and the ways in which a leasehold can be transferred or terminated.

Distinguishing Leaseholds from Other Interests

A leasehold is a present estate with the present right of possession. But the lease agreement that creates the leasehold may limit the tenant's possessory rights, and the leasehold itself may not last very long at all. So sometimes determining whether a person has a leasehold or some lesser, nonpossessory interest is hard to do. The following sections distinguish such lesser interests from leaseholds.

Licensing versus leasing

A *license* is permission to use land. The owner of a theater, for example, may grant licenses to people to enter the theater to watch a performance. Landowners also routinely grant licenses to people who deliver things or make repairs on their land.

A lease differs from a license because a lessee has the right to possess and control the premises, whereas a licensee merely has the permission to use the premises. A lessee, therefore, has the right to exclude other people from the premises; a licensee does not.

Some licenses look very similar to leases. A short-term rental of a vacation home, for example, may be a lease or a license. The fundamental question is whether the owner gives the other person the right to possess and control the premises or whether the owner has retained such control. Sometimes the parties' agreement grants some possessory rights and not others, making the agreement more difficult to characterize.

No one rule distinguishes a lease from a license. Courts just consider all the facts and decide which type of interest the parties created. Here are some facts that are often significant in such cases:

- ✔ **Exclusivity:** If the grantee of the interest has the exclusive right to possess the premises during the duration of the interest, it's a lease; if the interest isn't exclusive of others, it's a license. However, in some cases, a lease may not be exclusive of the landlord in that the landlord may retain the right to enter and use the premises for certain purposes. The more the grantor of the interest has such rights to occupy and use the premises, the less likely the interest is a lease.

- ✔ **Defined space:** A lease must be for a defined space, so if the interest doesn't define the space, it's probably a license.

- ✔ **Duration of interest:** The longer the interest lasts, the more likely it is to be considered a lease. But the duration alone isn't decisive, because theoretically you could create a lease that lasts only an hour.

- ✔ **Fungibility of property:** If the interest granted isn't really in a particular property but rather is in a particular type of experience — such as seeing a show or having lodging — then it's more likely to be a license.

✔ **Associated services:** The more services that accompany the interest in the land, the more likely it is to be a license, because those provided services indicate less control of the premises. For example, if a short-term rental includes utilities, linens, household supplies, and trash removal, it's more likely to be a license than a lease.

✔ **Consideration:** Many authorities say that payment of consideration in exchange for the interest tends to indicate a lease rather than a license. However, a licensee certainly may pay consideration for a license, and a lessor can give a leasehold to a lessee for free.

Comparing easements and leases

Like licenses, easements may be similar to leases. An *easement* is basically the right to use another's land in some way, such as to drive across it for access to neighboring land. I cover easements in detail in Chapter 6.

An easement differs from a lease in that the holder of the easement isn't a possessor of the land (for more about the idea of possession, see Chapter 2). The holder of an easement doesn't have the right to exclude others or a general right to use the land; she has only the right to use the land in certain specified ways. In the case of an express easement, the right of use is described in the grant of the easement. If the easement arises by implication or prescription, the right of use is limited by the use of the land that originally led to the existence of the easement.

Creating and Differentiating the Four Types of Tenancies

Parties can create four kinds of leaseholds, or *tenancies:*

✔ Fixed-term tenancy

✔ Periodic tenancy

✔ Tenancy at will

✔ Tenancy at sufferance

The difference among these tenancies is how and when they end. The following sections describe each of these tenancies in more detail.

Fixed-term tenancy

As the name suggests, the *fixed-term tenancy* has a definite term, or duration. The agreement creating the leasehold specifies a date on which the leasehold will automatically end. Neither party has to give notice to the other party to end the leasehold; it expires on the last day specified by the lease agreement.

A fixed-term tenancy is sometimes called a *tenancy for years,* but that label is misleading because a fixed-term tenancy can be created for any definite duration, no matter how short. On the other hand, many state statutes today do specify maximum terms for leases, such as 50 or 99 years.

Because a fixed-term tenancy exists only when the parties have specified an ending date for the leasehold, it can be created only by express agreement between the landlord and the tenant. Such agreements are subject to the *statute of frauds* — state statutes that allow enforcement of certain contracts only if there's written evidence of an agreement signed by the party denying its existence. Statutes of frauds vary among the states, but typically a lease agreement is subject to the requirements of the statute of frauds if it creates a lease term longer than one year.

Periodic tenancy

A *periodic tenancy* doesn't have a definite duration. The term of this type of tenancy is the period for which the tenant agrees to pay rent periodically, whether it's daily, weekly, monthly, annually, or some other period of time. The tenancy simply continues from period to period as long as the parties want. Because it never naturally expires, the periodic tenancy ends only when one of the parties notifies the other that she wants to end the tenancy. Generally, the terminating party must give such notice one rental period in advance, or six months in advance for a year-to-year tenancy. State statutes or the parties' lease agreement may specify when notice must be given to terminate periodic tenancies.

A landlord and tenant may expressly create a periodic tenancy by contract just as they may create a fixed-term tenancy. But parties may also create a periodic tenancy without an express agreement when the tenant pays periodic rent to the landlord and the landlord accepts those payments. One situation where parties may create a periodic tenancy without an express contract is when a fixed-term tenancy ends but the tenant keeps paying rent and the landlord keeps accepting it. Another time when the parties may create this type of tenancy is when they enter into a fixed-term lease that isn't enforceable because of the statute of frauds or some other reason. As long as the tenant pays the agreed-upon rent and the landlord accepts it, they have a periodic tenancy.

Tenancy at will

A *tenancy at will* exists when the tenant has possession with consent of the landlord, but the parties don't have an agreement on the rental to be paid or the term of the lease. It therefore has no defined duration or even a periodic term. For example, if someone sold a house but continued living there with the consent of the buyer, the seller would be a tenant at will until either the parties agreed on rental payments or the seller left.

Because a tenancy at will exists only when the parties haven't agreed on rent or term, parties rarely create a tenancy at will by express agreement. This type of tenancy generally exists only temporarily while the tenant has possession with consent but the landlord and tenant are deciding what to do next. The tenancy ends whenever either party chooses to end it — the common law requires no advance notice — or takes any action inconsistent with the tenancy at will, either by creating a different type of tenancy or by terminating the tenancy altogether.

Tenancy at sufferance

The *tenancy at sufferance* isn't really a tenancy. Rather, it describes the status of a possessor of land who rightfully held possession for a time and who stays in possession of the premises after her right ends. A tenancy at sufferance may arise when a lessee remains in possession after the lease ends or when a life tenant or the owner of a fee simple defeasible estate remains in possession after the end of her freehold estate. (Flip to Chapter 9 for details on estates.)

When a tenant stays in possession after the end of her lease and becomes a tenant at sufferance, the landlord has a reasonable time to choose one of two options:

- Notify the tenant that she'll thereafter be a periodic tenant with an obligation to pay a specified rent.
- Notify the tenant that she'll be a trespasser, subject to an ejectment action by the landlord if she doesn't leave.

Possessing the Leased Premises

Like the owner of any other present estate, the tenant has the right to possess the leased premises. The lease agreement may give the landlord the right to enter the premises for certain purposes, such as to inspect or make repairs, but the landlord doesn't have the right to possess the premises during the term of the leasehold.

In a multi-unit building, the tenant's right to possess the leased premises comes with an implied right (even if it isn't expressed in the lease agreement) to use *common areas* — areas that the landlord owns but that are for the use of all tenants generally, such as parking areas, hallways, and stairs.

The tenant can use the premises in any legal ways she wants to, unless the lease agreement limits the tenant's use. Such contractual limitations on the tenant's use are real covenants, which I tell you about in Chapter 5. The tenant doesn't generally have a duty to possess and use the land, just a right — although the parties can agree otherwise in their lease. In some commercial leases, for example, the tenant may covenant to occupy the premises and operate her business there in good faith.

The following sections examine the landlord's duties to ensure the tenant can enjoy possession during the lease term.

Delivering possession to the tenant

The landlord of course promises to give the tenant the legal right of possession when the leasehold begins. If the landlord doesn't have the legal right of possession and therefore can't convey it to the tenant at the beginning of the leasehold, the landlord has breached the lease.

But even if the tenant has the legal right to possess the premises, someone else, such as a former tenant, may still possess the premises, thus preventing the new tenant from physically entering into possession at the start of the leasehold.

The landlord usually has a duty to eject such a possessor so that the property is open for the tenant to take actual possession when the leasehold begins. Such a duty may come from one of three sources:

- ✔ The lease agreement may include an express promise that the landlord will deliver actual, physical possession at the start of the lease term.

- ✔ Statutes in a number of states declare that a landlord has a duty to deliver physical possession of the premises at the beginning of the lease term.

- ✔ Even in the absence of an express agreement or a state statute, most courts hold that the landlord has an implied duty to deliver physical possession of the premises at the start of the lease term. These courts reason that physical possession is the essential reason for the lease agreement and that the landlord is in a better position than the tenant to eject trespassers before the commencement of the tenant's lease term. (A minority of courts disagree, holding that the landlord isn't responsible for the trespass of a third party and that the tenant herself can bring an ejectment action to regain possession.)

Covenanting not to disturb the tenant's quiet enjoyment

The landlord also covenants that neither he nor anyone else with a superior right to possession will disturb the tenant's quiet enjoyment of the premises during the term of the leasehold. Simply entering into a lease implies this covenant, aptly called the *covenant of quiet enjoyment,* even if the lease agreement doesn't express it.

The covenant of quiet enjoyment isn't a promise to take action against trespassers. Rather, it's merely a promise that the landlord or a superior titleholder won't interfere with the tenant's possession. The tenant has to deal with trespassers herself. Furthermore, this covenant isn't a promise that no one has a superior title; rather, it's a promise that no such person, or the landlord himself, will interfere with the tenant's possession of the premises. Therefore, the covenant is breached only when such a person interferes with the tenant's possession. Such an interference is commonly called an *eviction.*

Here are some ways an eviction may occur:

- ✔ The landlord wrongly physically excludes the tenant from some or all of the leased premises.

- ✔ A prior tenant still has the right to possession, either because her lease term hasn't ended or she had a valid right to extend the lease term, and she lawfully prevents the tenant from possessing the premises.

- ✔ A mortgagee, whose mortgage encumbered the premises before the tenant leased them, forecloses the mortgage upon default and sells the premises at a foreclosure sale. When the foreclosure buyer takes possession and excludes the tenant, the landlord has breached the covenant of quiet enjoyment.

If an eviction does occur and the landlord breaches the covenant of quiet enjoyment, the tenant's remedies include the following:

- ✔ **Damages:** The tenant may recover consequential damages that result from the breach, such as relocation expenses, as well as the difference in value between the property she was promised and the property she actually received.

- ✔ **Withholding rent:** The tenant's duty to pay rent is conditioned upon the landlord's providing the promised quiet enjoyment of the premises. So if the landlord breaches the covenant of quiet enjoyment, the tenant has no duty to pay rent.

- ✔ **Termination of the lease:** The tenant can terminate the lease agreement altogether.

Maintaining the Leased Premises

Both parties have an interest in maintaining the leased premises. The tenant, of course, wants the premises to be in good condition during the term of the leasehold so that she can fully use and enjoy the property. Even though the landlord doesn't have the right of possession during the lease term, he'll eventually regain possession and will want the premises to be in good condition for future use.

The following sections clarify the landlord's and the tenant's responsibilities when it comes to maintaining the leased premises.

Understanding common law duties

Under traditional common law, the landlord generally has no duties to deliver the premises in a certain condition or to maintain the premises during the term of the lease. The landlord can't fraudulently misrepresent a material condition of the premises or actively conceal a defect from the tenant before entering into the lease, but he has no duty to provide premises of a certain quality. The tenant can inspect the premises before entering into the lease and decide whether she wants to lease them; if she does, she takes the property as it is.

The tenant, on the other hand, does have a common law duty not to commit waste. Just as other owners of present estates owe the duty to future interest holders not to commit waste, a tenant owes a duty to the landlord, who owns a reversion, not to commit waste. You can read about waste in more detail in Chapter 9, but it basically means the tenant has a duty not to damage the premises *(voluntary waste)* and not to permit damage to the premises *(permissive waste)*. The tenant, therefore, has a common law duty to make repairs that are necessary to prevent further damage to the premises, such as repairing a roof or otherwise keeping the building protected from the elements.

Contracting to maintain the premises

Because both parties have an interest in maintaining the premises but the common law imposes no obligation on the landlord and only a relatively narrow obligation on the tenant, landlords and tenants commonly contract to allocate maintenance duties between them.

If the landlord agrees by contract to make repairs, the tenant must notify the landlord of the need for such repairs and give him a reasonable time to make the repairs. In some leases, the tenant may agree to make some repairs, while the landlord agrees to make other repairs. But if such contract clauses are unclear, a court must interpret the scope of the parties' respective duties to repair. In interpreting repair clauses, a court may consider not just the language of the lease itself but also what the parties likely intended. A court is less likely to require a tenant to make repairs if

✔ The cost of the repair is large compared to the rental payments.

✔ The lease term is shorter, and therefore much of the repair's value will be enjoyed by the landlord.

✔ The repair is structural and unrelated to the tenant's specific use of the premises.

✔ The parties didn't contemplate the particular type of repair when they entered into the lease.

Taking a look at constructive eviction

If the landlord breaches contractual maintenance and repair duties, he'll be liable for damages to the tenant. Traditionally, the landlord's and tenant's covenants are independent, meaning that the landlord's breach of a repair covenant doesn't excuse the tenant's covenant to pay rent. Consequently, the tenant's only remedy for such a breach is damages.

However, over time courts developed the rule that the tenant's obligation to pay rent is conditioned on the landlord's performing his covenant of quiet enjoyment. If the landlord physically prevents the tenant from enjoying the premises, the tenant is not only entitled to damages but also excused from paying rent and can terminate the lease.

Courts have come to apply the same reasoning to breach of a landlord's contractual duty to maintain and repair the leased premises. If the landlord's breach significantly interferes with the tenant's quiet enjoyment of the premises, the landlord may have breached the covenant of quiet enjoyment, thereby entitling the tenant to withhold rent and terminate the lease, not just recover damages. Such a breach is called a *constructive eviction*.

To establish that the landlord has committed a constructive eviction, the tenant must prove the following:

✔ **Wrongful act by the landlord:** The tenant must prove that the landlord has breached a duty to the tenant. The covenant of quiet enjoyment and the constructive eviction doctrine themselves don't impose obligations on the landlord to maintain and repair the premises. So the tenant can't claim a breach of the covenant simply because the property is in bad shape; it has to somehow be the landlord's fault.

The tenant must identify some wrongful act by the landlord, whether because it breaches a contractual agreement, a tort duty, or even a statute. For example:

- The landlord has breached a lease covenant to maintain and repair the leased premises.

- The landlord has breached a lease covenant to provide utilities or other services to the leased premises.

- The landlord has not reasonably maintained the common areas.

- The landlord has tortiously interfered with the tenant's enjoyment of the premises, such as by maintaining a nuisance.

- The landlord has not taken action to prevent interference by other tenants, when such interference is in common areas or violates the tenants' leases. Some courts disagree, however, reasoning that landlords are not responsible for the wrongdoing of their tenants.

- The landlord has not maintained the property as required by a local statute, although some courts say this is only a public duty and therefore cannot be the basis for a claim of constructive eviction.

✔ **Substantial interference with enjoyment:** The tenant must prove that the wrongful acts by the landlord have substantially interfered with the tenant's use and enjoyment of the premises. Generally speaking, that means the wrongful acts must make the premises unsuitable for the tenant's use for a substantial period of time, not just temporarily.

✔ **Abandonment of the premises:** The interference with the tenant's use and enjoyment must be so substantial that it causes the tenant to leave the premises within a reasonable time. That's why it's considered equivalent to an eviction; the interference is so disruptive of the tenant's use that it's as though the landlord has physically evicted the tenant. If the tenant remains on the premises at all — even if the tenant abandons only part of the premises, like a flooded basement — then the tenant can't claim a constructive eviction.

Warranting habitability of the premises

In residential leases, the landlord implicitly warrants that the premises are habitable and covenants to maintain the premises in habitable condition throughout the term of the lease. Most states now have statutes that impose this warranty on landlords, but in some states, the courts have adopted the implied warranty of habitability by common law reasoning, without state legislation.

The implied warranty of habitability generally applies only to residential leases, but the covenant of quiet enjoyment applies to all leases. Because a claim for breach of the warranty of habitability is generally easier to prove than a claim for constructive eviction, residential tenants generally favor warranty of habitability claims. But except in a few states, commercial tenants don't have the option of claiming a breach of the implied warranty of habitability (which may be called an *implied warranty of fitness* or *suitability* when applied to commercial leases). So they still must rely on the older constructive eviction theory to withhold rent or terminate a lease when the landlord doesn't fulfill his obligations to maintain the premises.

Although specific aspects of the implied warranty of habitability vary among jurisdictions, I outline the general aspects of the rule in the next sections.

Proving an uninhabitable condition

All versions of the implied warranty of habitability agree that a violation of an applicable housing code that substantially affects the tenant's health or safety is a violation of the implied warranty of habitability. *Housing codes* are local ordinances and therefore vary from jurisdiction to jurisdiction, but they generally require landlords to meet minimum standards for residential buildings. They include not only requirements intended to ensure that buildings are safe and functional but also requirements of essential services such as heat and hot water.

Not all housing code violations substantially endanger tenants' health and safety. So a tenant can't just prove a code violation; he must also prove that the code violation endangers health or safety. On the other hand, some conditions may endanger health or safety even though they don't violate a housing code. Some courts have held that such conditions breach the implied warranty of habitability even though they don't violate a housing code; other courts have disagreed.

Many types of conditions may make residential premises uninhabitable, but some common types are

- ✔ Lack of heat, hot water, or other essential services
- ✔ Infestation by rodents or insects
- ✔ Leaking water, mold, and related problems
- ✔ Plumbing problems
- ✔ Nuisances by other tenants, like noise, or by the landlord, like those from construction activities

As you'd probably expect, the landlord isn't responsible for fixing problems that the tenant, or those for whom the tenant is responsible, has deliberately or negligently caused. Such problems don't breach the implied warranty of habitability.

Notifying the landlord

Courts and statutes generally agree that the landlord violates the implied warranty of habitability only if

- ✔ The tenant notifies the landlord within a reasonable time after discovery of the problem.

- ✔ The landlord doesn't make the needed repairs within a reasonable time after receiving the notice.

Waiver

Most courts and statutes say that the tenant can't waive the implied warranty of habitability. In these states, the warranty is mandatory and isn't just "implied" when the parties don't say otherwise. In other states, however, some tenants can waive some aspects of the warranty; for example, tenants of single-family houses may waive the warranty, and tenants may waive the protection of the warranty except as to matters required by the local ordinances.

Remedies

States vary in the remedies they provide to tenants upon breach of the implied warranty of habitability. Possible remedies include

- ✔ **Termination:** As with a constructive eviction that violates the covenant of quiet enjoyment, the tenant can vacate the premises and terminate the lease. Of course, the tenant must have notified the landlord of the breach, and the problems must continue until the tenant leaves.

- ✔ **Rent withholding:** In many states, the tenant may stop paying rent in whole or in part. The tenant may raise the breach of warranty as a defense or counterclaim if the landlord seeks to evict for nonpayment of rent or to recover unpaid rent; the court then determines how much the tenant ultimately must pay in rent. In some states, the tenant may be required to pay rent into escrow or apply the rent to fixing the habitability problems.

- ✔ **Damages or rent abatement:** If the tenant has paid full rent, she's entitled to recover some or all of the rent, but if the tenant hasn't paid rent, she's entitled to a judicial order reducing the amount she owes the landlord. In either case, jurisdictions vary in how they calculate damages:

- Some award the difference between the agreed contract rental and the actual rental value of the premises in their uninhabitable condition.

- Some award the difference between the market value of the premises if they were habitable and the market value of the premises in their actual uninhabitable condition.

- Some award the percentage of the agreed contract rental equal to the percentage by which the property is less valuable because of the uninhabitable condition.

✔ **Consequential damages:** The tenant can recover foreseeable *consequential damages,* expenses the tenant incurs because of the landlord's breach. These damages can include relocation expenses and the cost of making the repairs herself if the landlord failed to do so within a reasonable time after receiving notice.

✔ **Tort and punitive damages:** Although most courts don't allow them, some courts allow the tenant to recover tort damages for emotional distress, annoyance, damage to the tenant's personal property, and physical injuries. Some courts have also awarded punitive damages when the landlord's conduct is intentional, malicious, or in reckless disregard of the tenant's health and safety.

Protecting third parties from injury

The tenant is the possessor of the leased premises, so she traditionally has the same tort duties that other property owners have to third parties to prevent injury. Those duties traditionally depend on the status of the third party as an invitee, licensee, or trespasser and are generally the subject of courses in tort law rather than property law.

The landlord, on the other hand, isn't the possessor of the land, so he traditionally has no liability to the tenant or third parties for personal injuries resulting from the leased premises. However, in an increasing number of states (although still a minority), the landlord is liable for tort injuries to tenants or third parties resulting from his negligence. But traditionally (and still in most states), the landlord isn't liable in tort for physical injuries except in certain circumstances. The following sections describe those circumstances.

Landlord's duty of care in common areas

The landlord possesses the common areas, even though the tenants have the right to use them. Like any other possessor, the landlord has a duty to exercise reasonable care in maintaining those areas. Reasonable care means not only that the landlord performs needed repairs properly and in good time but also that the landlord reasonably discovers needed repairs and reasonably warns people of dangerous conditions.

Landlord's liability for latent defects

The landlord has a duty to disclose latent defects to the tenant at the beginning of the tenancy. The landlord is liable for injuries if the following are true:

- At the beginning of the leasehold, the landlord knew (or, in some courts, should've known) about the defective condition of the leased premises.
- The tenant didn't know about the defect.
- The defect causes injury to the tenant or a third party.

Landlord's failure to repair

Even though the landlord isn't the possessor of the leased premises, he may contractually agree to maintain and repair the premises in certain ways. If so, he's liable for negligence in fulfilling that contractual duty. Such a negligence claim requires proof that

- The landlord had notice of the needed repair.
- The landlord didn't make the repair within a reasonable time or with reasonable care.
- The unrepaired condition creates an unreasonable risk of harm.
- The unrepaired condition causes injury to the tenant or those she permits on the premises.

Landlord's negligent repair

If the landlord makes repairs to the leased premises, whether he's required to or not, he's liable for injuries resulting from his negligence in performing those repairs. Some courts hold the landlord liable for negligent repairs only if the repair made the condition more dangerous or only gave the appearance of being safe.

Landlord's failure to repair dangerous conditions in public areas

A landlord who leases property knowing that some or all of the property will be open to the public has a duty of care to the public. The landlord is liable to third parties if the following are true:

- At the beginning of the leasehold, the landlord knew or should've known about a defect that creates an unreasonable risk of harm to the public.
- The landlord didn't repair the condition or obtain the tenant's assurance that she would repair the condition before admitting the public.
- The dangerous condition causes injury to a third party.

Landlord's liability for crimes by third parties

Traditionally, landlords weren't responsible for other people's crimes on the premises. Today, however, most courts agree that landlords are liable for criminal attacks against tenants and others on the premises if the following are true:

- The landlord provides a service or maintains some aspect of the property, such as locks, alarms, or security guards, regardless of whether the landlord has a statutory or contractual duty to do so or simply does so voluntarily.

- The landlord provides the service or maintains the property negligently.

- The landlord's negligence contributes to the commission of a crime by making the crime easier to commit.

- The crime was reasonably foreseeable, usually meaning that the landlord knew of criminal activity nearby, if not on the premises themselves.

This liability is generally based on negligence in tort, not on breach of a contractual duty. A few cases, however, have suggested that failure to provide basic security measures such as door locks is also a breach of the implied warranty of habitability; therefore, a landlord may be liable in contract for foreseeable criminal injuries that result from such a breach.

Transferring the Leasehold

As Chapter 2 explains, the right to transfer property is a fundamental right of property ownership. The estates of landlords and tenants are transferable just like any other estates. The landlord can transfer his reversion in the fee to a new landlord, and the tenant can transfer her leasehold to someone else or even lease her present estate for a time to a new tenant. However, the parties can and often do restrain the tenant's freedom to transfer (and occasionally they restrain the landlord's freedom to transfer as well). Different types of transfers have different legal consequences for the parties involved.

Restraining the tenant's right to transfer

Lease agreements commonly include clauses that limit transfers by the tenant. Often, such clauses simply prohibit transfers by the tenant or prohibit them without the landlord's written consent. Another common clause, which is more favorable to the tenant, requires that the tenant obtain the landlord's consent but also says that the landlord may not unreasonably deny consent.

Many courts enforce these clauses by their terms. If the lease requires the landlord's consent to a transfer by the tenant and the landlord denies consent, the tenant can't transfer the leasehold — regardless of the landlord's reason. However, because these clauses restrain alienation and restraints on alienation are disfavored (as I explain in Chapter 9), courts construe them narrowly. For example, courts will construe a clause that prohibits "assignment" but doesn't say anything about "subleasing" to allow the tenant to sublease freely.

The policy against restraints on alienation doesn't invalidate all such restraints, but it does invalidate disabling restraints and allows only reasonable promissory and forfeiture restraints. The result of this general rule is that if the tenant transfers her interest in violation of a lease clause, the transfer will be effective despite the clause. The landlord can only recover damages (the remedy for breach of a promissory restraint) or, if the clause allows, terminate the lease for breach of the clause (the remedy for breach of a forfeiture restraint).

A growing number of cases apply the policy against restraints on alienation to require that a restraint on tenant transfers be reasonable. If the landlord doesn't have a good reason to object to the tenant's transfer, a court may refuse to enforce the restraining clause. A landlord has a good reason to object to a tenant who has fewer assets, less income, a history of breaching lease obligations, or otherwise seems more likely to breach. Especially in residential leases, a landlord may even have a good reason for objecting to a new tenant because the tenant seems less neighborly, because in a residential setting, people may live close together and relationships may be important even if the tenant performs the basic obligation of paying rent. In commercial leases, on the other hand, some courts have held that if the landlord doesn't have any commercially reasonable objections to the new tenant, then enforcement of the clause would violate the policy against restraints on alienation. Denying consent simply to demand additional rent or value in exchange for the consent, not because the new tenant puts the landlord in a worse position, isn't reasonable.

Some cases have also suggested that the implied duty of good faith and fair dealing, a general contract principle, requires that the landlord have a good reason for denying consent to transfer by the tenant.

Even if the landlord refuses to consent to the tenant's transfer, the landlord may implicitly consent (or waive the restraint) by accepting rent from the transferee. Furthermore, courts increasingly apply the general principle requiring mitigation of damages to deny recovery of damages for lost rent if accepting the transferee would've avoided such a loss.

Transferring all or part of the tenant's estate

A tenant can transfer all or part of her leasehold estate. Transferring the entire leasehold estate is called an *assignment;* transferring less than the entire leasehold estate is called a *sublease*. If a tenant assigns her leasehold, the new tenant becomes the landlord's tenant. On the other hand, if the tenant subleases her leasehold, the new tenant becomes the tenant of the original tenant. The following sections help you further distinguish between assignments and subleases.

Assigning

A tenant *assigns* her leasehold when she transfers her entire leasehold estate in some or all of the leased premises to another tenant. The *assignee,* the person to whom the tenant has assigned the leasehold, becomes the landlord's tenant. The landlord, therefore, can enforce the running covenants in the lease agreement directly against the assignee. Chapter 5 talks about when covenants run with the land instead of being merely personal to the original contracting parties.

Some covenants in a lease may be personal, but the usual and basic covenants regarding payment of rent and use of the land are running covenants that the landlord may enforce against an assignee. Furthermore, if the assignee promises the original tenant that he'll perform the covenants of the original lease, which is called an *assumption* of the lease, the landlord is a third-party beneficiary of that promise and can enforce all the covenants of the lease against the assuming assignee.

Subleasing

If the tenant transfers less than her entire estate, the transfer is a *sublease*. It's called a *sublease* because it's a new lease between the original tenant and the subtenant rather than an assignment of the existing lease between the landlord and the original tenant. (I fill you in on assignments in the preceding section.) If the tenant transfers anything less than the remainder of the lease term to the transferee, even retaining a reversion of just one day before the original lease term ends, the transfer is a sublease. In fact, some courts hold that even a transfer of the entire remaining lease term is a sublease if the transferring tenant retains a right of entry to terminate the transferee's interest.

A minority of courts have simply held that a transfer is an assignment if the parties intended to put the transferee in the original tenant's position but it's a sublease if the parties intended to create a new tenancy between the tenant and the transferee. These courts consider all the evidence of the parties' intent, including what they called the transfer, as well as the amount and form of payment and to whom payment is made.

Because the subtenant makes a new lease instead of taking over the existing lease, the subtenant doesn't have a direct property or contractual relationship with the landlord (called *privity*). The landlord therefore doesn't have the right to enforce the terms of the original lease against the subtenant at law.

This doesn't mean the subtenant doesn't have to worry about performing the original lease, however. As Chapter 5 explains, privity isn't required to enforce a covenant in equity as an equitable servitude. Consequently, the landlord should be able to specifically enforce land-related covenants against the subtenant, even though he can't obtain an award of damages for breach. Some states have statutes authorizing landlords to enforce the duty to pay rent against subtenants. Furthermore, as with an assignment, a subtenant may assume the obligations of the original lease by promising to perform the covenants of the original lease. In that case, the landlord is a third-party beneficiary of that promise and may enforce it against the subtenant. Finally, if the covenants of the original lease aren't performed, the landlord may have the right to terminate the lease, thus terminating the sublease as well.

The subtenant does have privity of estate and contract with the original tenant, of course. Thus, the subtenant is liable to the original tenant for breach of the sublease.

Holding transferring tenants liable for subsequent breaches of the lease

Whether the tenant assigns or subleases, the original tenant remains responsible to the landlord to perform her covenants under the original lease. So the landlord may sue either an assigning tenant or the assignee for breach of the real covenants in the lease.

The same is true for subsequent transferees who assume the tenant's obligations of the lease. By assuming the lease, they, too, have privity of contract with the landlord and are responsible to the landlord for performing the contract even if they later transfer the leasehold to someone else. Transferees who don't assume the lease, however, don't have privity of contract and have no more duties to the landlord after they transfer the leasehold to someone else.

Even so, the transferee who's in possession of the leased premises is primarily responsible to perform the duties of the lease. The tenant or assuming transferee who subsequently transfers is only secondarily responsible. As far as the landlord is concerned, if the lease is breached, the landlord may sue the original tenant, any subsequent transferee who assumed the lease, and/or the present assignee. But if a prior possessor who has transferred the leasehold is held liable to the landlord, that person has a claim against her transferee to recover whatever liability he incurred.

The only way a tenant or assuming transferee can be free of the lease duties to the landlord is if the landlord releases her. Merely consenting to an assignment or sublease doesn't release the assignor or sublessor. The landlord must expressly indicate an intention to release her from the obligations of the lease.

Terminating the Leasehold

Tenancies can end any number of ways. Some end automatically, while others require notice. A lease agreement can also authorize parties to terminate the leasehold if the other party breaches certain obligations. The sections that follow explore the various ways that leaseholds can end and explain the landlord's options if the tenant remains in possession after the leasehold ends.

Terminating pursuant to agreement

If the lease agreement creates a fixed-term tenancy, the leasehold automatically ends on the last day of the term as specified in the lease. Neither party has to notify the other of termination. If the tenancy is periodic, the leasehold ends after the required period of advance notice. A tenancy at will ends immediately whenever either party indicates the desire to end it, whether by notice or other action, although many state statutes specify that a terminating party must give the other party advance notice. (For a refresher on types of tenancies, see the earlier section "Creating and Differentiating the Four Types of Tenancies.")

Leases commonly include clauses that allow the landlord, and sometimes the tenant, to terminate the lease in certain circumstances. Most commonly, the lease gives the landlord the right to terminate the leasehold if the tenant breaches the duty to pay rent, commits waste, or commits other significant breaches of the lease. But if the tenant breaches, thereby giving the landlord a right to terminate, and the landlord subsequently acts as if the tenancy continues — most commonly by accepting rent — then the landlord waives the right to terminate for that breach.

Abandoning the leased property

Unless the lease says otherwise, the tenant has no duty to physically possess the leased premises. So the tenant doesn't breach the lease if she leaves the premises during the lease term, nor does her departure end her leasehold. However, if the tenant leaves the premises and stops paying rent, the landlord can choose to terminate the leasehold, relet the premises on behalf of the tenant, or in some states, simply continue to enforce the lease and demand the rent from the tenant. The following sections explore each of these options.

Rejecting the surrender and enforcing the lease

When the tenant abandons the premises and stops paying rent, it's called a *surrender* of the premises. The landlord doesn't have to accept the surrender. The leasehold belongs to the tenant for the lease term; the tenant can't end the leasehold early just by leaving and not paying rent.

Traditionally, and still in some states, the landlord can simply reject the surrender and continue to demand rent as it comes due. Eventually, the landlord may sue for the accumulated unpaid rent. Or the lease may authorize the landlord to immediately demand all the rent remaining to be paid during the lease term.

In most states today, however, whether by statute or judicial decision, the landlord can't recover rent from the tenant to the extent that the landlord could've reduced that loss by reasonably attempting to find a new tenant. When the landlord makes such attempts to reduce losses from another's breach, he's *mitigating* damages. The law has commonly required mitigation of damages in other contractual relationships, and states increasingly apply this doctrine to landlords as well.

Reletting the premises for the tenant

Whether mitigation is required or not, the landlord may choose to mitigate damages by finding a new tenant on behalf of the abandoning tenant. The abandoning tenant remains responsible for performance of her lease, so she still must pay the landlord the difference between the rent she owes and the rent the landlord collects from the new tenant. The abandoning tenant also must pay the landlord's reasonable costs of making repairs and finding a new tenant.

Accepting the surrender and terminating the leasehold

The landlord may choose to accept the tenant's surrender of the premises and thereby terminate the lease. In this case, the tenant has no more estate and no more duty to pay rent. Therefore, if the landlord wants to recover damages for lost rent from the tenant, the landlord should relet the premises for the tenant instead of accepting the surrender and leasing the premises for himself.

Whether the landlord chooses to relet for the tenant or accept surrender, the landlord retakes possession, fixes up the property, and finds a new tenant. Therefore, the landlord should clearly indicate his intention in writing — which usually is to relet for the tenant rather than accept surrender. If the landlord doesn't clearly indicate his intention, a court will infer his intention from all the circumstances. If the landlord enters into a new lease for a longer term than the abandoning tenant's remaining lease term, that situation generally indicates the landlord has accepted the surrender and isn't reletting for the tenant. Some cases have suggested that altering the property beyond what is necessary to relet also indicates acceptance of surrender.

Terminating the leasehold in other ways

Some other, less common ways that leaseholds may end include the following:

- ✔ **Death:** Unless the lease says otherwise, death doesn't terminate a fixed-term or periodic tenancy. The landlord's reversion and the tenant's leasehold are inheritable and devisable, meaning the owners can transfer them by will or, if they don't, their interests pass to their heirs by intestate succession. However, the death of either party terminates a tenancy at will.

- ✔ **Merger:** If the same person comes to own both the leasehold and the reversion, the estates merge and the leasehold ends.

- ✔ **End of landlord's estate:** If the landlord's estate ends, so does the leasehold. If the landlord has a life estate, for example, and leases that property for a term, as soon as the life estate ends, the leasehold also ends, even though the lease term may not have ended.

- ✔ **Damage or destruction:** The lease may provide that the tenant can terminate if the building is materially damaged or destroyed. If the lease doesn't say the tenant can terminate in such circumstances, the traditional rule is that the tenant leases the real property for the term, regardless of damage to or destruction of buildings. However, if the tenant rents only space in a building and not the land, the destruction of the building allows the tenant to terminate the lease. Likewise, some state statutes permit the tenant to terminate in the event of destruction or at least to terminate if the landlord doesn't rebuild. For residential tenants protected by the implied warranty of habitability, if damage or destruction to the building makes the premises uninhabitable, the tenant can elect to terminate if the landlord doesn't rebuild (see the earlier section "Warranting habitability of the premises" for details).

✔ **Eminent domain:** The government can exercise eminent domain to take leased property just as it can take any other property. If the government takes fee simple absolute ownership, it takes the reversion and the present leasehold and thereby ends the lease. The tenant has a right to the lost market value of her leasehold as just compensation, but if the rent is equal to the market value of the property, the tenant hasn't suffered a loss of market value. If the government takes the property only temporarily for less than the remainder of the lease term, then the leasehold doesn't end unless the lease says otherwise. The tenant continues to owe rent to the landlord and is entitled to just compensation from the government, measured by the property's fair market rental value.

Holding over after termination of lease

As I note in the earlier section "Creating and Differentiating the Four Types of Tenancies," if the tenant remains in possession after the leasehold ends (often called *holding over*), she becomes a tenant at sufferance. The landlord then has two choices:

✔ **Eviction:** The landlord can treat the holdover tenant as a trespasser and evict her from the premises. In such cases, the landlord is entitled to damages from the holdover tenant for the period of time during which she remains as a trespasser on the land, measured by the market value of the use of the land. (Some state statutes give the landlord two or three times the regular rent as damages for the period of holding over.)

✔ **Periodic tenancy:** The landlord can treat the holdover tenant as a periodic tenant and recover periodic rent from the tenant. The period of the tenancy is generally the period for which the tenant had been paying rent before holding over, and the other terms of the old lease continue to govern the parties' relationship. However, the lease can specify an increased rental payment that the tenant must pay if she holds over, or the landlord can specify an increased rental payment that the tenant must pay if she continues as a periodic tenant, as long as the amount is reasonable.

The landlord must make his choice within a reasonable time, but if he doesn't, the law is unclear whether the tenant is a trespasser, a periodic tenant, or even a tenant at will. The landlord may expressly indicate his choice, but often, he merely implies it by his actions. If the landlord brings a lawsuit to recover possession or leases the property to a new tenant, those actions obviously indicate the intention to treat the holdover tenant as a trespasser. On the other hand, accepting rental payments from the holdover tenant generally indicates the intention to treat the holdover tenant as a periodic tenant.

Applying and refunding security deposits

Lease agreements typically require the tenant to pay a *security deposit* to the landlord at the beginning of the lease term. The landlord holds the security deposit money to secure payment of debts that the tenant owes the landlord, such as unpaid rent and damages for harm to the property. The security deposit makes recovering such debts from the tenant easier because the landlord already has a fund of money in his control.

Most states have statutes that regulate the use of security deposits. These statutes, which usually apply only to residential leases, may include provisions such as the following:

✔ The security deposit may not be greater than the amount specified by the statute.

✔ The security deposit may only secure certain types of obligations specified by the statute and must specify what it secures.

✔ The landlord must keep the security deposit in a separate account and pay interest on the balance.

✔ If the landlord transfers his interest to another, his assignee is responsible for performing obligations connected to the security deposit.

✔ The landlord must give the tenant an itemized notice of amounts he withholds from the security deposit within a certain amount of time after the leasehold ends. Statutory remedies vary if the landlord doesn't return the deposit to the tenant or provide the required notice within the specified time period. For instance, the landlord may have to return the entire deposit, lose the right to recover claimed damages from the tenant, or owe the tenant some multiple of the amount that the landlord wrongfully withheld.

Evicting the Tenant

Even when a tenancy has ended and the landlord has the legal right to possession, the landlord may have to figure out a way to actually get the tenant off the property and retake possession. Obviously, the landlord can bring a lawsuit to eject the former tenant like any other trespasser, but the landlord has some other options as well, as I explain next.

Evicting by self-help

A landlord may try to get rid of the holdover tenant without going to court, which may be called evicting by *self-help*. Self-help eviction can be very tempting to landlords who want to save the time and expense of legal action. For example, a landlord may hope to regain possession by changing the locks while the tenant is away or by turning off the utilities. However, the rules and legality of eviction by self-help vary by jurisdiction.

In some states, the landlord has no right to enter the leased premises as long as the holdover tenant remains in possession, even though the landlord has elected to treat the holdover tenant as a trespasser. Some states have adopted this rule by statutes that apply only to residential leases, so in those jurisdictions, residential landlords have no right to self-help but other landlords do.

In other states, however, the landlord has a limited right to self-help. The majority rule is that the landlord doesn't commit a trespass if he peaceably enters the leased premises after the termination of the leasehold. Cases vary widely on what is "peaceable." Breaking in or directly confronting the tenant are unlikely to be peaceable. Entering while the tenant is away, through an unlocked door or with a key, is more likely to be peaceable. More important to the landlord is what he can do to exclude the tenant after he peaceably enters the property. By statute or judicial decision, in some jurisdictions, the landlord can't exclude the tenant by changing locks, turning off utilities, or performing other similar actions. Other jurisdictions allow such means of excluding the holdover tenant.

If the landlord excludes the tenant by self-help, he also has to do something with the tenant's stuff. Some states allow the landlord to use force that's reasonably necessary to evict, whereas others don't allow the landlord to use any force against people or their things.

The lease agreement may include a clause that gives the landlord the right to use self-help to evict the tenant. Some courts enforce these clauses, regardless of the applicable default rules about self-help, but others hold them to be void and apply the same rules to all landlords regardless of any lease clauses. So in some states, the lease is the first place to look to answer the landlord's questions about self-help; in others, you don't need to look at the lease at all.

Evicting by summary procedure

At least in large part because of concerns about violent conflicts arising from landlord self-help in evicting holdover tenants, all states have adopted statutes that provide a simplified judicial process for regaining possession of real property. The process goes by different names in different states but is often called a *forcible entry and detainer* action. The following sections shed light on the details of these summary procedures.

Defining forcible entry and detainer

As the label suggests, the forcible entry and detainer statute is meant to provide a process to quickly remedy forcible entries and detainers. A *forcible entry* is simply entering another's property forcibly without consent and without legal right, thereby ousting the rightful possessor. For example, a landlord forcibly enters when he uses self-help and changes the locks if he hasn't properly terminated the leasehold and the tenant therefore still has the legal right of possession.

If the trespasser retains possession, the rightful possessor may bring a forcible entry and detainer action to eject the trespasser. Even if the defendant lawfully and peaceably took possession initially, if she later wrongfully and forcibly retains possession, that possession is a *forcible detainer* and she's subject to a forcible entry and detainer action. A landlord seeking to evict a holdover tenant can allege a forcible detainer because although the tenant had the right to legal possession for a time, she then wrongfully retained possession after the leasehold ended.

The common label *forcible entry and detainer* suggests that the action applies only when the defendant has used some force. But states vary in whether force is required and, if so, what kind of force is enough to be subject to the statute. Variations include the following:

- ✔ Some states don't require any force. In those states, the plaintiff need only prove that the entry or detainer was unlawful and without the plaintiff's consent.

- ✔ Some courts have said that the plaintiff must prove actual force, not just implied force, in entering or retaining possession.

- ✔ Between these two extremes, some states do require force but define "force" to include threats of force or circumstances indicating that the other party won't surrender possession peaceably.

Simplifying the issues

The forcible entry and detainer statutes simplify the process of ejecting a holdover tenant or other trespasser who is subject to the statutory process. Just like any other lawsuit, the plaintiff initiates a forcible entry and detainer action against the defendant with a complaint, but the issues that the plaintiff can plead and litigate are limited. The statutes generally allow the parties only to plead and litigate the issue of who has the legal right to possess the premises. In fact, in some states, a plaintiff landlord can use the summary procedure only to regain possession for nonpayment of rent; if the landlord seeks to regain possession for other tenant breaches, the landlord must file an ordinary civil action.

Any other claims besides regaining possession, such as claims for damages for breaching lease duties, generally require a separate lawsuit. However, if the landlord alleges that he has the right to take possession of leased premises because the tenant has breached the duty to pay rent, then the court must decide whether rent is due in order to decide whether the landlord or tenant has the right to possess the premises. Some courts therefore have held that tenants can raise defenses to the obligation to pay rent, such as breach of the implied warranty of habitability. In most states, the landlord can also recover unpaid rent in a forcible entry and detainer action (and in some, he can even recover double rent as a statutory penalty), but in other states, the landlord can't recover any unpaid rent in a forcible entry and detainer action.

Speeding up the process

The forcible entry and detainer statutes speed up the usual judicial process by shortening the time between stages of the process. For example, the statute may require the plaintiff to first give notice to the defendant to cure her breach, if possible, or quit the premises, but the notice may only have to be given three to ten days before the plaintiff can file his complaint. The summons typically needs to be served on the defendant only a few days before the trial date. The U.S. Supreme Court's decision in *Lindsey v. Normet,* 405 U.S. 56 (1972), held that such a summary procedure doesn't violate the Due Process Clause.

Part IV
Acquiring and Transferring Property Rights

The 5th Wave   By Rich Tennant

"All I can say is, they better be familiar with the laws of adverse possession."

In this part . . .

Property law deals with how people become property owners. Get ready to discover how land is bought and sold as well as the circumstances in which you can become an owner simply by possessing property. I also explain how recording statutes protect buyers of land from property claims that they don't know about, how people use mortgages to facilitate buying land, and how foreclosures work when a buyer doesn't repay her loan.

Chapter 13

Acquiring Rights by Finding and Possessing Personal Property

∙ ∙

In This Chapter

▶ Considering what possession is and why it's important

▶ Resolving conflicts between competing possessors

▶ Understanding how one can become an owner by possessing unowned things

▶ Examining the rights and duties of possessors of things owned by another

▶ Evaluating claims by owners of land where another person found a thing

∙ ∙

*P*ossessing property is a fundamental attribute of ownership. By definition, if a person owns property, she has the right to possess it. Possession is also a way to acquire ownership in the first place. This chapter talks about acquiring ownership of personal property by possessing; for information on acquiring ownership of real property by possessing, turn to Chapter 14.

If personal property isn't owned by someone, you can become the owner simply by taking possession. Even if personal property is owned by someone, you can still acquire some ownership rights by taking possession. These rights vary depending on the circumstances. If someone else has a superior claim to the property, however, the person who takes possession also has duties to that superior claimant. This chapter discusses the rights and duties of someone who takes possession of personal property, owned and unowned.

Taking a Closer Look at Possession

Possession of personal property requires both physical control over the thing and the intention to exercise control or dominion over the thing. The necessary physical control depends on the circumstances. In simple cases, a person has physical control just by picking up the thing. But sometimes it isn't that simple. Sometimes legal rights depend on whether or when a person took possession of a thing. In such cases, the courts have to decide when a person's control has been enough to become possession.

A hunter would clearly have possession of a wild animal if he killed it and picked it up. After picking up the animal, he has complete physical control of the animal along with the required intent to exercise dominion. But he may have control even before killing it and picking it up. He has control as soon as he mortally wounds it as long as he continues in pursuit, because the animal will eventually die and the hunter will take it. Likewise, if he securely captures the animal in a trap, he has clearly taken possession. Even though he doesn't have his hands on the animal, he has brought the animal under his control enough to make it his.

Not only does a person have to reach a certain degree of control in order to take possession, but he must also have the power to continue controlling the thing. Again, sometimes this control is simple and obvious. If you pick up a feather and then set it down on your desk, you obviously have possession even though you don't keep holding the feather. But if you're chasing a wild animal, successfully grabbing it for a moment before it wriggles away may not be considered possession. You have to capture it.

After you've taken control of a thing, you don't have to keep holding the thing in order to keep possessing it, however. At that point, you continue to possess it as long as you have the intent and the ability to maintain control over the thing. Such possession is called *constructive possession.* You have constructive possession of chattels (tangible personal property) that you keep in your house, for example.

A person can also obtain possession of a thing through another person acting on his behalf. For example, employees who take possession of things within the scope of their employment generally take possession on behalf of their employers. Likewise, if someone hires an agent to perform some service and the agent finds and takes possession of a thing within the scope of her employment, the agent takes possession on behalf of the person who hired her. But if an employee or agent finds and takes possession of something outside the scope of her employment, she takes possession for herself.

Resolving Claims among Competing Possessors

Sometimes more than one person tries to take possession of a thing at the same time. If they all succeed at taking possession at the very same time, they take their rights as *tenants in common* (see Chapter 10 for details on tenancies in common). Otherwise, the first person to take possession acquires rights superior to the rights of a subsequent possessor. I describe the rights that come with possession later in this chapter. In this section, I identify some of the considerations in resolving disputed claims of possession.

Intending to control

Possession requires both physical control and the intent to exercise dominion. Two or more people can simultaneously or successively have physical control of unowned property without the intention to exercise dominion. The first person to combine control with the required intent owns the thing in question. Of course, proving when someone formed the required intent may be difficult, so if intent can't be assumed because of the value of the thing or the conduct of the people, expressions of intent may be the best evidence.

Imagine that two friends are on public land. One of them picks up a rock and thoughtlessly handles it as they talk. At some point, the other person takes the rock from her friend's hand, looks at it, and sees what may be a fossil. She points it out and says she's going to keep it. She owns the formerly unowned rock because she's the first to combine physical control with intent to exercise dominion, even though her friend picked it up first.

Determining whether someone interfered with possession

If one person has begun to take possession of a thing and another violently or wrongfully interferes with her taking possession, courts usually hold that the first person has the right to possess. Even though the second individual may have actually taken physical control rather than the first person, rules about possession should discourage violent conflict and not reward wrongdoing. So the person who violently or wrongfully interfered won't be considered a prior possessor.

Getting possession by trespassing

Ordinarily, the first to take possession of an unowned thing becomes the owner. However, if the unowned thing — say, a wild animal — is located on or under a person's private land, a trespasser on the land can't become the owner by taking possession of the unowned thing (unless perhaps the trespass is minor). The trespassing possessor still has the rights of possession and therefore some ownership rights against the rest of the world but not against the owner of the land on which the person trespassed. This rule removes a possible incentive to trespass and avoids rewarding a trespasser for wrongdoing.

Possessing sunken ships and treasure

Ships and their contents lost at sea may be governed by the law of salvage rather than the law of finders. The *law of salvage* states that whoever intentionally takes possession of property that is lost or in peril at sea, such as a sunken ship, is entitled to an equitable award from a court, while the owner of the property remains the owner. Basically, the law of salvage applies when property is lost at sea but not abandoned. The court considers all relevant factors, such as the value of the property salvaged and the investment and difficulty in salvaging it, to determine how much of the value of the property to award to the *salvor* (the person who's salvaging it).

A court in such cases may award finders a portion of the property's value as compensation. In such situations, multiple parties may attempt to recover the property, and their efforts may contribute to recovery of the property. A party can receive an award from the court even though the party didn't intend to acquire ownership of the property and even though it may not have obtained possession in the same sense required for a finder to obtain ownership rights of other personal property.

Similarly, when property lost at sea is abandoned, courts may hold that a finder possesses the property even though she hasn't actually obtained physical control over the property yet. For example, a company that locates a shipwreck, begins to recover property from the wreck, and has the demonstrated ability to continue doing so may thereby obtain sufficient possession to own the abandoned shipwreck.

Of course, if the property is generally open to the public, like a store is, a person isn't trespassing to enter the property. In that case, a person who takes possession of an unowned thing, like abandoned property, is considered the owner even though she took possession on private property.

Becoming an Owner by Possessing Unowned Property

In the U.S. legal system, there's no such thing as unowned land, but there are unowned things. Some things, such as people and protected species, are unowned because they can't be owned. Other things, like wild animals, are unowned until someone takes possession of them.

Still other things may be owned but become unowned. This happens when the owner of a thing abandons it, thereby giving up control and manifesting his intention to give up ownership. After a thing is abandoned, it's considered unowned. (I cover abandonment in greater detail in the later section "Protecting the owner's rights.") Similarly, if a wild animal is captured but then escapes back into the wild, it becomes unowned again.

A person becomes the owner of an unowned thing simply by taking possession. No one else has a claim to the thing, so the possessor has a claim superior to the rest of the world. Of course, someone may not become an owner if the law declares that the thing can't be privately owned. A person also may not become an owner by taking possession in an unlawful way, although she can still have rights of ownership against anyone else who interferes with her possession.

You can generally transfer ownership of personal property simply by transferring possession as long as you actually intend to transfer ownership. If you just give your property to someone else to use or take care of, you don't intend to transfer ownership and she doesn't become the owner by your transfer of possession.

Taking Possession of Owned Property

Numerous situations may result in a person taking possession of personal property that's owned by someone else. A person may find and take possession of a thing that the owner has lost or mislaid. She may borrow or rent a thing from the owner. Or she may steal it.

Even though the possessor of the owned property still has some rights as a possessor, the owner, of course, has the superior claim to own and possess the thing. The following sections describe the rights of the owner and the duties of the possessor in these situations.

Protecting the owner's rights

An owner doesn't lose ownership of her personal property simply because another person takes possession of it. She has the legal right to recover possession of her property from the possessor. However, the owner does lose ownership and can't recover the property in the following situations:

- **Abandonment:** If the owner abandons the property, she no longer owns it. Because the property then becomes unowned, the first person to take possession becomes the new owner. An owner abandons property when she voluntarily gives up possession or doesn't attempt to regain possession, with the intention not to reclaim the property. Often, the abandoning property owner isn't before the court, so the court must infer the owner's intentions from the circumstances. Courts commonly assume that an owner wouldn't abandon valuable property, so the court must find some affirmative evidence indicating that the owner didn't want to keep the property.

✔ **Adverse possession:** If someone else exclusively, openly, and continuously possesses property as an owner for a period of years specified by statute, she acquires ownership of the property by *adverse possession*. With chattels, the statutory period within which the true owner must bring a lawsuit to recover possession generally doesn't begin until the finder has notified the true owner that she has found the chattel or the true owner otherwise discovers that the finder has it. (For more details on adverse possession, see Chapter 14.)

Describing bailments and the possessor's duties to the owner

Not only does the owner have a superior claim to subsequent possessors, but those subsequent possessors also have a duty to take care of the property while they're in possession and to return it to the owner. A person who takes possession of another's personal property is called a *bailee*, and the owner is the *bailor*; their relationship is called a *bailment*. The extent of a bailee's duties depends on the circumstances, as the following sections explain.

Returning the property to the owner

A *true bailee* is a person who takes possession with the owner's consent. In such a bailment, the bailor gives possession of the property to the bailee to hold or to do something with (perhaps fix, as an auto mechanic would do). A true bailee must return the property to the bailor on demand or according to the terms of their agreement; if she doesn't, she's liable for damages regardless of the reason for her failure to return the property. Bailees may try to contractually limit or disclaim liability for not returning the bailed property, but courts may limit the enforcement of such clauses.

A person who takes possession without the bailor's consent may be called an *involuntary* or *constructive bailee*. Even though the possessor didn't voluntarily enter into a bailment with the owner, she acquires some of the duties of a bailee by taking possession of someone else's property. Because the bailor has the superior claim to the property, an involuntary bailee must, of course, return the property on demand. Even though the bailee has a right of possession against the rest of the world, she must keep the property for the bailor so she can return it.

Because the involuntary bailment created by finding lost property is for the benefit of the bailor, the finder (or involuntary bailee) is liable to the owner for loss of the property only if she did so intentionally or failed to exercise slight care over the property, meaning she was grossly negligent.

Taking care of the property

A bailee has a duty to care for the bailor's property while the bailee possesses it. Depending on the nature of the bailment, the bailee has the duty to exercise one of the following standards of care:

- **Extraordinary care:** If the bailor gives possession to the bailee for the bailee's benefit (so the bailee can make use of the property somehow), the bailee has a duty to exercise extraordinary care to prevent damage or loss while possessing the property. That means the bailee will be liable for any damage that results from even slight negligence.

- **Ordinary care:** If the bailor and the bailee both benefit from the bailment (as when the bailor pays the bailee for the service), the bailee has a duty to exercise ordinary care over the property. That means the bailee is liable for damages that result from not exercising the degree of care that a reasonably prudent person would have exercised in the circumstances if the property were her own.

- **Slight care:** If the bailee takes possession for the benefit of the bailor (such as when a person finds lost property and takes possession of it), the bailee has a duty to exercise slight care over the property. That basically means the bailee is liable if damage results from not exercising the degree of care an ordinarily careful person would exercise in caring for her own slightly important property, or from not exercising the degree of care that even a careless person would exercise for her own property.

Examining the Possessor's Ownership Rights against Third Parties

Even though an owner of personal property has a superior claim to a subsequent possessor, the possessor has a superior claim to everyone else. No one else can take the property from the possessor, and if someone else does, the possessor can legally regain possession.

In a legal action to recover possession, the possessor doesn't have to prove that she has complete ownership of the property in order to prevail. She only needs to prove that she has a better claim to possess the property than the other party in the lawsuit. Even if she's a thief, she's entitled to retain possession against any subsequent possessor. In other words, a subsequent possessor can't defend possession on the theory that the prior possessor didn't own the property.

Several people may successively possess a chattel. In general, everyone who possesses without abandoning has the right to possess against anyone who takes possession later. So you can have a hierarchy of claims to possession of the property, based on order in time, even though only one true owner exists.

Resolving Conflicts between a Finder and the Landowner

When a person finds and takes possession of a chattel on someone else's land, the landowner may also assert a claim to the chattel. Even though the landowner never directly possessed the chattel itself, the landowner may prevail in a contest with the possessor in some cases.

Often, courts explain such a result on the theory that the landowner constructively possessed the property before the finder actually possessed the property. *Constructive possession* means that the landowner didn't directly possess the chattel but had possession of the land where it was found and the circumstances suggest it would be better to award the property to the landowner than to the finder.

The following sections describe the situations in which the landowner may have constructive possession and win a contest with a finder of a chattel.

Keeping mislaid property with the landowner

The owner of the land where a chattel is found prevails against the finder if the previous possessor mislaid the chattel. A chattel is *mislaid* when the previous possessor

- ✔ **Intentionally put the chattel where it was found:** If the previous possessor unintentionally parted with possession, the chattel is *lost* rather than mislaid.

- ✔ **Intends to reclaim the chattel:** If the previous possessor doesn't intend to reclaim the chattel, the chattel is abandoned rather than mislaid and the previous possessor no longer owns it. (See the earlier "Protecting the owner's rights" section for details on abandoned property).

The landowner has a superior claim to a mislaid chattel because the previous possessor of the chattel still wants her property and presumably will return for it. Because the previous possessor intentionally put it somewhere, she may remember where she put it and go there looking for it. She may even have intended to leave the chattel in the custody and care of the landowner. The landowner, therefore, has the right to retain possession in the meantime to make it more likely that the previous possessor can find and retrieve the property.

Sometimes a chattel may be found in or on another chattel, which is found on a landowner's real property. In such a case, the parties may dispute whether the chattel or the real property is the place where the property was mislaid. For example, someone may find mislaid cash in a car while it's in a parking garage. The parking garage owner and the car owner may both claim that they should have the right of possession. The ultimate question for the court is where the previous possessor of the cash would go to find the cash. In these cases, the court can decide that the owner of personal property where a mislaid chattel is found has the superior claim.

Sometimes cases and other authorities say that a finder acquires no rights in mislaid property, but that isn't accurate. By definition, a finder of mislaid property is one who takes possession. One who takes possession has the right to continue possession against anyone else without a superior claim. So the finder does acquire rights in mislaid property — they're just inferior to, first, the rights of the true owner and, second, the owner of the land where the property is found.

Proving that the previous possessor mislaid a chattel may be difficult. Usually the previous possessor of the found chattel won't be available to testify whether she mislaid it; if she were, she would have a better claim to the chattel than either the finder or the landowner. So the court must infer from the available evidence whether the chattel was intentionally placed there and whether the owner intended to reclaim it.

Often the location of the chattel reveals pretty clearly whether the previous possessor placed it there intentionally. If the chattel was hidden or secured in some way, it was surely placed there intentionally. If it's just resting on the surface in the open, however, the placement was probably unintentional.

Determining whether the owner intended to reclaim the chattel or abandon it can be harder. The following evidence may be relevant to such a decision:

- **Illegality:** If the chattel is the fruits of illegal conduct, that fact may support an inference that the previous possessor abandoned the property for fear of being caught.

✔ **Passage of time:** The more time that has passed since the chattel was placed there, the more likely the previous possessor has abandoned it and doesn't intend to retrieve it. Of course, it may be hard to determine factually how long the chattel has been in a certain place before it was finally found.

✔ **Previous possessor's conduct:** Any actions inconsistent with the intent to keep ownership of the chattel may evidence abandonment. For example, if the finder publishes notice of the found chattel and no one appears to claim it, this may support an inference that the previous possessor has abandoned it.

✔ **Value of the chattel:** The more valuable and distinctive the chattel, the more likely the owner wouldn't intend to abandon it. In fact, courts often say that they won't presume that an owner would abandon valuable property, so only clear evidence of abandonment can overcome that presumption. On the other hand, if the chattel wasn't valuable at the time the previous possessor parted with it, a court may presume that the previous possessor abandoned it.

Possessing embedded property

A landowner's claim is usually found to be superior to a finder's if the found chattel is embedded in the land. When the chattel is buried in the ground or embedded in improvements to the land, possession of the land may be said to include possession of the embedded chattel. Even though the landowner didn't know about the chattel and therefore had no intention to exercise control over the chattel specifically, the landowner did have physical control of the premises, which includes the embedded chattel, and intended to exercise control over them.

However, intentionally buried property may instead be considered treasure trove. If so, the rules for treasure trove, discussed in the next section, would apply.

Recovering treasure trove

Treasure trove is money or treasure, such as gold and silver, that the true owner concealed for safekeeping so long ago that the true owner is unlikely to return for it. So the common law would call the property _mislaid_ at first, because the owner intentionally placed it somewhere without the intention of abandoning it. However, after a long passage of time, that property becomes treasure trove because it's likely that the true owner is dead and won't come back for it.

The finder of treasure trove owns it against the landowner and everyone else except the true owner. Even though the element of antiquity makes it unlikely that the true owner will appear to recover the property, the true owner's successors in interest still have the right to do so. But the finder prevails over the landowner, even though the treasure trove may have been embedded in the landowner's property.

Deciding that found property is treasure trove requires determining it to have been concealed in the location for a very long time, at least long enough that the true owner is likely dead. In making this decision, courts have considered evidence such as the following:

- ✔ **Dates found on coins or paper money:** Such dates obviously indicate how old the money is.

- ✔ **The age of the place where it's concealed:** For example, if the treasure is found inside a wall that was built 80 years ago, you can assume that the treasure has been there that long.

- ✔ **The condition of the place where it's concealed:** For instance, if the property is concealed in a metal container that has completely rusted away, you can assume the property has been in the container for a long time.

Some courts in more recent decades have rejected the treasure trove doctrine, which may encourage and reward trespass to find such treasure on another's land. Instead, these courts have held that the landowner owns property buried or otherwise embedded in her land, except against the true owner. Some state statutes have also been construed as abandoning the treasure trove doctrine.

Discouraging wrongdoing by the finder

The owner of the land where a chattel is found may prevail against the finder in circumstances where the finder's claim would seem unfair or wrongful. Such circumstances may include the following:

- ✔ The more extensively the finder trespassed on the landowner's property in the course of finding the chattel, the more likely the landowner will prevail against the finder.

- ✔ If the finder is an employee of the landowner or has otherwise agreed to give the found property to the landowner, the landowner will almost surely win.

> ✔ If the finder was permitted to enter the land for a limited purpose, the finder is less likely to win.
>
> ✔ If the real property where the chattel is found is private rather than open to the public, the finder is less likely to win.

Reforming the Common Law by Statute

Certain states have adopted statutes that change the common law rules regarding the rights of finders. The following sections detail some aspects of these statutes.

Finding the owner

Lost property statutes commonly require the finder to take specific actions to find the true owner of the found property. The finder typically must publish notice in a newspaper and otherwise publicize the discovery of the found property. Some statutes also require the finder to notify the police or other public officials or to deliver the found property to the police.

If the true owner claims the property within a specified time period after notice is published, such as six months or one year, the true owner gets to keep it. If she doesn't, she loses her claim to the property forever.

Rewarding the finder if the owner shows up

If the true owner does appear to claim her lost property within the statutory time period, lost property statutes typically reward or compensate the finder. Some require the true owner to compensate the finder for her expenses. Others require the owner to pay a percentage of the property's value to the finder as a reward.

Awarding the property to the finder if the owner doesn't claim it

If the true owner doesn't appear to claim the property within the specified time period, most statutes say the finder owns the property. However, some require the finder to give some of the property to the local government or other public body.

Most lost property statutes are more generous to finders than the common law in this way, because the finder owns the property completely free of claims by the true owner within a short time period after finding it. Under the common law, the finder must prove adverse possession over a longer time period, or abandonment, in order to become the owner. (You can read about adverse possession and abandonment in the earlier section "Protecting the owner's rights.") Unless and until the finder can do so, her use of the property is limited because she must keep it (and care for it) for the true owner or risk liability for not preserving the property and delivering it to the owner.

Determining when the lost property statute applies

Lost property statutes may not apply to all found property. Some statutes have been construed to apply only to property that is lost under the common law principles, meaning property that the owner unintentionally lost possession of. If the property is mislaid, abandoned, or treasure trove, the common law principles still apply. On the other hand, some statutes have been construed to end some or all of these distinctions and apply to any owned property found by another.

Escheating property to the state

State *escheat statutes* commonly provide that the state may claim property that has been abandoned by the true owner for a long period of time as well as when a person dies or disappears without heirs. The statutes don't terminate the true owner's title, but of course, in these situations, a true owner is unlikely to appear. So escheated property effectively becomes the property of the state. Although the state's right to claim abandoned property may appear to conflict with the right of a finder to abandoned property, courts generally construe these statutes narrowly to apply only in circumstances when no finder exists, such as when a bank holds funds that are abandoned.

Chapter 14

Becoming an Owner by Adverse Possession

....

In This Chapter

▶ Considering why adverse possession gives a person title to the land

▶ Examining the elements of an adverse possession claim

▶ Taking a closer look at the title obtained through adverse possession

....

*A*ccording to the doctrine of adverse possession, if a person continuously possesses land for a relatively long time in a way that manifests a claim of ownership, she becomes the owner of that property even though it wasn't hers before. I've dedicated this chapter to explaining why the adverse possession doctrine exists and which elements make up an adverse possession claim.

Getting Acquainted with Adverse Possession

Adverse possession may sound like a way for people to legally steal other people's land, but that's not the point of the doctrine, even though it might occasionally have that effect. The following sections reveal why adverse possession gives a person title and the resulting requirements of the doctrine.

Clearing up ownership on the ground

People often possess land in good faith, believing they have good title to it, but they really don't. Here are some examples of how this situation can happen:

✔ A deed or other legal document describes the boundaries of a person's property, but people have to locate those boundaries on the ground. Sometimes they don't get the boundaries right. So a person may end up mistakenly occupying some land that isn't really hers.

✔ A person may receive a deed to property and take possession of it, only to discover later that the deed is invalid because it wasn't in proper form, it wasn't executed or delivered correctly, or it's invalid for some other reason.

✔ A grantor correctly gives a grantee a deed to property, but the grantor doesn't actually have the right to transfer it to the grantee because of some prior and superior interest in the land.

The adverse possession doctrine gives the possessor good title after she possesses it for a long period of time. The doctrine thus harmonizes legal rights with what has actually happened on the ground, giving ownership to the person who has acted like an owner and whom people generally would think of as being the owner.

This may be unfortunate for the record owner, who loses ownership because of another's adverse possession, but adverse possession is helpful for many others, such as

✔ **The adverse possessor herself:** After all, she has relied on her ownership and made use of the property for a long time.

✔ **Other people who may have taken interests in the land or otherwise acted in reliance upon the adverse possessor's apparent ownership:** Their investments and expectations won't be disappointed.

✔ **The general public:** The public benefits from the adverse possessor's productive use of the land and from clearing up uncertainties about ownership.

Applying the statute of limitations to ejectment

Another way to think of adverse possession is as an application of the statute of limitations to ejectment actions. As Chapter 2 explains, *ejectment* is the cause of action by which a person with the right of possession can regain possession of real property from a wrongful possessor. Statutes of limitations apply to all types of actions, requiring a plaintiff to bring her cause of action within a certain number of years after she first discovers she has a claim. If the plaintiff doesn't bring her claim within that statutory time period, which varies for different types of claims, she loses her claim forever.

Adverse possession is simply the label given to the circumstances in which the statute of limitations bars an action to recover possession of real property. Some states have statutes that specify those circumstances; in other states, the adverse possession doctrine is a judicial application and extension of the statute of limitations. When the limitations period has passed and the adverse possession requirements are met, the record owner forever loses the right to eject the trespasser. Losing the right to eject someone else who is exclusively possessing the property really means losing ownership of the property. So when the requirements of adverse possession are met, the adverse possessor acquires title to the property. She doesn't obtain title from the former owner, but rather, she obtains a new title by virtue of her adverse possession.

Statutes of limitations generally aim to avoid trying to resolve claims too long after the relevant events have occurred. Sometimes courts seem to suggest that a plaintiff who isn't reasonably diligent in bringing her claim should lose her right to do so. But whether the plaintiff is considered blameworthy or not, courts have good reasons not to consider claims after a long time. For one, the evidence may be unreliable, increasing the risk of error in deciding the claim. Secondly, in various ways, the uncertainty about ownership harms the public in general. Statutes of limitations are often said to further a public policy favoring "repose" or stability and certainty.

Even so, statutes of limitations include exceptions that also apply to adverse possession claims. For example, a person can't obtain title to government-owned lands by adversely possessing them because the statute of limitations doesn't limit the time within which the government can bring claims to eject wrongful possessors of public lands. Similarly, the statute of limitations is said to be *tolled* in certain circumstances — that is, the statute says the time period for bringing a claim doesn't include the time during which conditions such as the following exist:

- ✔ The record owner is insane or otherwise legally incompetent.

- ✔ The record owner is a minor.

- ✔ The record owner is actively serving in the military.

- ✔ The record owner is imprisoned.

- ✔ The record owner dies. (If the plaintiff dies, some statutes extend the running of the limitations period for a specified time or until a personal representative is appointed.)

After these conditions pass, some statutes specify a shorter time period within which the person must bring her claim or be barred thereafter.

Exploring the Elements of Adverse Possession

To obtain title by adverse possession, courts generally say that the possessor must prove the following required elements:

- ✔ The person actually possessed the property.

- ✔ The possession was exclusive.

- ✔ The possession was open and notorious.

- ✔ The possession was adverse or hostile to the owner's title.

- ✔ The possession was continuous and uninterrupted.

- ✔ The possession described by the previous elements continued throughout the applicable statute of limitations period.

Sometimes courts use different terms, but these are the essential elements. They reflect the purposes and principles of the adverse possession doctrine. You can group them together in different ways, but here's how to group them according to the purposes they serve:

- ✔ The first two elements, actual and exclusive possession, establish that the possessor — sometimes called the *disseisor* because he takes away *seisin* (ownership) from the former owner — has used the land as an owner would.

- ✔ The second two elements, open and notorious and adverse possession, establish that the record owner — sometimes called the *disseisee* — has had notice of the possessor's apparent claim of ownership.

- ✔ The final two elements, continuous and uninterrupted use throughout the limitations period, establish that the record owner hasn't taken action to eject the adverse claimant throughout the statutory period of time.

I spend most of the rest of this chapter examining each of the required elements of adverse possession.

Analyze each of the elements separately; don't let your judgment about the satisfaction of one element influence your judgment or your discussion about the satisfaction of other elements. Sometimes students and lawyers mix elements together with confusing results. For example, in talking about whether particular activities constituted possession, you may be tempted to talk about the fact that they weren't continuous or they weren't open and visible, but those are different elements. Talk about each element separately and remember that an adverse possession claim requires proving all six elements.

Element #1: Actually Possessing the Property

No surprise here, but to adversely possess land, you have to possess it. But sometimes it's hard to determine whether a person's activities on the land really amount to "possessing" the land. Furthermore, even though courts say a person has to actually possess the land to obtain title by adverse possession, under some circumstances, a person may "actually" possess land that she doesn't physically occupy or use. I clue you in to when a person *actually* possesses land in the following sections.

The requirements for proving adverse possession are very similar to the requirements for proving a prescriptive easement (see Chapter 6). The difference, of course, is that a prescriptive easement is just the nonpossessory right to use another's land, whereas adverse possession results in title to the land. If the trespasser's use isn't substantial enough to constitute actual possession or if the use isn't exclusive of the record owner (see the later section on possessing exclusively), it may still satisfy the elements for a prescriptive easement. Such an easement entitles the person to continue using the property as she has been using it, even though she won't become the owner of the property. So be sure to consider the possibility of a prescriptive easement as well as the possibility of title by adverse possession.

Defining actual possession

Possessing property is a fundamental attribute of property ownership. By definition, an owner has the right to possess. Title by adverse possession arises when someone acts like an owner for a long period of time; you aren't acting like an owner if you don't possess the property.

Possessing real property means being physically present on the land and exercising physical control over it. Of course, property owners may not be physically present on the land all the time, and adverse possessors don't have to be physically present all the time in order to satisfy this element of the doctrine, either. But they do have to possess the land like an owner of such land would.

Because land and circumstances vary so much, it's hard to tell precisely what will count as possession and what won't count as possession. But here are a few observations about what counts as possession:

✔ Building substantial structures and other improvements is convincing evidence of possession.

✔ Fencing or otherwise marking boundaries tends to support a claim of possession, although it isn't essential to possession.

✔ Regular use of the land that is appropriate for the type of land generally counts as possession. For example, farming farmland is generally considered possession of the farmland.

✔ Irregular or sporadic use of the land may or may not be possession. Recreational uses of undeveloped land, harvesting timber or other natural products from the land, and grazing animals are examples of such uses that courts have sometimes held to be possession and other times have not.

✔ Some state statutes specify that a person may acquire title by adverse possession only if he encloses, cultivates, or improves the land in a usual way.

Determining the scope of possession

Because an adverse possessor acquires title to the land she adversely possessed, a court has to figure out exactly which land she possessed — which isn't always easy to do. It's a question of fact, of course, and it's up to the adverse possessor to prove exactly which land she possessed. Two things that can help determine the extent of her possession are

✔ **The adverse possessor's activities:** The possessor's activities may have been substantial on some parts of the property and only sporadic and insubstantial on others. For example, she may have built a house and made other improvements on some parts and simply walked across other parts of the property. In such a case, the possessor would acquire title only to the part of the land that she actually possessed.

✔ **Fences and other boundary signs:** In situations where the adverse possessor fences or otherwise encloses the property, courts will likely find that she possessed all the land within the enclosure. Even other indications of boundaries, like planting trees and shrubs or mowing grass, may support a finding that she actually possessed all the land within those boundaries, even though she didn't improve some parts of the property and used them less frequently.

Don't forget about underground! Possession of the surface is normally possession of the area underground, too. But if the minerals underground are owned by someone else, a possibility I cover in Chapter 4, then possessing the surface doesn't count as possessing the minerals underground. In such a case, the only way someone could actually possess the mineral estate is by extracting the minerals.

Possessing under color of title

Ordinarily, an adverse possessor obtains title only to the property she actually possesses. But the rule is different if she took possession under color of title. Taking possession under *color of title* means taking possession because the possessor received a deed or other legal document that purported to give her the property but that was invalid for some reason. In that case, the possessor possesses the whole property described in that document, even if she physically possesses only part of it.

However, if the document purports to convey parcels actually owned separately by different people, the possessor under color of title has possession only of the parcels that she actually occupies at least in part. If she doesn't physically occupy any part of one owner's parcel, then that owner wouldn't have any cause to eject her as a trespasser, and she can't be an adverse possessor of that parcel.

Paying taxes

Some state statutes require that an adverse possessor pay property taxes on the property to obtain title by adverse possession. In the absence of such a statute, an adverse possessor doesn't have to pay property taxes to obtain title by adverse possession. Payment of taxes isn't an act of possession because it isn't a physical act on the land itself. But it may be evidence of other elements of an adverse possession claim, such as hostility.

Element #2: Possessing Exclusively

To obtain title by adverse possession, a person must possess the land exclusive of others. As Chapter 2 notes, the right to exclude is one of the fundamental attributes of ownership; in fact, it may be the most fundamental attribute of ownership. So it's no surprise that the adverse possession doctrine requires that the adverse possessor exclude others just as an owner would; otherwise, the person wouldn't be acting like an owner at all.

Exclusive possession means that the record owner doesn't share possession with the possessor. If the record owner is still in possession, no other person can acquire adverse possession title — no matter how she uses the property.

The possessor must also exclude third parties as an owner would. Property owners don't exclude everyone, of course. They may invite and permit people to enter their land for various purposes. Likewise, such acts by an adverse possessor don't mean her possession wasn't exclusive. But the possessor must exercise control over who enters and who doesn't. If people enter the land without consent and the possessor does nothing about it, the possessor's possession isn't exclusive and she can't acquire title by adverse possession.

More than one person can adversely possess together and thereby become tenants in common and own the adversely possessed property together. (I cover tenancy in common in Chapter 10.) But if two or more competing people possess the land, then none of them are possessing exclusively and none can receive title by adverse possession.

Element #3: Possessing Openly and Notoriously

An adverse possessor must openly and notoriously possess the property. To *openly and notoriously* possess property, she must possess the property in a way that's so visible that a reasonably diligent owner would discover her possession. This requirement ensures that the owner knew (or at the very least should've known) about the apparent adverse claim of ownership by someone else so that he could take action within the limitations period to eject the trespasser.

If a reasonably diligent owner wouldn't discover the possession, then it isn't open and notorious. So if the possession is in an underground cave and a reasonably diligent owner wouldn't be aware of what was happening underground, then the possession can't result in title by adverse possession. But if the cave has a visible entrance on the surface and a reasonably diligent owner would observe the possessor coming and going, then the possession is open and notorious.

Similarly, at least some courts have held that if the possession is visible on the surface but is only a very small encroachment across the property line, a reasonably diligent owner wouldn't be aware of such an encroachment because he couldn't detect it without a survey. Therefore, the courts may not consider such an encroachment to be open and notorious.

A reasonably diligent owner periodically inspects his property. So if such an inspection would reveal the adverse possession, it's open and notorious. The owner can't defeat an adverse possession claim simply by saying he didn't live nearby and didn't actually know what was happening on the land.

Adversely possessing chattels

This chapter talks about adverse possession of real property, but you can obtain ownership of chattels by adverse possession, too. (*Chattels* are tangible personal property; see Chapter 2 for details.) The same rules generally apply. Because the possession must be open and notorious, the limitations period doesn't begin to run if possession is concealed or isn't reasonably discoverable by the record owner. In some states, the limitations period doesn't begin to run until the owner actually knows who has possession or where the chattel is. In fact, some courts have held that the limitations period doesn't begin to run until the owner demands that the possessor return the chattel.

Element #4: Possessing Adversely

Adverse possession must be adverse or hostile to the record owner's title. In other words, the adverse possessor must be a trespassing possessor who would be subject to an ejectment action. Otherwise, the record owner has no cause of action for the statute of limitations to bar. The following sections clarify when possession is adverse or hostile.

Possessing by right rather than permission

The essence of adverse possession is that it's adverse to, or in conflict with, the owner's title. So if the possessor's activities are consistent with the record owner's title, the possession isn't adverse.

Here are some circumstances in which someone other than the record owner is doing something that could appear possessory but that isn't considered adverse:

- ✔ The possessor entered the property by invitation or license from the record owner. Usually such permission has to be explicitly stated, although many courts have held that owners of undeveloped and unenclosed land implicitly give people permission to enter the land for uses compatible with the owner's title, such as recreational uses.

- ✔ The possessor is a tenant.

- ✔ The possessor is buying the property on a long-term installment contract with the contractual right to possess the property during the term of the contract.

✔ The possessor is a co-owner of the property. By definition, co-owners have the undivided right to possess the whole property that is co-owned. So if one co-owner possesses the property but the others don't, that possession is consistent with the rights of the co-owners and, therefore, not adverse or hostile.

These kinds of uses ordinarily aren't hostile or adverse, but they may become hostile or adverse if the possessor says or does something that indicates an adverse claim. Asserting an adverse claim may be called an *ouster*. A tenant or co-owner, for example, might simply declare to the landlord or other co-owners that she claims ownership for herself. Or one in possession may demonstrate such an intention by her conduct. For example, she may refuse to allow the record owner or co-owners to enter the property as they would otherwise have the right to do. At that point, the possession becomes adverse and hostile, and the ousted owner must take action to eject the possessor within the limitations period.

According to most authorities, the ousted owner can't simply declare that she gives permission to the possessor and thereby prevent the possession from being adverse. Once ousted, the owner knows that the possessor claims an adverse interest and that the possessor is exercising that interest, so the owner must bring a lawsuit denying that interest within the limitations period, or else he loses the right to do so.

Using the property as an owner

If the use isn't consistent with the owner's title in the kinds of ways described earlier, it's adverse and hostile. *Hostile* in this sense doesn't mean the parties must be in conflict somehow; it means only that the possession isn't consistent with the record owner's title. Because the record owner has the right of possession, any possession by someone else is inconsistent with the title unless the record owner can show that the possessor is there only because of the record owner's grant.

Sometimes courts and others say that possessing adversely means the possessor possesses under a *claim of right,* meaning she possesses as if she has the right to do so. This phrase may help you remember that this element requires only that the possessor act as an owner. The possession doesn't have to be contrary to the record owner's desires; it just has to be contrary to the record owner's title.

So if the record owner of 40 acres orally gave one of those acres to a friend, the friend's possession would thereafter be adverse because the possession is under a claim of right. The friend is possessing as if she has the right to do so. You could also explain that the possession is adverse because it's inconsistent with the record owner's title to all 40 acres. The possessor isn't in possession because of permission from the record owner; she's in possession because the owner gave the property to her — even though the grant was invalid because it didn't satisfy the statute of frauds. Although possession can be hostile even if not under color of title, someone who does possess property under color of title possesses adversely because she possesses by virtue of the purported grant, under a claim of right, rather than by revocable permission of the record owner.

On the other hand, using the phrase *claim of right* to describe adversity may cause confusion, too. The phrase can suggest that the possessor must believe that she has the right to possess the land. But most courts agree that the possessor doesn't have to subjectively believe that the property is hers; the possessor just has to objectively act as an owner would act so that the record owner is on notice of some possible conflict about the state of title and can take action to resolve that conflict. However, in some cases, courts have held that if the possessor doesn't subjectively mean to claim ownership of the possessed land, then she can't acquire title by adverse possession, especially if the possessed land is land adjoining her own and the parties have simply been mistaken about the location of the actual boundary between them.

Element #5: Possessing Continuously and without Interruption

An adverse possessor must continuously possess the property without interruption throughout the adverse possession period. This requirement does three main things:

✔ Ensures that the adverse possession has continued for the required length of time, during which the record owner didn't take action to stop it

✔ Helps to indicate that the possessor is acting as an owner would, because owners continuously possess

✔ Helps ensure that the record owner should've known about the possession because, if at any point the record owner had inspected the property, the record owner would've discovered the possession

The following sections explain in more detail what the possessor must prove to satisfy this element of an adverse possession claim.

Defining continuous possession

The possessor must possess the land continuously as an owner would. Owners aren't always present on their land, of course, so normal absences from the land don't make the possession discontinuous. But if the possession is occasional and irregular, then it isn't the kind of possession that typifies ownership and that will give a person title by adverse possession.

Like other elements of the adverse possession doctrine, the essential idea of the continuous possession element is that the possessor acted as an owner would act. So if the property is remote property that an owner would occupy only seasonally, then such seasonal adverse possession would likely be sufficiently continuous to satisfy this element of the claim.

If at any point during the limitations period the possessor leaves the property without intent to return, the possession is no longer continuous. Even if she returns to the property and resumes possession, the limitations period starts over.

Interrupting possession

If another person (the record owner or anyone else) interrupts the possession during the limitations period, then the possession isn't continuous and uninterrupted and won't give title by adverse possession.

Not every interference with the possession is an interruption. Only those interferences that are inconsistent with the possessor's exclusive possession defeat an adverse possession claim. The following examples help clarify when interferences count as interruptions and when they don't:

- ✔ If a third person trespasses and kicks the possessor off the land and the possessor successfully brings a lawsuit to regain possession, then the possessor's possession is still continuous and uninterrupted. But if the trespasser retains possession for a substantial period of time before the possessor takes action, then the possession is considered to be interrupted.

- ✔ If the record owner enters into possession of the land in asserting his own title, even for a brief time, he disrupts the continuity of possession, regardless of whether the record owner possessed the property exclusive of the possessor. Such possession by the record owner is inconsistent with the possessor's exclusive possession. On the other hand, if the record owner enters the property by permission of the possessor rather than by virtue of the record owner's hostile claim, then the possession isn't interrupted.

- ✔ If the record owner successfully sues to eject the possessor, the filing of the lawsuit interrupts the possession.

- ✔ Mere assertion of title by the record owner doesn't interrupt possession. So actions such as threatening the possessor, making demands, and posting signs don't interrupt possession; if anything, they merely highlight the fact that the possession is adverse. In fact, filing an ejectment action doesn't interrupt possession if the owner doesn't successfully prosecute the claim.

Element #6: Possessing for the Statutory Period

A possessor acquires title by adverse possession if she possesses actually, exclusively, openly, adversely, and continuously for the required period of time. At the moment she does so, the property becomes hers. The following sections explain how to determine when she has possessed the property long enough to acquire title.

Determining the required period

The common law adverse possession period was 20 years, but all 50 states now have statutes that specify the limitations period applicable to adverse possession claims. These periods vary but generally last between 5 and 20 years.

However, many state statutes specify shorter required time periods in certain circumstances, such as the following:

- The possessor entered into possession under color of title.
- The possessor paid property taxes on the possessed property.
- The possessor has enclosed or cultivated the possessed property.

In the absence of these circumstances, some statutes require an even longer period of possession than the common-law period of 20 years.

Combining periods of possession

Sometimes multiple people take turns adversely possessing property, with each person possessing the property for a period of time. These periods of adverse possession are combined, or *tacked,* as long as the successive possessors are in *privity,* meaning the successive possessor takes over possession from the predecessor instead of independently beginning her own possession. In other words, the prior possessor purports to transfer ownership of the adversely possessed property to the successor, even though the prior possessor doesn't legally own the property.

If the adversely possessed property is land adjoining property the possessor actually *does* own, then successive owners of the actually owned land are in privity even though the legal descriptions of the property in their deeds don't include the adversely possessed portion.

Consider the case of a person who enters into possession of some property under color of title — say, a void deed — and possesses the property for four years. Then she sells the property to another person, who takes possession for another four years. Then that person dies and her devisee takes possession for another four years. Say the applicable state statute requires possession for ten years. None of the three people individually possessed the property for the required ten years, but together they possessed the property for more than ten years. After they collectively have possessed the property for ten years, the current possessor (the devisee) acquires title, even though she has possessed it for only two years.

The same principle applies to the record owner: The adverse possession period runs cumulatively against successive owners of the adversely possessed property. If a person adversely possesses land owned by A for eight years and then continues to adversely possess that land for another two years after A transfers the land to B, the adverse possessor has adversely possessed the land for ten years. If the limitations period is ten years, the adverse possessor has acquired title by adverse possession, even though B personally had only two years to discover the adverse possession and eject her.

Understanding Title by Adverse Possession

As soon as the adverse possessor has actually possessed the land exclusively, openly and notoriously, adversely, and continuously for the statutory period, she owns the title to the property. Her title is a new title that originates from the fact that no one with a superior claim has the right to eject her from the property. The following sections explore the character of title obtained by adverse possession.

Quieting adverse possession title

After the requirements of adverse possession have been met, the adverse possessor is an owner like any other owner. She doesn't need to obtain a judicial decree to own the property, and she doesn't have to keep possessing exclusively, openly and notoriously, and so on. At that point, she could abandon the property and it would still be hers — unless and until someone else adversely possesses the property against her.

But even though the adverse possessor owns title automatically after she meets the requirements of the adverse possession doctrine, her title may be unmarketable. By its nature, adverse possession title is unrecorded. Such a title is also naturally subject to the uncertainty of litigation because parties may dispute the facts about whether the adverse possessor actually met the requirements of the doctrine. As a result, a reasonably prudent buyer may not be willing to buy such a property from the adverse possessor.

All real estate purchase contracts are conditioned upon the seller tendering marketable title to the property unless the contract says otherwise. (Chapter 15 explains what makes title marketable and unmarketable.) Some states have held that title based only on adverse possession is unmarketable because it's unrecorded and it requires litigation to resolve possible factual disputes about whether the adverse possessor really did satisfy the requirements. But other states have held that title based on adverse possession is marketable. In either case, the parties to a contract can specify for themselves which quality of title the seller must tender to the buyer. If the contract requires record title, then if the seller's title to some or all of the property is based on adverse possession, the seller's title doesn't satisfy the contract title condition.

The adverse possessor can ensure that her title is marketable by obtaining a judicial decree in a quiet title action. As Chapter 2 notes, a *quiet title action* is an action in equity to obtain a judicial declaration about a person's title to land. Even though the successful adverse possessor owns the property without a judicial declaration, a quiet title action results in a decree that resolves uncertainty and that provides a public record of the adverse possessor's title, thereby ensuring that her title is marketable.

Identifying the interests affected

Successful adverse possession bars the former owner from bringing a lawsuit to eject the adverse possessor, thus giving the adverse possessor ownership of the property. So adverse possession works against only those who would've had the right to bring an ejectment action against the possessor but didn't.

That means the adverse possessor may not obtain fee simple absolute in some cases (see Chapter 9 for discussion of fee simple absolute and other estates). The holder of a future interest, such as a remainder or an executory interest, doesn't have the right of present possession. Because a future interest holder couldn't have brought a lawsuit to eject the adverse possessor, the limitations period doesn't cut off his right to do so. If and when the future interest becomes possessory, the future interest holder would then have a right to bring a claim against the possessor and the limitations period would begin to run. In short, the adverse possessor generally obtains the present estate formerly owned by the disseised owner, so if the disseised owner owned just a life estate, that's what the adverse possessor has.

Similarly, adverse possession may not extinguish nonpossessory interests in the property, such as easements and covenants. If the adverse possession wasn't adverse to those interests, then the owners of those interests had no cause of action against the possessor, and the statute of limitations wouldn't bar them from asserting their interests in the future. But if the adverse possession was adverse to such interests, then the adverse possessor takes title free of them. In short, the adverse possessor must independently extinguish those nonpossessory interests by adverse possession of them because they aren't dependent on the owner's possessory title.

 For example, if someone has a right-of-way to pass across the adversely possessed property, he'll retain his easement if the adverse possessor didn't interfere with his use of the right-of-way during the adverse possession period, but he'll lose his easement if the adverse possessor prevented him from using it during that period.

Chapter 15

Contracting to Sell Land

*M*ost landowners get their land by buying it from previous owners. Almost all land purchases begin with a contract in which the seller and buyer agree on the terms by which they'll buy and sell the property at some time in the future, although such a contract isn't legally necessary. But the buyer and seller usually have a lot of work to do before they're ready to actually buy and sell anything. Among other things, the buyer probably needs to borrow money from a mortgage lender to pay the seller, and she may want to inspect buildings and survey the land. The buyer also needs to make sure that the seller has good title to the property, and the seller may have some work to do to clean up the title.

The buyer doesn't want to do all this work only to have the seller sell the property to someone else, and the seller doesn't want to do this work only to have the buyer change her mind and buy some other property. So both the buyer and the seller have reasons to enter into an enforceable purchase agreement before they invest time and money in preparing for the sale.

Because all sorts of things can go wrong before the parties complete the sale, such purchase agreements typically address what happens if various things do go wrong and include provisions intended to reduce the chances that they'll happen at all. Often, these contracts even include provisions that excuse either or both parties from completing the sale if certain conditions aren't met.

This chapter takes a look at all these typical aspects of real estate purchase agreements. It explains the parties' remedies if the other breaches the contract and examines duties that the seller may owe to the buyer that aren't created by their contract.

Creating an Enforceable Contract to Sell Real Property

Real estate purchase agreements are enforceable contracts just like any other contracts, and they're subject to the same general rules. Two parties form an enforceable purchase agreement only when one party makes an offer and the other accepts it. The agreement also must be supported by consideration, but the parties' respective promises to deliver a deed and to pay the purchase price are themselves sufficient consideration. (For details on all these generally applicable contract rules, see *Contract Law For Dummies* by Scott J. Burnham [Wiley].)

Real estate purchase agreements are also subject to the statute of frauds. Every state has a statute of frauds that generally says such contracts, as well as other types of legal documents specified in the statute, are unenforceable unless the purchase agreement, or some other documentary evidence of it, is in writing and signed by the party challenging its enforcement. The following sections explain the requirements of the statute of frauds and address an exception known as part performance.

Real estate purchase agreements go by many names, including the following:

- ✔ Sales contract
- ✔ Earnest money agreement
- ✔ Buy-sell agreement
- ✔ Binder
- ✔ Deposit receipt
- ✔ Marketing contract

Requiring a signed writing

Purchase agreements generally satisfy the statute of frauds because they're in writing and signed by both the buyer and the seller. But a purchase agreement may be enforceable even if it isn't in writing and signed by both parties. An unwritten agreement is enforceable in the following situations:

- ✔ **Written offer and acceptance:** Even if the parties never sign a purchase agreement, if one party submits a written offer and the other party signs that offer in acceptance, the written offer satisfies the statute of frauds as long as it includes the essential elements of the contract.

✔ **Other written evidence:** The statute of frauds permits enforcement of an unwritten purchase agreement if the party challenging it has signed some other writing (such as a letter, a deed, or instructions to an escrow agent) that sufficiently evidences the parties' contract. Even a check may satisfy the statute of frauds when the check includes notations that evidence the transaction, such as "10% deposit for Lot 8, Sunnyside Subdivision." Such written evidence may be combined to provide sufficient written evidence of the contract and its terms.

✔ **Defendant's admission:** Some states hold that the statute of frauds doesn't require a writing if the party challenging the enforcement of the contract admits in court documents or testimony that the parties had a contract.

Identifying essential elements of a writing

As with any kind of contract, the parties to the purchase agreement must agree on the essential terms in order to have an enforceable contract. The statute of frauds itself doesn't say which terms have to be in writing to satisfy the statute, so the courts have had to answer that question. The following elements must be included in the signed writings:

✔ **The signature of the party challenging the existence of the contract:** Usually this means the party has signed her name, but any other mark made for the purpose of authenticating the writing satisfies the statute. If the buyer seeks to enforce the contract against the seller, the seller must have signed the writing, and vice versa. In practice, both parties should sign the purchase agreement to ensure an enforceable contract. A few state statutes say only that the seller must have signed the contract, although even in those states a contract wouldn't be enforceable against a buyer who hadn't signed unless the seller can at least prove that the buyer accepted the contract.

✔ **Identification of the parties to the contract:** The writings must name or otherwise identify both the buyer and the seller. Even a reference to the "owner" of the described property is sufficient because you can determine who the owner is from public records.

✔ **Identification of the property:** In general, this required element is satisfied as long as a court can figure out from the writing which property the seller was selling to the buyer. A street address is generally sufficient, unless the parties don't specify the city and state, in which case some courts hold the identification of the land inadequate. As long as the writing has some description, the court may consider unwritten evidence to resolve ambiguity or uncertainty about the property's boundaries.

✔ **Indication of the intent to buy or sell:** The writings must indicate that the seller intends to sell and the buyer intends to buy the identified property.

✔ **Other essential terms:** People may disagree whether other terms are essential to a particular contract. For example, if the parties agreed on a purchase price for the property, some courts say the purchase price is an essential term that must be included in a writing to satisfy the statute of frauds. If the parties agreed that the seller would finance the purchase, many courts require the terms of the seller's financing to be included in a writing, too.

Amending or rescinding the purchase agreement

Even though the parties' agreement must be evidenced in writing, the parties can rescind it without a writing. The statute of frauds doesn't require contracts that rescind other contracts to be in writing.

Amending the agreement, however, generally does require a writing. Unless the parties change the agreement so much that they aren't selling and buying real estate anymore, a contract amendment must satisfy the statute of frauds just as an original contract must. So if an amendment isn't evidenced in writing, the original purchase agreement continues to bind the parties.

Even so, a party often can enforce unwritten amendments against the other party because of *promissory estoppel,* the principle that a promise is enforceable if the other person reasonably relies on the promise to her detriment. If the parties orally agree to change one of the party's obligations and that party proceeds to rely on that agreement to her detriment, the other is estopped to deny the amendment.

A purchase agreement may say that a buyer has 30 days to obtain a financing commitment from a lender. If the seller orally agrees that the buyer can take more time and the buyer proceeds to let the 30-day deadline pass in reliance on that oral agreement, then the seller couldn't thereafter rescind the contract or seek other relief because of the buyer's failure to meet the 30-day deadline. In fact, the parties' actions may implicitly modify the contract without their saying anything, and such implied amendments may be enforced by estoppel as well.

Making an exception when an oral agreement is partly performed

Even though the statute of frauds doesn't say so, courts agree that part performance of a purchase agreement makes it enforceable even if it doesn't comply with the statute of frauds. Courts differ in their explanations and application of the part performance doctrine, however.

One theory explaining this doctrine is that certain kinds of actions by the parties — some of which aren't really performing the contract at all — may take the place of a writing because they're sufficient evidence that the parties made a contract. The part performance doctrine considers the following types of actions as alternative evidence of the parties' contract:

- **Payment of the purchase price:** If the buyer pays some or all of the purchase price to the seller, the courts figure that they must have had a contract of some sort because the buyer wouldn't have just given the money to the seller for nothing.

- **Possession:** If the buyer takes possession of the property, that possession is pretty good evidence that the buyer did indeed contract to buy the property from the seller. Unlike payment of the purchase price, this action isn't really performance of the alleged contract because the buyer doesn't promise the seller that she will take possession. But it is an action that the parties may take because of the alleged contract.

- **Substantial improvements:** If the buyer makes substantial improvements to the property, those improvements are considered especially convincing evidence that the buyer had a contract to buy the property. Again, this action almost certainly isn't an act of performing the contract promises, but it's good evidence of the contract because the buyer wouldn't invest time and money in improving someone else's property.

A few courts require all three of these actions to enforce a purchase agreement that doesn't comply with the statute of frauds. But most of them simply look at all the actions in these categories and determine whether the evidence is sufficiently convincing that the parties did have a contract, despite the lack of written evidence. Most courts agree that payment of consideration alone isn't enough evidence because it's more likely than the other two actions to be ambiguous; the buyer may be paying money to the seller for all sorts of reasons that have nothing to do with a real estate sale, including an agreement to lease. Some courts require payment of consideration along with one of the other two types of actions.

Another explanation for the part performance doctrine is more like estoppel: If a party has taken action in reliance on the contract and those actions would be detrimental if the contract weren't enforced, then a court should, in fairness, enforce the contract. This explanation focuses on whether the actions would result in a hardship, not the evidentiary quality of the parties' actions. The more substantial the reliance, the more likely a court is to find part performance and excuse the absence of written evidence. Because the part performance actions are all actions primarily taken by the buyer — paying money to the seller, taking possession of the property, and building substantial improvements — this theory may seem to be more likely to find part performance when the buyer seeks to enforce the contract and the seller denies its existence. But the seller may also suffer harm from having allowed the buyer to take possession and build improvements.

When the part performance doctrine allows enforcement of a purchase agreement, courts generally say that it's enforceable only in equity, meaning that a party can specifically enforce the contract against the other but can't get damages for the other's breach (see the later section for more on breaches of contract).

Part performance is an exception to the statute of frauds. It isn't an alternative way of proving the existence of a contract. In any case, the party seeking to enforce the contract must prove that it existed, whether that proof is written or not.

Specifying Deadlines for Performance

A purchase agreement isn't a sale; it's an agreement to sell in the future. Therefore, it's an *executory contract,* meaning it's an agreement that requires the parties to do certain things they haven't done yet. The parties typically have a number of preliminary obligations to perform, such as applying for a loan or getting a title insurance commitment, and their primary obligations come at the end of the process: The seller will deliver a deed and the buyer will pay the purchase price.

Buyers and sellers almost always include in their contracts a date on which they will close the sale — when the seller will transfer the deed and the buyer will transfer the purchase price. They often include deadlines for other obligations and conditions, too. If they don't, the parties will have a reasonable time to perform their obligations, as a court decides under the circumstances.

Some obligations that have deadlines are conditional, meaning the parties have the obligation only if some condition is fulfilled. If the condition isn't fulfilled, then the failure to perform the obligation, whether on time or not, isn't a breach. Skip to the section "Conditioning the Parties' Obligations to Perform" for details on conditions.

The following sections reveal the consequences when a contract includes dates and deadlines for performance and one or both of the parties don't meet those deadlines.

Remedying an immaterial breach of a deadline

As long as applicable conditions have been fulfilled, if one party doesn't perform her obligation by the date specified in the contract, she has breached the contract. This is true whether the obligation is the ultimate obligation to close the purchase or a preliminary obligation to perform some preparatory step, like getting a mortgage loan.

However, the available remedies for the breach differ depending on whether the breach of the deadline is material. A breach is *material* if it prevents the nonbreaching party from enjoying the essential benefits of the contract. For example, the seller materially breaches the contract if she can't deliver legal title to the property when required. If a breach is material, the nonbreaching party can *rescind* (terminate) the contract; if it isn't material, the nonbreaching party is entitled to damages, but the contract is still enforceable.

Unless the parties agree otherwise, courts assume that deadlines for performing contract obligations are nonessential to the contract. As long as the party eventually performs her obligations within some reasonable time, the other party will still enjoy the essential benefits of the contract, even though it's later than expected. So such a breach wouldn't be material.

If one party immaterially breaches a deadline, damages are the other party's only remedy. The damages consist of whatever financial harm the nonbreaching party suffers because of the delay; if the other party never performs the contract, the nonbreaching party can recover damages for the loss of the benefit of the contract itself. The buyer's damages from delay may include lost rents or profits from the property; the seller's damages from delay may include extra insurance premiums, taxes, and interest the seller had to pay as a result. Of course, a delay in closing may also save each party some money, so those savings must be offset against the losses in calculating damages.

Remedying a material breach of a deadline

Although courts assume deadlines aren't essential to the contract, a delay in performance is a material breach in two situations:

- ✔ The delay is unreasonable.
- ✔ Time is of the essence.

Even though failure to perform an obligation by a stated deadline generally isn't a material breach, the breach becomes material if the party doesn't perform the obligation within a reasonable time afterward. The reasonableness of the delay depends on the circumstances.

A delay in performance is also a material breach if time is of the essence, meaning one or both parties have indicated that a particular deadline is essential to the performance of the contract. Here are the three ways that time may be of the essence:

- **Contract clause:** The purchase agreement itself may include a clause making time of performance essential. Merely stating a deadline doesn't make time of the essence; the purchase agreement must actually say "time is of the essence" or otherwise indicate that failure to meet the deadline is a material breach that excuses the other party from performing. The purchase agreement may declare time to be of the essence in general, meaning all the deadlines specified in the contract are essential terms, or it may say that time is of the essence with regard only to particular provisions, such as the closing date.

- **Extrinsic evidence:** Special circumstances of the transaction may indicate that time is of the essence. Such circumstances may include the parties' discussions about the importance of closing on time, economic reasons why prompt closing is essential (like a volatile market or a property that's declining in value quickly), or other transactions that one party plans and the other party knows about that depend on prompt closing.

- **One party's declaration:** Even if the purchase agreement doesn't say that time is of the essence, one party can make time of the essence by notifying the other party a reasonable time in advance. One party can make the originally stated deadline or an alternative date material, as long as she gives reasonable advance notice. But if the party doesn't give the other a reasonable amount of notice, breach of the deadline won't be considered a material breach. Reasonable notice depends on all the circumstances, including the amount of time and work required to meet the deadline and the parties' expectations.

If a breach of a deadline is material, the nonbreaching party may rescind the contract. She's thereby excused from her obligation to perform the contract, so the breaching party can't sue to specifically perform the contract. Alternatively, the nonbreaching party can recover damages for delay but still go forward with the contract. The nonbreaching party may also expressly or by implication waive her right to rescind the contract for delay. For example, by accepting late performance of some obligations, the nonbreaching party may waive the right to insist on timely performance of other obligations. Simply not objecting to delay may also be a waiver.

If time is of the essence and neither party tenders performance on the specified closing date, some courts say that either party may specify a new closing date by giving the other reasonable notice. Other courts reason that both parties have committed a material breach of the contract, so both of them are released from their obligations under the contract unless they indicate by words and actions that they waive the breach.

Conditioning the Parties' Obligations to Perform

Both parties to the purchase agreement promise to complete the sale in the future, but one of the biggest reasons for making such a promise in advance is to give the parties — especially the buyer — time to make sure the deal is feasible and desirable. If it turns out otherwise, the parties also want the right to abandon the deal.

Therefore, the contract may specify conditions that must be fulfilled before a party is obligated to perform the contract, called *conditions precedent.* The contract also may include *conditions subsequent,* which defeat or excuse a contractual obligation if they occur.

Whether a condition is precedent or subsequent, it's connected to an obligation to perform, excusing the obligation if the desired circumstances don't occur. Usually conditions benefit just one of the parties by making that party's obligations conditional, but a condition can also benefit both parties. Only a person who benefits from a condition can assert that condition. If a condition is unsatisfied, the benefited party can invoke the condition and decline to perform her conditional obligation, or she can waive the failure of the condition and perform the contract. She may waive the condition expressly or by actions that indicate that she's proceeding to perform the contract despite the failure of the condition. The nonbenefited party can't rescind the contract or otherwise take advantage of the unmet condition.

Some conditions may be within the parties' control; others may not be. To the extent that the parties do have control over whether a condition is met, the implied duty of good faith and fair dealing, which applies to contracts in general, requires them to try in good faith to meet the condition. Real estate purchase agreements often express such a requirement. If contracts didn't include such a requirement and the fulfillment of the condition were entirely within the control of a party, the contract would be unenforceable because the party could get out of the contract at will and the parties wouldn't have the mutuality of obligation required for an enforceable contract.

If the benefited party doesn't try in good faith to satisfy a condition to her own obligations or prevents the other party from satisfying such a condition, she can't excuse her performance because of the unmet condition. If the benefited party's obligation is conditioned on the other party's performance, the condition is met as long as the other party substantially performs her duty, even though it may not be completely or perfectly performed.

The following sections describe some of the common conditions found in real estate purchase agreements.

Tendering the deed and purchase price

The parties' main obligations — the seller to give a deed to the buyer and the buyer to give the purchase money to the seller — are conditioned on each other. Such conditions are called *concurrent conditions*. So if the seller doesn't or can't tender the required deed to the buyer, the buyer has no obligation to pay the purchase price. If the buyer doesn't or can't tender the purchase price to the seller, the seller has no obligation to give the buyer a deed. If neither party tenders her performance, then neither party has an obligation to perform and neither party has breached the contract — unless, some courts say, time is of the essence.

So if one party isn't ready to complete the sale, the other party has to tender her performance in order for the other to be in breach. A *tender* of performance is an offer to perform when the person is actually able to perform. For example, if the buyer doesn't have the money to buy the property at closing, the buyer is in breach only if the seller offers to deliver the required deed and actually has the required title.

The tendering requirement has a few exceptions. The nonbreaching party doesn't have to tender performance in the following situations:

- **Repudiation:** If the nonperforming party has *repudiated* the contract — meaning she has indicated by words or actions that she won't perform it — the other party may recover for breach without tendering his own performance.

- **Impossibility:** If the nonperforming party can't possibly perform, then the other party doesn't have to tender her performance. For example, if the seller has sold the property to somebody else, the seller can't possibly perform, so he's in breach regardless of whether the buyer tenders the purchase price.

Requiring marketable title

A condition about the quality of title is always included in a real estate purchase agreement. This condition benefits the buyer because the buyer doesn't have to go forward with buying the property if the seller can't convey the title she promised to convey. That's the whole point of the deal, so of course the buyer wouldn't have to buy something less than what the seller said she would sell.

Instead of including a title condition in the purchase agreement, the buyer could investigate the seller's title before entering into the agreement and decide then whether the title is acceptable. But determining the state of title isn't easy and generally involves paying someone else to research the title. So a title condition allows the buyer to enter into a binding purchase agreement and then proceed with investigation of the title.

If the title turns out to be unsatisfactory, the buyer doesn't have to buy the property, although she can waive the title condition and buy the property anyway if she wants to because the condition is for her benefit. If the title defect is relatively small, she may even be entitled to a judicial order reducing the purchase price to compensate for the title problem. In fact, the buyer may also recover damages or get other remedies from the seller because the title condition is not only a condition but also a covenant or promise by the seller to convey title of the specified quality.

The seller doesn't have to satisfy the title condition until closing. So unless the contract says otherwise, the seller has until that time to remove any title defects and satisfy the condition. In fact, the closing itself may be the means through which the seller makes the title marketable, such as by using the purchase price to pay off an existing mortgage or lien.

Furthermore, the buyer must notify the seller if she believes any title defects exist that prevent satisfaction of the title condition and allow a reasonable time — or a time that the parties agree to in their purchase agreement — for the seller to remove or fix the defects, unless the seller clearly can't fix the title problems anyway. If the seller doesn't fix the title problems within a reasonable time after receiving notice, the title condition excuses the buyer from buying the property.

The following sections describe implied and express title quality conditions and explain what they require.

Implicitly requiring marketable title

The contract usually states the title quality condition, but if it doesn't, such a condition is so fundamental that it's implied. As long as the purchase agreement says the seller will convey a particular estate to the buyer, the implied condition, in the absence of an express contract condition (see the next section), is that the title will be marketable. The only exception is if the contract doesn't require the seller to convey a particular estate and instead just requires what is usually called a *quitclaim deed* (Chapter 16 covers quitclaim deeds in detail). In that case, the seller doesn't claim to own anything at all but agrees to give the buyer a deed that conveys whatever right, title, and interest he has, if any. A purchase agreement to sell property by quitclaim deed would be rare.

The term *marketable title* can be a bit confusing because it doesn't simply mean a title that can be sold. As long as the seller has some interest in the land, however limited and however encumbered, he can sell it to someone else, and someone else would probably buy it for the right price. So the first thing to note about marketable title is that it means good title to whatever the seller contracts to convey. A life estate for the remaining lifetime of an elderly person, for example, may not be very marketable practically, but legally the life tenant may have marketable title to that life estate.

The implied marketable title condition, like any title condition, has two aspects:

✔ The title to be conveyed

✔ The required degree of certainty that the seller owns that title

The second of these two aspects is easier to summarize. The implied marketable title standard allows some uncertainty about the seller's title but requires that it be free from reasonable doubt, sufficiently certain that a reasonably prudent buyer would accept the uncertainties and go forward with the purchase.

The harder part is describing the title to be conveyed. When the implied marketable title condition applies, the title to be conveyed generally is the estate described in the contract free of encumbrances but with some exceptions. Probably the best way to understand what that means is to identify what makes title unmarketable:

✔ Lack of title to the estate promised

✔ Encumbrances on the estate

✔ Reasonable doubt about whether the seller has title or the property is encumbered

The seller obviously can't convey marketable title if she doesn't have title at all. So the seller's title is unmarketable if she doesn't own title to everything she agrees to convey in the purchase agreement. She may not own title for various reasons, such as a defect in the chain of title or the loss of the property to an adverse possessor (see Chapter 14 for details on adverse possession). But whatever the reason, if the seller doesn't have title to everything she promises to convey, the title is unmarketable.

If a seller says in the purchase agreement that she will convey an entire lot but she doesn't own title to the front 5 feet of that lot, she doesn't have marketable title. But if she says in the purchase agreement that she will convey all but the front 5 feet of the lot, then she does have marketable title.

Even when the seller owns title to the whole property described in the purchase agreement, her title isn't marketable if it's subject to encumbrances. _Encumbrances_ are nonpossessory interests that belong to other people. Following are some of the encumbrances that make title unmarketable:

✔ **Mortgages and liens:** As I note in Chapter 18, a _mortgage_ is an interest in the property given to another to secure repayment of a debt. If the debtor defaults, the mortgagee can sell the property at auction and apply the proceeds from the sale to the unpaid debt. A _lien_ is essentially an involuntary mortgage — the right of a third party to sell the property to satisfy a debt. For example, a person who gets a judgment for damages against another gets a judgment lien against her real property in that jurisdiction.

- **Easements:** An *easement* is a nonpossessory right to use the land in some way; see Chapter 6 for more on easements.

- **Covenants:** A *restrictive covenant* is the right to enforce a limitation on what the owner can do on the property. I cover covenants in detail in Chapter 5.

- **Leases:** Today a lease may be called an encumbrance on title, but it can also be considered a lack of title because in estate terms (which I cover in Chapter 9), the landlord owns only the future interest (called a *reversion*) and not the present estate. Either way, a lease makes title unmarketable.

- **Existing violations of zoning ordinances:** Even though a zoning ordinance doesn't technically affect title, some courts have held that an existing violation of a zoning ordinance makes title unmarketable.

- **Lack of access:** Some courts have held that lack of access from the land to a public street makes title unmarketable, even though the lack of access isn't really a title problem.

- **Encroachments:** Courts generally hold that title is unmarketable if the property has substantial improvements that significantly encroach on neighboring land or if neighboring land has such improvements that encroach on the property. This is true regardless of whether the limitations period has run to establish adverse possession or a prescriptive easement.

Even if the seller actually does have title free from encumbrances, title is unmarketable if there's reasonable doubt about the existence of a title defect. If someone else has a claim to an interest in the property that would require litigation to resolve and a reasonable buyer would object to it, the title is unmarketable.

For example, if someone else has been possessing some part of the property for a substantial period of time, title may be unmarketable because the buyer would have to bring a lawsuit to eject the possessor and the possessor may have acquired title to part of the property through adverse possession, which would require a lawsuit to resolve.

Similarly, if the seller's own title to the property is based on adverse possession, by himself or by a predecessor in title, some courts would say that his title is unmarketable unless the adverse possession claim is settled by a court in a quiet title action. Even though the seller may have good title, some courts reason that his title is unmarketable because it's subject to the uncertainty and burden of litigation in order to resolve the adverse possession claim for sure.

Not all encumbrances make title unmarketable. Courts have noted the following exceptions:

✔ **Visible easements:** Some courts say that if an easement was apparent to the buyer before she contracted to buy the property and the buyer agreed to buy the property anyway, then the buyer must have agreed to buy the property subject to that easement. This same reasoning may lead a court to hold that any encumbrance known to the buyer before contracting doesn't make title unmarketable.

✔ **Beneficial easements:** Easements that actually make the property more valuable may not make title unmarketable. For example, utility easements do limit the property owner's freedom of use in some ways, but they actually make the property more valuable by allowing the property to receive utility services.

✔ **Superfluous covenants:** Some courts have held that covenants don't make title unmarketable if they merely prevent the owner from doing things that a zoning ordinance or other public regulation prohibits anyway.

✔ **_De minimis_ defects:** Some courts hold that a title defect doesn't make title unmarketable if it's very minor or unlikely to be asserted.

Contracting about title quality

Most purchase agreements include express title quality conditions. Buyers and sellers almost always specify the title to be conveyed because the seller knows that his title isn't perfect and wouldn't satisfy the implied marketable title condition. The seller obviously doesn't want to promise to convey better title than he owns; if he did, he'd be asking for a lawsuit. So the seller instead agrees that he'll convey the title he actually has — although, of course, he may not know the extent of his actual title. Buyers and sellers also may specify a different standard of confidence or certainty that the seller has the described title, but that's less common.

The purchase agreement may describe the title to be conveyed by listing known title defects as exceptions to the title the seller will convey. For example, "seller will convey good fee simple absolute title to the property, subject to the recorded covenants of Sunnyside Subdivision and an easement in favor of Utility Company." Or it may describe exceptions categorically, such as "seller will convey good fee simple absolute title to the property, subject to easements and covenants of record." The buyer needs to be wary about agreeing to such a provision, because the buyer doesn't know which easements and covenants are recorded until she has a title search performed after she signs the purchase agreement.

If a real estate purchase agreement doesn't include some description of the title the seller will convey, even quite ordinary and acceptable title defects, like a subdivision's restrictive covenants, may make the title unmarketable.

The parties also sometimes specify different standards of confidence required. However, courts generally construe such standards as equivalent to the marketable title standard, unless they're clearly different. For example, some purchase agreements say that the seller must have "good" title. Many courts say that standard is the same as the marketable title standard. Others say it means a title that is in fact valid, even if it's doubtful and would require litigation to settle.

One fairly common contractual alternative that's different from the marketable title standard is an agreement that the promised title be "insurable." Such a standard may be easier to meet, because a title insurance company may be willing to insure against technical or minor title risks that would make title unmarketable.

When the contract requires the title to be insurable, confusion can result from not keeping the two aspects of the title quality condition separate. An insurable title condition is satisfied only if the title insurer agrees to insure the full title that the purchase agreement says the seller will convey to the buyer. The title insurer may agree to insure the title subject to an exception for a certain title problem that the purchase agreement doesn't describe as an exception to the title the seller would convey. In such a case, the title condition hasn't been met. For example, the purchase agreement may say that "the seller will convey insurable title to the property, subject to recorded easements and covenants." If the title insurer finds that someone else owns a lien on the property, the insurer may agree to insure the title generally but make an exception for losses resulting from the lien. Even though the title insurer is willing to insure some title, it isn't willing to insure the entire title that the seller promised to convey in the purchase agreement.

Another common contractual agreement is that the seller will convey good or marketable title "of record." That means that the public real property records must evidence the seller's title. Some states say that the implied marketable title standard requires the title to be of record anyway, but others don't. In those other states, this contractual agreement is different from the default implied marketable title standard. If the seller's title to some or all of the property derives from adverse possession and hasn't been settled by a quiet title action, his title may be good, but it isn't of record and thus doesn't satisfy the contract title condition. Or if some link in his chain of ownership isn't recorded, his title doesn't satisfy this condition.

Obtaining financing

The buyer often needs to borrow money to pay the purchase price. So the buyer includes in the purchase agreement a condition that she's excused from purchasing the property if she doesn't get the required mortgage loan. This condition doesn't benefit the seller, who has no reason to care how the buyer gets the purchase price, so if the buyer wants to waive this condition and go forward with the purchase, the seller can't object.

The terms of such financing conditions may be simple or detailed. If the condition just says the buyer must receive an acceptable or satisfactory loan, most courts would say the buyer must receive a loan that's commercially reasonable — in other words, one that a normal borrower would accept. The parties can avoid uncertainty and conflict by being more detailed in describing this condition. For example, the financing condition can specify a minimum loan amount the buyer must receive, a maximum interest rate, and the maximum costs the buyer may have to pay for the loan.

Sometimes the buyer can't get the required financing and the seller offers to finance some or all of the purchase so that the sale can go forward. Ideally, the parties say in their purchase agreement whether seller financing satisfies the financing condition. If they don't, courts tend to reason that seller financing doesn't satisfy the condition because borrowing from an individual is so different from borrowing from an institutional lender like a bank.

Even though the buyer can't ensure satisfaction of the financing condition, her actions can certainly make a big difference in whether the financing condition is fulfilled. So the buyer has an implied, often express, duty to make reasonable efforts to get the required financing. Generally, that means promptly applying for a loan from at least a few different lenders and cooperating with their reasonable requests. But the buyer doesn't have to make futile efforts, so if a lender would clearly decline the loan because of the application of standard criteria in the industry or because the lender has already indicated its intention, the borrower doesn't have to go through the motions of applying to satisfy her duty to diligently seek financing.

A buyer's efforts to obtain financing may be a condition to the seller's obligation to go forward with the purchase. So, for example, the purchase agreement may say that the seller may rescind the contract if the buyer doesn't apply for a mortgage loan within ten days of signing the agreement.

Considering other conditions

Purchase agreements can include many other conditions besides the ones I list in the preceding sections. For instance, the parties can include very specific conditions because of their unique circumstances, such as a condition that the buyer is obligated to buy only if she passes the bar exam. Most conditions, such as the ones in the following list, are for the benefit of the buyer, ensuring that the buyer doesn't have to go forward with the purchase if the deal turns out to be undesirable:

- ✔ A building inspection shows that the improvements on the land are in good condition.
- ✔ An inspection shows that the property isn't infested by pests.

✔ A survey confirms the boundaries of the property and the lack of encroachments or other title defects.

✔ The buyer gets zoning approval for her intended use, a required building permit, or other governmental approvals.

✔ The buyer sells her present house.

✔ The seller's existing mortgage lender consents to the buyer's assuming the existing mortgage loan.

The purchase agreement may also include conditions for the benefit of the seller. Here are some examples of such conditions:

✔ The seller's obligation to sell is conditioned on his successfully buying another house.

✔ The seller can rescind the contract if before closing he loses his new job that requires him to relocate to a different city.

✔ The seller can rescind the contract if the buyer doesn't make diligent efforts or complete preliminary steps within a specified time to fulfill a condition to the buyer's obligations. For example, if the buyer's purchase is conditioned on selling an existing house, the purchase agreement may say that the buyer will list the house for sale within ten days and have a contract to sell the house within 90 days, or else the seller may rescind the contract.

Managing the Risk of Loss

Real property is always subject to various risks that it will be damaged or that it will lose value. Fires, floods, tornadoes, and alien invasions may physically damage the land and its buildings. Changes in zoning and housing ordinances may impair the property's value. Or the government may take the property through its eminent domain power.

Such risks don't take a vacation just because a buyer and seller have a contract pending. Of course, the buyer and seller would both like to avoid such losses. But if such a loss occurred, the buyer would likely want to get out of the contract or get the seller to pay for the loss. The seller, on the other hand, would want the buyer to bear the cost and go forward with the purchase. Because of this difference in interests, a purchase agreement may include provisions intended to reduce and allocate such risks between the parties. If the purchase agreement doesn't include a relevant provision, a court may have to decide the consequences of the loss.

The following sections clarify how courts resolve risk-of-loss issues when the purchase agreement doesn't answer the question and how purchase agreements may reduce and allocate these risks.

Allocating risk by equitable conversion

If the purchase agreement doesn't address what happens in the event of damage or loss, most states apply the common law doctrine of *equitable conversion*. According to this doctrine, the buyer becomes the equitable owner of the property as soon as the parties have signed a purchase agreement that could be specifically enforced in equity. The seller still has legal title until he gives the buyer a deed, but the buyer's equitable title is the real ownership interest.

The equitable conversion doctrine means the buyer bears the usual risks of ownership, including the risk that the property will be damaged or lost. In other words, the buyer still has to go forward with the purchase of the property, even if such a loss occurs; it's as if the buyer has already bought the property. Like any property owner, the buyer enjoys the benefits of anything that happens to increase the value of the property, since the seller can't refuse to sell the property in accordance with the purchase agreement. Likewise, the buyer suffers the burden of any losses. Of course, if a third party causes the loss, the buyer may sue that person for damages. If the seller's negligence causes the loss, the buyer may pay a reduced price or rescind the contract.

Characterizing the parties' interests

In addition to making the buyer bear the risks of ownership, the equitable conversion doctrine may answer questions about the parties' interests in the property to be sold, like whether the parties' interests in the property are subject to judgment liens. Most states have statutes that say a judgment against a person becomes a lien against her real property in the jurisdiction. The statute itself may clearly say whether a seller's or buyer's interest is subject to such a lien, but if it doesn't, a court may rely on the equitable conversion principle. Most courts would conclude that the buyer's equitable title is real property subject to a judgment lien. But perhaps surprisingly, most courts would hold that the seller's legal title is also real property subject to a judgment lien.

Another such question courts sometimes answer with the equitable conversion doctrine is who gets the buyer's or seller's interest if she dies before closing. If the buyer dies, her equitable title is generally treated as real property and passes to the *devisees* or *heirs* — the people who by will or intestate succession receive her real property. The personal property of the estate must pay the remaining purchase price, however, which leaves less for the *legatees* or *next of kin* — the people who by will or intestate succession receive her personal property.

If the seller dies and the contract was signed after the will was made, courts generally reason that the seller no longer owns the real estate, but just a personal property right, namely the contract right to receive payment for the land at closing. So the legatees or next of kin would receive the payment. However, if the will was made after the contract was signed and it specifically devises the land being sold to someone, courts usually honor the testator's intention and award the purchase price to the devisee instead of concluding that the testator didn't own the land anymore and giving the devisee nothing.

Many have criticized the equitable conversion doctrine because the buyer may not expect to bear such losses and because the seller is generally in a better position to avoid and insure against them until closing. Some courts have avoided the application of the doctrine in particular cases by holding that the buyer didn't bear the risk of loss because a condition precedent hadn't been performed yet or because the seller didn't yet have the required title at the time the loss occurred.

Some states don't follow the traditional equitable conversion rule at all. For instance, some courts hold that the buyer can either rescind or have the price reduced if the property isn't in substantially the same condition on closing as it was when the parties signed the purchase agreement. Other states have adopted the Uniform Vendor and Purchase Risk Act, which allows the buyer to rescind the contract if a material loss occurs before the buyer has taken legal title or possession.

Contracting about risks

Most buyers and sellers agree not to follow the equitable conversion doctrine (described in the preceding section), perhaps because this traditional rule is inefficient and contrary to expectations. For example, the seller may agree by contract to deliver the property at closing in the same condition it was in when the parties signed the purchase agreement. Or the purchase agreement may say that if the property is substantially damaged by fire or other specified causes, the seller will fix the damage or the buyer can cancel the contract.

The parties can allocate risks however they want to in their purchase agreement. Some contracts are very specific about different kinds of risks. For example, the purchase agreement may say the buyer has the right to rescind if there's physical damage costing more than 50 percent of the purchase price to repair, that the buyer may not rescind but the seller will repair any damages costing between 20 and 50 percent of the purchase price, and that the buyer will bear the cost of any smaller damages; that the buyer has the right to rescind if there are unfavorable zoning changes that interfere with an intended use; and that the buyer may not rescind if the government takes the property but does get to keep the award of just compensation.

Insuring against risks

Insuring against the risk of loss is one way to reduce that risk. Both the buyer and the seller have an interest in the real property, so both parties can insure against losses. The purchase agreement may require one of the parties to insure the property until closing; such a contract clause may indicate that the insuring party is to bear the risk of loss as well.

If the party bearing the risk of loss has insurance, then the insurance policy will compensate her for her losses, and all is well. But sometimes the party bearing the risk of loss doesn't have insurance, while the other party does. This situation is much more likely to happen when the buyer bears the risk of loss, as is the case under the traditional equitable conversion rule, and the seller has insurance because he has been insuring the property throughout his time of ownership and simply hasn't cancelled the policy yet. In such a case, most courts agree that the seller can't keep the insurance proceeds and force the buyer to complete the purchase. The seller holds the insurance proceeds in a constructive trust for the buyer, and the seller can either use the insurance proceeds to repair the property or apply the proceeds to the purchase price.

A court will likely take a similar approach if the buyer is insured but the seller bears the risk of loss. If the buyer had insurance because the purchase agreement required it, then the insurance was also for the benefit of the seller, and if the buyer rescinds the contract, the seller should get the insurance proceeds. If the purchase agreement didn't require the buyer to have insurance before closing, the buyer may not have any claim to insurance proceeds if she chooses to rescind and therefore suffers no loss. If the buyer does claim insurance proceeds, they'll likely have to be applied to offset an abatement of the purchase price or to repair the property.

Remedying Breaches of Contract

If one of the parties breaches the purchase agreement, the other party may have a variety of remedies. The two main remedies available to the buyer and seller are damages and specific performance:

- **Damages:** Either party may recover damages if the other party breaches the contract. If the breach isn't material, like a delay in performance when time isn't essential, damages are the only available remedy. But either party may choose to recover damages for a material breach as well.

- **Specific performance:** Unless the contract says otherwise, the nonbreaching party may seek *specific performance,* a judicial decree requiring the breaching party to perform the contract. The general rule is that a court will order specific performance only when the remedy at law — an award of damages — would be inadequate.

The next sections offer more details on both types of remedies.

Calculating damages

The general measure of damages for a complete loss of the transaction is the favorable difference between the contract price and the market value of the property when the breach occurs. For the seller, that's the contract price minus the market value; for the buyer, it's the market value minus the contract price. If the seller soon sells the property to somebody else, the new contract price helps prove the value of the property at the time of the breach. Likewise, if the buyer had a contract to sell the property to someone else, that contract price can help prove the value of the property at the time of the breach.

If the seller breaches because he doesn't have the required title, even though he's acted in good faith, some courts hold that the buyer can't recover damages for the lost benefit of the bargain. Instead, the buyer can recover only her earnest money and any other out-of-pocket costs she has incurred, with interest.

In any case of total breach, the nonbreaching party may also recover foreseeable expenses in reliance on the contract and even foreseeable, proven lost profits that depended on performance of the contract.

Liquidating damages

If the buyer breaches, the seller instead may want to keep the buyer's deposit or earnest money as damages for the breach. The purchase agreement often expressly authorizes the seller to do so, but some courts hold that the seller may keep the earnest money as damages even if the purchase agreement doesn't directly say so.

Keeping the earnest money as damages is an example of *liquidated damages* — a fixed damages amount to which the parties agree by contract before a breach ever happens. Most courts say that liquidated damages are enforceable if the following two things are true:

- ✔ **The seller's actual damages would be difficult or impossible to measure.** Courts generally seem to assume this is true of a seller's damages for breach of the buyer's contract to buy real property.

✔ **At the time of the contract, the liquidated damages amount was a reasonable estimate of the actual damages the seller might suffer if the buyer were to breach.** Earnest money often isn't an estimate of damages at all but rather a traditional percentage of the purchase price, such as 10 percent. Still, most courts hold that a normal earnest money amount is enforceable as liquidated damages. But if the seller received a large deposit, and especially if the seller's actual damages turn out to be much less, a court may hold that the deposit isn't enforceable liquidated damages but rather an unenforceable penalty for breach.

The purchase agreement may say that the seller's only damage recovery is keeping the earnest money, or it may say that the seller has the option to keep the earnest money or recover actual damages. The latter is obviously more favorable to the seller. Some courts enforce such a clause; others don't.

The seller generally can decide not to seek damages at all and instead to specifically enforce the contract. However, the purchase agreement may indicate that liquidated damages are the seller's only remedy or that the buyer has the choice whether to buy the property or forfeit the deposit.

Specifically performing the contract

The buyer is almost always entitled to specific performance against the seller. Because courts reason that all properties are unique in some way, an award of market value could never fully compensate for the loss of the specific property the buyer is entitled to buy. As a result, damages are generally inadequate for a buyer, and she's entitled to specific performance.

Sellers usually can get specific performance against a breaching buyer, too. Of course, an award of damages is more likely to adequately compensate the seller than it is the buyer because the seller's interest in the transaction is getting money, not property. Even so, courts generally assume a seller is entitled to specific performance. Sometimes they offer the doubtful explanation that if the buyer is entitled to such a remedy, the seller should be, too. Others suggest that difficulties in measuring the harm to the seller justify specific performance.

Disclosing Latent, Material Facts

A real estate purchase agreement may include representations by the seller about the condition of the property. If those representations are untrue, the buyer is entitled to damages for the resulting loss of value.

The seller may make such representations outside of the purchase agreement, too. If the seller knowingly makes a false statement of material fact about the property, the buyer can recover damages or rescind the contract. In fact, some courts say the buyer can rescind the contract even if the seller innocently misrepresents a material fact or actively conceals a material fact in a way that prevents the buyer from discovering it.

The buyer may also rescind the contract or, probably, recover damages if the seller fails to disclose material facts in certain situations. Most courts today agree that a seller has a duty to disclose when the following circumstances are true:

- **The seller knows about a condition of the property.** This may include not just physical facts about the property; it also may include past events on the property, such as flooding, and conditions in the neighborhood, such as the occurrence of violent crime.

- **The condition is material.** A condition is material if it significantly impairs the value of the property or the seller knows that it would be important to the buyer's decision to enter into the contract or to continue performing it when she had the choice to rescind. Some cases suggest a narrower disclosure duty — that the seller must disclose only if the condition would affect health or safety.

- **The condition is latent.** A *latent defect* is a defect that a reasonably prudent buyer wouldn't discover by inspecting the property and matters of public record. The buyer may include in the purchase agreement a clause that allows her to inspect improvements and rescind if she discovers objectionable defects. If the buyer includes such a clause, however, she has the obligation to discover whatever such inspections would discover and cannot sue the seller for not disclosing such facts.

Some states have statutes that require the seller to disclose certain types of facts about the property and allow the buyer to sue the seller if the seller misrepresents or doesn't disclose the required information.

Implicitly Warranting Workmanship and Habitability

Most states today recognize two implied warranties by builders who sell new homes:

- **The warranty of good workmanship:** The builder-seller used reasonably good materials and performed the construction with reasonable skill and care.

- **The warranty of habitability:** The house is safe, clean, and fit for human habitation.

In many cases, a defect in a house violates both warranties, but the two warranties aren't identical. The warranty of good workmanship includes conditions that don't make the house unfit for habitation, such as cosmetic brick problems or a poorly built driveway. The warranty of habitability, on the other hand, includes conditions that the builder-seller didn't create himself but reasonably should've known about as an expert, such as soil problems or bad water.

If the buyer knows about the defect before closing or if it was readily discoverable before closing, the defect doesn't violate the implied warranties. In that case, courts reason that the buyer accepted the defect by closing the purchase.

Because these implied warranties are based on contract, most courts agree that only the original buyer of the home can sue the builder-seller for breach of the implied warranties. Successive buyers don't have a contractual relationship with the builder-seller who made the implied warranties.

If the builder-seller breaches the implied warranties, the buyer can recover the cost of fixing the problem or have the builder-seller fix it. If fixing the problem is impossible or too expensive, the buyer can recover the resulting loss in the property's market value. Some courts allow the buyer to rescind if the house is unfit for habitation.

Even well-meaning builders would like to avoid the risk of litigation about these implied warranties. Most states say builders can disclaim the implied warranties, as long as they do so clearly and conspicuously in their agreement with the buyer. Some states don't allow builders to disclaim the warranties, however.

Construction defects may not appear for a long time after the house is sold. In some states, the statute of limitations begins to run as soon as the house is sold, so after the limitations period, say five years, the buyer can't sue the builder-seller for breach of the implied warranties. In other states, the limitations period doesn't begin to run until the plaintiff discovers that she has a claim against the builder-seller, which may be many years after the house was first sold. This is sometimes referred to as the *discovery rule.*

Especially if the state also allows successive buyers to sue the builder-seller for breach of the implied warranties, the discovery rule means that builder-sellers are exposed to the possibility of warranty claims for many years after finishing construction. As a result, many states have also adopted *statutes of repose,* statutes that require any claim for construction defects to be brought within a certain number of years — such as 10 or 15 years — after construction is completed, regardless of when the defect is discovered.

Chapter 16

Conveying Title by Deeds

· ·

In This Chapter

▶ Merging deeds and purchase agreements

▶ Drafting valid deeds

▶ Delivering and accepting deeds

▶ Warranting title

· ·

*T*itle to land means ownership of land, so saying that a person has title doesn't mean that she possesses a legal document; it means she's the legal owner.

Although there are other ways of obtaining title to land, the most common way that people get title is by a deed. Unlike title, a *deed* is a legal document, a way to convey title from a grantor to a grantee. A deed may do more than convey title, however. Deeds also commonly include warranties or covenants of title from the grantor to the grantee. Deed warranties are essentially the grantor's promises to pay damages to the grantee for certain title problems.

In this chapter, I present the requirements for a deed to validly transfer title as well as the ways in which deeds may warrant title.

Merging a Purchase Agreement with a Deed

The buyer and seller of real estate typically sign a *purchase agreement,* an executory contract that obligates the parties to buy and sell the real estate on certain conditions. They may make various promises and representations in their purchase agreement, as I explain in Chapter 15.

The purchase agreement governs the parties' relationship until *closing,* when the seller gives a deed to the buyer and the buyer gives the purchase money to the seller. At that point, the purchase agreement is said to *merge* with the deed, although maybe it would make more sense to say that the deed replaces the purchase agreement. By delivering a deed and the purchase money, the parties indicate that the conditions of the purchase agreement have been met or that they waive the failure of any conditions that haven't been met. They also indicate that they accept the other party's performance of its obligations under the purchase agreement. That indication is especially strong when the deed addresses the same subject as the purchase agreement.

If either party feels that a condition hasn't been met or that the other party has breached a covenant in the purchase agreement, she must demand performance before closing, waive the objection, or expressly agree with the other party to go forward with the closing and resolve the objection after closing.

The merger doctrine has some exceptions. Even after closing, a party may enforce terms of the purchase agreement in the following situations:

- ✔ **Express intent to survive closing:** The parties can enforce a term of the purchase agreement if the parties clearly indicated their intent that the term would be enforceable after closing, such as by a clause saying that the particular term would survive closing.

- ✔ **Promises to be performed after closing:** The parties can enforce purchase-agreement promises that are intended to be performed after closing. A simple example is a promise in the purchase agreement that says the seller will make certain repairs on the house within a certain time period after closing. The parties obviously would intend that promise to be performed and enforceable after closing.

- ✔ **Collateral provisions:** The deed transfers title and possession to the grantee and may warrant that title. The deed doesn't generally include any other types of promises. So if the purchase agreement includes promises that aren't related to the transfer of title and possession, and if the deed says nothing about those promises, there's no reason to think that the deed was meant to take the place of those provisions of the purchase agreement.

- ✔ **Fraud:** A party can sue the other for fraud after closing, despite the merger doctrine. For example, if the purchase agreement represented that the heating system worked and the seller lied in telling the buyer that she recently had the heating system inspected and it worked fine, the buyer could sue the seller for fraud even after closing.

- ✔ **Mutual mistake:** A mutual mistake exists when both parties share a mistaken belief and their written agreement therefore doesn't reflect their actual agreement. For example, a drafting mistake in the deed's legal description of the conveyed property may be a mutual mistake, and a party may have the deed reformed after closing to reflect the parties' actual agreement.

Recognizing the Formal Requirements for a Deed

A deed is generally a pretty short and simple legal document, maybe just a couple of pages long. Sometimes deeds use exotic-sounding, or archaic-sounding, legal terminology. But the formal requirements for a valid deed are pretty simple. A deed must be in writing because the statute of frauds requires a writing for the transfer of any interest in land other than short-term interests. Additionally, a written deed must always

- ✔ Identify the parties involved
- ✔ Identify the land being conveyed
- ✔ Express the grantor's intent to convey the land to the grantee
- ✔ Include the signature of the grantor

I cover each of these elements of a valid deed in the following sections.

Identifying the parties

The deed must name or otherwise sufficiently identify the grantor and the grantee. Some state statutes require the parties' addresses and marital status in addition to their names, and some courts have held that the grantor's signature (a required component of a valid deed) doesn't sufficiently identify the grantor.

Perhaps surprisingly, most courts have held that a deed in which the grantee's name is intentionally left blank, to be filled in later, is valid as soon as the grantee's name is written in. But if there's no grantee, the deed is void, because it can't very well transfer an interest to a nonperson.

Identifying the land

The deed must identify the land conveyed. If the deed doesn't describe the land in a way that can be identified on the ground, it's void and doesn't convey anything. The following sections describe several ways the deed may legally describe the land.

Understanding a deed's traditional parts

Deeds traditionally contained more than the elements required today. You may still run into these traditional components, so it's good to be familiar with them:

- ✔ **Premises:** The premises are the parties' names, a statement of consideration paid, the legal description of the property conveyed, and a clause granting the property to the grantee. Today courts agree that consideration doesn't have to be paid for a deed, so there's no need to state the consideration paid. But in a few states, a statement of consideration creates a rebuttable presumption that the grantee did pay consideration, which may help the grantee establish her right to the protection of the recording statute.

- ✔ **Habendum clause:** *Habendum* is the beginning of the Latin phrase meaning "to have and to hold." You may still see deeds using this phrase. The clause limits the estate being granted. For example, a habendum clause may limit the grant to a life estate by saying, "To have and to hold during her natural life." The habendum clause thus may limit or qualify the interest conveyed by the granting clause, but traditionally, if

a habendum clause contradicts the estate named in the granting clause, the granting clause prevails. Nowadays, though, courts are likely to try to determine the grantor's intent from the deed as a whole.

- ✔ **Reddendum clause:** A reddendum clause is a clause by which the grantor reserves some interest in the property, like a life estate or mineral estate. For example, a reddendum clause could reserve mineral rights by saying something like, "All minerals are reserved and excepted from this conveyance."

- ✔ **Warranties of title:** Warranties of title are still common, although they're often made without expressly reciting the warranties of title in the deed. Instead, if the deed uses granting language specified by state statute, the use of that language has the effect of making the warranties of title even though they're not included in the deed.

- ✔ **Execution:** A deed ends with the *execution*, or the signatures of the grantors. A deed commonly includes a certificate of acknowledgement by a notary and maybe signatures of other witnesses.

Metes and bounds: Describing with direction and distance

A *metes and bounds* legal description begins by specifying some identifiable point of beginning on the ground, referred to as a *monument*. This starting point may be a natural monument, like a tree, or an artificial monument, like a road or a stake placed by a surveyor. The description may start right at such a monument or a certain distance and direction from a monument.

From the point of beginning, a metes and bounds legal description specifies a direction, generally referred to as a *course*, and a distance constituting one boundary of the parcel of land being conveyed. Courses are generally expressed as deflections from north and south. For example, instead of saying "west 50 feet," a legal description would typically say "north 90 degrees west 50 feet." Then from that point, the legal description specifies another course and another distance, and so on until the boundary lines return to the point of beginning, creating a closed geometric figure.

Sometimes a metes and bounds description has errors. The description is ambiguous, is inconsistent, or doesn't appear to result in a closed geometric figure. In such cases, courts have to try to figure out what the parties intended. Extrinsic evidence may clarify the boundaries of the land that the parties intended to convey. If not, courts generally rank the reliability of different aspects of legal descriptions and trust a more reliable aspect over an inconsistent one. Here's the usual ranking of reliability:

1. Natural monuments

2. Artificial monuments, including surveyors' markers

3. Boundaries of adjacent tracts of land

4. Courses

5. Distances

6. Area

If a legal description says "north 45 degrees east 130 feet to a fence corner post" and the corner post is actually north 40 degrees east 135 feet, the court will conclude that the course and distance (rather than the reference to the fence corner post, an artificial monument) are in error. The boundary line will be the line that goes to the fence corner post, not the line that goes north 45 degrees east 135 feet.

Government Survey System: Designating sections and townships

The Government Survey System is a federal land survey system that has been applied to most of the land added to the United States since the system was adopted in 1785. It divides the land into square *townships.* A township, which is 6 miles on each side, is divided into 36 square-mile *sections.*

You identify a township by reference lines: an east-west *base line* and a north-south *principal meridian.* Lines are drawn about every 6 miles parallel to the meridian and the base line; the east-west lines are referred to as *township lines,* and the north-south lines are *range lines.* So a township is identified by specifying how many townships it is north or south of the base line and how many ranges it is east or west of the principal meridian. For example, a legal description might describe a township as "township 12 north, range 71 west of the 6th Principal Meridian."

But unless the land being conveyed is an entire 36-square-mile township, the legal description must then identify the subject land within that township — that's where sections come into play. Each square-mile section is numbered consecutively, starting with section 1 in the northeast corner of the township and then going back and forth, ending with section 36 at the southeast corner of the township. So the legal description can identify the relevant square-mile section simply by the section's number within the identified township.

Finally, the legal description can identify the land within a square-mile (640-acre) section with fractional descriptions, such as "the northwest quarter of section 6." Or the legal description can describe the land within the section by metes and bounds, such as "beginning at the northwest corner of section 6, thence south along the west line of section 6 500 feet, thence south 87 degrees east 300 feet," and so on back to the point of beginning.

Putting these elements of the description together, a simple legal description using the Government Survey System might go like this: "The south half of the northwest quarter of section 6, township 12 north, range 71 west of the 6th Principal Meridian."

Subdivision plat: Referring to recorded lot numbers

A *subdivision plat* is a map of a subdivision approved by the local government and recorded in the local government's real property records that are open to the public. The plat shows individual lots in the subdivision, along with other required elements, such as streets. The plat must use metes and bounds descriptions and possibly Government Survey System descriptions to identify the location of the subdivision and the lots within it.

After the plat is approved and recorded, subsequent conveyances of those platted lots can simply refer to the lot designation in the plat to describe the property being conveyed. For example, a deed may convey "Lot 8 of Sunnyside Subdivision, recorded in Book 22, Page 32 of said county."

Other land descriptions

Legal descriptions may include some other approaches. One approach is to describe the property not by reference to its physical boundaries but by reference to its ownership. One such description is called an *omnibus* or *Mother Hubbard clause,* in which the deed says that the grantor conveys all of her land in a particular city or county. You obviously can't tell what land that is just from the deed. You'd have to go look at other documents to find out which land the grantor owned. Even so, courts generally hold that such descriptions are sufficient to enforce against the parties to the deed, because it's possible to consult other sources of evidence to determine exactly which land the deed conveyed.

Another descriptive approach is to describe a portion or fraction of a described parcel of land. Here are some examples:

- ✔ **Fractions of the parcel:** For example, a deed may refer to "the south half of Lot 8 of Sunnyside Subdivision." Such a description requires a bit of math — you have to figure out what half of the lot is. When the parcel is square or rectangular, that's easy. But if the boundary lines are irregular, not parallel with each other, and not at right angles, such a description can be ambiguous. And if the deed doesn't specify the location of the fraction within the larger described parcel, a court may hold that it simply can't figure out what the parties intended and therefore that the deed is void.

For example, a deed that conveys "half of Lot 8" would probably be void because you can't tell which half the deed conveys — unless a court concludes that the parties intended to create a tenancy in common, with each party owning an undivided half share of Lot 8.

✔ **A specified width along a boundary of the parcel:** The deed may say something like "the south 100 feet of Lot 8 of Sunnyside Subdivision." Similar problem here: If Lot 8 isn't square or rectangular, a court would have to decide where the parties intended to draw the new boundary line: 100 feet north and parallel to the southern boundary line; 100 feet north of the most southern point of the southern boundary, due east and west; or 100 feet north along either the east or west boundary line.

✔ **Area:** The deed may specify "7 acres in the northwest quarter of section 6, township 12 north, range 71 west of the 6th Principal Meridian." A quarter of a section is 160 acres, so a deed with such a description is probably void unless the deed also contains some indication of how to locate which 7 acres the deed conveys. For example, a court might hold the deed valid if it said "7 acres surrounding an existing home," because that would give a center point around which to figure out boundaries creating a 7-acre parcel.

Expressing intent to convey

The deed must somehow express that the grantor intends to convey the interest to the grantee by means of the deed. The words "grants" and "conveys" make it pretty clear that the grantor is conveying the named interest to the grantee.

Sometimes drafters of deeds seem to feel that there must be one magic word to use, but they aren't sure which word it is — so they use every synonym they can think of, like "grantor hereby grants, conveys, bargains, sells, transfers, sets over, and delivers" the property to the grantee. That's overkill — one word will do.

A state statute may specify some magic words for a different purpose — words that, when used in a deed, have the effect of making certain warranties of title, not just conveying title. You do need to know what those words are so that you don't make warranties of title when you don't mean to. I talk about these statutes in the later section "Warranting generally."

Any word that indicates a present conveyance will do, but sometimes drafters have written that the grantor "warrants" title without ever saying the grantor actually conveys title. Sometimes drafters also have got in trouble because they used words that indicated an intent to convey in the future rather than in the present.

Witnessing, acknowledging, and recording a deed

In almost all states, a notary must witness or acknowledge the grantor's signature in order to have the deed recorded in the public real property records. Some states also require witnesses in order to record a deed. But a deed is valid between the grantor and grantee even if it's unacknowledged, unwitnessed, and unrecorded. Recording is important only to give notice of the transaction to the rest of the world. (For information on recording deeds and other documents, see Chapter 17.)

Signing the deed

For a deed to be valid, the grantor must sign it. She can sign her name or make any other mark intended to validate the deed, and she can even have her agent sign for her. But if she doesn't sign the deed somehow, the deed is void.

The grantee doesn't need to sign the deed for it to be valid; only the grantor needs to sign.

The Handoff: Delivering and Accepting a Deed

Even a valid, signed deed doesn't convey title until it's delivered and accepted. If a deed isn't effectively delivered, it's void. That means that even if someone else later buys the property from the grantee in the deed, that buyer owns nothing even if she couldn't reasonably have discovered that the previous deed was never delivered. But if the grantor was somehow negligent in allowing the grantee to get possession of the deed and make it appear that the deed was validly delivered, the grantor may be estopped from denying that the deed was delivered.

The following sections talk about delivery and acceptance in more detail.

Performing acts intended to make a deed effective

Delivering a deed means taking some action intended to make the deed effective presently. What that action is doesn't really matter, but one obvious action is for the grantor to hand the deed to the grantee. Physically handing the deed to the grantee commonly creates a presumption of a delivery, whereas retaining possession may create a presumption of nondelivery.

The important part of delivering a deed is the grantor's intent to make the deed effective by his action. The grantor may deliver the deed simply by gesturing to it or even by saying that it's now effective. On the other hand, even actions that would surely appear to be a delivery — such as physically handing it to the grantee — aren't an effective delivery if the grantor manifests an intention for the deed not to be presently effective. For example, the grantor hasn't delivered a deed if he hands it to the grantee with the intent that the grantee deliver it to an escrow agent, who will keep the deed until the grantee finishes paying for the property. The grantor hands the deed to the grantee but doesn't intend for the deed to be effective until later.

A deed doesn't have to convey a present estate. The grantor can effectively deliver a deed that conveys a future interest. If the grantor hands over a deed that gives the grantee the right to take possession at the end of the year, that's a valid conveyance of a future interest. On the other hand, if the grantor hands over a deed that purports to give the property to the grantee immediately, but the grantor says that it isn't effective until the end of the year, the deed isn't effective because the grantor hasn't delivered it. As if that's not confusing enough, consider this: If the grantor is still alive when the year ends and doesn't repudiate his delivery before then, he'll have effectively delivered the deed at the end of the year even without taking any further action.

Courts reach different results when the grantor hands over a deed to the grantee and indicates that the deed is effective only upon the occurrence of some condition in the future. Some courts hold that the grantor intended the delivery to be effective, albeit conditional, and that the grantor can't impose such conditions on the grantee, so the grantor effectively delivered the deed. Such decisions simply disregard the conditions. Other courts hold that the grantor hasn't delivered the deed at all, because he didn't intend the delivery to be presently effective. And some courts enforce the condition and hold that the deed conveyed title if the condition was fulfilled.

However, if the condition is that the deed will be effective when the grantor dies, courts generally agree that the deed is void because the grantor's intent is to convey property at his death. Conveying property at death, which I cover in Chapter 3, requires compliance with the formalities of the Statute of Wills.

Delivering by escrow

A grantor may effectively deliver a deed in the future by an escrow. An *escrow* is a deed (or other thing) given to a third party, called an *escrow agent*, to hold and then deliver to the grantee when specified conditions are met.

The parties may close a real estate sale by using an escrow agent. The grantor can give the deed to the escrow agent with instructions to deliver the deed to the grantee when the grantee delivers the purchase price to the escrow agent. Likewise, the grantee can deliver payment to the escrow agent with instructions to give it to the grantor when the grantor gives the deed to the agent and the rest of the contract conditions are fulfilled, such as getting an acceptable title insurance policy. The escrow agent also may manage the closing in other ways, like allocating expenses and recording documents. All of this makes closing easier and more convenient for the parties involved.

When a deed is delivered by escrow, it conveys title when the escrow conditions are met. Most would say that is true even if the escrow agent delays physically delivering the deed to the grantee. The parties may give the escrow agent written instructions detailing the conditions, or they may simply instruct the escrow agent to close the escrow when the conditions of the parties' purchase agreement are met.

The escrow agent's delivery to the grantee is said to *relate back* to the date that the grantor entrusted the deed to the escrow agent. That means that the grantor has effectively delivered the deed even if the grantor dies or is incapacitated before the conditions are fulfilled and the escrow agent delivers the deed to the grantee. The delivery relates back to the grantor's delivery to the escrow agent only when the following are true:

- ✔ **The buyer and seller have an enforceable contract of sale.** Even if the parties have a contract, the delivery doesn't relate back if the contract doesn't satisfy the statute of frauds, unless written escrow instructions or other documents can satisfy the requirement of a writing.

- ✔ **The seller hasn't reserved a legal right to take the deed back from the escrow agent.** A delivery is essentially a final act by which the grantor gives up control of the property, so if the grantor can recall the deed from the escrow agent, he hasn't really delivered the deed yet.

If these conditions aren't met, the escrow agent's delivery upon fulfillment of the conditions is still effective; it just doesn't relate back to the grantor's earlier delivery. That also means that up until the escrow agent delivers the deed to the grantee, the grantor can take the deed back from the escrow agent.

Up until closing, the escrow agent is an agent of both the grantor and the grantee. The escrow agent has a duty to both parties to perform its duties with reasonable care, skill, and loyalty. The agent must comply strictly with the parties' joint instructions and is liable for damages from failure to do so. If the parties disagree about whether the escrow conditions have been met, the escrow agent shouldn't disregard one of the parties' directions but instead should *interplead* the escrow, initiating a judicial action to have the court determine what the escrow agent should do with the deed and the purchase money.

Delivering by escrow at death

Through a *death escrow,* the grantor may give a deed to an escrow agent to deliver to the grantee on the condition that the grantor dies. A death escrow is effective as long as two things are true:

- ✔ The only condition is the grantor's death.
- ✔ The grantor doesn't retain the legal right to take the deed back out of escrow. Death escrows typically aren't purchases, but gifts that take the place of wills. So the grantor may give the deed to the agent without telling the grantee about it, and if the grantor asks the agent to give it back, the agent may likely do so. But the death escrow is still effective as long as the grantor has no explicit right or power to do so. For example, the death escrow isn't effective if the grantor puts the deed in a safe deposit box with instructions to an agent to deliver the deed at his death but keeps a key to the box that would enable him to take the deed back before his death.

No matter who the grantor is, he's certain to die, so the grantor's conveyance isn't really conditional. In fact, that's why courts reason that as soon as the grantor delivers the deed to the escrow agent, the deed is effective to transfer the property interest to the grantee. Of course, the interest isn't to take effect until the grantor's death, so it's a future interest. Like a normal escrow, the delivery to the escrow agent therefore is the effective date of delivery — not because it relates back, but rather because the delivery to the escrow agent itself completed the delivery of a deed to a future interest.

Accepting delivery of a deed

After the deed is delivered, the grantee must accept it before title is conveyed. Of course, the grantee almost always wants the property. In fact, courts presume that the grantee accepts a deed if the property conveyed is valuable. But if the grantee doesn't want the property, she may indicate her lack of acceptance in any way she wants and thereby avoid taking ownership of it.

Warranting Title in a Deed

A deed always conveys title to a grantee; that's what makes it a deed. But a deed also often includes covenants, or warranties, about the title it conveys. These covenants promise the grantee that if the grantor's deed can't convey the described title to the grantee (whether in whole or in part), the grantor will pay damages to the grantee. The following sections describe the details of deed covenants or warranties of title.

Covering the various covenants

Grantors typically make broad promises about the quality of title and then customize those promises by making exceptions for title defects that they anticipate or already know about. All title defects can be grouped into two categories:

✔ Possessory interests belonging to other people

✔ Nonpossessory interests belonging to other people

Different covenants address these two categories. Some covenants promise that no such defects exist; others promise that no one else will assert such rights. In all, grantors commonly include six title covenants in their deeds. The following sections cover each of those covenants in detail.

Covenants of seisin and right to convey

The *covenant of seisin* is essentially a covenant that the grantor owns the estate that the deed says it conveys to the grantee. This covenant promises that no one else has any conflicting possessory interests, present or future. If someone else owns some part of the described land, that would violate the covenant of seisin. Likewise, if a deed says it conveys a fee simple absolute (defined in Chapter 9), but someone else owns a future interest in the property, that future interest would violate the covenant.

The *covenant of right to convey* is similar. As the name suggests, it's a promise that the grantor has the right to convey the described estate. Obviously, if the grantor doesn't own all of the described estate, then she doesn't have the right to convey it all.

In general, the same title defects breach both the covenants of seisin and right to convey. But in some situations, the grantor has seisin but not the right to convey, such as when the property is subject to a valid covenant preventing the grantor from conveying the property to the grantee. On the other hand, the grantor may have the right to convey but not seisin, such as when the grantor is acting as an agent for the owner.

Covenant against encumbrances

An *encumbrance* is any title problem that isn't a lack of title that would breach the covenants of seisin and right to convey (see Chapter 15 for details on encumbrances). Mortgages, liens, easements, and covenants are all encumbrances. The *covenant against encumbrances* is a covenant against encumbrances. Plain and simple. It's a promise that no such interests encumber the property.

Of course, few properties are unencumbered, so a grantor would almost certainly not promise that the property is free from encumbrances. Rather, the deed would say that the grantor covenants that there are no encumbrances except for certain specified encumbrances, which the deed then proceeds to name. The deed may do so specifically, as in "subject to an easement in favor of Utility Company." Or it may do so generally, as in "subject to easements, covenants, and other interests of record."

In some situations an encumbrance doesn't violate the covenant even though the deed doesn't exclude it from the covenant. Here are some of those situations:

- ✔ **The grantee knew of the encumbrance.** If the grantee knew about an encumbrance when the grantor gave her the deed, some courts would hold that the encumbrance doesn't violate the covenant, even if the deed doesn't say that the encumbrance is an exception to the covenant. However, most courts would say that the deed covenant means what it says and that the grantee's knowledge of an encumbrance doesn't negate the grantor's covenant to pay damages for the existence of the encumbrance.

- ✔ **The encumbrance was visible.** Courts commonly hold that an encumbrance that's open and visible, like an easement for a public street, doesn't violate the covenant against encumbrances, even though the encumbrance isn't mentioned as an exception. Such decisions reason that the grantee must have intended to accept the property subject to such encumbrances, or she wouldn't have gone forward with the purchase. But the lawyer drafting a deed should be explicit about which encumbrances the grantor doesn't covenant against.

- ✔ **The encumbrance is beneficial.** Some courts have held that encumbrances that make the property more valuable, like utility easements, don't breach the covenant against encumbrances. They figure that the covenant was meant only to protect the grantee from harm resulting from title defects, so if an encumbrance actually benefits the grantee, it doesn't breach the covenant.

- ✔ **Code violations exist.** Some cases have held that existing violations of local building, housing, and zoning codes may breach the covenant against encumbrances. However, most courts agree that such violations don't violate the covenant because they don't affect title to the property at all.

Covenants of quiet enjoyment and warranty

Like the covenants of seisin and right to convey, the covenants of quiet enjoyment and warranty go together because they're essentially the same. But why make only one covenant when two will do the job just as well?

✔ **Covenant of quiet enjoyment:** A covenant that the grantee can use and enjoy the property without interference by the legal claims of other people who have valid interests in the property

✔ **Covenant of warranty:** A covenant that the grantor will warrant and defend the grantee's title against the legal claims of other people who have valid interests in the property

Both covenants promise that other interest holders won't interfere with the grantee's use and enjoyment. Such interference may result from a possessory interest, like someone else actually owning title to some portion of the land the deed purported to convey, or a nonpossessory interest, like an easement or covenant. In either case, if the owner of such an interest interferes with the grantee's use of the property, the covenants are breached.

Covenant of further assurances

The *covenant of further assurances* is a promise that, upon demand by the grantee, the grantor will execute any additional documents in the future that are needed to fix any defects in the grantee's title. This covenant applies only when the grantor himself has the power to fix a title defect.

Distinguishing present and future covenants

The covenants of seisin, of right to convey, and against encumbrances are called *present covenants.* The other three covenants — the covenants of quiet enjoyment, warranty, and further assurances — are called *future covenants.* (For details on what these covenants say, see the earlier "Covering the various covenants" section.) The following sections explain why and detail the differences between the two types of covenants.

Breaching present and future covenants

The present covenants all promise that title defects don't exist at the time that the grantor gives the deed to the grantee. The mere existence of a title defect breaches these covenants. That's why they're called present covenants, because they're covenants about the present state of title. The grantor doesn't promise that title defects won't arise in the future, of course — the grantor has no control over what happens with title to the property after he conveys it to the grantee. He promises only that such defects don't exist at the moment that he hands the property over to the grantee. That means that a present covenant is breached at the moment the deed conveys title, if ever. At that moment, either breaching title defects exist or they don't.

The future covenants, on the other hand, promise that no one with a valid interest in the property will interfere with the grantee's use of the property. So these are covenants about the future — promises that after delivery and acceptance of the deed, no such owner of a valid legal interest will come along and interfere (or in the case of the covenant of further assurances, that the grantor will comply if the grantee demands reasonable further assurances).

Future covenants therefore are breached only when a valid interest holder interferes with the grantee's use of the property. This kind of interference is commonly called an *eviction,* although it doesn't mean that the grantee has to be kicked off the property. Even if a grantee discovers a serious title defect, such as an easement that effectively prevents the grantee's intended development and use of the land, the defect itself doesn't breach the future covenants. They're breached only when the owner of the easement asserts the interest in some way that interferes with the grantee's use. And if it turns out that the person interfering didn't actually have a valid interest in the property that she could enforce against the grantee, then the covenants weren't breached at all. Even the covenant of further assurances requires an eviction in order for the grantee to obtain damages for breach.

Here are some examples of circumstances that qualify as evictions:

- ✔ The interest holder lawfully interferes with the grantee's use and possession.

- ✔ The interest holder *constructively evicts* the grantee by asserting his rights in the property somehow.

- ✔ The grantee gives up possession to, or buys the rights of, a valid interest holder.

- ✔ Some courts say that the grantee's inability to perform her contract to sell good title to another is an eviction; others say it isn't.

- ✔ The grantee subsequently gives a warranty deed to someone else, and when the title defect emerges, the grantee pays damages for breach of her own deed covenants to the subsequent grantee.

- ✔ The government holds a valid legal interest in the property. Normally the interest must be asserted somehow, but the government's mere ownership of a legal interest in the land is considered a breach of the future covenants.

- ✔ The grantor wrongfully interferes with the grantee's use and possession. Wrongful interferences by third parties — interferences that aren't the result of a valid interest in the property enforceable against the grantee — don't breach the future covenants. But the grantor's own wrongful interference does violate the covenants of warranty and quiet enjoyment.

Authorities often say that the future covenants are covenants against interference by "paramount" or "superior" titleholders. That doesn't mean that the interference must come from someone who has a more substantial interest than the grantee. It simply means that the interference must come from someone who has an interest in the property that's enforceable against the grantee. The owner of even a small right-of-way evicts the grantee simply by using her easement, even though an easement isn't a more substantial interest than the grantee's fee simple ownership.

Applying the statute of limitations to deed covenant claims

Because only an eviction breaches the future covenants, the statute of limitations period doesn't begin to run until an eviction occurs. So the grantor may remain exposed to the possibility of such a claim for many years.

A claim for the breach of the present covenants, on the other hand, arises when the deed is delivered and accepted. At that moment, the grantee has a claim because the mere existence of a title defect breaches the covenant, so that's when the statute of limitations begins to run. If the owner of the conflicting property interest doesn't assert it somehow, the grantee may never discover the title defect until after the statute of limitations has passed. In that case, the grantee never has a chance to sue the grantor for breach of the present covenants and may get relief only if she's evicted and can sue for breach of the future covenants.

Enforcing title covenants against earlier grantors

Future covenants run with the land, meaning they may be enforced against a grantor even by successive grantees, whereas present covenants don't run with the land.

Present covenants aren't ongoing promises. They're promises about the state of title at the moment the deed conveys title to the grantee. So at the time of the conveyance, the grantee either has a claim or doesn't. If the grantee subsequently conveys the property to someone else, that subsequent grantee has no claim against the earlier grantor for breach of the earlier grantor's present covenants, even if the subsequent grantee discovers a title defect and brings a claim within the statute of limitations period. In theory, the grantee could assign to her subsequent grantee any undiscovered claims against the grantor, but so far most courts haven't presumed that grantees do so.

Future covenants, on the other hand, run with the land. That is, subsequent grantees can sue any prior covenanting grantor, not just their immediate grantor, for breach of future covenants. Unlike the present covenants, the future covenants clearly are promises about future events. Here are the basic requirements and reasons the future deed covenants run with the land (see Chapter 5 for information about running covenants):

✔ **Horizontal privity:** The grantor and the grantee created the future deed covenants in the instrument that conveyed the benefited land to the grantee.

✔ **Vertical privity:** If the grantee subsequently transfers her land to someone else, that subsequent grantee has vertical privity with the original benefited party.

If the grantee actually owned nothing at all, because her grantor didn't actually have title to any of the land, you could say that subsequent grantees have no vertical privity with the original grantee because they have no estate at all. But courts still hold that subsequent grantees can sue the prior grantor for breach of the prior grantor's future deed covenants.

✔ **The covenants touch and concern the land:** The future deed covenants are promises about the title to the benefited land, so the benefit of those covenants can run to successive owners of the benefited land. However, the grantor remains obligated to perform the future deed covenants; the burden doesn't pass to any successor. The future deed covenants don't touch and concern any land that the grantor owns, so they're personal to the grantor.

✔ **Intent to run:** The grantor and grantee presumably intend the future deed covenants to benefit not just the grantee but any subsequent owners. The parties know that an eviction might happen long in the future, after the grantee has conveyed the property to someone else, yet they don't say in the deed that only the grantee can enforce the covenants.

Limiting or omitting warranties: Distinguishing types of deeds

A deed may include all, some, or none of the deed covenants. It also may qualify and customize those covenants as the parties agree in their purchase agreement. The purchase agreement may specify exactly which title covenants the grantor's deed must include, but typically the agreement uses general labels indicating the types of title covenants that will be included in the deed. The four common labels are as follows:

✔ General warranty deed

✔ Special warranty deed

✔ Bargain and sale deed

✔ Quitclaim deed

The following sections explain how each of these types of deeds are created and how they differ from each other.

Warranting title generally

A *general warranty deed* includes deed covenants warranting title against valid claims by anyone other than the grantee. Typically, a general warranty deed includes all six of the deed covenants I describe earlier in "Covering the various covenants" or all but the covenant of further assurances. But the parties can agree that the grantor will give a general warranty deed that includes fewer of the deed covenants. What makes a warranty deed "general" is that the deed covenants warrant "generally" that no one else — other than owners of any interests specifically excepted in the deed, of course — has a claim to which the grantee's title will be subject.

The general warranty deed is probably the most common type of deed. Courts generally assume that if a purchase agreement says the grantor will give the grantee a "warranty deed," that means a general warranty deed.

A general warranty deed may expressly state the general warranties. The following are examples of how each of the covenants may be expressed:

- ✔ **Covenant of seisin:** "The grantor covenants that he is lawfully seized of the property in fee simple absolute."

- ✔ **Covenant of right to convey:** "The grantor covenants that he has the right to convey the property to the grantee."

- ✔ **Covenant against encumbrances:** "The grantor covenants that the property is free from all encumbrances except as described herein."

- ✔ **Covenant of warranty:** "The grantor, the grantor's heirs, and personal representatives will forever warrant and defend the foregoing title in the grantee, her heirs, and assigns against all lawful claims and demands."

- ✔ **Covenant of quiet enjoyment:** "The grantor guarantees the grantee, her heirs, and assigns in the quiet enjoyment of the premises."

- ✔ **Covenant of further assurances:** "The grantor will execute such further assurances of the property as reasonably requested."

A deed may be a general warranty deed without expressly stating the warranties. The statute of frauds requires that title covenants be written, but many states have statutes that say a deed using certain words, such as "conveys and warrants" or even "grants" has the effect of making the deed covenants of title, even though the covenants aren't stated in the deed. Lawyers drafting and reviewing deeds need to look for such a statute and make sure they use language consistent with their clients' intentions.

Warranting title specially

A *special warranty deed* warrants title only against title defects that the grantor created or allowed to be created, not title defects that existed before the grantor owned the property. It's "special" because the warranties are limited in this way, not because it's better.

Like a general warranty deed, a special warranty deed may include all the title covenants or just some of them. A deed may make any of the covenants generally or specially. In fact, a deed can make some covenants generally and other covenants specially.

A special warranty deed may expressly make the warranties specially. It usually does so by saying something like "the grantor covenants and warrants the following against the claims of the grantor and all persons claiming by, through, or under the grantor." Then the deed lists the covenants using the same kind of language used in a general warranty deed (see the preceding section). The types of promises are the same; the difference is that the special warranty deed makes no covenants about title defects that preceded the grantor's ownership.

Some state statutes specify language that makes special warranties without stating them in the deed. For example, a state statute may say that if a deed says the grantor "warrants specially" the property, then it makes the usual deed covenants specially. Or a statute may say that if the deed says that the grantor "conveys and warrants [the property] against all who claim by, through, or under the grantor," the deed thereby makes the usual deed covenants specially. Lawyers must know the applicable state statutes or risk using words that produce unintended effects.

Granting title without warranties

A deed doesn't have to make any deed covenants. Some authorities use different labels to distinguish between two types of deeds that make no covenants of title:

- **Bargain and sale deed:** This label may describe a deed that says it conveys a particular estate to the grantee but that doesn't warrant title to that estate.

- **Quitclaim deed:** A *quitclaim deed* doesn't purport to convey any particular estate at all. Instead of saying the grantor conveys fee simple absolute or some other estate, the quitclaim deed just says that it conveys whatever right, title, or interest the grantor may have in the described property.

Quitclaim deeds are commonly used for gifts, when the grantee isn't paying anything for the property and the grantor has no incentive to warrant title. They're also used to clear up title problems. If title is uncertain, the person seeking to get clear title may get quitclaim deeds from possible conflicting claimants. In such cases, the grantor may not own anything at all, so he uses a quitclaim deed to indicate that he gives the grantee whatever rights he has in the property, if any.

Whether these labels are used or not, there may be an important difference between bargain and sale deeds and quitclaim deeds. If the deed says that the grantor conveys a particular estate, courts are more likely to hold that if the grantor later acquires some or all of that estate, it automatically passes to the grantee. Why? Because the deed estops the grantor from denying that the grantee owns it. If the deed doesn't convey a particular estate but just says that the grantor gives whatever he owns in the property, if anything, then courts are less likely to apply the estoppel by deed doctrine. For details on estoppel, see the later sidebar "Estopping the grantor."

Remedying breaches of title covenants

Damages are the grantee's remedy for breach of a deed covenant. The grantee can also specifically enforce the grantor's covenant to provide further assurances.

The grantee is generally entitled to get her money back from the grantor if she paid for something she didn't get from the grantor. That means that the most the grantee can recover is the purchase price she paid for the property. It also means that the grantee's damages are generally measured by the value of the property at the time of the grantor's conveyance, not when the covenant is breached or the grantee brings her claim. The deed covenants are more like a money-back guarantee on consumer products than an insurance policy.

If the grantee recovers the entire purchase price paid, the grantor is entitled to get back from the grantee whatever title the grantee actually received. Courts figure that if the grantee got all her money back, she shouldn't be able to keep any of the title that the grantor did actually have power to convey to the grantee.

Usually when a grantee receives property for free, the grantor doesn't warrant title. But a grantee may receive a warranty deed even though she didn't pay anything for the property conveyed. Some courts allow such a grantee to recover damages up to the market value of the land at the time of the conveyance.

Additionally, a grantee can sue previous grantors for breach of their future deed covenants. When the grantee wins such a claim, she can't recover more than the prior grantor received for the property, even if she paid more than that. The covenanting grantor's liability is always limited by the amount she received for the property. But cases disagree on how much the grantee may recover if she paid less for the property than the prior grantor received. Some cases say that the grantee may only recover what she paid for the property, whereas other cases say that the grantee may recover her actual loss up to the amount that the prior grantor received for the property.

The next sections walk you through the measure of damages that grantees can recover when a deed covenant is breached.

Measuring damages for lack of title

The grantor's lack of title, in whole or in part, breaches the present covenants of seisin and right to convey; it also may breach the future covenants if the valid title holder evicts the grantee. Whether the grantee successfully sues for breach of present or future covenants, the grantee is basically entitled to get back the money that she paid for property she didn't get (not the current value of the property).

If the grantor actually didn't own the property at all, the grantee can recover the entire purchase price she paid. If the grantor had title to some but not all of the property conveyed, then the grantee is entitled to recover whatever she paid for the part not conveyed. For example, if she paid $200,000 for 40 acres and the grantor didn't actually have title to one of those acres, then the grantee would get back $5,000, which is 1/40 of the purchase price.

The grantee's recovery for breach of the deed covenants is limited in this way even if she invested money in improving the property. If she bought undeveloped land and then built buildings on the land, the property may be worth much more than when she bought it. However, even though the grantee can't recover the value of the improved property from the covenanting grantor, the grantee in this situation may get relief through rules about mistaken improvements. In general, if a person improves land in good faith, mistakenly believing she owns the land, the person who does actually own the land must pay her for the increased market value of the land or sell the land to the improver for its unimproved value.

Measuring damages for encumbrances

The existence of an encumbrance breaches the present covenant against encumbrances. The assertion of a valid encumbrance that interferes with the grantee's use and enjoyment of the property breaches the future covenants. In either case, the grantee is entitled to recover the amount of the purchase price that she paid for value she didn't receive — in other words, the difference in the market value of the property at the time she bought the property.

There's an important alternative for the grantee, however. The grantee can instead recover the reasonable cost of removing the encumbrance, although she still can't recover more than her total purchase price. If the encumbrance is a mortgage, the grantee can recover the amount of the mortgage debt.

Recovering litigation costs

If the grantee reasonably contests the claim of another interest holder and loses, the grantee may recover her attorneys' fees and other litigation costs. Likewise, the grantee can recover attorneys' fees for negotiating to buy out a valid interest holder. Some courts may award attorneys' fees only if the grantee first notified the grantor and asked her to defend the title.

Estopping the grantor

The doctrine of *estoppel by deed,* or *after-acquired title,* may provide an additional remedy for the grantee. In this case, the grantor's deed, which purports to convey an interest, estops him from asserting that interest against the grantee if he acquires it later.

The rule applies when a deed purports to convey something but doesn't because someone other than the grantor has a valid prior interest in the property. If the grantor later acquires that valid prior interest, the after-acquired interest automatically passes to the grantee, unless the grantee prefers damages.

Some courts say that only a deed containing all the deed covenants will estop the grantor. Others say that a deed will estop the grantor as long as it includes the covenant of warranty. And some say that any deed estops the grantor as long as it purports to convey a particular estate, even if the deed doesn't include title covenants.

However, the grantee can't recover attorneys' fees she pays for a dispute between the grantee and the covenanting grantor. And if the grantee wins a lawsuit against someone claiming an interest in the property, then she isn't entitled to attorneys' fees or any other damages from the grantor — the grantee's successful lawsuit establishes that in fact the claimant didn't own a valid interest in the property and the deed covenants therefore weren't breached.

Chapter 17

Recording Title

. . . .

In This Chapter

▶ Understanding priority and why it matters

▶ Considering what can be recorded

▶ Indexing recorded documents

▶ Examining the kinds of recording statutes and whom they protect

▶ Eliminating certain title risks by statute

. . . .

Various people can have different interests in the same real estate at the same time. One person may own a life estate in the property, another may own a remainder, a third may own an easement, a fourth may have a lease, a fifth may own a lien, and so on. Sometimes the creation or exercise of one interest conflicts with other interests in the property.

An owner of the property may even convey an estate to one person and then purport to convey it again to another. In this situation, too, the interests of the two grantees obviously conflict.

Such conflicts are generally resolved by statutes that allow parties to give notice of their real property interests to the rest of the world and, when they don't give such notice, protect those who bought interests in the property without notice of earlier interests. This chapter fills you in on the requirements for recording documents in the public records and identifies the circumstances in which the recording statutes protect people who didn't know about an unrecorded interest.

Understanding Priority Disputes

Priority problems arise when a property owner creates conflicting interests in the property. Probably the simplest example is when the owner conveys her property to one person by deed and later gives another deed to the same property to a different person. But similar conflicts can happen when the owner creates lesser interests. For example, the owner leases the property to a tenant and later mortgages the property. If the owner subsequently defaults and the mortgagee forecloses, the foreclosure buyer and the tenant may have a conflict about whether the lease continues in effect.

In either case, the baseline common law principle to resolve these conflicts is simple and intuitive. The owner can't give away any part of what she doesn't own. So after she has conveyed a property interest to one person, she has no power to convey the same interest to another person. For example, after the owner has given away a leasehold to a tenant, she has no power to take any of that interest away from the tenant (unless the lease otherwise provides, of course). All the landlord can mortgage is what she still owns, which is the reversion that will take possession after the leasehold ends.

The bottom line is that if the owner creates inconsistent interests, the later interest is subject to the prior interest, but the prior interest isn't subject to the later interest. This principle is often referred to as "first in time, first in right."

Recording Documents

The principle of first in time, first in right may seem unquestionably right and fair. Someone shouldn't be able to give away someone else's property rights. But selling an interest that conflicts with a prior interest may also be unfair to the later grantee. If the grantor doesn't tell the later grantee about the prior interest and the later grantee can't reasonably discover the prior interest, then the later grantee may innocently and reasonably pay value for a property interest that turns out to be impaired or useless. He might be able to sue his grantor for damages, but a judgment against the grantor may not be collectible and may not be a satisfactory substitute for the desired property interest.

If a prior interest isn't reasonably discoverable, the later grantee can't do anything to avoid the unfair result. But the prior grantee can do something, and it's pretty easy. A simple way to avoid unfairness to the later grantee is to have the prior grantee notify him of the prior interest. The prior interest holder knows she has an interest in the property, and she knows that other people may consider acquiring interests in the property, too. She doesn't know who those later grantees may be, of course, but she knows that such people may come along. If she can give notice to the world generally, she can avoid the unfairness to a later grantee.

That's what the recording system does. In all 50 states, a person who acquires an interest in real property can give notice of that interest to the world by filing a document with the local government where the real property is located. Thereafter, anyone who considers acquiring an interest in real property can search those recorded documents to see whether any conflicting prior interests exist. From those records, he can determine whether his intended grantor actually owns the interest she's offering to sell and whether that interest is encumbered.

The following sections talk more about the requirements for a document to be recorded and how it's recorded.

Identifying recordable documents

State statutes specify the requirements for recording a document. Generally, any conveyance of any interest in land may be recorded. Typically, the state statute doesn't require recording in order for a document (often generically called an _instrument_) to be valid, but if an instrument isn't recorded, then a later interest may not be subject to the unrecorded prior interest.

Any document affecting ownership of real property may be recorded. Following are some of the common types of documents that may be recorded:

- **Deeds:** The grantee of any deed should record it to give notice of her interest.

- **Mortgages and deeds of trust:** A mortgage includes the right to sell the land at auction if the borrower defaults on the mortgage debt (see Chapter 18 for details). A deed of trust is similar to a mortgage, except it gives title to a trustee with the power to sell the property in the event of default.

- **Installment contracts:** Sometimes called _contracts for deed,_ installment contracts are long-term purchase agreements. The buyer pays installments of the purchase price over a long period of time and receives a deed when she finishes paying the full purchase price. Even though she doesn't have legal title until she receives a deed, she has a valuable interest in the land, which can be called _equitable title._

- **Options:** Some courts say an option doesn't create an interest in land and isn't recordable; others say that it is recordable.

- **Leases:** A lease is a possessory estate in land and may be recorded in most states. However, if the lessee is in actual possession of the land, any later grantee will have notice of her leasehold anyway. Therefore, many leases aren't recorded, or sometimes parties record a simple notice of the lease rather than the lease itself.

- **Contracts concerning real property:** Courts generally construe recording statutes broadly to allow recording of any document that affects the ownership of interests in land. So other kinds of contracts that create rights concerning real property (such as an agreement among tenants in common that restricts their right to sell their fractional interests) may be recorded.

- **Judgments about land:** A judgment, such as a decree in a quiet title action, may affect ownership of real property. Some statutes require such a judgment to be recorded in order to give constructive notice, whereas others allow it but don't require it. In the states that don't require recording of judgments in order to give notice, the public court records give notice of judgments even if they aren't also recorded in the real property records.

✔ **Liens:** Parties claiming statutory liens against the property, such as tax liens or mechanics' liens, may record a notice of the lien in the real property records.

Complying with conditions for recording

A person records a recordable document by taking it to a county official, who has the duty to maintain such real property records concerning property in the county. The county official doesn't evaluate the legal validity of the document. If the document meets the basic requirements, the county official will record the document, index it (as I explain in the next section), and return it to the person who filed it.

Here are the three requirements that must be met in order to record any document affecting real property:

✔ The document affects ownership of land within the county.

✔ A notary public or other authorized official witnessed and verified the signatures of the parties to the document. (Some statutes may have different witness requirements.)

✔ Any necessary document-recording fees have been paid. (Some states don't consider the document legally recorded if the fee isn't paid.)

The county recorder used to record documents by including a copy of the instrument in a book. Documents were included in the book as received, so they were kept in chronological order. Deeds might be included in one book, mortgages in another book, and other interests in yet another book. So when a deed or other document refers to a recorded instrument, you'll often see a reference to a book or volume number and a page number within that book, where a copy of the recorded instrument may be found. As you'd expect, today county recorders generally make electronic images of the documents instead of putting them in books.

Using Indexes to Find Recorded Documents

The recording system helps people determine the state of title before buying an interest in land. A buyer wants to know, for example, whether someone has an outstanding mortgage that will result in the land being sold if a debt isn't paid — that mortgage obviously makes the land worth less to the buyer.

The county official who records documents keeps an index so people can find relevant documents. Two main types of indexes exist:

- ✔ **Grantor-grantee index:** This is the most common type of index. It actually involves two indexes: an index in which documents are listed alphabetically by the name of the grantor, with accompanying notations about the type of document and where it can be found in the county's records, and an index in which the same documents are listed alphabetically by the name of the grantee.

    These indexes used to be kept in books, so if you search title you'll likely need to look through a series of such index books covering different years. Today computer databases allow you to search all documents included in the database, but older documents may not be included in the database.

- ✔ **Tract index:** Also referred to as a *parcel index,* this type of index is less common. It organizes recorded documents by the location of the property, such as by subdivision name or quarter-quarter of a Government Survey System section (more on this system in Chapter 16).

To examine relevant documents using a grantor-grantee index, you first search backwards in the grantee index, starting with the name of the person whose title you're trying to confirm. When you find her name as a grantee, you see the name of her grantor as well, and then you continue searching back in time, looking for that person as a grantee. You continue finding each grantor until you get to the original grant from the sovereign. In some states, a statute or a bar association title standard says you have a reliable chain of title after you've confirmed title a certain number of years back in time, like 40 years.

Then you use the grantor index. You go through each of the identified grantors in the chain of title and search for their names during their period of ownership in the grantor index. You may even need to search for their names in the grantor index before and after their period of ownership. Searching for each owner's name in the grantor index allows you to find any other interests each owner may have created, such as mortgages and easements, or even a conflicting conveyance of the property to someone outside the chain of title.

Searching title with a tract index is easier than with a grantor-grantee index. You start by looking through the relevant part of the tract indexes where the property is located and finding all the documents that may deal with the property. Then you simply look up all those documents.

If you're evaluating title, you still have to actually look up the indexed documents that you identified and examine them to see whether they're signed and otherwise facially valid, whether they actually relate to the property in question, and what interests they create. And a title search doesn't end there. You also have to look at other sources of public documents that relate to title, such as records of judgments kept by the courts, probate records dealing with transfers upon death, and the tax records that include tax liens and sales.

Distinguishing the Three Types of Recording Statutes

Although recording acts differ among the states, all recording acts make an unrecorded prior interest unenforceable against a later interest in some situations. So even though you don't have to record an instrument in order for it to be valid, you generally should record it. Otherwise, someone else may later acquire a conflicting interest that will prevail against your interest. In all states, if you do record your valid interest, your interest is enforceable against any interests that arise after your interest was recorded.

Following are the three types of recording statutes and the circumstances in which they protect a later interest from a prior interest:

- ✔ **Notice acts:** About half the states have recording statutes called *notice* acts, which protect a later purchaser of an interest if she didn't have notice of the prior interest, whether through actual notice, by means of the public records, or otherwise.

A notice statute may say something like this: "No interest in real property shall be good against subsequent purchasers for a valuable consideration and without notice, until the same be recorded according to law."

- ✔ **Race acts:** Only a few states have the kind of recording statute known as a *race* act. These statutes make a prior interest void against a later interest if the later interest is recorded first.

A race statute may say something like this: "No conveyance of an interest in real property shall be valid against third parties until it is recorded according to law."

- ✔ **Race-notice acts:** The most common type of recording act is the *race-notice* act, which combines the requirements of the notice and race acts. That is, a prior interest is void against a later interest if the later interest holder paid value without notice of the prior interest and recorded her interest first.

A race-notice statute may say something like this: "Every conveyance of real property is void as against any subsequent purchaser or mortgagee of the same property, in good faith and for a valuable consideration, whose conveyance is first duly recorded."

Determining Whether an Interest Is Recorded

All three types of recording acts (described in the preceding section) protect later interests against prior interests only when the prior interest isn't recorded. So if a prior interest *is* recorded before a later interest is created, the answer is always the same: The later interest is subject to the prior interest. The recording acts don't change the usual principle of first in time, first in right.

However, a document may be filed with the county recorder but still be treated as unrecorded when the document

- ✔ Doesn't comply with the requirements for recording
- ✔ Is hard or impossible to find using the indexes

The next sections offer more insight into each of these situations when a document is filed with the county recorder but isn't treated as recorded.

Recording a document improperly

A document is recorded only if it complies with the statute. If an instrument is recorded but actually isn't entitled to be recorded, it's legally unrecorded. So if a document isn't the type of document that the statute allows to be recorded, it isn't recorded even if the county recorder mistakenly accepts it. Likewise, if the document doesn't comply with the prerequisites for recording (which I describe in the earlier "Complying with conditions for recording" section), it isn't recorded.

If an instrument is unrecorded, the recording act may protect a subsequent purchaser against it. But in some states, a subsequent purchaser who actually finds the document may still have constructive notice of the prior interest and therefore won't be protected by the recording act. I discuss this exception in the later "Constructive notice" section.

Being unable to find a recorded document

Even a recorded document that's entitled to be recorded and that satisfies the prerequisites for recording may still be treated as unrecorded if it can't reasonably be found. If a document can't reasonably be found, then it's no better than if it weren't recorded at all. And because the person who files the document with the county can check after recording to make sure it can be found in the indexes, many courts hold that if the document can't be found, the subsequent purchaser is innocent, the prior interest holder could've avoided the subsequent purchaser's reliance, and therefore the document is unrecorded.

Here are some situations in which some courts hold that an actually recorded document is legally unrecorded because it's hard or impossible for a subsequent purchaser to find:

- **Documents are improperly indexed.** In a grantor-grantee index, if the county recorder indexes the instrument under a wrong or misspelled name, a subsequent purchaser who searches title may have no chance of finding it. For example, if the grantee's name is Wilson but the recorder indexes and spells it as Vinson, a reasonable title search would never find the document. But if the first letters of the name are spelled and indexed correctly, a misspelling is less likely to prevent discovery of a document, such as if the grantee's name is misspelled and indexed as Robertson instead of Robertsen. Similarly, in a tract index, if the recorder indexes an instrument in the wrong location, a title searcher has no reasonable way to discover the instrument.

- **Links are missing.** In a grantor-grantee index, even if the prior interest is recorded, a searcher can't find it if it isn't properly connected in the same chain of title back to a common predecessor in title. Courts agree that such a deed, sometimes referred to as a *wild deed,* is unrecorded. For example, suppose A gave a deed to B that wasn't recorded and then later gave a deed to C that was recorded. A subsequent purchaser through C wouldn't be able to find any interest that B or B's successors subsequently created, even if recorded, because the subsequent purchaser would search in the grantee index to C, then to A, and so on; the subsequent purchaser would never discover that A had previously conveyed the property to B.

A person recording her instrument can avoid the missing-links problem simply by researching title to confirm that not only is her interest recorded but so are the previous instruments in her chain of title.

- **An earlier recorded document creates an interest in the property.** A title searcher in a grantor-grantee index searches for successive owners backward in time in the grantee index and then checks each of those owners in the grantor index during their time of ownership. That means if one of those owners conveyed an interest before her ownership, even though it was recorded, a title searcher normally wouldn't find that interest.

That may sound crazy, because why would someone convey an interest in property before she owns it? But it can happen, maybe because of a mistake, maybe because of fraud. Whatever the reason, if A gives a warranty deed to B before she acquires the property and then later does acquire it, the property automatically transfers to B under a doctrine called *estoppel by deed,* which I cover in Chapter 16. If A later conveys the property to C, a subsequent purchaser through C normally wouldn't find that earlier deed to B even though it was recorded. Some courts therefore say that the deed is legally unrecorded; others say it's recorded and that title searchers simply have to check the grantor indexes further back in time if they want to check for earlier recorded deeds.

✔ **A later recorded document creates an interest in the property.** This problem is similar to the problem of the earlier recorded document. Suppose that O sells property to A, and A doesn't record her interest immediately. Instead, A records it after some other person, B, acquires the property and records, knowing of A's prior interest. Except in the race states, B wouldn't be protected by the recording statutes. But if B sold the property to C, C wouldn't normally find A's recorded interest. C would start with her seller's name in the grantee index, finding the recorded conveyance to B. She would then find the conveyance from O to B and keep going back in time in the grantee index. Then she would search each of those names in the grantor index during the time each owned the property, ending with B. She wouldn't find that O had previously sold the property to A, because the deed to A wasn't recorded during the time that O appears to have actually owned the property; the deed to A was recorded only after O had given a recorded deed to B. Most states say that the later-recorded document prevails, which means that a prudent title searcher should search for each owner's name in the grantor index not just for the time the grantor appears to have owned the property but afterward as well. Others treat such a later recorded document as unrecorded.

✔ **Deeds create interests in other property.** Not only may a deed convey a particular parcel of land, it may also create an interest in some other parcel of land. For example, a deed may give the grantee an easement over adjoining land the grantor still owns. A person who later acquires the grantor's retained land may not discover from a title search that the land is subject to an easement. If a grantor-grantee index says the earlier deed creating the easement concerns a different parcel of land, the title searcher will pass by that entry in the index, looking for entries dealing with the parcel she is buying. Some courts say that skipping the other entries is reasonable and that the easement is unrecorded. Other courts say the easement is recorded and that a title searcher should search any documents involving the previous owners to see whether they create such an interest in the relevant property, even though the index doesn't say that the deed relates to the relevant property. The problem is even worse in a tract index system: If the deed is indexed only as relating to the land conveyed and not the burdened land retained, the title searcher won't find an index entry for that deed at all.

Paying Value for Property Interest

All recording acts but two of the race statutes protect a later interest from a prior interest only if the owner of the later interest paid value for it. The recording statutes are generally meant to protect people who would be harmed by the lack of notice of an existing interest in real property. In other words, the statutes protect those who would rely on the state of title in deciding to pay substantial value and would lose some of that value if a prior unrecorded interest were valid against them. Those who pay no value for their property interests don't lose any investment if it turns out that their interests are impaired or useless because of prior conflicting interests.

A person pays value for a property interest by giving anything of substantial economic value in exchange for the property interest, such as the following:

- ✔ **Money:** The subsequent purchaser doesn't have to pay the full value of the property in order to be protected by the recording statute. Courts generally agree that a purchaser is protected if she pays some substantial amount compared to the value of the property and not an amount that's nominal or grossly inadequate. A person who receives a property interest by gift, will, or inheritance isn't protected by the recording statute.

  A mere promise to pay money, even giving a mortgage to secure such a promise, isn't payment of value. However, giving a promise to pay in the form of a negotiable instrument is payment of value if circumstances would make it enforceable regardless of whether the promisor receives good title to the property.

- ✔ **A loan:** Many statutes expressly say that mortgagees are protected against unrecorded interests if they satisfy the other requirements of the statute. But even if the recording act doesn't say that, courts all agree that a lender who loans money to a borrower and takes a mortgage to secure repayment has paid value as required for the protection of the statute.

  However, if the lender has already made an unsecured loan and then later takes a mortgage to secure repayment, the lender hasn't paid value and isn't protected by the recording act. In this situation, the lender didn't pay value relying on the state of title, unless she agrees to somehow change the borrower's obligation in a way that's detrimental to the lender, like by extending the time for repayment.

  Likewise, a person who acquires a statutory lien against the property doesn't pay value for her lien and therefore isn't protected by the statute. For example, a person who gets a judgment against another automatically gets a statutory _judgment lien_ against her real property, which allows her to sell the property to satisfy the judgment. Some recording statutes expressly protect those who hold judgment liens, but in most states a judgment lienor isn't protected because she didn't pay value to receive her lien.

- ✔ **Canceling an obligation:** Canceling an existing debt or accepting a deed as performance of an outstanding obligation can be payment of value.

Taking Property Interest without Notice

Notice and race-notice recording statutes protect a subsequent purchaser only if she paid value without having notice of the prior interest. Some statutes say the subsequent purchaser is protected only if she pays value "in good faith," which means the same thing — she paid value without notice of the prior interest. Therefore, such a purchaser may be called a *bona fide* or *good faith purchaser.*

If the recording act protects the holder of a later interest against a prior interest, she can transfer her interest to others free of the prior interest, even if her grantees have notice of the prior interest. This rule is often called the *shelter rule.* Without it, a good faith purchaser wouldn't be able to sell the property to anyone else if the prior interest was then recorded, dramatically impairing the property's value to the good faith purchaser.

So if A buys property without notice of a prior unrecorded conveyance, and then after she buys it the prior conveyance is recorded, anyone to whom A might subsequently convey the property would have constructive notice of the prior conveyance from the real property records. But the shelter rule says that A can sell her property to someone else, and her grantee will still be free of the prior interest, even though now it's recorded.

The following sections explain the different ways a subsequent purchaser may have notice and therefore not be protected by the recording act.

Actual knowledge

This point may sound like a no-brainer, but a person has notice of a prior interest if she actually knows about the prior interest. She may learn about the prior interest from the seller, the owner of the prior interest, or neighbors. Or she may learn about it by searching title, inspecting the property, or some other way. If she pays value for her property interest after getting such actual knowledge of a prior interest, the recording act won't protect her, and her interest will be subject to the prior interest.

However, sometimes the recording act protects a subsequent purchaser even if she has actual knowledge of a prior interest. Some cases hold that if an instrument was improperly recorded, the subsequent purchaser legally doesn't have notice of it even if she actually finds the instrument.

Constructive notice

A person may have notice of the prior interest even though she doesn't actually know about it. Such notice is called *constructive notice*. It's as if she received a notice in the mail but never opened it. She was sufficiently notified of the prior interest, but she wasn't sufficiently careful to actually get the message. A person may receive constructive notice from two main sources:

- ✔ Public records
- ✔ The property itself

The next sections describe how each of these sources may give constructive notice of a prior interest.

Constructive notice from public records

The recording acts protect a later interest against a prior interest only when the prior interest isn't recorded. So it may seem that either an interest is recorded, in which case the recording act doesn't apply, or it's unrecorded, in which case the subsequent purchaser couldn't possibly get notice from the real property records anyway. But there are situations in which even though a prior interest is unrecorded, the subsequent purchaser had constructive notice of the prior interest from the real property records.

This can happen when a reasonable title search would discover an instrument that refers to some other prior interest. Even though the prior interest itself is legally unrecorded, the title searcher would have constructive notice of the interest as long as she could reasonably identify the interest from the instrument that was recorded.

For example, a recorded deed to lakefront property might say that the conveyance of the property is subject to an existing easement belonging to the adjoining parcel to the south to cross the property to get to the lake. Even though the easement itself is unrecorded, a subsequent purchaser of the property would have constructive notice of the easement.

Furthermore, other public records may give constructive notice of an interest that isn't recorded in the real property records. A judgment lien may not be recorded in the real property records, for example, but unless a statute requires it to be recorded, a subsequent buyer may have constructive notice of the judgment lien from court records. Similarly, a subsequent buyer may have constructive notice of unrecorded interests from property tax records, bankruptcy court records, and probate records.

Constructive notice from the property

A buyer of an interest in real property has constructive notice of whatever she would discover from visiting the property and talking to whoever is in possession of it.

If the seller possesses the property, then the buyer has no reason to investigate further. But if someone else possesses the property, then the buyer has notice of the possibility that the possessor has some prior interest in the property. The buyer can't reasonably rely on the seller's explanation of why someone else is in possession, because the seller has a big temptation to lie. Rather, the buyer must directly ask the possessor why she is in possession. If the buyer were to do so, the possessor would surely tell the buyer whether she has a prior interest in the real property, and the buyer would thereby acquire actual knowledge of the prior interest. If the buyer doesn't ask the possessor, then the buyer has constructive notice of the possessor's interest rather than actual knowledge.

However, if the real property records show that the possessor used to own the property, especially if she owned it quite recently, then some courts figure that a reasonable buyer would assume the former owner was still in possession simply because the present owner has given her permission to stay there temporarily. In that case, the buyer doesn't have constructive notice if it turns out the possessor actually is possessing the property pursuant to some property interest she still owns.

The possession must be sufficiently visible, open, and clear so that a reasonable buyer would have notice that someone other than the seller may have an interest in the land. In some cases, someone other than the seller may be in possession, but that wouldn't be evident to a reasonable buyer visiting the property. In such cases, the buyer doesn't have constructive notice of the possessor's interest.

Even if the possessor is only occasionally present on the land, improvements on the land may give notice that someone other than the seller is possessing the property. For example, if a building on neighboring land encroaches on the property, a reasonable buyer would think that the neighbor may actually own that part of the property and ask the neighbor about it. But if the improvements don't indicate that someone else is possessing the property but are equally consistent with the seller's claim of title, then the buyer has no constructive notice of the prior interest.

If the possessor is a tenant, most courts hold that a reasonable buyer has notice of whatever interests she would discover from talking to the tenant. Even if the lease is recorded or otherwise known to the buyer, she still has constructive notice of whatever interests she would discover by talking to the tenant. That's because the tenant may have acquired rights that don't appear in the written lease, such as an option to buy the land or a right to extend the lease term. Buyers often condition their obligation to purchase leased land on receiving satisfactory statements from the tenants indicating that they don't have further rights in the property.

Inquiry notice

Someone may have notice of a prior interest through inquiry notice. A person has *inquiry notice* when the following things are true:

✔ She actually knew or had constructive notice of something that suggested the possibility of the prior interest.

✔ A reasonable investigation of that information would've discovered the prior interest.

Inquiry notice may arise from the real property records. One such situation occurs when a document refers vaguely or incompletely to another prior interest. A title searcher has inquiry notice of the prior interest if a reasonable investigation would've discovered it.

Suppose a prior deed to the property says the conveyance is subject to covenants in favor of the neighboring owner. Even though the title searcher can't know from that reference what the covenants are, or even who has the benefit of those covenants, if she could discover the covenants by asking the neighbors — maybe if she asked, one of the neighbors would produce a copy of the covenants — then she has inquiry notice of them.

If the reference to a prior interest is too vague, however, then a reasonable title searcher might not investigate at all and would have no inquiry notice.

Inquiry notice could arise out of facts discovered from other sources, such as an inspection of the property, comments by neighbors, the appearance of the neighborhood suggesting uniform covenants, news stories, and any other source if it's sufficiently reliable and definite that a reasonable buyer would investigate further.

Protecting Subsequent Purchasers from Unlikely Claims

A title search may uncover some old title defects that are unlikely to result in conflicting claims to the property. A buyer might conclude that such title risks are acceptable and go ahead with the purchase. But some state statutes go further and eliminate such risks altogether, reasoning that the value of greater certainty and marketability of title outweighs the possible elimination of meritorious claims.

One such way of eliminating old title claims is adverse possession. If a person possesses land openly, exclusively, continuously, and adversely for the statute of limitations period, she gets clear title to the possessed property, eliminating any title interests to which the possession was adverse. Of course, a buyer who isn't sure about the validity of an earlier claim may not like the idea of buying the land and hoping to possess the land ten years without interruption in order to have clear title. In some cases, she may feel confident that previous owners have satisfied the adverse possession requirements, although confirming satisfaction of the requirements would be difficult. (For information on adverse possession, see Chapter 14.)

The following sections describe three types of state statutes that are intended to eliminate old and unlikely title claims:

- ✔ Title curative acts
- ✔ Statutes eliminating specific types of old interests
- ✔ Marketable title acts

Curing defects by title curative acts

Some states have title curative acts that eliminate claims based on certain defects in recorded instruments after a certain number of years. Typically, *title curative acts* say that after the specified number of years, maybe five or ten years, an instrument is validly recorded and no claim may be based on things like the following:

- ✔ Defects in execution
- ✔ Defects in or the absence of witnessing or acknowledgment
- ✔ Defects in recording
- ✔ Improper exercises of a power of attorney or power of appointment

Eliminating specific old interests

Some states have statutes that eliminate specific types of interests after they're very old, unless the holder of the interest records a notice that she owns the interest and wants to preserve it. The most common type of this statute eliminates old mortgages, which after the specified time period from the due date will almost certainly no longer be valid and asserted. Some state statutes similarly extinguish old future interests that the rule against perpetuities wouldn't extinguish, like rights of entry and possibilities of reverter, after a long period of time. (For details on future estates and the rule against perpetuities, see Chapter 9.)

Applying marketable title acts

A substantial minority of states have adopted marketable title acts. In general, the *marketable title acts* extinguish all claims arising before the *root of title* — a recorded instrument that's at least a specified number of years old, generally 20 to 40 years old.

So in a state with a marketable title act and a root of title period of 40 years, a buyer searching title would need to search title back to a conveyance that was at least 40 years earlier. The buyer is still subject to any title claims discovered back to that conveyance, but the marketable title act extinguishes any claims arising before it, so the buyer doesn't have to worry about searching any further, right?

Not quite. The marketable title acts all have a number of exceptions, claims that aren't extinguished even though they're older than the root of title. Such exceptions may include

- ✔ An interest that's specifically referred to and identified in the root of title or an instrument in the chain of title more recent than the root of title
- ✔ The reversion of a lessor
- ✔ Easements that are clearly observable or certain types of easements, like utility, railroad, and road easements
- ✔ Rights of a party in possession
- ✔ Rights of the federal or state government
- ✔ Water and mineral rights
- ✔ Claims that are re-recorded after the root of title or notices of which are recorded after the root of title as permitted by the statute

Marketable title acts might not entirely relieve a title searcher of the need to search title further back than the root of title, but they do extinguish many old interests that are unlikely to be asserted.

Chapter 18

Mortgaging Real Property

*B*uyers of real property often borrow money to make the purchase. A promissory note obligates the borrower to repay the loan, of course. But if the borrower defaults, the lender may find that the borrower simply doesn't have the money to pay the debt. The lender may reduce the risk of nonpayment by taking a *security interest* — either a *mortgage* or a *deed of trust* — in the borrower's real property. A mortgage or deed of trust gives the lender the right to sell the real property at auction and apply the proceeds of the sale to the unpaid debt. This chapter describes this process, called *foreclosure,* as well as other rights the lender may have to protect its interests.

By reducing the risks for lenders, mortgages make loans more available and cheaper for borrowers. But if a borrower defaults, she may lose her property. State legislatures have responded to concerns for borrowers by adopting statutes intended to protect borrowers from abuses and unnecessary hardship. This chapter also covers these statutory protections.

Finally, this chapter considers transfers by both borrowers and lenders. The borrower may want to transfer her property to another even though a mortgage is attached to it. The lender likewise may want to transfer its promissory note and mortgage to another. This chapter examines some legal issues connected with such transfers.

Introducing Mortgages and Deeds of Trust

A *mortgage* is the right to sell property in the event of default on a debt or other obligation and then apply the proceeds to the satisfaction of the obligation. The person who owes the debt or obligation gives a mortgage to secure her performance. Usually her performance is to repay a loan, but a mortgage can secure other types of obligations too, as long as the obligation can be quantified. Because she gives the mortgage to her creditor, she's called the *mortgagor,* and the creditor who holds the mortgage is called the *mortgagee.*

A mortgage is an interest in land. In fact, some jurisdictions say that the mortgagee actually has title to the mortgaged property until the debt is satisfied and the mortgage is released. This theory is commonly referred to as the *title theory.* Other jurisdictions say that a mortgage is merely a lien on property, not title to property. This theory is called the *lien theory.* In either case, the mortgagor has the right to possess the property as long as she pays her debt and doesn't default.

A *deed of trust* is similar to a mortgage. It conveys the property to a *trustee,* who holds the property in trust for the lender, who is called the *beneficiary.* The trustee has the right to sell the property in the event of default by the borrower, called the *trustor,* and to apply the proceeds to the debt owed the beneficiary, just as with a mortgage.

The rules I present in this chapter apply to deeds of trust and mortgages alike, except where otherwise indicated.

Possessing the Property before Foreclosure

The mortgagor has the right to possess the property as long as she doesn't *default.* The mortgage agreement specifies what constitutes default, but generally acts of default include failure to repay the debt as agreed and breach of other important obligations, such as paying property taxes.

The fundamental right of a mortgagee is to sell the property in foreclosure if the mortgagor defaults. But the lender/mortgagee may not want to foreclose immediately when the borrower/mortgagor first defaults. And even if the mortgagee does want to foreclose immediately, the process of foreclosing can take a while. In the meantime, the mortgagee wants to make sure the property's value doesn't decline and thereby reduce the amount the mortgagee can recover if and when it ultimately forecloses.

The mortgagor who defaults may not have the money to manage the property well, and the mortgagor who expects to lose the property in foreclosure may stop taking care of the property. The mortgagee therefore may want to protect the property by having someone else possess and manage it. The mortgagee may do this in two ways:

- ✔ It can take possession itself.
- ✔ It can have a court appoint a receiver to take possession.

Taking possession

If the mortgagor defaults, the mortgagee may have the right to take possession of the property. In a title theory state, the mortgagee can immediately take possession upon default. And in some lien theory states, the mortgagee can take possession upon default if the mortgage agreement gives the mortgagee the right to do so. In other lien theory states, however, the mortgagee has no right to take possession before foreclosure.

If the mortgagee does take possession, it doesn't simply become the owner of the property with the right to do whatever it wants to do with the property. Rather, the mortgagee acts as a sort of trustee for the mortgagor. The mortgagee must manage the property prudently for the benefit of the mortgagor, including making repairs and paying essential expenses with the available income from the property. The mortgagee in possession is also liable in tort to third parties, just as an owner would be. So taking possession has some benefits, allowing the mortgagee to protect the property and manage the rents or other income from the property, but it also has some risks of liability to the mortgagor or third parties.

Appointing a receiver

A *receiver* is a person appointed by a court to take possession of the property and manage it, such as maintaining it and collecting rents from tenants. As the preceding section explains, in some situations the lender itself can't take possession, so a receiver is the only way to take possession from the mortgagor. Even if the mortgagee could take possession itself, having a receiver appointed may be easier, and doing so avoids the duties and risks that come with taking possession, which I describe in the preceding section.

The mortgage agreement may specify circumstances in which the mortgagee is entitled to have a receiver appointed. Some courts will enforce such agreements, but other courts reason that the appointment of a receiver is an exercise of the court's equitable discretion, so they either disregard the mortgage clause entirely or apply their own criteria differently if the mortgage clause would authorize appointment of a receiver.

Even if the mortgage agreement doesn't say anything about appointment of a receiver, a mortgagee may still ask the court to appoint a receiver. In that case, the court will of course apply its own criteria for deciding whether to appoint a receiver. And once again, even if the mortgage agreement does specify grounds for appointment of a receiver, some courts will still apply their own criteria.

Courts vary in the requirements for appointment of a receiver, but generally they consider the following:

- ✔ **Waste:** Some courts appoint a receiver only if the mortgagor has committed waste or threatens to commit waste. Other courts simply consider waste as one factor in deciding whether to appoint a receiver. Chapter 9 talks more about *waste,* which essentially occurs when the present owner of the property acts in some way that impairs the value of the property in which another has a future interest. Damaging or neglecting the property in a way that reduces its value is waste. Failure to pay taxes, to pay mortgage interest, or to apply rents to the mortgage debt may also be waste, because doing so increases the debt secured by the mortgage and therefore reduces the extent to which the mortgagee's debt is secured. If there's no threat of waste, courts figure there's no reason to think that a receiver is needed to protect and preserve the property — the mortgagor can do it herself.

- ✔ **Inadequate security:** Some courts will appoint a receiver only if the security is inadequate; others consider inadequate security as a factor. The security is inadequate if the market value of the property isn't enough to ensure that the mortgagee can get the debt fully repaid by foreclosing. If the property is worth well more than the outstanding debt, courts reason that a receiver isn't needed because the mortgagee can simply proceed with foreclosure and thereby get its debt fully repaid.

- ✔ **Default and mortgagor's financial ability:** Some courts require that the mortgagor be in default before appointing a receiver. Others don't require default, but they do consider the mortgagor's financial circumstances that may make a default likely. If the mortgagor is in financial distress, that supports the mortgagee's argument that a receiver is needed to ensure the property is well managed.

- ✔ **Other considerations:** If the mortgagor has somehow committed fraud, the court may conclude that a receiver is needed to ensure the property is managed properly, even if the mortgagor hasn't committed waste. A court also may consider what alternatives to a receiver are available to the mortgagee, wanting to avoid the harsh remedy of taking away possession from the mortgagor who, after all, owns the property. The court may compare the harms to the parties in deciding whether to appoint a receiver.

The receiver is an agent of the court, not of one of the parties. But she does have a duty to both parties to manage the property with reasonable care, skill, and loyalty. The mortgagee has no duty to fund the receiver's activities, and the receiver has no duty to spend her own money to manage the property. The receiver's duty is just to use the money from the property itself or money that the interested parties give the receiver for that purpose.

Selling Property in Foreclosure

If the mortgagor defaults, the mortgagee can *foreclose*, meaning the mortgagee can sell the mortgaged property and keep as much of the proceeds as needed to pay off the mortgagor's debt. The mortgagee may initiate a judicial action to have a public official sell the property at auction. Or, if the mortgage or deed of trust authorizes it, in some states the mortgagee may have the property sold without a judicial action. State statutes specify required notices and sale procedures for such private, nonjudicial foreclosure sales. The following sections explain the process of selling property in foreclosure.

Curing default or exercising equity of redemption

Before a foreclosure sale can occur, the mortgagor must have defaulted and not permissibly cured the default or exercised the equity of redemption. The following sections talk about these legal issues preceding foreclosure.

Defaulting

The mortgagee can foreclose only if the mortgagor materially breaches the contract, which is called a *default.* Not all breaches of the contract are acts of default; the mortgage agreement generally specifies what constitutes a default. Typical acts of default include the following:

- ✔ **Failure to make a required payment of principal and interest when scheduled:** Commonly mortgages allow a grace period after the due date, such as 15 days, but after that time, the mortgagor is in default.

- ✔ **Failure to pay property taxes and public assessments on the property:** These unpaid taxes and assessments may result in liens that allow the government to sell the property to satisfy the unpaid taxes and assessments.

✔ **Failure to maintain property insurance:** The lack of insurance creates the risk that the property will be damaged with no source of money to repair it.

✔ **Significantly damaging the property:** Damage obviously reduces the property's value as security for the mortgagee.

Accelerating the debt

A foreclosing mortgagee virtually always starts the process by accelerating the debt, although doing so isn't technically necessary to foreclose. Before default, the mortgagor's obligation typically is to pay an installment of principal and interest each month. But the mortgage usually provides that, if the mortgagor defaults, the mortgagee can *accelerate* the debt, which means demanding immediate payment of the entire unpaid principal and other amounts owed under the parties' agreement. Then the mortgagee can foreclose and use the sale proceeds to pay off the entire debt and not just unpaid monthly installments.

However, regardless of what the mortgage says, most courts don't allow the lender to accelerate if it would be unconscionable because the harsh consequences are unjustified by the mortgagor's default. Here are some circumstances in which courts may consider acceleration unconscionable:

✔ The default was technical and minor, not causing any real injury to the mortgagee or jeopardizing the mortgagee's security.

✔ The mortgagor tried in good faith to perform her obligations but unintentionally and innocently committed the default.

✔ The default was brief, and the mortgagor promptly tried to cure the default.

✔ The default was caused by fraud or conduct in bad faith by the mortgagee.

One thing that isn't on this list is the personal or financial circumstances of the mortgagor. The mortgagor's circumstances don't make acceleration unconscionable even though one might empathize with her plight.

The mortgagee also may not accelerate the debt if it has waived the right to do so. Probably the most common waiver occurs when the mortgagee has previously accepted late payments from the mortgager, resulting in waiver of the right to accelerate the debt when a payment is late. The mortgagee also may waive the right to accelerate the debt, or be estopped from doing so, by assuring the borrower that it won't accelerate the debt for a particular reason. To avoid waiver of the right to accelerate, mortgages often contain anti-waiver clauses that say the mortgagee's acceptance of late payments or other acts of forbearance won't waive the mortgagee's right to accelerate the debt for such reasons in the future. Courts generally enforce such anti-waiver clauses.

The mortgagor has the right to cure the default up until the mortgagee effectively accelerates the debt. So if the mortgagor defaults by not making a couple of monthly payments, the mortgagor can prevent acceleration and foreclosure by tendering the late payments to the mortgagee any time before the mortgagee accelerates the debt.

At the very least, the mortgagee must take some action, such as giving notice to the mortgagor or filing a foreclosure action, in order to accelerate the debt. Often, state law or the mortgage agreement requires the mortgagee to give notice of its intention to accelerate the debt 30 days or some other time before actually accelerating, giving the mortgagor time to cure her default. Some state statutes and mortgage agreements also allow the borrower to cure default even after acceleration, sometimes even up until the moment of a foreclosure sale.

Exercising the equity of redemption

Even if the debt is accelerated and the mortgagee begins foreclosure proceedings, the mortgagor always has the right to exercise the *equity of redemption,* which is the right to pay off the entire outstanding debt and thereby extinguish the mortgage and avoid a foreclosure sale.

The mortgagor always has this equitable right, no matter what the mortgage agreement says. Anything inconsistent with the equity of redemption is simply invalid. The mortgagee's only interest is in being fully repaid, so if the mortgagor pays the entire debt, along with any other damages and charges she agreed to pay, then the mortgagee has received everything it bargained for and has no further interest in the property. The mortgagor can exercise the equity of redemption at any time up until the moment the property is sold by a foreclosure sale.

Extinguishing junior interests

The foreclosing mortgagee has the right to sell the same title that the mortgagor owned at the time she gave the mortgage to the mortgagee. After the mortgage is created, the mortgagor may convey other interests in the property, such as leases, easements, or even other mortgages. But such interests are *junior* to the earlier mortgage, meaning the mortgage isn't subject to such interests. Except as I explain next, the foreclosure sale simply wipes out those junior interests so that they no longer exist.

In a judicial foreclosure action, the mortgagee's lawsuit must name all the owners of junior interests in order to extinguish their interests. That includes owners of any interest in the property that came later in time, including owners of easements, covenants, liens, other mortgages, and leases. If these owners aren't parties to the foreclosure lawsuit, their interests aren't extinguished by the foreclosure sale and will still encumber the property now owned by the foreclosure buyer.

However, upon discovering the omission, the foreclosure buyer — which may be the mortgagee or someone else — may have several options (unless the mortgagee is the foreclosure buyer and intentionally omitted the junior interest). Those options include the following:

- ✔ **Paying off the junior interest:** The foreclosure buyer can extinguish the junior interest simply by paying the amount of the junior debt to the junior interest holder.

- ✔ **Conducting another foreclosure sale, this time including the omitted junior interest:** For this purpose, the buyer is considered to have bought the revived foreclosed mortgage, so the foreclosure buyer can foreclose and apply the proceeds to the revived mortgage debt; the junior interest will then get any excess up to the amount of its debt.

- ✔ **Getting a court order giving the junior interest holder a specified time to redeem:** To *redeem* is to pay the outstanding debt that was secured by the foreclosed mortgage and thereby take title to the property. With this option, if the property has value beyond the amount of the outstanding debt, the junior interest holder can capture that value by selling the property on the market. Some courts make such an order only in certain circumstances, including when the buyer bought in good faith and the junior interest holder knew of the impending foreclosure sale but didn't disclose its interest, or when the property isn't worth more than the foreclosed mortgage debt.

In a nonjudicial foreclosure sale, there's no lawsuit and therefore no occasion for the mortgagee to name junior interests as parties. However, a state statute may require the foreclosing mortgagee to notify the junior interests so that they can participate in the sale to protect their interests.

Distributing the proceeds of a foreclosure sale

In a foreclosure sale, the mortgaged property is sold to the high bidder in a public auction. If the property is foreclosed in a judicial action, a sheriff or other public official may conduct the sale; if it's foreclosed in a nonjudicial action, the trustee conducts the sale. State statutes specify when and where such sales may be held, but the location is often the courthouse.

The money paid by the highest bidder is distributed as follows:

1. **The costs of the sale and the debt owed to the foreclosing mortgagee are paid first.**

The mortgagee's only interest in the property is to be fully repaid, however, so if any money is left over, the mortgagee doesn't get to keep it.

2. **The surplus is distributed to owners of junior interests in order of priority (which is generally the order in which the interests were created).**

The sale extinguishes junior interests in the property, so these parties have a claim against the proceeds to compensate them for their loss.

3. **The mortgagor gets to keep any money that's left after paying the junior interests.**

Imagine that after mortgaging her property, the mortgagor sold an easement to a neighbor and then gave a second mortgage to secure a home equity loan. If the first mortgagee forecloses, the proceeds of the foreclosure sale are first used to pay the costs of sale and to pay off the outstanding debt on the foreclosed mortgage. If any money remains, the easement holder receives the market value of her lost easement. Any remaining surplus is applied to the home equity loan. And if that loan is fully paid and money still remains from the foreclosure sale, the mortgagor keeps the rest.

The mortgagor may complain that the high bidder at the foreclosure sale bid an unfairly low amount. In general, however, a low winning bid invalidates a sale only if it's grossly inadequate, something like 20 percent of the property's market value or less. But if the foreclosure proceedings were irregular in some way that caused a low bid, a court may invalidate the sale even though the bid was a higher percentage of the property's market value. Courts have invalidated sales for reasons such as the following:

✔ The foreclosing mortgagee didn't provide correct notices as required by statute.

✔ The high bidder colluded with other prospective bidders to reduce the amount bid, such as by agreeing to share profits or paying them money not to bid.

✔ The foreclosing mortgagee misrepresented the property's condition or title or otherwise suppressed bidding by others.

✔ The foreclosing mortgagee sold multiple mortgaged parcels in combinations or in an order that wasn't the most beneficial to the mortgagor.

✔ The party conducting the sale was the high bidder.

Any interests that are senior to the foreclosed mortgage — interests that were created earlier in time — are not affected by the foreclosure sale. Those interests simply remain attached to the property now owned by the high bidder at the foreclosure sale. Because the owners of the senior interests aren't affected by the foreclosure sale, they have no claim to the proceeds of the sale.

The foreclosing mortgagee can and usually does bid at the foreclosure sale. If the foreclosing mortgagee is the high bidder, it essentially pays itself up to the amount of its debt by canceling the debt to the extent of its bid. The foreclosing mortgagee only has to come up with cash if it bids more than the amount of its debt.

Recovering deficiency from borrower

The foreclosure sale may not result in a surplus at all. In fact, the high bid may be less than the amount of the outstanding debt, resulting in a deficiency on the debt. Sometimes a mortgage loan is *nonrecourse*, meaning the mortgagor isn't personally liable to pay any deficiency remaining after a foreclosure sale. But in the absence of such an agreement, the mortgagor still has a contractual duty to pay the full debt to the mortgagee, so the mortgagee can get a *deficiency judgment* against the mortgagor to recover the still-unpaid debt, unless a statute prevents it (the situation I describe in the next section).

If the foreclosing mortgagee wins with a low bid and then sues the mortgagor for a deficiency, a court is more likely to invalidate the sale because of an inadequate winning bid and procedural irregularities. In that situation, not only does the low bid deprive the borrower of the benefit of paying off junior interests and/or receiving a surplus, but it also results in a greater claim against the borrower by the mortgagee.

Protecting Mortgagor by Statute

A defaulting mortgagor can suffer serious consequences. If she can't pay her debt, she'll lose her property in a foreclosure sale. The winning bid will almost surely not be as much as the property would be worth if sold normally. Not only that, but if the winning bid is less than the outstanding debt, the defaulting mortgagor may still be subject to a lawsuit to recover the rest of the unpaid debt.

States have an interest in protecting borrowers from such consequences. Not only do states want to avoid unfair losses to a person who has paid a substantial amount of money to buy property and then is unable to complete the purchase, but states also want to avoid the economic consequences and public burdens that may result from foreclosures. Many states therefore have adopted various statutes intended to protect mortgagors. The following sections clue you in to three common statutory protections:

- Anti-deficiency statutes
- One-action statutes
- Statutory rights of redemption

Anti-deficiency statutes

Selling the property at auction to the high bidder is intended to maximize the value paid for the property and thus reduce the mortgagor's debt as much as possible. Often, however, the mortgagee is the only bidder at the sale. Not only may the mortgagee bid less than the property is actually worth, but the mortgagee may bid even less than the amount of the unpaid debt, intending to try to collect the remainder of the unpaid debt in other ways.

To encourage higher bids and avoid unfairness to the mortgagor, states have adopted several kinds of statutes that limit deficiency judgments. Some statutes prohibit deficiency judgments altogether in certain situations, such as the following:

- ✔ If a seller finances the purchase herself, taking a mortgage from her buyer, the seller can't sue for a deficiency after foreclosure.

- ✔ If the mortgagor resides on the property, the mortgagee can't get a deficiency judgment after selling the property at a foreclosure sale.

- ✔ If the mortgagee sells the property by a nonjudicial foreclosure, the mortgagee can't get a deficiency judgment. So if the mortgagee thinks the property may sell for less than the debt and wants to get a deficiency judgment, it should instead foreclose judicially.

Other statutes don't prohibit deficiency judgments, but they do limit the amount. One common version allows the lender to recover a deficiency judgment only to the extent the unpaid debt exceeds the fair market value of the mortgaged property at the time of the foreclosure sale. So if the property actually isn't worth enough to secure the unpaid debt, the statute allows a deficiency for the difference. But if the property is worth enough to pay the debt, the lender can't bid less than the debt and the fair market value of the property, get the property to resell, and sue the mortgagor for a deficiency, thereby getting more value than the unpaid debt.

The same limitation applies if a junior mortgagee purchases at the foreclosure sale. A junior mortgagee who is the high bidder at the foreclosure sale has the same temptation and opportunity to bid low to get the property for less than it's worth and then still get a judgment for the remainder of the debt against the mortgagor. So the same limitation applies.

Another version of fair value legislation requires a court to certify that the winning bid at the foreclosure sale is equal to the fair market value of the property in order for the mortgagee to get a deficiency judgment. So if the winning bid was less than fair market value, the mortgagee can't recover any deficiency judgment. Some states also have statutes that limit the time period within which a mortgagee can bring an action for a deficiency judgment.

A mortgagee might try to avoid the limitations of an anti-deficiency statute by suing the mortgagor for damages resulting from waste rather than suing for breach of the contract to repay the debt. Courts have held that an anti-deficiency statute still applies to such an action if the waste is the result of the mortgagor's not having the money to maintain the property or make required payments. Even if the mortgagee would otherwise have an action for waste, if the mortgagee is the high bidder at the sale and bids the full amount of the debt, the mortgagee hasn't suffered a loss from the waste and can't recover anything for waste.

A mortgagee also might try to avoid an anti-deficiency statute by requiring the mortgagor to waive the protections of the statute in the original mortgage agreement. In general, courts hold such waivers to be void.

One-action statutes

One-action statutes prohibit a lender from bringing separate actions for foreclosure and for breach of the contract to repay the debt. Rather, the mortgagee must seek a deficiency judgment in a foreclosure action or forfeit the right to recover a deficiency.

The effect of these statutes is to require the mortgagee to recover as much value as possible from the mortgaged property first. Otherwise, the mortgagee might first get a judgment and try to get as much value as possible from the mortgagor's other assets before foreclosing. The one-action rule protects the mortgagor's basic expectation that the primary source of repayment in the event of default will be the sale of the mortgaged property. It also protects the mortgagor from having to deal with two separate actions.

Statutory rights of redemption

The value of the property in excess of the debt encumbering it is often referred to as the mortgagor's *equity*. If the mortgaged property is sold at foreclosure for less than it's worth, the mortgagor loses equity that otherwise would've paid off junior debts or been returned to the mortgagor.

Anti-deficiency statutes don't protect the mortgagor against the loss of equity. They protect the mortgagor only against excessive out-of-pocket payments on the debt when the value of the property should've resulted in paying off more of the debt. Even with an anti-deficiency statute, the property may be sold in foreclosure for less than it's worth so that the mortgagor loses her equity; instead, the foreclosure buyer enjoys the excess value that it bought for cheap.

Of course, the mortgagee and foreclosure buyer might reply that the mortgagor lost her equity only because she breached her contract. As long as she pays her debt as she agreed, she won't lose the property at all. Even if she defaults, she may have the opportunity to cure her default for a time. And even after the debt is accelerated, she can avoid losing the property, and avoid losing her equity, by paying the outstanding debt.

Even so, a majority of states provide one more opportunity for the mortgagor to avoid losing her equity even after the foreclosure sale. In most states, statutes provide that the mortgagor can *redeem* the property after the sale, meaning the mortgagor can essentially buy it back from the foreclosure purchaser. The following sections detail the essential elements of these statutory redemption schemes.

Redemption price

A few statutes require the redeeming party, or *redemptioner,* to pay the whole debt secured by the foreclosed mortgage. All the other statutes require the redemptioner to pay the foreclosure buyer the amount she bid for the property, plus costs and interest. That encourages bidders at the foreclosure sale to bid higher and closer to market value, because the lower the winning bid, the more likely a redemptioner will be to have the money and incentive to redeem the property.

Who can redeem

The primary reason for statutory redemption is to allow the mortgagor to recapture her equity and keep the property. By paying the foreclosure purchase price, she can fully compensate the winning bidder but get the property back. If the property is worth more than the winning bid, the redeeming mortgagor can thereby recapture that extra value.

Some of the statutes also allow junior interest holders to redeem. A junior interest holder doesn't have the primary claim to the equity in the property, of course; the mortgagor does. The mortgagor therefore has the primary right to redeem, and if she does so, no junior interest holder can. But if the mortgagor doesn't redeem, in some states a junior interest holder can redeem because doing so enables the junior interest holder to apply excess value to the debt the mortgagor owes her.

Time to redeem

State redemption statutes vary in the time allowed for redemption, ranging from a few months to a couple of years after the foreclosure sale. Some statutes provide longer redemption periods for larger parcels of land or agricultural land, and some provide shorter periods for redemption when a purchase-money mortgage was foreclosed or the property is abandoned. Some provide a time period during which only the mortgagor may redeem, and afterward, junior interest holders may redeem within a specified time if the mortgagor doesn't.

Possessing the property

Many of the redemption statutes allow the mortgagor to retain possession of the property during the statutory redemption period that follows the foreclosure sale. Legislatures included such provisions so that mortgagors could keep making use of their property and thereby have a better chance of redeeming their property.

Sales from which property can be redeemed

Some states allow statutory redemption only when the property is sold in a judicial foreclosure or only when the property is sold in a nonjudicial foreclosure. Such statutes affect which type of foreclosure mortgagees will choose, because one method of foreclosure removes the possibility of statutory redemption after the sale and thereby makes the property more marketable.

Waiver

The possibility of statutory redemption may discourage bidders at the foreclosure sale, who may have to wait until after the redemption period to take possession and in any event face some uncertainty about their continued ownership until the period passes. So mortgagees have a reason to want mortgagors to waive the right to statutory redemption. However, in some states, by statute or judicial decision, waiver isn't allowed. In other states, sometimes expressly by statute, waiver is allowed.

Transferring Mortgaged Property

The owner of mortgaged property can transfer her property just like any other owner. But she can't change the rights of the mortgagee. Because a mortgage is an interest in land, it stays with the land even if the mortgagor transfers the property to someone else, just as a running covenant or appurtenant easement would stay with the land (see Chapters 5 and 6 for more on covenants and easements, respectively). And of course, that means the property isn't worth as much as if there weren't any mortgage encumbering the property.

The following sections talk about some of the legal issues related to transferring mortgaged property.

Restricting transfer

Even though the right to transfer is a fundamental attribute of property ownership, mortgagees may have good reasons to be concerned about transfers of the mortgaged property. After the mortgagor transfers the property, the new owner is expected to make the payments on the mortgage loan, and the original mortgagor no longer has the same incentive to make sure the payments are made, because she doesn't own the mortgaged property anymore. The new owner may not be as creditworthy and reliable as the original mortgagor, and therefore a transfer may increase the risk of default.

The new owner also may not take good care of the property, and the property therefore will decline in value, reducing the mortgagee's security.

Mortgages therefore often include clauses restricting transfer, typically a *due-on-sale clause* that says the mortgagee may accelerate the debt and foreclose if the mortgagor transfers the property without the mortgagee's prior written consent. (See the earlier section "Accelerating the debt" for more information.) Some states held that such clauses are invalid restraints on alienation, an issue I cover in Chapter 9. However, a 1982 federal statute preempts state law and makes such due-on-sale clauses enforceable except in certain situations. In most cases, if a mortgagor wants to transfer mortgaged property without paying off the loan, she must first get the lender's written consent because of a due-on-sale clause. Otherwise, the lender may exercise its right to demand immediate payment of the remaining debt.

Assuming mortgage debt

If the mortgagor transfers the mortgaged property and doesn't pay off the mortgage loan in the process, the property is still subject to the mortgage, assuming it's recorded or the new owner of the property otherwise has notice of the existing mortgage. The original mortgagor no longer owns the property and so won't keep making the mortgage payments. Instead, the new owner will have to make the mortgage payments, or else the mortgagee can foreclose and sell the property.

However, the new owner isn't personally liable for the unpaid debt simply because she bought property that was subject to a mortgage. If there's a default on the loan, the mortgagee can foreclose but can't sue the new owner for a deficiency on the loan itself.

When she buys the property from the mortgagor, the buyer of the mortgaged property can expressly agree to be personally liable on the debt. Such an agreement is called *assuming* the loan. In that case, the mortgagee is a third-party beneficiary of the buyer's promise to the mortgagor and can directly sue the new owner for breach of the obligation to pay the debt.

Enforcing a mortgage against the transferor

The mortgagor remains liable on her contract to repay the mortgage loan even if she transfers the property to another, and even if that buyer assumes the loan. Her agreement with her buyer can't change the rights of the mortgagee, which has a contract with the mortgagor requiring her to pay the debt.

Even if the mortgagee consents to the transfer, the mortgagor remains liable for performance of the loan obligation. However, the mortgagee can expressly *release* the mortgagor from the debt, after which the mortgagor is no longer liable.

The mortgagor is also released from the debt if the mortgagee and the new owner modify the loan in some way that increases the risk of default and liability without the mortgagor's consent. For example, if the mortgagee and the new owner agree to extend the term for repayment or to increase the interest rate, such changes would increase the risk of liability on the debt and would release the mortgagor from the obligation if she hadn't consented to such changes.

If the buyer assumes the mortgage but the mortgagor isn't released and remains liable on the debt, the buyer is said to have the *principal* obligation and the mortgagor is a *surety* for the buyer's performance. That means that the buyer is primarily liable and the mortgagor is secondarily liable. In the event of default, the mortgagee can sue either or both of them. But if the mortgagor pays the debt, she can recover that payment from the assuming buyer who is primarily liable to repay the debt. If she pays off the debt, she steps into the shoes of the mortgagee and can even foreclose on the property to recover the amount she paid to the mortgagee.

Transferring Mortgage

The mortgagee can transfer its interest in the property, the mortgage itself. Mortgagees often sell mortgages to get more money to make more loans. Some entities buy large numbers of mortgages, which may in turn be sold to a number of investors or used as security assuring payment on bonds, as a way to provide more funds for mortgage lending.

The mortgagee may transfer the mortgage simply by transferring the promissory note. The mortgage is inseparably connected to the promissory note that it secures, so the mortgage is automatically transferred with the note. Some notes, called *negotiable instruments,* may be transferred only by the holder signing the note and transferring possession to the grantee. Nonnegotiable notes may also be transferred by a separate document.

Even though transferring the note also transfers the mortgage, the parties to such a transaction typically sign a document assigning the mortgage to the grantee. That document can be recorded to give notice to others that someone else owns the mortgage now.

Part V
The Part of Tens

The 5th Wave

By Rich Tennant

"...and then, sadly, just before the divorce, my husband's part of the house burned to the ground."

In this part . . .

The other four parts of this book examine the legal rules of property law. Here, I offer a few lists from my experience and perspective that may help you in studying property law as a whole.

Even though this book is about legal rules rather than cases, the first list is ten property cases that are worth reading and remembering because they're landmark cases or especially helpful illustrations of property rules. The second list may be especially helpful if you're a student: It's a list of ten mistakes that property law students often make. (You might as well learn from others' mistakes and find new mistakes to make.) If you're preparing for the bar exam, you'll be interested in the final list, a list of ten subjects commonly tested in bar exams — although all I can promise you is that property law will be on your bar exam.

Chapter 19

Ten Notable Property Cases

*M*ost property law is state law. In some areas of property law, states apply very different property rules. So most property law cases that law students study are just examples. In practice, you'll be most interested in cases from your own jurisdiction, and you won't have any reason to revisit many of the property cases you studied in law school.

Some property cases are worth remembering, however. Some are worth remembering because they're constitutional decisions from the U.S. Supreme Court and are therefore relevant in all U.S. jurisdictions. Others may be worth remembering because they're landmark cases that are often cited even by other states' courts or because they consider unique and important issues. Some may simply help you remember and illustrate fundamental property law concepts.

There are certainly more than ten property law cases worth remembering, but in this chapter, I talk about ten that I think are especially notable. I summarize the basics of each case here, but if you really want to know the case, look up the opinion.

Spur Industries, Inc. v. Del E. Webb Development Co.

494 P.2d 700 (Ariz. 1972)

Law school property classes often study *Spur Industries, Inc. v. Del E. Webb Development Co.*, a nuisance case from Arizona. In 1956 some owners of property west of Phoenix developed cattle feedlots in an agricultural area that had many similar operations nearby. In 1960 Spur Industries acquired the feedlot property and began to expand it from 35 to 114 acres. In the meantime, Del E. Webb Development Co. bought two ranches nearby for a large retirement community called Sun City and began selling units in 1960.

At first the Sun City homes were a couple of miles away from Spur Industries' feedlot. But as the Sun City development progressed closer to the feedlots in the following years, it became clear that people didn't want to buy the closer lots because of odors and flies from the feedlot. Some people who had already bought Sun City homes complained that the odors and flies interfered with their enjoyment of their homes and made being outside unpleasant.

The Supreme Court of Arizona affirmed the judgment that the feedlot was both a private and a public nuisance because of its effects on Sun City residential properties. However, the court also held that Del E. Webb Development Co. had to pay Spur Industries the cost of moving or shutting down. Because of the harm to those who had bought homes in Sun City, the court was unwilling to hold that the feedlot wasn't a nuisance even though the developer had knowingly developed a large residential community in an agricultural area. But the court reasoned that an injunction is an equitable remedy, so while enjoining the feedlot from continuing, it could also require Del E. Webb to pay the costs that its development decisions had caused Spur Industries to suffer. Spur Industries had done nothing blameworthy, the court said, and Del E. Webb had taken advantage of lower land values for large tracts of land in this agricultural area and should indemnify landowners who had to leave because of the change in the character of the area.

The case is notable because of its attempt to achieve a better balance between the competing land uses by enjoining the nuisance but requiring the plaintiff to pay the cost. Ordinarily, a court balances all the considerations, which I present in Chapter 4, and decides whether on balance the challenged activity is reasonable or unreasonable. If it's reasonable, it has the property right to continue; if it's unreasonable, the plaintiff has the property right not to be invaded, and it must cease. However, if the injury is slight, a court may award damages rather than enjoining the nuisance. Spur Industries offers another option: The court can enjoin the nuisance but make the plaintiff who is more responsible for the conflict bear the costs.

Tulk v. Moxhay

41 Eng. Rep. 1143 (1848)

To this day, American courts quote *Tulk v. Moxhay*, an 1848 decision by the English High Court of Chancery, as a leading case on the subject of enforcing covenants in equity.

In 1808, Charles Augustus Tulk sold the central garden in Leicester Square to Elms with a covenant that Elms and his successors would maintain the square garden for the benefit of Tulk's tenants who rented houses he owned on Leicester Square. Moxhay eventually came to own the property years later and planned to alter the garden. Tulk still owned several houses on the square and asked the court to enjoin Moxhay from altering the garden in violation of the covenant.

Under the current law in the United States, this covenant would have run with the land. But under English law of the time, Tulk and Elms didn't have horizontal privity because including the covenant in a deed transferring the burdened parcel didn't count as horizontal privity. Moxhay therefore argued that he wasn't bound by Elms's covenant.

The court, however, said it didn't matter that the covenant wouldn't run with the land. Rather, the court said that it would be inequitable for a person to buy land knowing that a prior owner had restricted its use and then use it contrary to that restriction. The subsequent owner who has notice of the restriction is in the same equitable position as the person who originally agreed to the restriction, so he's likewise bound by it.

Consequently, one may enforce a covenant against successors in equity despite the lack of privity, as long as the parties intended successors to be bound, the covenant touches and concerns the land, and the successor had notice of the plaintiff's covenant right before buying the property. You can read more about covenants in Chapter 5.

Sanborn v. McLean

206 N.W. 496 (Mich. 1925)

This Michigan Supreme Court decision is an early case that contributed to establishing the theory of implied covenants. The McLeans owned a house in a residential neighborhood in Detroit. They decided to build a gas station on the rear of their lot, but the neighbors objected that the gas station was a nuisance and would violate a restrictive covenant allowing only residential uses. The McLeans' lot, Lot 86, had never been the subject of an express restrictive covenant. However, their lot was one of 91 lots on the same street that had been owned a few decades earlier by the McLaughlins. The McLaughlins had sold many of those lots subject to express residential covenants before they sold Lot 86 to the original buyer in 1893.

The court held that Lot 86 was therefore burdened by an implied covenant, which it called a *reciprocal negative easement*. The court explained that when common owners, like the McLaughlins, sell multiple lots with a plan for a common scheme of covenant restrictions, then each time the common owners sell one of those restricted lots, they implicitly make a reciprocal identical promise to the buyer. Therefore, when the McLaughlins sold those earlier lots with express covenants, they had already implicitly covenanted that Lot 86 would likewise be used only for residential purposes.

Of course, the court acknowledged that the subsequent purchasers, like the McLeans, would be bound by that implied covenant only if they had actual or constructive notice of the covenant when they bought their property. When the McLeans bought Lot 86 in 1910 or 1911, they could see that the neighborhood was uniformly residential. They also had an abstract of title, which the court said revealed that there were many other lots in the subdivision and also revealed the common owners. So the court reasoned that the McLeans had sufficient notice to inquire whether the property was subject to a reciprocal covenant, and if they had they would've quickly discovered that it was.

Sanborn v. McLean is often cited because it describes the circumstances in which courts may find implied reciprocal covenants: When a common owner sells lots subject to a common plan of restrictive covenants, the common owner makes implied reciprocal promises with each sale pursuant to that common plan. The case also illustrates that not only may the common plan result in finding an implied covenant but also the common plan, as revealed by title records as well as by development on the ground, may give constructive notice to subsequent buyers that their property may be subject to such an implied covenant.

Village of Euclid v. Ambler Realty Co.

272 U.S. 365 (1926)

The U.S. Supreme Court's opinion in *Village of Euclid v. Ambler Realty Co.* held that the village's newly adopted zoning ordinance was a constitutional exercise of the police power. The opinion settled the validity of this new form of land use regulation, which is so pervasive today.

Ambler Realty owned 68 acres in Euclid, Ohio, between Euclid Avenue on the south and the Nickel Plate Railroad on the north. In 1922, Euclid adopted a zoning ordinance for the first time, as many cities were starting to do. The ordinance zoned the southern 620 feet of Ambler's property U-2, which allowed one- and two-family dwellings along with some other uses considered appropriate and compatible. The next 130 feet to the north was zoned U-3, allowing the U-2 uses and also apartment houses, hotels, museums, and such, but not general commercial or industrial uses. The rest of Ambler's property was essentially unrestricted, except for some land uses that were prohibited in the city altogether.

Ambler complained that it had held its vacant property for industrial development, for which it was well suited because of being by the railroad, but the zoning ordinance dramatically reduced the value of its land that was zoned U-2 and U-3. Ambler therefore claimed that the ordinance deprived it of property without due process of law, among other things.

The Supreme Court held that the zoning ordinance didn't deny Ambler Realty due process of law. The Court said that the ordinance was valid under the Due Process Clause unless it was "clearly arbitrary and unreasonable," without any "substantial relation to the public health, safety, morals, or general welfare." (Chapter 8 talks about this substantive due process doctrine.) The Court explained the various public benefits that Euclid reasonably expected to result from separating commercial and industrial uses from residential uses and even from separating apartment houses from some residential zones. (Chapter 7 explains how such zoning ordinances work.)

The Court noted that even though in some cases specific prohibited uses might not be incompatible with a residential zone, the government can make general classifications to make the law effective without being unconstitutionally arbitrary. However, the Court also acknowledged that when a zoning ordinance is applied to specific properties and uses, some applications of the zoning ordinance may be arbitrary and unreasonable. Because Ambler Realty challenged the zoning ordinance itself and not any specific application of the ordinance, the Court didn't have to consider such an issue. So the *Euclid* decision pretty much settled the validity of zoning ordinances generally, but property owners continue to challenge specific applications of zoning ordinances as irrational and arbitrary.

Penn Central Transportation Co. v. City of New York

439 U.S. 883 (1978)

Courts continue to quote the U.S. Supreme Court's opinion in *Penn Central Transportation Co. v. City of New York* as the authoritative expression of the predominant regulatory takings test. Chapter 8 talks about the regulatory takings principles expressed in *Penn Central*, so you can refer to that chapter for details on the Court's opinion.

Penn Central, which owned the Grand Central Terminal in New York City, wanted to build a 50-story tower on top of the terminal. But New York City's Landmarks Preservation Law established a process for designating historic landmarks and districts and allowed the property owner to alter or add to the exterior of a historic landmark only if the owner first got permission from a Landmarks Preservation Commission. The Commission had designated the Grand Central Terminal as a historic landmark, so the law required Penn Central to get permission to build the planned tower. The Commission denied permission because the tower would overwhelm the landmark and significantly impair its aesthetic value.

The Supreme Court held that the restriction on Grand Central Terminal didn't take Penn Central's property without just compensation. The Court explained that there's no "set formula" for determining when a regulation is a taking and that such decisions are "ad hoc, factual inquiries." But it noted these "factors that have particular significance":

- ✔ "The economic impact of the regulation on the claimant, and, particularly, the extent to which the regulation has interfered with distinct investment-backed expectations"
- ✔ "The character of the governmental action"

Considering these factors, the Court held that the restriction didn't take Penn Central's property, observing the following:

- ✔ Penn Central could get a reasonable return on its investment in the terminal even without building the tower. Its primary expectation was continuing to use the terminal as it had been.
- ✔ In evaluating the economic impact of regulations, courts must consider the "parcel as a whole," not just the discrete segment of property subject to regulation. So the Court noted that the landmark site still had substantial value even though the regulation prevented Penn Central from building higher.
- ✔ The law gave Penn Central transferable development rights that allowed them to build higher on other properties in the area and thus mitigated the economic impact of the regulation.
- ✔ Even though Penn Central was burdened more than benefitted by the law, that didn't make the law a taking.

Lucas v. South Carolina Coastal Council

505 U.S. 1003 (1992)

This Supreme Court decision makes some important additions to the regulatory takings law described in *Penn Central* (see the preceding section). David Lucas bought two undeveloped residential lots on the Isle of Palms in South Carolina, intending to build houses on them. Two years later, however, the state adopted the Beachfront Management Act, which prohibited Lucas from building any "occupiable improvements" on the lots. The state trial court found that this law made the two lots valueless.

The Supreme Court reaffirmed statements in earlier opinions that a regulation is a taking whenever it denies "economically viable use" of the land. In this case, the trial court's factual finding that the lots were valueless invoked this rule. In order to prove a taking without application of the ad hoc, factual inquiry described in *Penn Central,* many property owners have since tried to persuade courts that regulations made their properties valueless.

The state court had reasoned that the law wasn't a taking in this case, despite making the property valueless, because the law was preventing a serious public harm to the beach. But the Supreme Court rejected this idea, stating that a regulation certainly must produce some public benefit in order to be valid, but characterizing the public benefit as preventing harm doesn't mean the regulation isn't a taking requiring compensation. Otherwise, the Court argued, no regulations would be takings because any regulation can be characterized as preventing harms.

However, the Supreme Court offered a different principle that can avoid compensation no matter how dramatic or complete the economic impact of a regulation. The Court said that the government doesn't have to pay compensation if "the logically antecedent inquiry into the nature of the owner's estate shows that the proscribed use interests were not part of his title to begin with." That is, if the owner didn't have the property right to do something in the first place, a regulation that prohibits her from doing it hasn't taken anything away from her. The Court explained that "background principles" of state property law, such as nuisance law, define the extent of a person's property rights. So the Court remanded for the state court to determine whether such background principles would mean that Lucas didn't have the property right to develop his property in these circumstances; if he didn't, the Beachfront Management Act didn't take anything away from him.

The idea of background principles has had a major influence on regulatory takings cases. Governments argue that challenged regulations aren't takings because background principles of state law prohibited the owner's use anyway. Courts continue to consider when a change in property law becomes a background principle that defines the scope of a person's protected property rights.

Javins v. First National Realty Corp.

428 F.2d 1071 (D.C. Cir. 1970)

This decision by the U.S. Court of Appeals for the D.C. Circuit is a leading early case recognizing the landlord's implied warranty of habitability. The implied warranty of habitability, which I examine in Chapter 12, is an especially important change in the traditional rights and duties of landlords and tenants.

First National Realty Corp. was the landlord of an apartment complex called Clifton Terrace. First National filed lawsuits to regain possession after Ethel Javins and two other tenants failed to pay their rent. All three of them argued that they should owe no rent or otherwise shouldn't be evicted because of hundreds of violations of the District of Columbia's housing regulations.

The court agreed, holding that the landlord who rents residential property implicitly warrants that the property will be habitable throughout the lease term. The court offered several reasons, including the following:

- ✔ A modern residential lease should be treated like other contracts for goods and services. In such contracts, courts commonly had found implied warranties that the goods and services would be fit for their ordinary purposes.

- ✔ Residential tenants today reasonably expect that they're renting habitable premises, not just land.

- ✔ The landlord has more opportunity, ability, and incentive to maintain the rental property.

- ✔ Because of the shortage of housing, tenants don't have the leverage to bargain for better housing.

- ✔ The District of Columbia Housing Regulations required landlords to maintain residential premises, so a residential lease agreement is a contractual undertaking to provide and maintain premises that comply with the regulations.

The court held that the obligation to pay rent is conditioned on the landlord's compliance with the implied warranty of habitability. So the court remanded for the trial court to determine whether the tenants owed any rent in light of the alleged violations of the Housing Regulations. At the time, only a few courts had recognized this implied warranty of habitability. Today, almost all 50 states have adopted the implied warranty, either by statute or judicial decision.

Armory v. Delamirie

93 Eng. Rep. 664 (1722)

Armory v. Delamirie is an old English case about found property. Texts and treatises often cite it as an early case establishing the rights of a finder. It's a simple and memorable case to help recall those rights, which Chapter 13 discusses in detail.

A chimney sweeper's boy found a piece of jewelry and took it to the defendant's goldsmith shop. He gave it to the goldsmith's apprentice to find out its value, and the apprentice took out the jewels. The boy refused the offered payment, but the apprentice only gave him back the empty socket.

The court held that the boy acquired a property right in the jewel by finding it. His property right wasn't absolute, because the rightful owner would have a better claim to it. But the boy was the owner of the jewel in relation to everyone else, with the right to keep it and the right to recover its value from the goldsmith.

Pierson v. Post

3 Cai. R. 175 (N.Y. 1805)

This case is notable because the majority and dissenting opinions thoughtfully consider the principles that justify protection of private property and when those principles should protect a hunter's property in a hunted animal. But the case is probably even more notable because the story and opinions are colorful and because so many law students have studied it over the years. If you tell a lawyer you're studying property and have read *Pierson v. Post*, there's a good chance she'll remember the case.

Lodowick Post complained that he was hunting with dogs and hounds "upon a certain wild and uninhabited, unpossessed and waste land, called the beach," when he found and pursued a wild fox. While Post was pursuing and in sight of the fox, Jesse Pierson shot the fox and took it. Post claimed Pierson had trespassed on his personal property in the fox.

The court held that Post didn't own the fox, so Pierson had done him no legal wrong, though he may have been "uncourteous or unkind." The court agreed with both Pierson and Post that a wild fox would become Post's property only if he had taken "occupancy" of the fox. Until someone takes possession, the animal is unowned. The court held that mere pursuit of a wild animal is not occupancy of the animal, and pursuing the fox is all that Post had done. The court said that Post, or anyone, could possess or occupy a wild animal and thereby become the owner in the following circumstances:

- He actually seizes the body of the animal.
- He mortally wounds the animal and is in continued pursuit.
- He traps the animal so that it may not escape.

Along the way, the court indicated some reasons for property rules. The court explained that a person who traps or mortally wounds a wild animal with continued pursuit should thereby acquire a property right because he has shown the intention of owning the animal and deprived the animal of its natural liberty, removing it from the state of nature. The court also said that merely finding and pursuing an animal shouldn't give someone a property right because such a rule would cause uncertainty about rights and would "prove a fertile source of quarrels and litigation."

The dissent, on the other hand, urged a different rule and considered other reasons for property rules protecting things as property. The dissent said that a hunter has a property right in a wild animal if the hunter has a reasonable prospect of taking the animal and has revealed the intention to take possession of it. The dissent stressed that Post and other "votaries of Diana" invest substantial effort in capturing wild foxes, perhaps suggesting that the effort of finding and pursuing are enough to make a claim of natural right to the fruits of those labors. But mostly the dissent reasoned that the court should adopt a property rule that would give "the greatest possible encouragement" to kill foxes because they're "pernicious and incorrigible" in their "depredations on farmers and on barn yards." The dissent thus concluded that the property rule should recognize a right to any wild animal once the hunter has a reasonable prospect of taking it because otherwise hunters wouldn't have as much incentive to hunt in the first place.

Stambovsky v. Ackley

572 N.Y.S.2d 672 (1991)

Stambovsky v. Ackley is notable because it goes beyond then-existing New York law to adopt a new rule requiring sellers to disclose known, latent, material facts impairing the value of the property. It's also notable because the material fact was that the house was haunted.

Jeffrey Stambovsky contracted to buy Helen Ackley's riverfront Victorian house in Nyack, New York. Before closing the sale, Stambovsky learned that Ackley and her family had seen ghosts in the house numerous times and that the house was widely reputed to be haunted. He asked the court to rescind the purchase agreement because Ackley hadn't told him about the haunting before entering into the agreement.

The trial court dismissed the complaint because New York law didn't recognize a claim for not disclosing facts about property being sold. The Appellate Division held that the prevailing rule was inequitable when a buyer couldn't reasonably discover the facts. The court therefore held that the buyer could rescind the contract in equity when the seller didn't disclose facts to the buyer in the following circumstances of this case:

- ✔ The seller has created a condition that "materially impairs the value of the contract" to the buyer.

- ✔ The condition is "peculiarly within the knowledge of the seller or unlikely to be discovered by a prudent purchaser."

As Chapter 15 notes, in recent years most courts have adopted and even expanded this duty to require the seller to disclose any material conditions that she knows about and that the buyer couldn't reasonably discover.

Chapter 20

Ten Common Mistakes in Applying Property Law

In This Chapter

▶ Identifying some common mistakes in applying property law

▶ Understanding how to avoid these common mistakes

*E*veryone makes mistakes. In fact, people often make the same mistakes. This chapter is all about ten common mistakes property law students make in applying property law. Now, I don't have any evidence that these are the most common mistakes, but I've certainly seen them a lot in my experience teaching. Not only can this list help you avoid making these mistakes yourself, but it can help you better understand what's right.

Misapplying the Rule against Perpetuities

There are so many ways to mess up in applying the rule against perpetuities that I could use half this list of ten just listing rule-against-perpetuities mistakes. Or I could just say the common mistake is not applying the rule correctly and send you to Chapter 9 for help. But I'll be more specific.

The *rule against perpetuities* says that no interest is good unless it must vest, if at all, not later than 21 years after some life in being at the creation of the interest. Here are some of the most common mistakes in applying this rule:

✔ **Confusing vesting and taking possession:** To be good, a remainder doesn't have to be certain to take possession within 21 years of a life in being at the creation of the interest; instead, the remainder is good as long as it's certain to vest or fail within that period of time.

✔ **Calculating the perpetuities period from the moment the prior estate ends rather than the moment the future interest was created:** A future interest is created when the grantor delivers the deed that creates the future interest or when the testator whose will creates the future interest dies. The interest isn't possessory until sometime in the future, but the interest has already been created. So for the rule against perpetuities, the question is whether at the moment the future interest is created there is someone alive within whose lifetime plus 21 years the interest is certain to vest, if it ever vests at all.

✔ **Considering only the lives of particular people in deciding that a future interest is void:** If the interest is good under the rule, you only need to identify one person (or group of people) within whose lifetime plus 21 years the interest is certain to vest or fail and explain why that is. But if the interest is void under the rule, you have to explain why there's no one alive at the time of the conveyance within whose lifetime plus 21 years the interest is certain to vest or fail. It isn't enough to say that the interest isn't certain to vest or fail within 21 years of the lifetime of the life tenant, which is probably the most common mistake of this kind. You should consider all the possible lives-in-being at the creation of the interest whose lifetimes might be connected to the occurrence of the vesting condition.

✔ **Considering what actually happened after the conveyance:** The rule against perpetuities is unaffected by what actually happens after the interest is created. The question is whether, at the moment of creation, you could've looked into the future and been certain that it would vest or fail within 21 years of some living person's lifetime. So unless you're told to consider a "wait and see" variant of the rule against perpetuities, events after the interest was created don't count.

Mislabeling Present and Future Estates

Law students often mislabel estates. Mislabeling sometimes isn't a big deal, as long as you understand who has the right of possession and in which circumstances. But it's still important to correctly describe to others who owns what kind of estate, and sometimes labeling mistakes lead to substantive mistakes, too.

One common labeling mistake is to conclude that an estate is determinable or on condition subsequent when really it's subject to an executory limitation. The mistake results from the difference in how the condition of defeasibility is expressed when the estate is determinable rather than on condition subsequent:

✔ When an estate is determinable, words of duration express the condition of defeasibility: "to A as long as the property is not used to host a circus." If A does host a circus on the property, it will revert to the grantor.

✔ When an estate is on condition subsequent, the condition of defeasibility uses words of condition: "to A, but if used to host a circus, the grantor may re-enter and take possession."

The mistake is to read words of duration describing a condition and assume that the estate is determinable. Students may become so focused on the differences in how a condition is expressed that they forget to consider who will get the estate. If the grant says "to A as long as the property is not used to host a circus, then to B," the property doesn't revert to the grantor; it goes to a third party, B, on occurrence of the condition. That means A has a fee simple subject to an executory limitation and B has an executory interest.

If the property goes to a third party rather than the grantor, the estate is never determinable or on condition subsequent. Those estates are followed by reversionary interests in the grantor. If the property goes to a third party after the occurrence of a condition of defeasibility, the future interest is either a remainder or an executory interest — those are the only two future interests created in third parties.

When labeling a defeasible estate, first check whether the grant says the property will revert to the grantor after the condition occurs or whether it will go to a third party. If it goes to a third party, it doesn't matter how the condition of defeasibility is expressed; the estate is subject to an executory limitation, and the third party owns an executory interest. You need to differentiate words of condition from words of duration only if the grant doesn't specify a third party who gets possession when the condition occurs.

A grant may create two or more future interests in succession, sometimes resulting in all sorts of confusion and mislabeling of the future interests. The key is to think through and label one estate at a time, in chronological order. A grant can create only one present estate, and that's the place to start. Correctly labeling the present estate will tell you which type of future interest must follow it, as Chapter 9 details. After you label the first future interest, consider which type of present estate that person will own when her future interest becomes possessory. That tells you what the next future interest must be. Continue until you identify the last person in line — someone who has a future interest in a fee simple absolute.

Misunderstanding Hostility

Hostility or adversity is one element of claims for title by adverse possession as well as claims for prescriptive easements. A common mistake is to reason that use isn't hostile or adverse because the record owner has acquiesced or agreed to the use or possession. But the record owner's acquiescence or agreement doesn't necessarily mean the use or possession isn't hostile in the way these rules require.

Use or possession is *hostile* or *adverse* if it's objectively inconsistent with the record owner's title. It doesn't have to be inconsistent with the record owner's desires. If someone uses or possesses the property simply because the record owner gave permission — that is, she has a license — then that use or possession is consistent with the record owner's title. But if someone uses or possesses the property because the record owner agreed to give her an easement or to give her ownership (or if the record owner assented to her assertion of an easement or ownership), that use is hostile or adverse because it conflicts with the record owner's title, even though the record owner agrees and even welcomes the use or possession.

Don't make the mistake of asking whether the record owner agreed to the use or possession or opposed it. Instead, ask whether the record owner would have reason to think that the user was acting as if she had an easement that she could keep using even if the record owner were to object. Or in adverse possession cases, ask whether the record owner would have reason to think that the possessor was acting as if she owned the property and could keep possessing it even if the record owner were to object. See Chapters 14 and 6 for more information on this requirement.

Considering the Intent to Create a Covenant Rather than Intent to Run

A covenant is said to *run with the land* when successive owners of the relevant lands are bound or benefitted by the covenant. One requirement for a covenant to bind a successor to the original covenantor is that the original parties intended successive owners of the burdened land to be bound. Likewise, one requirement for a covenant to benefit a successor to the original covenantee is that the original parties intended successive owners of the benefitted land to have the right to enforce the covenant.

A common mistake is to talk about the original parties' intent to create a covenant rather than their intent to bind or benefit successors. This mistake seems to happen especially when talking about implied covenants. It isn't enough to observe that the original parties intended to create a covenant; you must consider whether the original parties intended for the covenant to run with the relevant property interest. You can read more about running covenants in Chapter 5.

Considering Only Notice of a Covenant's Burden

To enforce a covenant in equity, the burdened party must have had notice of the benefitted party's covenant right. Often law students talk only about the burdened party's notice that the land was burdened by a covenant, but that doesn't satisfy the notice requirement.

The burdened party must have notice that the person seeking to enforce the covenant was a benefitted party. Here are a couple of ways to remember that:

- **Remember that a covenant isn't just a burden; it's a legal right to enforce a promise against the burdened property.** So knowing that the property is burdened is only half the story; unless you know who owns the right to demand performance of the covenant, you don't really know about the covenant. Having notice of a covenant always means having notice that person X has the right to enforce a promise against person Y.

- **Think about the reason for the notice requirement.** The burdened party must know to whom she owes the obligation of performing the covenant. A stranger to the covenant and the properties — like me — obviously couldn't take the burdened party to court to make her comply with her covenant. That right belongs only to benefitted parties. If the burdened party wants to use the property in a way not allowed by the covenant, she has to know who to talk to and get permission from. So it wouldn't be equitable for a person to enforce the covenant against her if she had no notice that she owed the duty to that person.

Applying Estoppel or Part Performance without Evidence of an Agreement

The statute of frauds generally makes an easement agreement unenforceable if it's not evidenced in writing. But there are two relevant exceptions to the statute of frauds that allow an easement agreement to be enforced without a writing: estoppel and part performance.

Sometimes law students make the mistake of arguing that a person has an easement because she has satisfied the requirements for estoppel or part performance, without even talking about whether the parties had an easement agreement in the first place. The estoppel and part performance doctrines don't create an easement contract when the parties never formed a contract. The party claiming an easement must still prove that the parties had a contract giving an easement to her (even though they may not have called it an easement). The estoppel and part performance doctrines simply allow that contract to be enforced even though there isn't the required written evidence of it. You can read more on easements in Chapter 6.

Deciding a Joint Tenancy Exists without the Four Unities and Express Intent

A joint tenancy can exist only when all the joint tenants have unity of time, title, interest, and possession. (Chapter 10 explains what each of those unities means.) But when a grant expressly says that someone's a joint tenant, it's easy to conclude that she's a joint tenant without considering whether she's eligible to be a joint tenant. For example, if the grant says "1/3 to A and 2/3 to B as joint tenants with right of survivorship and not as tenants in common," A and B can't be joint tenants; their different fractional interests mean that they don't have unity of interest. So before concluding that a joint tenancy exists, you must consider both whether the grant expressly indicates the intention to create a joint tenancy and whether the four unities are present.

You can make a mistake the other direction, too. Sometimes students argue that because the four unities are present, the co-owners are joint tenants. That's not enough, either. The grant creating the co-ownership must expressly say it creates a joint tenancy to overcome the presumption of a tenancy in common.

Applying the Equitable Conversion Doctrine Where It Doesn't Apply

The *equitable conversion doctrine* (covered in Chapter 15) says that if a buyer has an enforceable contract to buy land, equitably she is already the owner of the land, even though she hasn't completed the purchase and received a deed yet.

A common mistake is to apply the doctrine of equitable conversion where it doesn't belong. As the equitable owner, the buyer bears the risk of damage to the land and must go forward with the purchase even if the property is physically damaged before closing. But the equitable conversion doctrine doesn't apply to other types of risks and doesn't trump other covenants and conditions of the contract. For example, if a loss results from a title defect during the executory contract period, the buyer doesn't bear the risk of loss under the equitable conversion principle; the implied marketable title condition — or an express title condition in the contract — excuses the buyer from purchasing if the title isn't marketable or doesn't meet the contract standard title.

Failing to Identify the Landlord's Wrongful Act in a Constructive Eviction

A landlord may breach the covenant of quiet enjoyment by constructively evicting the tenant (see Chapter 12 for details). A constructive eviction requires proof of all three of the following:

- ✔ The landlord commits a wrongful act.

- ✔ The act substantially interferes with the tenant's enjoyment of the leased premises.

- ✔ The substantial interference causes the tenant to abandon the premises.

A common mistake in applying this rule is to overlook or misunderstand the first requirement, that the landlord commits a wrongful act. The wrongful act must be an act in violation of some legal obligation. So if you're arguing that the landlord has constructively evicted a tenant, you must identify the source of some duty that the landlord has breached. The covenant of quiet enjoyment itself doesn't create duties to maintain or repair the premises or any other duties in relation to the condition of the leased premises.

If the failure to maintain and repair has caused the tenant to abandon the premises, that's a constructive eviction only if the contract says the landlord has a duty to maintain and repair in that way. With residential leases, you might instead argue that the landlord breached a statutory duty to maintain the premises in a habitable condition as required by local housing codes, although some courts say that's a public duty and can't be the basis for a constructive eviction.

Applying Purchase Agreements after Closing and Deeds before Closing

Chapter 16 explains the merger doctrine that a purchase agreement generally isn't enforceable after closing, when the seller gives a deed to the buyer and the buyer gives the purchase money to the seller. The deed effectively takes the place of the purchase agreement, and the parties indicate by going forward with closing that the other party's performance is acceptable and that they waive any unfulfilled conditions to their obligation to perform.

When a dispute arises after closing, students sometimes mistakenly suggest that the buyer could rescind the purchase because of a failure of a condition in the purchase agreement, such as a failure of marketable title. However, after closing, it's too late for such a remedy. The buyer's only contract-based claims are for breach of the deed covenants of title — if the deed includes them. The merger doctrine doesn't apply in some situations, however, as I note in Chapter 16. If a dispute does arise after closing, you should consider whether any of those exceptions would allow a claim based on the purchase agreement — but don't talk about such claims unless you first explain why merger wouldn't prevent the claim.

Sometimes people make mistakes the opposite direction, too. When a dispute arises before closing, sometimes people mistakenly argue about whether the deed covenants of title have been breached. The deed covenants of title aren't made until closing, even though the purchase agreement may say that the seller will give a warranty deed to the buyer when closing occurs. If a title problem arises before closing, the buyer's remedy is to rescind the contract or possibly abate the purchase price, as I note in Chapter 15. The buyer can't sue for damages under the deed covenants of title.

Chapter 21

Ten Property Subjects Commonly Tested in Bar Exams

*Y*ou may wonder what property law you need to know in order to pass the bar exam. If only the bar examiners would tell you the questions beforehand, you'd be sure to find the right answers and know what they want you to know, right? If only.

The coverage of state bar exams varies, but all include some property law subjects. You can find many online descriptions of state bar coverage, although often without enough detail to tell which specific property law subjects are likely to be tested. Almost all the states have adopted the Multistate Bar Exam, however, and many states have also adopted the Multistate Essay Exam. The website of the National Conference of Bar Examiners (www.ncbex.org), which administers these multistate exams, includes outlines of the subject matter covered by the exams. The Multistate Bar Exam, a multiple-choice exam, has 33 property law questions out of the total 200 questions on the exam.

This chapter highlights ten property law subjects that commonly show up on bar exams, both state and multistate. It doesn't aspire to predict which property issues you'll be tested on, but it may help you think about some areas you shouldn't neglect as you study for the bar.

Because a first-year property law course surveys a broad range of issues, it can't cover all property law issues in depth. Other courses in the law school curriculum offer more detailed study of many of these subjects, so this chapter also mentions other courses that can deepen your understanding.

Purchase Agreements

Real estate purchase agreements are generally one of the most heavily tested property subjects on bar exams. The National Conference of Bar Examiners says that 20 percent of the Multistate Bar Exam property questions are about real property contracts.

The Property Law course in the first year of law school usually includes some coverage of real estate contracts, but you often need upper-level courses in real estate transactions to really know the subject. Chapter 15 of this book discusses real estate contracts.

Mortgages

Mortgages are another commonly tested topic. In fact, mortgages account for another 20 percent of the Multistate Bar Exam questions.

The details of mortgage law are often left for upper-level law school courses on real estate finance. For a refresher on mortgages, see Chapter 18.

Deeds

Property transactions — the kinds of things that real estate lawyers deal with — seem to dominate the property law coverage in bar exams. And titles, which include deeds, make up (you guessed it) 20 percent of the Multistate Bar Exam questions.

To brush up on deed basics, refer to Chapter 16. For more-detailed information, consider a real estate transactions course.

Recording Acts

Recording acts, which I discuss in Chapter 17, are also commonly tested on bar exams. State recording acts vary, so knowing the recording act of the state in which you're taking the bar exam is especially important. But the Multistate Bar Exam also may include questions about all three types of recording acts as part of the property law questions dealing with titles.

A course in real estate transactions may cover recording and title searching beyond the coverage in the first-year property law course.

Landlord-Tenant Law

Landlord-tenant law, the subject of Chapter 12, is commonly tested on bar exams. On the Multistate Bar Exam, landlord-tenant questions are included in a category called "ownership," which includes another 20 percent of the questions. Landlord-tenant law also seems to be a common subject for essay questions.

Some law schools have upper-level courses in landlord-tenant law.

Estates

Estates, which you read about in Chapter 9, are generally well covered in bar exams. The Multistate Bar Exam includes questions on estates along with landlord-tenant law and concurrent ownership under the "ownership" heading.

Remainders and the rule against perpetuities may be worth special attention. Don't overlook restraints on alienation either, which may be both an estate issue and a covenant issue, as Chapter 9 explains. Courses on wills, trusts, and estates offer more study of estates.

Concurrent Ownership

Concurrent ownership is commonly tested along with present and future estates. Many states don't recognize tenancy by the entirety anymore, so in those states, you only need to study tenancy in common and joint tenancy. Wills, trusts, and estates courses may also study more about concurrent ownership. For concurrent ownership basics, turn to Chapter 10.

Covenants

Covenants seems to be a hard subject for students, and it's often tested. The last 20 percent of the property questions on the Multistate Bar Exam deal with "rights in land," including covenants, easements, fixtures, and zoning.

You may focus on the requirements to apply covenants to successors at law and in equity, but don't neglect the rest of the issues about covenants, including interpretation and termination. The first-year property course is usually the primary direct coverage of this subject in the law school curriculum. You can read about covenants in Chapter 5.

Easements

Easements, which I cover in Chapter 6, are commonly tested along with covenants. The study of easements often focuses on the creation of easements, but you may see questions on scope and termination as well.

As with covenants, the law school curriculum doesn't usually include advanced study of easements, although some upper-level subjects may deal with particular kinds of easements.

Adverse Possession

Adverse possession, the subject of Chapter 14, is a pretty likely subject for bar exam testing. The Multistate Bar Exam includes adverse possession in the "titles" category of questions, along with recording acts and deeds.

You may run into adverse possession in some other law school course, but the first-year property course is where it's taught.

Index

• F •